A BRIEF HISTORY OF CANADA

A BRIEF HISTORY OF CANADA

ROGER RIENDEAU

☑®

Facts On File, Inc.

A BRIEF HISTORY OF CANADA

Facts On File, Inc.
11 Penn Plaza
New York NY 10001

Library of Congress Cataloging-in-Publication Data

Riendeau, Roger E., 1950-
    A brief history of Canada / by Roger Riendeau.
        p.   cm.
    Includes bibliographical references (p.   ) and index.
    ISBN 0-8160-3157-6 (acid-free paper)
    1. Canada-History.   I. Title.
F1026.R58   19999
971-dc21   99-23494

Facts On File books are available at special discounts when purchased in bulk quantities for businesses, associations, institutions or sales promotions. Please call our Special Sales Department in New York at 212/967-8800 or 800/322-8755.

You can find Facts On File on the World Wide Web at http://www.factsonfile.com

Text and cover design by Evelyn Horovicz

Printed in the United States of America

MP FOF 10 9 8 7 6 5 4 3 2 1

This book is printed on acid-free paper.

TABLE OF CONTENTS

PREFACE

History is essentially a story. So Professor J. M. S. Careless, an eminent and influential Canadian historian, told me when I was one of his graduate students at the University of Toronto a quarter-century ago. Professor Careless, whose own history of Canada, written nearly a half-century ago, was entitled *Canada: A Story of Challenge* (Macmillan, 1953), was trying to convey to me that history is not merely a collection of past events highlighting the great achievements of great people, that history must be more than an account of past politics and, above all, that history must not succumb to the temptation of serving the interests of current politics. The central role of the historian is to instill a sense of order out of the chaos of the past and to make the past come alive so that it can inform the present and the future. How can we intelligently judge where we are and determine where we are going if we do not have a clear understanding of where we have been? I have endeavored to heed this advice in telling my story of Canada.

True to its title, *A Brief History of Canada* undertakes the ambitious challenge of recounting in a single volume the development of a somewhat enigmatic land in the northern half of North America from the prehistoric emergence of Native civilization to the rise of a modern urban and industrial nation at the end of the second millennium. To attempt to accomplish this objective in such a compact volume suggests that this work is meant to be introductory in nature, aimed particularly at general readers who may have little familiarity with Canadian history. The hope is that this book will provide both Canadian and non-Canadian readers with the incentive to become more interested in Canada and to appreciate its complexities and subtleties. Indeed, Canada is a fascinating country because of its paradoxical qualities. On the surface, it appears to be a northern extension of the United States, with many similarities in historical origin, geographical features, cultural background, political system, and socioeconomic values. However, when one probes beneath surface appearances, numerous subtle differences that help to account for the existence of two distinct nations in the northern half of North America emerge. The recent North American Free Trade Agreement (NAFTA) has generated increased interest in the similarities and differences between Canada and the United States.

The book is divided into five sections to reflect the various stages of Canadian development. The first section (Chapters 1–2) — "Exploring the Northern American Frontier"— presents a brief overview of the lesser-known presettlement era. For thousands of years, before the North American frontier was politically divided into national domains, the natural divisions of geography prevailed and the vast and varied landscape, along with climatic conditions, virtually dictated the course of social, economic, and political development. So long as the land remained in a state of wilderness, the Native peoples were masters of their own destiny, developing their distinct cultures and societies and eventually serving as indispensable partners to unacclimatized European explorers, traders, missionaries, and settlers. The serendipitous European rediscovery of North America initially around the turn of the second millennium and again in the late 15th and 16th centuries set the stage for settlement and imperial rule.

The second section (Chapters 3–5)—"The French Empire in Northern America, 1608–1760"—focuses on the imperial competition between France and Britain before a national distinction between Canada and the United States became clear. The opening of a lucrative market for beaver fur hats and coats in Europe in the early 17th century induced French traders to explore the interior of North America via the St. Lawrence–Great Lakes waterways and to establish colonies in Quebec and Acadia (Nova Scotia). Early French colonial development was hampered not only by warfare with the Iroquois but also by clashes between the fur traders—who preferred to leave the land in its wilderness state—and Catholic missionaries, who desired to spread Christianity by promoting settlement. The establishment of a paternalistic and authoritarian style of government and feudal social institutions within a North American frontier environment ensured that New France would evolve unlike its English colonial counterparts to the south and in relative isolation from France. The westward expansion of the French fur-trading frontier by the mid-18th century led to a military collision with the English-owned Hudson's Bay Company to the north and the embryonic American settlement frontier to the south. The struggle for the North American frontier was not settled on the battlefield so much as on the balance sheet, as English willingness to protect the valuable thirteen colonies ultimately exceeded the French desire to sustain what the philosopher Voltaire called "a few acres of snow."

The third section (Chapters 6–10)—"The British North American Colonies, 1760–1867"—traces the adjustment of French colonists to British rule, the growth of English-speaking settlement through American and British immigration, the development of a staple-based economy, and the establishment of British political institutions. As the pioneer communities of the Atlantic and St. Lawrence regions developed socially and economically, they came to demand greater political freedom just as Britain was seeking to shed the burdens of empire in the late 1840s. The prospect of independent survival and growth outside the protection of the empire and in the shadow of the expansionist United States induced the various British North American colonies to join forces to form a nation under a constitutional framework that combined British parliamentary democracy with American-style federalism. The marriage of economic and political convenience that became the Dominion of Canada in 1867 proved as difficult to arrange as it was to sustain.

The fourth section (Chapters 11–15)—"The Foundations of Canadian Nationhood, 1867–1931"—starts by explaining the nature of the Canadian national constitution, the expansion of Canada into a transcontinental nation from the Atlantic to Pacific shores, the origins of the modern national political party system, and the implementation of an economic development strategy known as the National Policy. The first three decades of Canadian nationhood were marked by the persistence of regional and cultural conflict, which reflected the uncertainty and dissatisfaction with this bold national experiment. However, Canada's economic fortunes took a turn for the better in the first three decades of the 20th century as millions of immigrants, largely from overseas, came to settle on the western prairie wheat lands and in the eastern manufacturing centers. The opening of the vast northern resource frontier was a further boost to urban and industrial growth, in addition to promoting closer economic ties with the United States. With economic and territorial expansion came a growing national self-confidence that demanded a greater voice in the conduct of foreign policy, which had remained under British control after Confederation. Britain's decline as a world power and Canada's outstanding performance during World War I set the stage for the achievement of full national autonomy within the new British Commonwealth under the Statute of Westminster in 1931.

The fifth and final section (Chapters 16–20)—"Affluence and Anxiety in the Modern Era"—follows the course of Canadian development from the perilous 1930s to the present. The Great Depression brought prolonged and widespread economic and social distress and also altered attitudes toward the appropriate role of the state in Canadian life. The outbreak of World War II in 1939 dictated continued state intervention as Canada impressively mobilized its own armed forces by asserting its diplomatic and military independence from Britain and reinforcing its continental defense strategy through alliances with the United States. The postwar boom featured the rapid growth and diversification of the Canadian population in the wake of the resumption of mass immigration, the rise of the "welfare" state, and the emergence of Canada as a "middle power" in an increasingly polarized world order. The so-called Quiet Revolution of the 1960s brought Quebec's growing sovereignty aspirations to the forefront of national politics that were already divided by divergent concepts of federal-provincial relations. By the end of the century and millennium, the search for an elusive national unity continued, although Canadians could take pride in the many outstanding achievements of its citizens and a level of stability and affluence that has been the envy of the rest of the world.

The story of Canada is about determined, opportunistic, and talented men and women working together to overcome natural adversity and obstacles in order to make valuable contributions to national and international progress. The evolution of Canada as a prosperous and peaceful community in the northern half of North America has been based on a tolerance of diversity, whether expressed regionally, politically, culturally, socially, linguistically, or religiously. Indeed, the sometimes harsh and triumphant realities of the Canadian experience offer abundant inspiration for an interesting and revealing portrait of a unique land and its people.

The development of this book benefited from the assistance and advice of several people, some of whom deserve special acknowledgment. Heather MacDougall, my long-time colleague and friend from the Department of History at the University of Waterloo, was a constant source of encouragement and insight. Douglas Francis of the University of Calgary, the coauthor of a major textbook on Canadian history, offered his interesting perspective on the challenges of writing national history. Miriam Grant, also of the University of Calgary, contributed scholarly perspectives from the standpoint of a geographer. Dennis Duffy, Cynthia Messenger, and Donald Boere, distinguished colleagues at Innis College, University of Toronto, kept me in tune with the Canadian literary, music, and arts scene. Special thanks should go to Mary Kay Linge, senior editor at Facts On File, Inc., for her persistent interest and patience in guiding this book to press. I am also grateful to Sharon Fitzhenry and Richard Dionne of Fitzhenry & Whiteside for their faith in the value of this book. Finally, for her unwavering support, caring, and love, I owe a greater debt than I can ever repay to my wife, Diane Searles, to whom I dedicate this book.

PART ONE

EXPLORING THE NORTHERN AMERICAN FRONTIER

CHAPTER 1

THE NATURAL DOMAIN

A little more than a century ago, Goldwin Smith, a former Oxford and Cornell University history professor, pessimistically anticipated the destiny of Canada as an independent nation in his book *Canada and the Canadian Question* (1891):

> Whether the four blocks of territory [the Maritime provinces, southern Ontario and Quebec, the Prairie provinces, and British Columbia] constituting the Dominion can for ever be kept by political agencies united among themselves and separate from their Continent, of which geographically, economically, and with the exception of Quebec ethnologically, they are parts, is the Canadian question.

Arguing that "Canada is a political expression" forced to develop in defiance of nature, Smith concluded unequivocally that the young nation could not possibly survive on its own and could only fulfill its destiny through a "reunion" with the larger and more powerful United States: "The idea of a United Continent of North America, securing free trade and intercourse over a vast area, with external safety and internal peace is no less practical than it is grand."

Paradoxically, Smith's analysis of Canada's destiny proved to be at once prophetic and misguided. On the one hand, he accurately predicted that Canada's economic fortunes and military security would be inextricably bound up in greater continental integration, as reflected in the North American Free Trade Agreement (NAFTA). On the other hand, he underestimated the strength and resilience of a Canadian nationality derived from a shared experience of the past and the willingness to respond to the challenges of geographic limitations, regional economic disparity, social and cultural diversity, political compromise, and international diplomacy. Canada has survived as a distinct national community since 1867 because its people, whether they are descended from the aboriginal, French, Anglo-Saxon, other European, Asian, African, or Latin American cultures, have the collective will to recognize themselves as part of a common experience. Even those who have contemplated leaving the national community from time to time have been reluctant to lose the benefits of being Canadian. The uniqueness of the Canadian experience becomes more apparent and appreciated as its story unfolds.

IN DEFIANCE OF NATURE

Goldwin Smith had ample reason to question the geographical viability of Canadian nationhood. Canada is a vast country, extending over 4,000 miles from east to west and upwards of 3,000 miles from north to south. With an area of 3,850,000 square miles, it is the second-largest nation in the world, exceeded in size only by Russia. Yet only about one-eighth of the land is considered habitable, and only about one-twelfth is cultivable, largely accounting for the fact that Canada's population has consistently been about one-tenth the size of that of the United States, even though Canada's land area is slightly larger than that of its southern neighbor. Furthermore, because of the limited quantity of arable land available for settlement, well over 90 percent of the Canadian population lives within 300 miles of the U.S. border. Smith recognized the implications of this physical reality for national unity in terms that are no less pertinent today than they were a century ago:

> The habitable and cultivable parts of [Canada] . . . are not contiguous, but are divided from each other by great barriers of nature, wide and irreclaimable wilderness or manifold chains of mountains. . . . Each [part], on the other hand, is closely connected by nature, physically and economically, with that portion of the habitable and cultivable continent to the south of it which it immediately adjoins, and in which are its natural markets. . . .

Indeed, the fact that the lines of geographic division in North America tend to run north and south across the entire continent while the direction of discovery and development has tended to be east and west across the northern half of the continent has fostered a continuing tension between nationalism and regionalism in Canada. Geographically, Canada is divided into seven regions, each with its distinct patterns of landform and natural resources.

The Atlantic Region

On the East Coast is the Atlantic or Appalachian region, including the four provinces of Newfoundland, Nova Scotia, New Brunswick, and Prince Edward Island as well as parts of eastern Quebec south of the St. Lawrence River. The landscape of this region is dominated by the Appalachian Highlands, ancient worn-down mountains and plateaus seldom exceeding 4,000 feet above sea level. As the Appalachian Highlands extend southward into the New England states, the coastal plain widens, with the result that the Atlantic Provinces can accommodate only about one-tenth as many people as their southern counterpart, even though the two regions cover basically the same land area. The generally poor soil of the Appalachian Highlands has restricted agricultural settlement in the Atlantic Provinces to the river valleys and the narrow coastal plain, while the rugged terrain has been a barrier to land transportation both within the region and with the rest of Canada. The fact that, throughout most of their history, the Atlantic Provinces have had easier contact with the New England states than with the other Canadian provinces has been a constant source of political discontent.

On the other hand, the Appalachian Highlands have endowed the Atlantic Provinces with significant forest and mineral wealth, notably coal, which sustained economic interest in the region well into the 20th century. But the foremost natural resource of the Atlantic region is derived from its maritime location. The deeply indented coastline with numerous excellent harbors became the launching point for one of the world's greatest fishing grounds, including the once-renowned cod fisheries of Newfoundland's Grand Banks. The lure of the sea in addition to a ready supply of timber enabled the region to become a prolific shipbuilding and shipping center by the middle of the 19th century. Ultimately, nature would prove to be less generous to the Atlantic region than it was to other regions to the west and south. A shortage of fertile land remained a deterrence to population growth, and a limited resource base could not withstand human exploitation.

The St. Lawrence Lowlands

A stark contrast to the limited resources of the Appalachian region is the natural abundance of the St. Lawrence Lowlands to the west. Encompassing most of southern Quebec and southern Ontario, this predominantly flat fertile plain occupies less than 2 percent of Canada's total area but accommodates over 60 percent of the nation's population. Blessed with a favorable climate, excellent soil, and easy access by land and water, the upper St. Lawrence Valley and Great Lakes basin was the original agricultural heartland before becoming the commercial, industrial, and financial center of the nation. Indeed, the contrasting fates of the St. Lawrence and Atlantic regions demonstrate the importance of agriculture in laying the foundation for future economic and population growth in Canada.

Transportation was another key to development. From the outset, the St. Lawrence River and the Great Lakes formed a vital water highway linking the Atlantic Ocean with the continental interior. Ironically, this east-west route proved to be an agent of both continentalism and nationalism. On the one hand, the waterway facilitated the movement of people and goods to and from New York and Pennsylvania as well as the Ohio-Mississippi Valley, a natural extension of the St. Lawrence lowlands. On the other hand, the St. Lawrence–Great Lakes system launched a succession of explorers and traders along a transcontinental course leading to the northwest and Pacific regions, later followed by the railroad. Thus, the St. Lawrence region emerged as a hub of transportation and trade, thriving as a beneficiary of the north-south pull of the United States and as a catalyst for east-west integration within a national economic framework.

The Canadian Shield

The dominance of the St. Lawrence region was reinforced by still another geographical factor—access to a resource frontier to the north and west. Initially, the vast wilderness to the north, known as the Canadian Shield, was considered to be the chief obstacle to Canadian development. This expanse of Precambrian rock, worn down by millions of years of glaciation, covers almost half of Canada's land surface, including much of the northern frontiers of Quebec, Ontario, Manitoba, and Saskatchewan, as well as Nunavut and the eastern edge of the Northwest Territories. The rugged terrain of the Shield is interspersed with forest, scrub bush, muskeg swamp, numerous lakes and streams, and isolated pockets of arable land that offered little or no attraction to the farming pioneer. Thus, until the late 19th century, the Shield remained a colossal barrier to the spread of settlement westward from the St. Lawrence region. Only the fur trader voyaging by canoe and portage was capable of regularly negotiating the 1,000-mile trek.

Advancing technology and industrialization, however, would transform the Shield from an uninhabitable wilderness to a valuable hinterland. The building of the Canadian Pacific Railway during the 1880s not only regularized transportation and communication across this barrier but also uncovered a treasure house of natural resources. Minerals both base and precious, pulpwood for paper production, and hydroelectric power harnessed from the fast-flowing rivers and streams have greatly enhanced industrial development, particularly in southern Ontario and southern Quebec, and have provided another exportable commodity for the increasingly important U.S. market. Furthermore, the forest areas of the southern Shield, with their numerous lakes and rivers, have become an attractive sporting and vacation land in the leisure-conscious 20th century. While the opening of the northern resource frontier has led to the establishment of small communities around centers of activity, the lack of cultivable land in addition to a less favorable climate has limited population growth to less than 5 percent of the national total.

The Hudson Bay Lowlands and the Arctic Region

To the north of the Shield lie two other sparsely settled regions that together encompass nearly one-third of Canada's land area. Surrounding Hudson and James Bays along the northern edges of Manitoba and Ontario, the Hudson Bay Lowlands make up an infertile plain, locked in permafrost and characterized by marshes, peat, and innumerable ponds. The vast Arctic region, including the northern coastal mainland of Canada and the Arctic islands, is mostly treeless tundra and rock, frozen eight to nine months of the year. Aside from the indigenous population, the region has sustained small-scale fur trading posts and whaling stations since the mid-19th century. In recent times, the region has taken on strategic value as a location for weather and radar stations. The future also holds out the promise of significant mineral and energy resources, but the cost of northern development and exploration tends to place a considerable strain on an economy sustained by a population of scarcely 30 million. In the final analysis, the vast expanse of northland, including the Shield, the Hudson Bay Lowlands, and the Arctic region, is a major factor contributing to the population discrepancy between the two North American nations.

The Great Central Plains

Nowhere are the limiting and divisive effects of geography more evident than in the Great Central Plains region to the west of the Canadian Shield. A northern extension of the great continental plain that stretches unbroken and ever-widening from the Arctic Ocean toward the Gulf of Mexico, this region is almost evenly divided into two distinct subregions. The portion immediately north of the international boundary consists of the flat, treeless Prairie triangle extending 750 miles from eastern Manitoba to the foothills of the Rocky Mountains and projecting 400 miles northward into Alberta. The Prairie region—including the dry belt in southeastern Alberta and southwestern Saskatchewan where the American desert reaches across the border—represents three-quarters of the cultivable land in Canada. The area to the north of the main Prairie region is generally characterized by more undulating forested land of low agricultural potential and deteriorating climate conditions, although fertile pockets of land that are difficult to access can be found in the Peace and Mackenzie River valleys. While this northern parkland was attractive to the early fur traders, the grain-growing potential of the southerly Prairie region was the catalyst for national development in the late 19th and early 20th centuries and a source of sectional discontent thereafter.

Distance from major markets and suppliers, dependence on fluctuating world prices, and vulnerability to the hazards of nature, including cyclic droughts and an erratic growing season—have all combined to make Prairie farming a precarious occupation. Within this context, Prairie farmers have grown resentful of national government policies that appear to serve the interests of central Canadian manufacturers and bankers at their expense. The prosperity generated by discovery of oil and natural gas in Alberta and Saskatchewan in the mid-20th century and subsequent disagreements between the provincial and national governments over pricing and marketing policies have intensified western discontent over central Canadian "imperialism." This political alienation has reinforced a prevailing sense of physical isolation caused by formidable mountain barriers to the east and west. Thus, prairie inhabitants invariably feel a closer affinity to the plains dwellers south of the border than to their fellow Canadians to the east, west, or north.

The Western Cordilleras

Western alienation and isolation is compounded by the imposing Cordilleras, a mountain system extending the length of the Pacific coast of North and South America. The Canadian part of the Cordilleras, which covers about one-sixth of the nation's total area, dominates the landscape of British Columbia and the Yukon Territory to the north. Unlike those of the Canadian Shield and the Appalachian Highlands, these are young mountains rising to a height of 13,000 feet. Early travelers from the east faced the daunting prospect of surmounting the Rockies, which loom majestically over the Alberta flatlands. Before reaching the Pacific shores they had to cross three other formidable ranges—the Selkirk, Coast, and Cascade—rising parallel to one another. It is therefore not surprising that this region, like the Canadian Shield, remained the private domain of the fur traders and the indigenous people until the completion of the Canadian Pacific Railway in 1885.

Thereafter, the development of British Columbia paralleled that of the Shield region with the recognition of its abundant mineral, forest, and hydroelectric power potential for industrial production, in addition to its coastal fisheries. But unlike the Shield region, British Columbia is blessed with fertile soil and a temperate climate in its southern river valleys, which proved attractive for agricultural settlement. In particular, the Fraser Valley in the southwest corner contains over half of the province's population even though it covers less than 1 percent of the province's area. As a result of this concentration of population close to the U.S. border, along with the mountain barriers and the vast distance from central Canada, British Columbians have developed a distinctly Pacific outlook with stronger connections with the people of California and the nearby American northwestern states than with their fellow Canadians to the east.

Given the prevailing geographic realities, it seems remarkable that Canada could have been conceived as a transcontinental nation in the modern sense, let alone enduring and even prospering for the past 130 years. Not only have Canadians had to overcome the challenges of geography but they have had to resist the temptation to follow the dictates of nature and to cast their lot with a better endowed and more powerful neighbor, as Goldwin Smith urged them to do. In choosing to defy nature for the sake of nationalism, modern Canadians have effectively pursued a course somewhat different from that of their indigenous ancestors who also sought an independent existence but one essentially in harmony with nature.

IN HARMONY WITH NATURE

The original inhabitants of North America left no direct written account of their evolution prior to sustained European contact beginning in the late 15th century. But archaeological evidence suggests that they migrated from Siberia to Alaska via a land bridge known as Beringia toward the end of the last ice age at least 10,000 years ago. Even when the glacial ice sheets melted and Beringia was submerged by the present-day Bering Sea, it was still possible to make the approximately 50-mile crossing between Siberia and Alaska. As many as 10 million people may have gradually spread across the continent in search of more favorable hunting and fishing sites. To these first peoples, North America was truly a boundless frontier; their freedom of movement was restricted only by geographical barriers or by clashes with more powerful enemies. Unencumbered by political boundaries in the modern sense, the indigenous people tended to cluster in small, culturally diverse tribes or bands wherever it suited their needs.

The estimated 250,000 to 500,000 indigenous people who roamed the Canadian territory probably belonged to even more than the 11 linguistic families speaking at least 53 distinct languages that currently exist among the Native people of Canada. Although common language and customs could form the basis of tribal organization, the nomadic lifestyle of the Native people and the extent of territory over which they wandered often worked against political or cultural unity on this basis. A more enduring and distinguishable basis of unity was more often evident among those Native bands who adapted their way of life to the conditions and resources of the regions that they occupied. Thus, Native cultural divisions tend to coincide with Canada's geographic divisions.

Eastern Woodlands

The dense forests of the Appalachian Highlands, the St. Lawrence Lowlands, and the lower fringes of the Canadian Shield in Quebec and Ontario provided a common environment for a Native population that belonged to two unrelated linguistic families. An estimated 30,000 to 40,000 Algonquian-speaking people occupied the Maritime and lower Shield regions. Most notable among the eastern Algonquians were the Micmac of Nova Scotia and the Malecite of New Brunswick, and perhaps the now-extinct Beothuk of Newfoundland. The Algonquians further inland included the Montagnais along the lower St. Lawrence Valley, the Algonquin of the Ottawa River valley, the Nipissing in the Lake Nipissing region, the Ottawa on Manitoulin Island in Lake Huron, and the powerful Ojibwa or Chippewa along the north shore of Lakes Huron and Superior.

Depending on their location, the nomadic Algonquians hunted deer, moose, caribou, bear, seal, and walrus as a source of food, clothing, tools, and weapons. They gathered wild rice and an assortment of berries, nuts, tubers, and plants, in addition to harvesting maple and birch sap. Agriculture as a subsistence activity was either marginal or nonexistent among most of the Algonquians. To assist one another in obtaining food, several closely related families joined together to form a band, and the band-village led by a hereditary male chief became the principal political unit. Band-villages, however, were not strictly demarcated, and all members had equal access to basic subsistence resources. To navigate the waterways of the St. Lawrence–Great Lakes system, the central Algonquians became skilled in making and handling the birch-bark canoe, which later European traders and explorers would find indispensable in opening up the Canadian frontier.

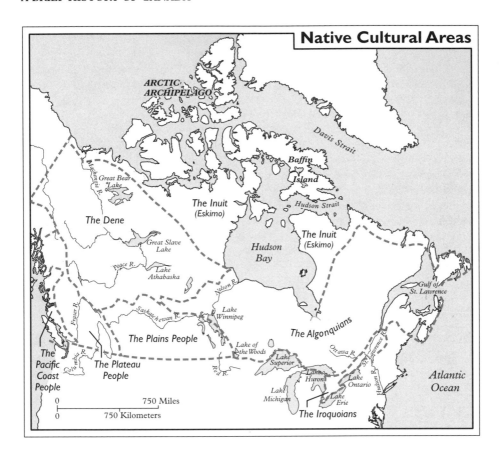

Native Cultural Areas

An estimated 70,000 to 90,000 Iroquoian-speaking people inhabited much of the St. Lawrence lowlands and the neighboring New York, Pennsylvania, and Ohio regions. The Huron, Neutral, Petun, and Tobacco tribes inhabited the southern Ontario frontier while the Seneca, Cayuga, Onondaga, Oneida, and Mohawk formed the League of Five Nations or the Iroquois Confederacy along the southern shore of Lakes Ontario and Erie and the upper St. Lawrence River. After prolonged warfare, the Five Nations Iroquois drove out their northern kinfolk by the mid-17th century.

Initially a traditional hunting and fishing people like the neighboring Algonquians, the Iroquois evolved into a primarily seminomadic and agricultural people. While men were responsible for hunting, fishing, trading, warfare, and clearing the land for cultivation, women assumed the responsibility of planting, cultivating, and harvesting the farm crops, notably corn, beans, squash, and tobacco. The fertility of the soil, therefore, became the major criterion for choosing the sites of the stockaded villages around which their cultivated fields were located. The village sites inevitably had to be moved every 10 to 15 years when the soil and available firewood became exhausted.

The semisedentary life of the Iroquoian agricultural existence necessitated dwellings more comfortable and permanent than the conical birch-bark tipis or domed wigwams hastily built by their roving Algonquian neighbors. Accordingly, within stockaded villages of 1,500 to 2,500 people, 10 to 30 families belonging to the same clan lived together in dwellings known as longhouses. These single-story, apartmentlike rectangular complexes, constructed of a framework of small timbers and covered with sheets of elm or cedar bark, stretched upwards of 60 yards in length by 12 yards in width, with a 10-foot corridor running down the middle of the house. Residence in these households was matrilocal. A man could only marry a woman from outside of his clan, whereupon he would move into his wife's longhouse as a kind of guest. Moreover, descent, inheritance, and succession followed the female line. Several matrilineages comprised a clan, and three to 10 clans whose members were scattered in various villages comprised a tribe.

The tribe formed the basis of the highly developed political organization that became the Five Nations Confederacy by the late 15th century. Formed to promote common action in external affairs, the Five Nations Confederacy was governed by a council of 50 permanent and hereditary chiefs who dealt with disputes among the tribes, conducted negotiations, and decided on peace or war. The Huron adopted a similar political system to counteract their Iroquois enemies. The confederacy gave the Iroquois a degree of political coherence that enabled it to emerge as the most powerful military force among Canada's Native people. But foreshadowing the future Canadian Confederation, the central council could not always control the ambitions of individual tribal leaders who were all too willing to assert their authority in domestic affairs and to advance their parochial interests at the expense of national unity.

Plains

Unlike their Iroquois and Algonquian neighbors to the east, the indigenous people of the western Prairie region had little or no direct contact with European explorers and traders until well into the 18th century. The estimated 30,000 Natives of the Canadian plains belonged to three linguistic families. The Algonquian-speaking people included the Blackfoot of southern Alberta and the Plains Cree and Plains Ojibwa in the Saskatchewan River valley and the Lake Winnipeg region. The Assiniboine and Sioux of southern Manitoba and Saskatchewan spoke the Siouan languages. The numerically small Scarcee tribe in the Rocky Mountain foothills spoke an Athapascan tongue.

Although they occupied the rich agricultural prairie lands, the Plains people had neither the tools, the knowledge, nor the necessity to till the fertile soil. Instead, the immense herds of buffalo that roamed over and fed upon these grasslands was the foundation of Plains culture. Buffalo meat was the dietary staple, either cooked directly or ground and mixed with fat and berries to produce pemmican. Buffalo hide was used for clothing, footwear, shields, and cover for the conically shaped tipis that served as homes. Buffalo bones, hooves, and horns provided tools, weapons, and utensils. Buffalo hair and sinew was used for thread and bowstrings. Buffalo dung was a source of fuel on the treeless plain.

The dependence on hunting buffalo along with antelope, deer, and grouse dictated a nomadic existence. The constant search for buffalo herds inhibited extensive social or tribal organization. Most tribes consisted of loosely organized and independent bands. Only in midsummer, when the buffalo were concentrated in large herds, would the bands come together for a few weeks in one large communal hunting drive. Once the well-organized buffalo hunt ended, the bands dispersed to their own encampments to prepare for the harsh winter. Intertribal trade and raiding brought the horse to the Canadian plains by the end of the 17th century. The immediate result was an improvement in hunting technique, as people no longer had to follow the buffalo herd on foot. But in addition to enhancing the mobility of the Plains people, the use of the horse intensified their sense of independence from each other, which in turn would render them vulnerable to European encroachment.

Pacific Coast and Plateau

Almost half of the Native population of Canada lived in modern-day British Columbia on the eve of European contact. Moreover, the coastal and interior regions of British Columbia had the most linguistically diverse indigenous population. Despite their proximity to one another, the peoples living along the Pacific coast and in the interior plateau region evolved as distinct cultural communities primarily because of the isolating effects of the towering Cordilleran mountain ranges.

The people of the Pacific belong to five unrelated language families consisting of 19 distinct languages. Among the major tribes strung along the coast from north to south are the Tlingit and the Haida of nearby Queen Charlotte Island, each of whom speaks a unique language that has no known relationship to any other. Immediately to the south of the Tlingit are people who speak three languages of the Tsimshian language family. The Kwakwala or Kwakiutl to the south of the Tsimshian and the Nootka on the western coast of Vancouver Island are part of the Wakashan language family, while the southwest coastal Salish and the inland Bella Coola are members of the large Salishan language family.

The coastal people made good use of the abundant marine and forest resources of their region. They were capable fishers and sea hunters, depending largely on salmon, seal, and sea otter for food, clothing, and tools. The dense forests also provided them with ample deer, elk, bear, and mountain goat, in addition to giant cedar and fir timbers for their long dugout canoes. These seaworthy canoes, with a capacity of as many as 50 adults, enabled them to travel great distances to raid and trade with their neighbors. The giant timbers were also split with antler wedges into wide, smooth planks and used to build massive communal houses. The tall, straight trunks were worked with stone and later iron tools (derived from trade with Europeans) into elaborately sculptured totem poles that depicted the crests and legendary histories of the chieftains' families.

The abundance of resources encouraged the Pacific coast peoples to live in relatively permanent villages close to navigable water under the leadership of two or three hereditary clan chiefs. United by kinship, dialect, or common territorial interest, villages were generally independent of each other, although in times of war a chief of commanding personality and fighting skill might form a temporary alliance with other villages in the area. Village society was organized on the basis of a rigid class system, in which people were generally divided into three ranks—nobles, commoners, and slaves—that did not customarily intermarry. Similar to European feudal society, property was a basis of ranking and a measure of affluence. The noble families claimed possession of all the land and places for hunting, fishing, and gathering while the mass of the common people sought their protection and employ. The slaves were either prisoners of war or their offspring. They had no civil rights and could be sold at their noble owner's will. To enhance their prestige, the chiefs and nobles would organize a potlatch, a special kind of feast that involved a distribution of gifts according to the rank of the invited guests. Potlatches were celebrated on all possible occasions, and noble families often competed against each other to provide lavish gifts as a sign of their wealth and generosity.

The indigenous peoples of the interior plateau region were less populous and more scattered than their Pacific coast neighbors, primarily because of the difficulties of communication in this rugged area between the coastal mountains and the Rockies. Included among the Plateau societies are the Interior Salish of the Fraser River basin, an eastern extension of the Salishan linguistic family; the Kutenai (Kootenay) in the Kootenay River basin to the east; and the Athapascan-speaking people to the north, the largest of whom were the Carrier tribe.

Somewhat like their coastal neighbors, the seminomadic Plateau people depended on salmon fishing and hunting for bear, caribou, moose, deer, and mountain goat. But in custom, dress, and housing, they resembled the people of the Plains far more than they did those to the west. Moreover, Plateau community life resembled the simple organizations of the nomadic hunting people of the Eastern Woodlands. A group of families related by blood or marriage formed a band led by a hereditary chief or headman whose advice was sought and who would represent the group in an informal council of older men and prominent hunters. Each band had its own hunting and fishing territory, held in common by all its families, who generally wandered and hunted together. Wherever they came into contact with their stronger and more advanced coastal neighbors, the inland people tended to adopt their ways of life, including the hierarchical clan system and the potlatch. Unlike the Pacific coast people who expressed their heritage through their art forms, the Plateau people carried on a remote existence until the initial European contact in the late 18th century.

Subarctic and Arctic

The inhospitable climate and terrain of the upper Canadian Shield, the Hudson Bay Lowlands, the Mackenzie and Yukon River valleys, and the northern reaches of the western Cordilleras have sustained a widely scattered and sparsely populated Subarctic cultural group. In fact, Subarctic population densities were among the lowest in the world, as little more than 60,000 Natives occupied an area in excess of 2 million square miles on the eve of sustained European contact. Most of the Subarctic people were not organized politically into tribes; but neighboring bands, speaking a common language dialect, exploiting the resources of the same territory, or closely related by family ties or marriage tended to form identifiable groups. Broadly speaking, the Subarctic peoples belong to two regionally based language families. The Algonquian-speaking people of the eastern Subarctic include the Innu (Montagnais-Neskapi) of northern Quebec and Labrador, the Cree in the Hudson Bay Lowland and upper Shield regions of Quebec and Ontario, and the Ojibwa northwest of Lake Superior. More than 20 Athapascan languages are known to be spoken among the people of the western Subarctic who are known today as the Dene. Among the major groups spread across the Northwest and Yukon territories from Hudson Bay to Alaska were the Chippewyan, Slave, Beaver, Dogrib, Sekani, Tutchone, and Kutchin.

The Subarctic peoples were primarily hunters and forest dwellers who lived in bands of 25 to 30 members. With no permanent villages, each band moved frequently within a defined territory in search of caribou, beaver, and hare in the northern districts and bear, moose, and buffalo in the southern districts. When game was in short supply, they fished in the numerous rivers and lakes. During the summer, several local bands often resided together to take advantage of prime hunting and fishing sites. Most Subarctic bands did not have formal chiefs prior to European contact; instead, they followed the leadership of a senior male who took the initiative in undertaking particular tasks such as trading, warfare, and communal hunting. All adult males and females had a voice in the decision-making process, and families or individuals who disagreed with decisions affecting the band were free to join another band. Such a degree of personal autonomy and flexibility in social organization helped the Subarctic peoples respond to the opportunities and challenges of their environment.

Overcoming the limitations of the environment was an even greater challenge for the Native people of the Arctic region. Historically known as Eskimos, an Algonquian word roughly meaning "eaters of raw meat," the Arctic people in recent times have preferred to call themselves Inuit, simply meaning "people." They speak one common language, Inukitut or Eskimo-Aleut, although as many as six dialects are spoken throughout the Arctic region. The Inuit are divided into eight main tribal groups, some of which are named after the regions in which they are located: the Labrador, the Ungava of northeastern Quebec, the Baffin Island, the Iglulik along the northwestern shore of Hudson Bay, the Caribou along the mainland coast west of Hudson Bay, the Netsilik along the Arctic coast west of Hudson Bay, the Copper of Victoria Island and the adjacent mainland region, and the nearly extinct Mackenzie whose territory in the Mackenzie River delta was taken over in the 20th century by Alaskan Natives to form the Western Arctic Inuit community.

Over thousands of years, the Inuit developed from their Paleoeskimo ancestors, notably the Dorset and Thule cultures, a special ability to adapt to their barren and polar environment by making inventive use of meager local resources. They hunted caribou, polar bear, seal, and whale not only for their food but also for all the various necessities of life. The skins of these animals, for example, were used to make clothing and footwear, tentlike summer shelters, and both single-seated water craft known as kayaks and larger vessels called umiaks. From bone and ivory, the Inuit made bows and arrows, spears and harpoons, knives, fishhooks, and runners for sleds pulled by dogs over snow and ice. From seal, walrus, and whale, they derived oil for fuel and lighting. Out of blocks of ice and snow, they constructed their dome-shaped winter dwelling known as the igloo.

The need to wander incessantly over land, ice, and water in search of game and sea mammals made for rather transitory community organization. Approximately 20,000 Inuit were scattered in small communities throughout the nearly 1 million square miles of Arctic frontier on the eve of sustained European contact in the late 18th century. The most important social and political unit was the regional band, several of which together constituted a tribal group consisting of 500 to 1,000 members. During the winter, regional bands tended to congregate in groups of 100 to 200 people to hunt seal. But in the summer they would disperse into smaller bands of two to five families to pursue their own destinies and occasionally to form new groupings in response to social needs and desires to interact with kin living elsewhere. Although elder men whose strength of character and physical skills gave them prestige in the community that allowed them to wield a certain amount of influence, they were not chiefs and possessed no real authority over their own or neighboring groups. Such a loosely knit community organization reflected the precariousness of life in an environment where human settlement was governed by seasonally available food resources.

Prior to sustained European contact, in essence, the Native peoples had already laid the foundation for future human development in the northern half of North America in three significant respects. First, a sustainable economy was based on the exploitation of abundant, albeit unevenly distributed, natural resources. Traditional Native technology negated the possibility of resource depletion or of refinement of resources for industrial production. Second, society was invariably multicultural and multilingual. Vast distances, geographical barriers, and limited transportation technology often prevented an intermingling of these diverse native cultures. Third, geography dictated the persistence of regionalism as the basis for political or social organization. Accordingly, lines of communication and exchange for the Native peoples were more often north and south than east and west. Into this context came Europeans with their modern technology and peculiar concepts of property ownership and nationally based political organizations, which over a period of five centuries would profoundly alter the natural domain of Canada.

CHAPTER 2

ACCIDENTAL REDISCOVERY

Although Canada was originally discovered by anonymous Native peoples, the first attempts to record the process of exploring and identifying the unknown land were undertaken by European navigators and adventurers. Yet the earliest moments of European contact are almost as mysterious as the prehistoric period. A partial explanation for this ambiguous beginning lies in the serendipitous nature of the European "rediscovery" of the "New World" and the disappointment that inevitably followed. In *The Oxford History of the American People*, historian Samuel Eliot Morison points out:

> America was discovered by a great seaman who was looking for something else; when discovered it was not wanted; and most of the exploration for the next fifty years was done in the hope of getting through it or around it.

While Morison was referring to Christopher Columbus's discovery of the West Indies in 1492, similar circumstances and sentiments surrounded the early European landings in Canada. Disillusioned by their failure to fulfill their destiny, the early explorers tended to make a cursory note of Canada's existence and continued hopefully in their quest for more rewarding discoveries.

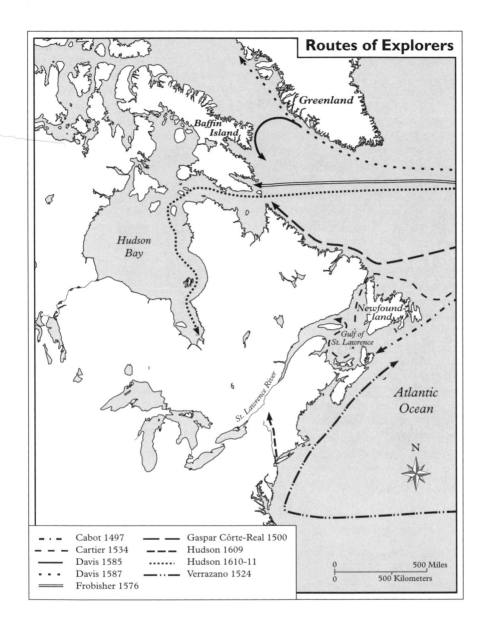

Routes of Explorers

Greenland

Baffin Island

Hudson Bay

Newfoundland

Gulf of St. Lawrence

St. Lawrence River

Atlantic Ocean

N

— · — Cabot 1497	— — Gaspar Côrte-Real 1500	
— — — Cartier 1534	— — — Hudson 1609	
——— Davis 1585	········ Hudson 1610-11	
· · · Davis 1587	— ·· — Verrazano 1524	
═══ Frobisher 1576		

0 — 500 Miles
0 — 500 Kilometers

THE NORSE VOYAGES

The accident and ambiguity of the European rediscovery of Canada is epitomized by the Norse voyages of the late 10th and early 11th centuries. In search of more farmland, Scandinavian mariners, known as Norsemen or Vikings, had ventured northwestwardly from the European mainland to discover and colonize Iceland about 874 and Greenland in 985. According to ancient Norse sagas, trader Bjarni Herjolfsson was blown off course on his way from Iceland to Greenland in 986 when he became the first known European to sight the mainland of North America. Having likely reached the coast of Labrador, he decided against landing, purportedly concluding: "This land is unwinsome and ungainsome." In other words, the first recorded opinion about North America was that it was neither pretty nor profitable.

While Herjolfsson apparently had no desire to explore the lands he sighted, his reports about its dense forests generated some interest in Greenland, where wood was in short supply. Around 1001, Leif Eriksson, the son of Greenland colonizer Erik the Red, sailed west to investigate the resources of this strange territory. He and his crew therefore became the first known Europeans to set foot on North American soil. Norse sagas indicate that Eriksson's expedition first landed in a place which he called Helluland, meaning "land of flat stones," now believed to be either the southern coast of Baffin Island or the northern coast of Labrador. The expedition then sailed southward, landing at a place that Eriksson called Markland, or "wooded land," probably the central or southern coast of Labrador. The third landfall was called Vinland, which could mean "wine land," "vine land," "fruitful land," or "grassland." Modern historians and geographers have variously located Vinland from southern Labrador to Florida. After wintering in Vinland and exploring the area further, Eriksson and his crew returned to Greenland with a cargo of timber, vines (valued as fasteners in shipbuilding), and "wineberries" (likely currants, gooseberries, or cranberries).

While Leif Eriksson never returned to Vinland, several Norse expeditions were launched from Greenland to establish settlements in the new western lands during the first decade of the 11th century. Leif Eriksson's brother Thorvald led an expedition to Vinland in 1004. The following year the first recorded contact between Europeans and native North Americans ended in violence. As they explored the coastline, Eriksson and his men encountered and murdered a small group of "skraelings," as the sagas called them, a word that may be translated as "wretches" or, as later Europeans would say, "savages." In an ensuing retaliatory skirmish, Eriksson was killed by a native arrow, and his men retreated to Greenland.

Perhaps the most ambitious colonizing venture was led by Icelander Thorfinn Karlsefni, who brought over 160 settlers about 1011. The colonists bartered with local Natives, but conflict again erupted, and the Norse were driven back to Greenland within two years. A final attempt to colonize Vinland was led by Leif Eriksson's half-sister, Freydis, but it too ended in bloody confrontation among the settlers and the Natives. Although there were no further colonizing efforts, Norse traders from Greenland periodically returned to acquire timber until about the mid-14th century when the Greenland settlements were abandoned.

Knowledge of the western exploits of the Norse was derived from the *Greenlanders' Saga* and *Erik the Red's Saga*, both of which consist of stories passed down orally from generation to generation before they were written down in the late 12th and middle 13th centuries, respectively. Accordingly, the sagas were designed to serve more of a literary than a historical purpose, with the result that the distinction between fact and legend often became blurred. Not until 1960 did archaeologists unearth indisputable evidence of Norse settlement at L'Anse aux Meadows on the northern tip of Newfoundland. Whether this site was Leif Eriksson's Vinland, the Karlsefni colony, or some other unknown settlement, it was clear that the Norse had visited Canada at least five centuries earlier than had any other Europeans.

RENEWED EUROPEAN INTEREST
IN THE NEW WORLD

In the late 15th century, Europeans discovered the New World for a third time. Because the native experience was unrecorded and the Norse sagas had disappeared until they were rediscovered at the end of the 16th century, European explorers beginning with Columbus had to approach the New World with little or no awareness of the routes and discoveries of their predecessors. The revival of interest in the New World once again originated by accident rather than by design. In fact, the grand design of the age was not to find a new world but to reach an ancient world. Since ancient times, the Indies—an all-encompassing term for southern and eastern Asia including India and China—had been a source of goods that Europeans valued highly: silks and other fine textiles, precious gemstones, and pungent and fragrant spices. Peppers, nutmeg, cinnamon, and cloves were vital in preserving and improving the taste of food, and especially in the aging of meat in the absence of refrigeration. But European access to these desirable commodities was restricted by the rising Islamic empire that had gained control of the overland routes to East Asia used by Marco Polo and other Europeans in the 13th century. To the increasingly powerful nation-states of 15th-century western Europe, economic and military supremacy was bound up in the quest for a direct sea route to the Indies that would bypass the intricate and costly Muslim trade monopoly.

Portugal took the lead in the race to the east when Bartholomeu Diaz successfully circumnavigated the southern tip of Africa in 1488, and within 10 years Vasco da Gama had crossed the Indian Ocean to reach India. Meanwhile, rival Spain supported the expedition of Italian navigator Christopher Columbus who maintained that, because the world was round, it was possible to reach East Asia by sailing west. He was so convinced that he had reached India at the end of his first voyage in 1492 that he called the Native people "Indians," a designation that remains common. Columbus's voyage not only intensified the maritime rivalry between Spain and Portugal but also raised questions about the rights of the two Catholic nations to evangelize the Native peoples of the recently "discovered" territories. Accordingly, in 1493 Pope Alexander VI established a "line of demarcation," modified slightly by the Treaty of Tordesillas the following year, whereby all lands lying to the west of the line were under the jurisdiction of Spain while those lying to the east belonged to Portugal. This division placed some of the Atlantic region of Canada and much of Brazil within the Portuguese sphere of influence.

Having actually discovered the Caribbean Islands, Central America, and South America during his four voyages, Columbus still believed that he had reached Asia by the time another Italian navigator, Giovanni Caboto (subsequently anglicized as John Cabot), sailed from England on a westward voyage across the north Atlantic in 1497. On June 24, 1497, Caboto landed somewhere along the coast of Labrador, Newfoundland, or Cape Breton Island, thus marking the first recorded landfall on the North American mainland since the Norse voyages. Claiming the land for England (although he planted the flags of both England and Venice), Caboto explored what he believed to be the northeastern coast of China. He did, however, make two discoveries that would spur him on to further exploration and that would be significant for the future development of the continent. First, he found the Grand Banks of Newfoundland, a fertile breeding ground for cod. The sea so swarmed with fish that the crew could catch them with baskets let down on ropes from the deck of the ship. Second, Caboto came upon a large passage, the Gulf of St. Lawrence, which he believed was a direct route to the heartland of China. Encouraged by these findings, he returned triumphantly to England, whereupon the king rewarded him for reaching this "new found land" by sponsoring a second voyage in 1498. The expedition never returned, and it is believed that Caboto likely perished somewhere off the coast of Newfoundland. Despite the failure to reach Asia, Caboto's voyages are significant for establishing England's claim to the Atlantic Coast of North America and for stimulating further interest in pursuing a northern sea route to Asia.

The rich cod fishing grounds discovered by Caboto soon attracted Portuguese, Spanish, English, French, and Basque fishing fleets seeking to satisfy a market created in predominantly Catholic Europe, where abstinence from meat was decreed for more than 150 days a year. From March to October of each year, upwards of 10,000 fishermen would gather in the waters off the coast of Newfoundland and Cape Breton Island before returning to Europe with their catch. The Portuguese and Spanish fishing fleets, using the "green" or "wet" method of preservation, remained offshore where they caught and heavily salted the fish directly onboard ship. The French and English fleets, using the "dry" or "shore" method of preservation, took their catch ashore to be dried on racks or "flakes," which meant that the fish needed only a light salting to avoid spoilage during the long voyage home.

The huts and storehouses that the "dry" fishermen built as they tended their cod-strewn drying racks during the summer in effect became the first semblance of European settlement, however impermanent and anonymous, since the Norse efforts five centuries before. The French fishing stations were scattered along the northern and southern shores of Newfoundland and perhaps on the Cape Breton and mainland Nova Scotia coasts, while the English concentrated on the eastern coast of Newfoundland, particularly around the Avalon Peninsula. The cod fishing fleets were joined by Basque whalers who from July to mid-January established their own shore stations in the Strait of Belle Isle between the Newfoundland mainland and Labrador. Whale oil found a ready market in Europe as a source of light; an all-purpose lubricant; and an additive to drugs, soap, and numerous other products. To these temporary fishing and whaling stations, local Natives came to exchange their furs and beaver robes for European metal goods and textiles, a prelude to the trading links that would open up the northern American frontier in the next century.

While countless fishing and whaling fleets singularly operated in relative historical obscurity throughout the 16th century, the quest for a northern sea route to Asia continued to capture the public imagination in Europe. The Portuguese, believing that the Atlantic Coast of North America lay east of the papal line of demarcation and was therefore under their sphere of influence, sought to complement their eastward route to India around Africa with a westward passage. An expedition led by Gaspar Côrte-Real explored the North Atlantic coastline from Greenland to Newfoundland in 1500. He identified the forests of the region as a valuable supply of timber for masts and ships and the Native peoples as promising sources of slaves comparable to west Africa. When he returned to the Labrador coast in 1501, Côrte-Real abducted 57 Natives and shipped them back to Portugal with his brother Miguel. Like Caboto, Gaspar Côrte-Real and his crew never returned from this second voyage, and the same fate befell his brother, who came back to search for him in 1502. Around 1520 João Alvarez Fagundes explored the southern coast of Newfoundland and the Gulf of St. Lawrence with a view toward establishing a colony called Cabo Bretão. Probably located on Cape Breton Island, this colony appears to have been short-lived as a result of clashes with the local Natives. Although no trace of the colony has ever been found and little is known about it, Portugal's Cabo Bretão seems to have been the first European colony established north of Florida since the time of the Norse. But after the failure of this colony, the Portuguese—except for those seafarers who annually fished the Grand Banks and the coastal waters off Newfoundland—lost interest in North America.

By the 1520s it was becoming clearer that the land that Columbus and Caboto had discovered was not an extension of Asia. When Spanish explorer Vasco Núñez de Balboa crossed a narrow strip of land in Panama and sighted the Pacific Ocean in 1513, it became apparent that a land mass of undetermined size lay between Europe and Asia. Ferdinand Magellan's ill-fated voyage around the world from 1519 to 1522, during which he traveled westward around the southern tip of South America and across the vast expanse of the Pacific Ocean before reaching Southeast Asia, was further confirmation that America was a distinct continent. Still to be determined was the northern extent of this continental land mass.

At this point France decided to enter the race to East Asia after having long focused its foreign policy on the Mediterranean. The first French voyages to North America had been made by Jean Denys and Thomas Aubert, each of whom explored the eastern coast of Newfoundland in 1506 and 1508, respectively. The seven Beothuk whom Aubert apparently brought back to France were objects of curiosity, but not enough to sustain the interest of the French monarchy. Magellan's expedition, however, stimulated the interest of King Francis I who sought to challenge his arch rival, Emperor Charles V of Spain, by finding a more direct route to the riches of Asia than by the circumnavigation of South America. Thus, Francis I gave his support to an expedition led by yet another Italian mariner, Giovanni da Verrazzano, who in 1524 explored the Atlantic coastline from Florida to Newfoundland. Verrazzano hoped to find either an isthmus dividing the Atlantic Ocean from the Pacific, such as Balboa had found in Panama, or a strait across the northern tip of the continent corresponding to the one Magellan had discovered at the southern end. But after exploring nearly 2,000 miles of continental shoreline, Verrazzano came to the disappointing, albeit important, conclusion that the Atlantic and Pacific Oceans were not connected in the northern hemisphere, and in fact that they were separated by a body of land not connected to Asia. In effect, Verrazzano heralded the existence of a new continent, North America.

Because most of this new continent lay west of the papal line of demarcation, Spain was anxious to investigate its potential. Spain immediately hired Portuguese navigator Esteban Gomez to explore the Atlantic coast from Newfoundland to Florida in 1524–25. Like the Côrte-Reals, Gomez abducted several Native people along the New England or Nova Scotia coast and took them back to Spain to sell as slaves. The Spanish king was not impressed and freed the 58 Natives who reached Spain alive. Disappointed with the results of its northern expeditions, Spain soon found it more profitable to concentrate its exploration and colonization efforts south of Florida.

While the existence of North America was common knowledge in western Europe by the 1530s, the nature and extent of the new continent, beyond a superficial awareness of its eastern coastline, remained a profound mystery. Being as much entrepreneurs as adventurers, these early explorers were more anxious to bring back the "riches" of Asia that their financial backers expected than they were in recording and mapping their discoveries. The sense of disappointment that pervaded their voyages may account for the failure of the explorers to keep precise records of their findings or of succeeding generations to ensure the survival of vital historical documents and artifacts. As a result, the story of the earliest moments of the European rediscovery of the northern American frontier is little more than a rough sketch pieced together from diverse fragments of empirical evidence, deductive reasoning, and educated speculation. Fortunately, the story becomes a little clearer with the voyages of Jacques Cartier.

THE VOYAGES OF JACQUES CARTIER

Unlike his recent predecessors who had sought to circumnavigate North America, Jacques Cartier set sail from Saint-Malo, France, on April 20, 1534, with the intent of finding a sea route through the continental land mass to Asia. In the process, he became the first European to penetrate inland and to leave a detailed surviving account of his adventures, beginning with *Voyages au Canada en 1534.*

Having likely accompanied Verrazzano on his voyages in the previous decade, Cartier, with his expedition of two ships and 61 men, reached Newfoundland within 20 days. When he passed through the Strait of Belle Isle and into the Gulf of St. Lawrence 10 days later, he was in waters previously uncharted by Europeans. He surveyed the southern coast of Labrador, referring to it as "the land God gave Cain," after the biblical wasteland. Following the west coast of Newfoundland, he then veered southwestward to explore the coasts of Prince Edward Island, eastern New Brunswick, and the Gaspé Peninsula. On July 3, his hopes of finding a passage to Asia were aroused by the sight of a large opening in the shoreline, which turned out to be Chaleur Bay, dividing New Brunswick from the Gaspé Peninsula of Quebec.

Here, Cartier met the native Micmac people, who "set up a great clamour and made frequent signs to us to come on shore, holding up to us some furs on sticks." The eagerness of the Natives to trade their furs for metal goods suggests that Cartier's expedition was probably preceded by European fishermen who left no record of their contact. Nevertheless, Cartier's visit represents the first recorded exchange of furs between Natives and Europeans and the first trading exchange of any kind since the Norse voyages. Proceeding north to the Bay of Gaspé, which briefly appeared to be the elusive passage to Asia, Cartier encountered Iroquoian people who had come from the interior to fish and hunt seal. When he raised a cross to claim possession of the land for France on July 24, Cartier not only established trade relations with the Iroquois but also persuaded a reluctant Chief Donnacona to allow his two sons to make the return journey to France so that they could serve as interpreters and guides on the next voyage.

From the Natives, Cartier heard highly embellished but intriguing tales of a great waterway leading to the west and the rich kingdoms to be found in that direction. When he sailed north to Anticosti Island, Cartier gazed upon the St. Lawrence River, which he mistook as a strait leading to the Pacific Ocean. Despite the visions of fantastic Oriental empires offering gold, silver, jewels, and spices, it was now August, and concerns over the approach of autumn storms on the Atlantic prompted the decision to turn back to France.

Cartier's exploits, while falling short of expectations, sufficiently intrigued King Francis I, especially when supported by the imaginative stories of Donnacona's sons, Taignoagny and Domagaya. The king therefore endorsed Cartier's request to undertake a larger expedition of three ships and 110 men, which left Saint Malo on May 19, 1535. After a journey of 50 days, Cartier reached the Gulf of St. Lawrence and explored its north shore for several weeks in search of a passage to Asia. On August 13, as he approached Anticosti Island, Taignoagny and Domagaya informed him that the route to *kanata,* an Iroquoian word meaning village or settlement, lay to the south of the island. In fact, they were referring to their own village of Stadacona, on the future site of Quebec City. But Cartier misinterpreted "Canada" to be the name of the territory ruled by Donnacona, chief of Stadacona. Realizing that it was not a strait as he had surmised on his first journey, Cartier also referred to the river he was entering as the "Rivière du Canada." But three days earlier, he had named a bay north of Anticosti Island "Saint-Laurent," after the Christian martyr whose feast day it was. By the next century, the entire gulf and the great river were commonly referred to as the St. Lawrence.

Cartier continued up the St. Lawrence River to Stadacona where on September 7, he renewed his acquaintance with Chief Donnacona. Viewing the French as powerful and valuable trading partners, Donnacona objected to their intention to proceed inland to a larger Iroquois village at Hochelega. The Stadaconans apparently had the customary right to a monopoly over upriver traffic, and Donnacona recognized the advantages of assuming the broker's role in the trade of furs from the interior Native groups for precious European metal goods. Ignoring Donnacona's wishes and thus foreshadowing future European reaction to Native land and trading rights, Cartier arrived at Hochelega on October 2. There he climbed to the summit of a nearby hill, which he called "Mont Réal" (Mount Royal), and gazed in the distance at the "Lachine" (meaning China) rapids that ended any hopes of further progress by ship. Now nearly 1,000 miles inland, Cartier learned from his Native informants that the St. Lawrence River stretched another three months' journey westward, thereby giving Europeans their first sense of the vastness of the continent. He also learned from the Natives at Hochelega about the Ottawa River, which led to a "land of gold and silver." Allowing for the fertile Native imagination and wishful European interpretations, stories of the rich inland kingdoms probably had some factual basis, referring to the mineral deposits of the Canadian Shield.

With the dream of finding a passage to Asia fading, Cartier returned downriver to Stadacona, where he would make a grim discovery. Too late in the year to risk the return voyage to France, Cartier decided to spend the winter at Stadacona, blissfully unaware of its length and severity. Deceived by the heat of past summers and a latitude more than two degrees south of Paris, Cartier and his men were not prepared for a nightmarish five-month winter in which their fort and ships were buried under several feet of snow and ice. Furthermore, one-quarter of Cartier's crew died of scurvy before they learned of a native cure consisting of boiling white cedar bark and needles to make a herbal tonic rich in ascorbic acid (vitamin C). In preparing for a spring departure, Cartier strained relations with the natives even further by abducting Donnacona, his two sons, and seven of their companions in order to retain tribal support in anticipation of a third French expedition to the St. Lawrence region. Eventually, Donnacona agreed to accompany Cartier to France on the promise that the 10 Iroquois would return safely the following year. None of the Iroquois would survive to return to their homeland.

So unimpressed was King Francis I with the accomplishments of Cartier's second voyage that five years would pass before a third expedition received royal support. In the meantime, Francis I continued to be preoccupied with waging war against Spain, which was challenging French rights to exploit the wealth of the New World on the basis of tradition. In response, the French monarch invoked the new doctrine of imperialism to assert his right to exploit lands not previously occupied by another Christian power. In essence, Francis argued, national claims to territory in the Americas and elsewhere would henceforth rest not on papal decrees but on prior discovery, conquest, and settlement.

Accordingly, to retain exclusive rights to the resources of Canada, France decided to establish a strategically located colony. The king sought to enhance the stature of this endeavor by designating a nobleman, Jean-François de la Roque de Roberval, to lead the expedition and relegating Cartier, a common sea captain, to commander of the fleet. The recruitment of potential colonists, however, proved to be so difficult that the royal prisons became a major source of Canada's first French settlers.

With Roberval's three ships expected to join him later, Cartier left Saint-Malo with five ships on May 23, 1541, and reached Stadacona exactly three months later. Cartier admitted to the Iroquois that Donnacona, an old man, had died of natural causes but falsely announced that the other nine Iroquois whom he had taken to France were not only alive and well but also had become so prosperous that they preferred to remain there permanently. Unsure of whether or not the Iroquois believed him, Cartier decided to settle his 150 colonists at Cap Rouge, some 10 miles upriver from Stadacona. This distance was insufficient to prevent cultural conflict. The Iroquois kept the French under constant siege and eventually killed 35 colonists. After a vain attempt to get past the rapids below Hochelaga and a winter as bitter as the one six years before, Cartier and the remaining colonists set sail for France in June 1542 with a cargo of what they believed to be gold and diamonds extracted from the nearby cliffs. Encountering Roberval's expedition at St. John's harbor in Newfoundland, Cartier ignored orders to return to Cap Rouge and escaped during the night to continue his trip to France. In a final note of bitter irony, the gold and diamonds that he triumphantly offered the king of France turned out to be iron pyrite and quartz.

Meanwhile, Roberval, oblivious to Cartier's ordeal, reestablished the colony at Cap Rouge and resumed the futile attempts to get past the Lachine Rapids. Further discouraged by Iroquois hostility and another harsh winter during which 50 out of 200 colonists died of scurvy, Roberval abandoned the settlement in the summer of 1543. The dismal failure of the first French colony in the New World fostered an image of Canada as an inhospitable and uninhabitable country with little of value to offer the economy of France. When not distracted by civil war and conflict with Spain, French imperial interest for the rest of the century focused on the tropical and subtropical regions to the south, in the Caribbean. Only the fishing fleets that came annually to the Grand Banks of Newfoundland and the Gulf of St. Lawrence sustained the French presence in 16th-century Canada.

QUEST FOR THE NORTHWEST PASSAGE

Fishermen seasonally attending to their dry fishery on the eastern Avalon Peninsula of Newfoundland represented the extent of the English presence in North America for more than three-quarters of a century after Caboto's disappointing voyages. But with England's rise as a great sea power, heralded by Sir Francis Drake's voyage around the world from 1577 to 1581, came a renewed interest in northern discovery. The year before Drake embarked upon his epic global journey, Martin Frobisher undertook his first of three voyages in search of a northwest passage to Asia through the uncharted Arctic waters of Canada. For the next 330 years, the quest for a northwest passage would capture the imagination and daunt the spirit of numerous British oceanic explorers.

In July 1576, after a fairly routine crossing of the north Atlantic, Frobisher and his crew sailed past Greenland into a wide stretch of water that appeared to divide two continents. He named this waterway Frobisher Strait in the belief that, like the Strait of Magellan at the southern tip of South America, it would lead to the Pacific Ocean. As he explored this "strait" for nearly a month, he presumed that he was passing through the gap between the northern coastlines of America and Asia. Unbeknownst to Frobisher, he had not discovered a strait but rather a long, wide bay at the southeastern end of Baffin Island that would one day bear his name. Before he had a chance to realize his mistake, Frobisher encountered Inuit people who apparently had already been trading furs for metal goods with European vessels of the Newfoundland-Labrador fishing and whaling fleets. In the midst of trade relations, misunderstandings ensued and fighting broke out between the Inuit and Frobisher's crew. Having incurred the wrath of the local Natives and mindful that it was late August, Frobisher decided it would be prudent to return to England whereupon he could report triumphantly that not only had he discovered the passage to Asia but the mysterious black rock that he had brought back contained evidence of gold.

The excitement generated by these discoveries persuaded Queen Elizabeth I to provide three ships and a crew of 120 for a second voyage in 1577. Frobisher returned to Baffin Island in July and August, more concerned with mining than exploration. He loaded nearly 200 tons of rock onto his ships before renewed hostilities with the Inuit and the fear of advancing ice prompted his return to England. The four Inuit captives whom Frobisher brought along did not survive more than two months. Furthermore, tests conducted on the new ores led to the hasty conclusion that they contained a quantity of gold and silver sizable enough to warrant a third voyage.

The 15 ships that left England on May 31, 1578, represented the most ambitious overseas speculation of the age and indeed the largest expedition ever sent to the Canadian Arctic. Frobisher was instructed to establish a colony of 100 men to serve as a base for a gold-mining operation. After straying off course into a waterway that Frobisher dubbed "Mistaken Strait" (later known as Hudson Strait) and dogged by ice and stormy weather, the expedition finally reached the site of his earlier excavations on Baffin Island at the end of July. Too late to establish a colony, Frobisher concentrated on setting up an efficient mining operation, which produced over 1,200 tons of ore by the end of August when it became necessary to depart. Back in England, smelters spent the next five years in a futile attempt to extract gold or silver from the ore. In keeping with the adage that "all that glitters is not gold," Frobisher, like Cartier before him, had actually brought back iron pyrite, aptly known as "fool's gold."

Despite the failure of Frobisher's gold-mining venture, the search for a northwest passage to Asia continued. In 1583 Sir Humphrey Gilbert, an early champion of the idea of a northwest passage, attempted to establish a colony in the Avalon Peninsula of Newfoundland to serve as a base from which the search for the passage could be launched. After formally taking possession of Newfoundland for England, he perished at sea and the colonizing mission was abandoned. In 1585 English navigator John Davis continued the quest by sailing to the waters west of Greenland, crossing the strait that would bear his name, and eventually reaching Cumberland Sound, north of Frobisher Bay on Baffin Island. Sailing into Cumberland Sound for about 150 miles, Davis was forced to turn back by stormy weather. Convinced that he had located the passage to Asia, he returned to Baffin Island in 1586. In fog and poor weather, he strayed off course and ended up along the coast of Labrador. On a third attempt, in 1587, Davis sailed up the western coast of Greenland through Davis Strait and into Baffin Bay, reaching farther north than had any other previous navigator. He crossed westward to

Baffin Island before proceeding south to explore Cumberland Sound, but never ascertained whether it was a closed inlet or an open sea.

War with Spain distracted English interest in the northwest passage until 1610 when Henry Hudson sailed into Frobisher's "Mistaken Strait," which was subsequently renamed Hudson Strait. In early August he came upon a huge body of water that he felt certain would lead to Asia. Following its southerly course, he reached the bottom of what came to be known as Hudson Bay and James Bay, where his ship became trapped by ice. During the winter, scurvy made its appearance and supplies ran low. When the ice thawed in the spring, Hudson wanted to continue his exploration, but his men, ravaged by scurvy and a shortage of supplies, did not share his enthusiasm. Mutiny ensued and Hudson, his son, and a few loyal crew members were cast adrift in an open boat, never to be seen again. One of the mutineers, Robert Bylot, who guided Hudson's ship back to England, was pardoned and returned with Thomas Button to search for Hudson in 1612–13. After exploring the western shore of Hudson Bay and finding no prospect of a passage, Bylot accompanied William Baffin in a renewed search for a northerly route in 1615. On their second voyage in 1616, Bylot and Baffin surpassed Davis's northern penetration when they reached the top of Baffin Bay and sailed into the entrance of Lancaster Sound, which they did not realize was the eventual gateway to the northwest passage. On the threshold of conquering the elusive passage, England's interest in far northern discovery was waning, with the result that the records of the Bylot and Baffin discoveries slipped into obscurity and more than two centuries would pass before their feat would be duplicated.

Similarly, enthusiasm for finding a northwest passage via Hudson Bay diminished considerably when Danish naval captain Jens Munk lost 61 out of 64 of his men during a horrifying winter at the mouth of the Churchill River in 1619–20. A final effort was made in 1631, when rival expeditions led by Luke Foxe and Thomas James set sail from England two days apart to explore the western shore of Hudson Bay. Foxe followed a northerly course that led him out of Hudson Bay and into the channel and basin that bear his name, while James proceeded in a southerly direction to explore the bay that is named after him. Both explorers concluded that a western sea route out of Hudson Bay did not exist and that the climate and terrain of the surrounding area rendered colonization inconceivable. Thus, exploration of the Hudson Bay area ceased for the next four decades, while the lure of the northwest passage faded for the next two centuries.

Indeed, the European rediscovery of North America was a multinational affair motivated by the pursuit of commercial goals, notably a western sea route to Asia. The failure to achieve this goal or at least to find the kinds of resources that were valued in western Europe prompted the Scandinavian countries, Portugal, Spain, France, and England to despair over the developmental prospects of the vast, mysterious, and seemingly inhospitable continent by the end of the 16th century. With Portugal and Spain fading fast as imperial powers and preferring to exploit the subtropical regions to the south, the entrepreneurs and missionaries of the two emerging rivals for European supremacy, France and England, would give the northern American frontier a second look in the 17th and 18th centuries and comprehend the potential resources that could be exploited—and the souls that could be converted to Christianity.

PART TWO

THE FRENCH EMPIRE IN NORTHERN AMERICA

1608–1760

CHAPTER 3

THE COLONIZATION OF NEW FRANCE

The development of the northern American frontier in the 17th and 18th centuries was a product of intense imperial rivalry between two emerging European powers. The rivalry between Protestant, democratic Britain and Catholic, feudal France occasionally erupted into international warfare that often spread to the far corners of their expansive empires. Even when the nations were ostensibly at peace, the ferocity of their economic, political, and religious competition inevitably influenced the destiny of the Canadian frontier, which until the mid-18th century stood at the outer margins of imperial expansion. France took the initiative in exploiting the resource potential of the northern American frontier, as its fur traders and missionaries reached Hudson Bay in the north, the Gulf of Mexico in the south, and the foothills of the Rocky Mountains in the west. But the perils of ruling over such a far-flung empire while containing domestic political unrest would prove to be overwhelming in the face of a British adversary, which, standing on the threshold of industrial power, ultimately placed greater value on the long-term developmental prospects of North America.

Yet the inspiration for the colonization of the northern half of North America spoke neither French nor English; indeed, it spoke no human language. A small fur-bearing animal, the beaver, revived French interest in the region discovered and explored by Cartier almost a half-century earlier. The quest for new sources of fur lured traders deeper into the continental interior, sustained friendly and hostile contact with the Native people, initiated permanent settlement along the shores of the St. Lawrence River, and prompted the French government to regulate trade through monopolies granted to private companies. Paradoxically, the fur trade would prove to be both a blessing and a curse to French colonization, for the industry that gave rise to New France was also chiefly responsible for its slow development, particularly during its first half-century of existence.

IN SEARCH OF A COMMERCIAL OUTPOST

While France was plagued by the anarchy of religious and civil warfare, the French presence in North America in the half-century after Cartier's voyages continued to be maintained by the growing number of fishing fleets that sailed every spring to the Grand Banks off the coast of Newfoundland, to the Gulf of St. Lawrence, and to the Bay of Fundy. As they waited on shore for their fish to dry, crew members routinely came into contact with the local Native population, with whom they casually traded knives, axes, pots, and other ironware and trinkets in exchange for furs. The increasing demand of the western European and Mediterranean markets for cod and the fierce international competition in North Atlantic American fisheries necessitated the establishment of permanent shore bases. At these fishing bases, men were left over the winter to guard the more favored sites and the drying racks in addition to making preparations for the following season. Initially, French fishermen maintained good trade relations with the Native people out of sheer necessity. However, these trade relations took on added economic significance as the beaver felt hat became fashionable in late 16th-century Europe.

Since the supply of European beaver was by this time extremely limited, the excellent quality beaver pelts that the fishing fleets brought back to France commanded a high price. With the huge profits to be made in the fur trade, French ships came in larger numbers and soon pushed farther up the St. Lawrence River, seeking out the Native traders before other competitors reached them. By the end of the 16th century, a thriving trade in beaver pelts had developed at Tadoussac, located at the mouth of the Saguenay River where it flows into the lower St. Lawrence. So intense and potentially ruinous was the competition for beaver fur in the Gulf of St. Lawrence region that enterprising merchants appealed to the Crown to grant them trading monopolies. A royal charter of monopoly granting exclusive rights of trade and control over a designated region was considered necessary to stabilize prices at a profitable level in an industry burdened by uncertain supplies and markets as well as risky and costly transatlantic voyages. For his part, King Henry IV was quite willing to grant such a privilege in exchange for a commitment to establish and develop colonies that would reassert the French claim to sovereignty overseas without significant cost to the royal treasury. This merger of private enterprise and public support would be the hallmark of French imperialism in North America, and colonial destinies would inevitably be shaped by the shifting balance of commitment within this fragile partnership.

The early efforts of French monopoly holders to establish colonies as year-round trading bases in the St. Lawrence and Maritime regions around the turn of the 17th century proved to be no more successful than Cartier's earlier voyages. In 1598 the Marquis de La Roche deposited 40 to 50 convict settlers on Sable Island, 90 miles off the southern coast of Nova Scotia, but after five years only a dozen survivors returned to France. Pierre Chauvin de Tonnetuit failed in his attempt to establish a permanent trading post at Tadoussac as only five of 16 settlers survived the severe winter of 1600–01. Having obtained the monopoly over the fur trade of the St. Lawrence Valley, Vice Admiral Aymar de Chastes commissioned François Gravé Du Pont along with Samuel de Champlain to explore the region's commercial and settlement potential in 1603. Journeying up the St. Lawrence as far as Lachine, west of present-day Montreal, they learned much about the inland areas farther north and west as a result of their contact with the Algonquians, whose trading network extended well into the lower Great Lakes. Impressed with the potential of the region and the possibility that the St. Lawrence River and the Great Lakes could be a water route across the continent to the Pacific Ocean, Gravé and Champlain returned to France only to find that de Chastes had died and that the monopoly was transferred to Pierre de Gua, sieur de Monts.

De Monts did not share Champlain's enthusiasm for the St. Lawrence Valley, which he felt was too distant and inclement for settlement and too competitive with traders who refused to respect the royal monopoly. Preferring the more accessible and southerly Atlantic shores, de Monts enlisted Champlain and Gravé to accompany him on an expedition that sailed into the Bay of Fundy in 1604 and wintered on a small island near the mouth of the St. Croix River, now on the border between New Brunswick and Maine. Not only was the island's sandy soil unsuitable for agriculture but a shortage of water and timber added to the misery of a bitterly cold winter. Nearly half of the expedition's 79 men died of scurvy before spring, while the remainder suffered from near-starvation. In 1605 the struggling colony was moved across the Bay of Fundy to Port Royal on the west coast of Nova Scotia, which was then known to the French as Acadia. Situated in the fertile Annapolis Valley, Port Royal became the first European agricultural settlement on Canadian soil. Life in the colony was enhanced by the burlesque pageantry and feasting of the Ordre du bons temps (Order of Good Cheer), the first social club in Canada, along with the first Canadian theatrical production, Théâtre de Neptune, presented by Marc Lescarbot in 1606. Nevertheless, de Monts remained dissatisfied with this colonial venture. The quest for furs and mineral resources in the region was insufficiently profitable, and the search for a westward passage through the continent proved futile. When he received word that the king had cancelled his monopoly, de Monts abandoned the colony in 1607 just as the English were establishing their first permanent settlement in North America at Jamestown, Virginia.

De Monts succeeded in persuading the king to extend his fur-trading monopoly for one more year to allow him a final opportunity to recoup at least part of his investment. Realizing the limitations of Acadia, in 1607 he relinquished Port Royal to his chief associate, Jean de Biencourt de Poutrincourt, who had no immediate plans to continue the colony. Port Royal was deserted and Acadia remained undeveloped except for a few fishing stations until de Poutrincourt returned three years later with a group of settlers, including two Jesuit priests who hoped to start a mission to convert the Micmac. The revived colony struggled along until 1613 when it was destroyed by a Virginia-based expedition led by Samuel Argall, who claimed that English sovereignty extended that far up the Atlantic coast. About 20 French fur traders and fisherman stayed on at Port Royal, but after a few years the base fell into disuse.

Meanwhile, de Monts decided to follow Champlain's advice by focusing his attention on the St. Lawrence region. In 1608 Champlain and Gravé, under the auspices of de Monts's company, led an expedition up the St. Lawrence River to establish a commercial colony in the region the French called Canada. In an attempt to forestall the summer traders at Tadoussac, Champlain set up his trading post 130 miles farther upstream where the river narrows suddenly before widening out once more. This site, which Champlain called Quebec (*Kebec* is the Algonquian word for "where the river narrows"), would prove to be one of the best natural military strongholds in North America. Not only did the river narrow sufficiently at this point to allow cannons to dispute the passage of enemy ships, but the cliffs of Cape Diamond towering above the shoreline offered a natural citadel to guard the great water highway into the interior. Indeed, whoever controlled Quebec would control access into the interior of the continent. But as past experience had shown, strategic location was not enough to sustain a colony. The seeds of French colonialism had been planted before but had persistently failed to take root. What would enable Quebec to achieve the distinction of being the first permanent settlement in Canada was the visionary leadership of its founder.

As autumn approached, Gravé left Quebec with a shipload of furs, leaving Champlain and 27 men ill-prepared to confront the severe winter. By the following spring only eight of them had survived, with two-thirds of the deceased falling victim to scurvy and one-third to dysentery. But unlike the earlier winterers at Quebec and Port Royal, the stout-hearted Champlain was not discouraged. When Gravé returned in the spring with supplies and reinforcements, Champlain renewed his determination to fulfil his mission "to lay the foundation of a permanent edifice, as well for the glory of God as for the renown of the French."

THE EARLY FRENCH FUR TRADE AND NATIVE RELATIONS

As the founder of New France, Champlain embodied the spirit of 17th-century French imperialism. He was inspired by a sense of patriotism that desired to promote the greatness of France and by a religious zeal to spread the Catholic faith to the "pagan" world. He was also motivated by a passion for adventure, with a special fascination for the discovery of new lands and the search for the unknown. For all his devotion to religion and his skills as a navigator and geographer, Champlain realized that he was first and foremost an agent of a business enterprise. Above all, Champlain was keenly aware that the commercial investors on which he depended for his colonial success were more interested in profits and dividends than in empire-building and the promotion of new settlements.

To keep his colonial dream alive, Champlain had to devote much of his energy to defending and promoting the monopoly principle that was so vital to determining the fur trade's margin of profit in the face of opposition or disinterest in France. After the cancellation of de Monts's monopoly in 1609, Champlain successfully negotiated with various noble sponsors who not only influenced the king to renew the monopoly but also recruited financial supporters. Champlain made frequent trips back to France to plead for more aid and settlers for his struggling colony of scarcely 20 men. In 1617, for example, he appealed to the French Chamber of Commerce to undertake a major colonization program that would bring 400 families and 300 soldiers to settle in Quebec. The Chamber of Commerce expressed interest in his request but thought it more appropriate for the Crown to undertake. With the threat of religious conflict with the Huguenots looming, the French king felt that he could spare neither fiscal nor human resources to transform a distant trading post into a thriving colony.

Champlain did succeed in persuading retired Parisian pharmacist Louis Hébert to bring his family to Quebec in 1617 to become the first permanent settlers dedicated to the cultivation of the land. Hébert's wife, Marie Rollet, is believed to be the first European woman to till the Canadian soil. But the successive fur-trade monopolists who effectively controlled the destiny of Canada had no interest in encouraging others to follow the lead of the Héberts. Bringing out settlers was expensive and would lead to the clearing of the forest in which the beaver lived and the fur trade thrived. More settlers would also render the monopoly more difficult to enforce since they would inevitably prefer the quicker profits to be realized in the fur trade to the arduous work of clearing and cultivating the land. This inherent conflict between the fur trade and settlement would persistently undermine Quebec's evolution from outpost to colony.

When he was not traveling back to France to court potential monopolists and investors, Champlain was preoccupied with inland exploration in search of furs and a western route through the continent. Initially, his main concern was to forestall the competition of the summer traders at Tadoussac by sending men upriver to meet the Algonquian and Huron middlemen coming down with their furs, thereby ensuring that they went no further east than Quebec. Since the time of Cartier's expeditions, the Algonquians, notably the nomadic hunting Montagnais and Algonquin, had moved from the north to drive the Iroquois south of the St. Lawrence into the present-day states of New York and Pennsylvania. The Montagnais maintained their base of operation in the vicinity of Quebec, while the Algonquins occupied the Ottawa River region and the Huron were stationed to the south in present-day southern Ontario. To establish good trade relations with these northern and western tribes, Champlain agreed to join them in raids against their long-standing Iroquois enemies in 1609. The expedition gave him the opportunity to follow the Richelieu River flowing south from the St. Lawrence (just below present-day Montreal) to the lake that now bears his name. In the ensuing encounter, a few shots from French muskets quickly scattered the Iroquois war party, which had never previously seen guns. However, this apparently easy victory had the unexpected effect of mobilizing a powerful and relentless foe: the Iroquois would imperil French colonization throughout the century.

The significance of this brief skirmish became even more far-reaching less than three months later, in September 1609, when Henry Hudson sailed up the river that bears his name and traded with the Iroquois. Within five years, the Dutch had established a trading post—Fort Nassau—where Albany, New York, is now located. Rival European trading nations now controlled the two main navigational arteries that offered access to the heart of the continent. The Dutch (and later the English) supplied the Iroquois with European firearms in exchange for furs via the Hudson and Mohawk rivers; the French could similarly trade with the Algonquians and Huron via the St. Lawrence and Ottawa Rivers. The injection of European technology and economic motives had the further effect of intensifying the nature and scope of intertribal warfare in North America. Quick raids by small bands engaging in hand-to-hand combat to inflict relatively limited casualties and to capture a few prisoners for ceremonial torture would give way to sustained, larger-scale military campaigns featuring the use of firearms and steel weapons that resulted in unprecedented brutality and death.

Champlain's commitment to a commercial alliance with the Algonquians and Huron necessitated his participation in another successful attack on the Iroquois near the mouth of the Richelieu River in 1610. In a further effort to persuade the northern and western tribes to bring their furs to Quebec, he inaugurated the practice of sending young company representatives to live among the Native people to learn their language, customs, and values. The diplomatic Champlain recognized the value of showing due respect to his Native business partners, on whose goodwill, knowledge, and skill French colonists were so dependent. For the French were not only enormously outnumbered by the Native population but had also learned from their Native allies about the geography of the country and basic tactics for survival in the wilderness, including the manufacture and use of such essential items as canoes, snowshoes, and toboggans. In 1610 Champlain arranged for young Etienne Brulé to live with the Huron. As one of the first coureurs de bois (runners of the woods), the adventurous Brulé became a skillful interpreter and intermediary during his five years among the Huron. Traveling with his adopted people, he extensively explored their trading area and thus was likely the first European to see the Great Lakes.

In 1615 Brulé served as Champlain's interpreter as they accompanied another Huron and Algonquian war party on a raid against the Iroquois, who were obstructing the flow of furs to Quebec. In addition to continued trade, Champlain hoped that supporting the Huron-Algonquian war effort would help overcome their reluctance to lead him into the interior. In July 1615, Champlain and 12 others journeyed up the Ottawa River, which he had explored two years previously, but this time he continued westward along the entire route leading to Georgian Bay on Lake Huron. Traveling south along the shore of Georgian Bay, the expedition reached the heart of the Huron village encampments near present-day Midland and Penetanguishene. During the month that he spent in what became known as Huronia, Champlain learned much about life within the Huron Confederacy, an alliance of several tribes with a population exceeding 30,000 living in villages containing upwards of 2,000 people each. The trade network of the Huron, by virtue of their good relations with the Algonquians, extended as far as Lake Superior to the west and James Bay to the north. In early September, the Huron war

Despite its limited accuracy, Samuel de Champlain's map of New France (1632) was a major contribution to European geographical knowledge of eastern Canada.

party with Champlain set out on its southeasterly trek by way of the Severn and Trent river systems, reaching and crossing Lake Ontario at its eastern narrows, and landing near present-day Oswego, New York, a month later. On this occasion, however, the Iroquois, now equipped with Dutch firearms, were able to turn back this assault on their fortified village of Onondaga near Lake Oneida, and a wounded Champlain retreated to Huronia with his Native allies.

Despite the military setback, the expedition of 1615 had far-reaching significance for the development of Canada. Although the fear of an Iroquois attack prevented the Huron from guiding Champlain back to Quebec by way of the shorter St. Lawrence route, and thus compelled him to winter in Huronia and return by the Ottawa route, he had gained much knowledge about the relationship between the St. Lawrence River and

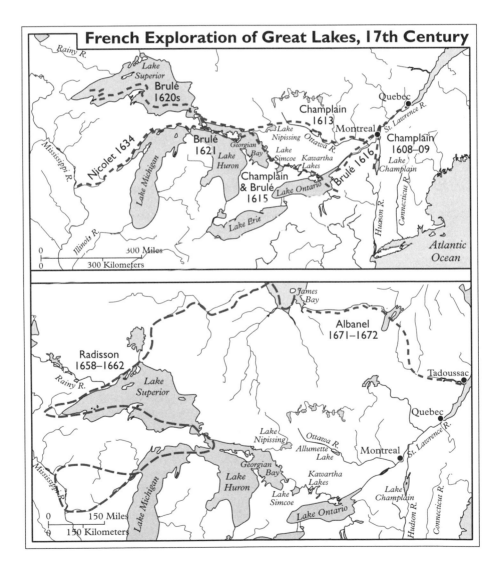

the Great Lakes, thereby opening the way for further westward exploration. His return to Quebec in 1616 marked the end of Champlain's explorations, but his quest for a western sea was continued by his young protegés. Brulé reportedly reached Sault Ste. Marie in 1621–22 and perhaps Lake Superior. Jean Nicolet set out from Quebec on his western trek in 1634, and within four years he had reached Green Bay and approached the headwaters of the Mississippi River, thus becoming the first European to explore the American Northwest.

Certainly, Champlain's active support of the Huron-Algonquian campaign against the Iroquois paid commercial dividends, as this alliance supplied upwards of two-thirds of the French fur trade by the 1620s. On the other hand, the Iroquois, inspired by their victory in 1615 and empowered by their trade connection with the Dutch, took the offensive. For the remainder of the century, the Iroquois would threaten the French fur trade empire either by disrupting interaction with the western tribes or by assaulting the base at Quebec. Yet French fur traders displayed little inclination toward peaceful relations with the Iroquois out of a concern that they might allow the northern and western tribes access to Dutch trading posts on the Hudson or serve as brokers for them. So long as the Iroquois remained a barrier between these tribes and the Hudson traders, the St. Lawrence traders held the upper hand in the competition to control the North American fur trade. In effect, the Native people, in their role as go-betweens and suppliers for the fur trade, had become willing pawns of European imperialism.

CATHOLIC MISSIONS AND THE FAILURE OF COMPANY RULE

Despite the advance of fur traders into the interior of the continent, no more than 80 people lived permanently at Quebec by the mid-1620s, and less than 20 acres there were under cultivation. With the state and private enterprise unable or unwilling to encourage settlement, Champlain turned to the Catholic Church for support. To stem the rising tide of the Protestant Reformation, the Catholic Church was eager to spread the faith to the emerging colonies of the New World. The French Catholic clergy, following the example of their Spanish and Portuguese counterparts, had a vision of converting the pagan hordes of America to Christianity. As early as 1615, four Recollets missionaries arrived at Quebec and went to live at Huronia and among the Montagnais at Tadoussac. A devout Catholic, Champlain hoped that the missionaries would inspire the Algonquians and Huron to form settlements, to farm the land, and to intermarry with the French people. The Recollets, however, experienced difficulty adjusting to wilderness conditions, language barriers, and general hostility or indifference to the Christian message. The Native people already had an enduring religious tradition that adequately met their needs, and they had no wish to abandon it. Accordingly, the Recollets sought the assistance of the Society of Jesus (commonly known as the Jesuit Order), which sent eight missionaries to Quebec in 1625–26.

The collaborative efforts of the Recollets and Jesuits were immediately hampered by the Huguenot traders, who had no desire either to establish settlement or to convert the natives to Christianity. In 1627 Cardinal Richelieu, the chief adviser of King Louis XIII, stepped in to ban the Huguenots from New France and to inaugurate an ambitious policy to develop French colonies overseas. Impressed by the success of the English colonies of Virginia and New England, which had about 2,000 and 300 inhabitants, respectively, as well as the Dutch colony of New Netherlands with about 200 settlers in the Hudson River valley, Richelieu was determined to promote agricultural settlement and missionary activity along the St. Lawrence. In accordance with the prevailing economic philosophy of mercantilism, he hoped that New France could fulfill the typical colonial function of enriching the imperial power by exporting raw materials and by importing its manufactured products. The highly influential Richelieu formed the Company of One Hundred Associates (also known as the Company of New France), whose investors were motivated more by religion and patriotism than by expectations of profit. In return for a monopoly on all commerce and title to all the land that France claimed in North America, the company agreed to bring out 4,000 French and Catholic settlers within 15 years, and to promote missionary activity. This most ambitious colonizing venture yet undertaken by France began in earnest when the company sent 400 settlers with the necessary supplies to Quebec in May 1628. However, renewed imperial hostilities overseas would spill over into North America to interrupt French colonization and missionary efforts for the next four years.

When hostilities broke out between France and England, the buccaneering Kirke brothers—David, Thomas, and Lewis—took advantage of the opportunity to seize Tadoussac in 1627, to capture the French ships that were bringing the settlers sent out by the Company of New France in the following year, and to attack Quebec in 1629. Cut off from France and lacking in food and supplies, Champlain and his garrison had no choice but to surrender. Champlain returned to France only to discover that the war between England and France had ended three months before with the capitulation of Quebec, which now, like Acadia, was officially an English possession.

England was mildly interested in Acadia because of its fisheries and its strategic approach to the St. Lawrence. In 1621 Scotsman Sir William Alexander persuaded King James I of England to grant him title to all of the land of Acadia so that he could establish the colony of Nova Scotia. In 1627 his son succeeded in bringing about 70 colonists to Port Royal, most of whom were merely interested in the quick profits of the fur trade and the fisheries. The settlement had already disbanded by 1632 when the Treaty of St.-Germain-en-Laye restored all the French territories that the English had seized in North America.

Having successfully campaigned for the restoration of Quebec to French rule, Champlain returned in 1633 to rebuild the colony plundered by the Kirke brothers and to resume his effort to bring out settlers on behalf of the reorganized Company of New France. Upstream from Quebec, he built another fur-trading post called Trois-Rivières (Three Rivers) at the mouth of the St. Maurice River, one of the main routes to the north. Within a few years, the Jesuits established a mission there, and settlers began clearing the adjacent land. But three decades of frustrating colony-building finally took their toll on Champlain, who died on Christmas Day in 1635. The passing of its founder and first governor at a time when the Company of New France was losing interest in colonization left Canada in a precarious situation. The various proprietors of the company did not object to settlement as such, only to its interference with trade or to any attempt to make them subsidize it. Within the French government, Richelieu became absorbed by the Thirty Years' War in Europe, and his successors were plagued by recurring civil unrest. For nearly three decades after Champlain, then, effective colonial leadership passed by default to the Catholic Church, particularly the Jesuit missionaries.

After the restoration of French rule in 1632, Cardinal Richelieu had given the Jesuits a monopoly over the mission field of New France. The following year, Father Paul

Le Jeune undertook to minister among the Algonquin and Montagnais but found that their nomadic lifestyle offered only a barren field for missionary effort. The most successful mission among the Algonquians was St. Joseph de Sillery (southwest of Quebec), which contained about 150 baptized Montagnais by 1641. However, the threat of Iroquois attack, continued resistance to Catholicism and the French way of life, and the outbreak of European-based diseases such as smallpox and measles led to the demise of the mission by the end of the decade. Although similar problems plagued efforts at Huronia, the more sedentary Huron proved to be slightly more receptive after Father Jean de Brébeuf established the first permanent mission there in 1634. Sainte-Marie was constructed in 1639 to serve as the headquarters for the 11 other mission stations scattered throughout Huronia by 1648.

French fur traders considered the missions in Huronia to be valuable in consolidating their commercial alliance with the Huron Confederacy. But the fur trade itself proved to be responsible for bringing the missionary work at Huronia to a bloody end. When the Iroquois had exhausted the furs of their own region, they invaded Huronia to capture the northern trade route and thereby maintain their vital traffic in European goods. In 1648 and 1649, the Iroquois unleashed their fury on Huronia, obliterating both the Native population and the French missionaries. The martyrdom of Brébeuf and his associates in Huronia, however, did not end the work of the missionaries in evangelizing the Native people. The priests continued their efforts among the Montagnais and extended them to such eastern tribes as the Micmac and Abenaki. The Jesuits also spread westward, establishing a mission at Sault Ste. Marie as they sought to maintain contact with their disciples among the dispersed Huron. The Recollets and Sulpicians joined them in following the path of the fur traders and explorers as they penetrated the continent, together extending the frontiers of religion, commerce, and French imperialism.

The religious orders pursued their Native conversion efforts within the context of colonial expansion and attending to the spiritual and social needs of the French settlers. The Jesuits became the principal agency for recruiting colonists and encouraging them to clear the land. To this end, and to stimulate donations for their missionary work, they published the annual *Jesuit Relations*, which from 1632 to 1673 reported on their activities in New France and praised the merits of life in the new country. In addition to their value as immigration propaganda, the *Jesuit Relations* would later prove to be a useful source of information about the early history of New France. The Jesuits established a college at Quebec to educate colonists and natives alike as early as 1635, a year before Harvard University was established in Massachusetts. When Marie de l'Incarnation's Ursuline nuns arrived in 1639, they founded a school for girls and a hospital at Quebec. Missionary zeal also motivated Sieur de Maisonneuve to lead some settlers, including Jeanne Mance, Canada's first nurse, to establish Ville Marie in 1642. Strategically located at the confluence of the Ottawa and St. Lawrence Rivers, the mission settlement was destined to evolve into the commercial center of Montreal over the next two decades.

Although the intervention of the Catholic Church helped to increase the population of Canada to nearly 1,000 by the mid-1640s, colonial development continued to be hampered by a lack of secular leadership and the precariousness of frontier life. In 1645 the nearly bankrupt Company of New France ceded the fur trade monopoly to a group of local entrepreneurs known as the Compagnie des habitants (Company of the habitants). In response to general dissatisfaction with the new company's rule, a royal decree created the first form of local and representative government in the colony. In place of a governor appointed by the king on the nomination of the monopoly-holding company, local authority rested in a council composed of the governor of the colony (who resided at Quebec), the local governor of Montreal, the Superior of the Jesuits, and syndics, or elected representatives of the people of the three areas of settlement. Despite several modifications to this structure over the next 15 years, the colony continued to be plagued by a weak and divided administration.

The most persistently divisive issue—the sale of liquor to the Native people—pitted commerce against religion. Alcohol had been unknown to the Native people until the arrival of Europeans, but they quickly acquired an appreciation for its intoxicating effects and demanded it eagerly. Indeed, French traders found that they could obtain more furs for a relatively small amount of alcohol than they could for larger quantities of other goods. On the other hand, the clergy, appalled at the social and moral consequences of excessive consumption by Natives who had not yet developed a physical tolerance for alcohol and who refused to take responsibility for their behavior while intoxicated, wanted its sale outlawed, and declared such trade to be a mortal sin. The arrival of Bishop Laval in 1659 and his subsequent government appointments intensified quarrels between the governor, who invariably supported the fur trade, and the bishop, who saw himself as the protector of society and the arbiter of morality.

Above all, the slow growth of population in the St. Lawrence colony by the mid-17th century was directly related to the daunting prospects of life in the Canadian wilderness. To start with, prospective immigrants were confronted with the dangers of the Atlantic crossing, which could take anywhere from three weeks to three months depending on headwinds and weather. Problems with food supply, sanitation, and scurvy onboard ship often meant that upwards of 20 percent of the passengers did not survive the transatlantic journey. Those who did arrive safely faced the arduous task of clearing the dense hardwood forest, building log shelters with crude implements, and clearing land to plant crops. Even when settlers had progressed that far, they faced the threat of Iroquois attacks.

The settlements along the St. Lawrence had been largely immune from Iroquois assaults until the early 1640s, when the escalation of competition for control of the inland fur trade and French expansion westward rendered them more vulnerable. By the 1650s Canada was in a virtual state of siege, with the result that small detachments of French soldiers began regularly patrolling the St. Lawrence from Trois-Rivières to Montreal, the most exposed settlement. A mass invasion of Montreal was thwarted by Adam Dollard des Ormeaux and his 16 companions, whose heroic stand to the death at Long Sault on the Ottawa River kept the Iroquois from completing their mission of destruction in 1660. The fear of the Iroquois was heightened in 1664 when the English captured the Dutch colony of New Amsterdam and renamed it New York. The Hudson River route was thenceforth controlled by an ominous alliance of France's most powerful European enemy and its most relentless Native American adversary. The prospect of both the English and the Iroquois turning their aggressive designs on the St. Lawrence colony appeared to seal the fate of the French empire in North America.

The plight of Acadia was even worse than that of Canada. After restoration to French rule in 1632, France took a momentary interest in the colony as Cardinal Richelieu sent his cousin Isaac de Razilly with about 300 colonists to revive Port Royal and to establish a new settlement at La Hève (along the southeast coast), both on behalf of the Company of New France. De Razilly's death in 1636, however, proved to be a major setback for the colony, plunging it into civil strife by the rival claims of successors who vied for control over the fur trade of Acadia. While Charles de Menou d'Aulnay laid claim to Port Royal as de Razilly's cousin, Charles de la Tour felt that his connection with the de

Poutrincourt family entitled him to govern Acadia from his fort at the mouth of the Saint John River (in present-day New Brunswick). Armed conflict between the two rivals, marked by raiding, plundering, and destroying each other's posts, persisted until 1645 when d'Aulnay captured de la Tour's headquarters while he was in Boston enlisting more support for his cause. D'Aulnay remained the sole authority in Acadia until his death in 1650, thereby opening the way for de la Tour's return. Ultimately, the long-standing feud was resolved in typical European fashion when de la Tour married d'Aulnay's widow in 1653. The next year, however, an expedition from Massachusetts led by Francis Nicholson captured Acadia, and once again the colony was part of the English empire.

Acadia, in essence, was a victim of geography and imperialism. Because of its strategic but exposed position between the principal French and English colonies, Acadia was a primary target for conquest in times of imperial conflict. But once those hostilities subsided, Acadia's limited resources rendered it unworthy of further contention. Consequently, the colony was tossed back and forth between empires, with little or no concern for its development.

After half a century, the French empire in North America rested on a precarious foundation. Acadia had been lost through sheer neglect, and the survival of the larger St. Lawrence colony remained in jeopardy. Under the rule of private fur-trading companies, both colonies were too weak in numbers, resources, and administration to defend and sustain themselves, let alone to attract more settlers and entrepreneurs. With the complete failure of company rule, only decisive and unprecedented state intervention could save New France from extinction.

CHAPTER 4

ROYAL GOVERNMENT AND A DISTINCT SOCIETY

For the first half-century of its existence, New France was like an orphaned child in desperate need of parental support. But France could only afford to give attention to its overseas empire on a sporadic basis. When measured against recurring international warfare and civil unrest featuring religious dissension and royal succession crises, the affairs of a distant colonial frontier with scarcely 3,000 people could easily fall to the bottom of the public agenda of a major world power. But at a critical moment, the interests of France and its struggling Canadian colony converged, even if only temporarily. From 1663 to 1672, King Louis XIV and one of his chief advisers, Jean-Baptist Colbert, took over the control of New France, instituting a new form of government, providing for the defense of the colony, giving impetus to settlement, and encouraging the development and diversification of the economy. Although events in Europe would continually distract the attention of the French Crown, New France was effectively transformed from a struggling colony at the mercy of the fur trade to a viable agrarian society distinct from that of France and any other that would blossom on the North American frontier.

A GRAND IMPERIAL DESIGN AND AUTHORITARIAN RULE

The assumption of government control by Louis XIV in 1661 ushered in the golden age of French imperialism. More than his predecessors, the young king appreciated the potential value of his overseas empire not just as a source of wealth but also as a symbol of the power of France throughout the world and the glory of its absolute ruler. King Louis XIV launched his grand imperial design under the able direction of Colbert, who as minister of the marine was responsible for the financial well-being and economic development of the nation and all of its colonies. Like Richelieu before him, Colbert was deeply committed to the principles of mercantilism, which held that the key to national wealth and power was the maintenance of a favorable balance of trade. By exporting more than it imported, a nation could achieve a level of economic self-sufficiency that promoted prosperity in peace and security in war. By supplying raw materials and serving as markets for finished products, colonies reduced the imperial power's dependence on foreign trade and enhanced its shipping and shipbuilding industries. While the French colonies in the East and West Indies offered the most promising opportunities for commercial expansion, Colbert was convinced that the marginal colony of New France could also make a valuable contribution.

In addition to furs, Colbert expected New France to provide France with timber and ship masts, which were then being imported from Russia and Scandinavia. He also hoped that the colony could become an agricultural producer and thereby become part of a triangular trade network with the French West Indies and France. Manufactured goods could be shipped from France for consumption in New France; the same ship could then proceed from New France with a cargo of grain, peas, and fish to feed the slaves on the French West Indies plantations; from there the ship could return to France with rum, molasses, and sugar. In this regard, Colbert was inspired by the English, who were already developing a similar triangular trade with their American and West Indian colonies.

Before Colbert could fully implement his mercantilist plan, New France had to be placed on a more stable, secure, and self-sufficient footing. Colbert wanted New France to become a "compact colony" concentrated in the St. Lawrence Valley rather than being spread across the continent. Achieving this goal would require a strong centralized administrative framework closely controlled from France. Colbert initiated the process of administrative reorganization by revoking the charter of the Company of New France in 1663. A royal edict established a new form of government based on the absolute authority of the king and modeled along the lines of the administration of a French province, but with modifications to take into account the uniqueness of the North American frontier environment.

Under the edict, the king delegated authority over the royal colony to the minister of the marine, who formulated policy on the advice of the senior administrators in the colony—the governor, the bishop, and the intendant. These three locally based officials comprised the Sovereign Council (replacing the Council of Quebec) along with a number of minor officials—five councillors, the attorney general, and the clerk. The Sovereign council (renamed the Superior Council in 1703) was the sole governing authority in the colony, acting as a legislative, administrative, and judicial body. As a legislative body, the council had the authority to pass local regulations concerning finance, law and order, and trade, subject to amendment and veto by the king on the advice of his minister. As an administrative body, the council was confined to registering, proclaiming, and enforcing royal ordinances, since all major decisions were made in France. As a judicial body, the council exercised the authority to establish lower courts and to act as a court of appeal in criminal and civil cases, although the royal council in Paris was the final court of appeal.

The three major officials of the Sovereign Council were assigned specific duties in a manner designed to prevent any one of them from becoming too powerful. The nominal head of government—the governor—was customarily a noble and a soldier who was responsible chiefly for military affairs and diplomatic relations with the neighboring Native tribes and the English colonies to the south. He tended to be most powerful in times of war and could exercise considerable control over the fur trade. While the governor could veto the actions of the other officials, he had to justify his actions to the minister of the marine, who often did not take kindly to interference with the other officials. Second in rank was the intendant, who was responsible for justice, finance, economic development, and general administration. In effect, he was the day-to-day business manager of the colony, and the scope of his role became more wide-ranging as the colony grew. An increasingly important function of the intendant was to organize the entire male population into militia units and to appoint captains from among the most respected men in the community to command them. In addition to their military function, these captains of militia served an important civilian role as the liaison between the intendant and the rest of the population.

When the Sovereign Council was first formed, the bishop ranked directly below the governor in political power by virtue of his responsibility for attending to the social and spiritual needs of the colony and for evangelizing the neighboring Native population. But the powers of the bishop were significantly reduced with the advent of royal government. Because the Jesuits had effectively run the colony for most of the three decades prior to 1663, Louis XIV and Colbert were concerned about the excessive authority of the church and instructed the governor and intendant to make the church subordinate to the authority of the state.

Despite the best efforts of Colbert, the functions of the three officials occasionally overlapped, thereby leading to jurisdictional and personal friction among them. Although the governor remained the supreme authority in principle, the expanding functional realm of the intendant enhanced his power to the point where he could exert more influence depending on the circumstances. Although the bishop's power steadily declined, controversial moral issues such as the sale of liquor to the Natives could lead to clashes of interest with the governor and intendant. Furthermore, leaders with strong personalities such as Governor Louis Buade, comte de Frontenac (1672–82, 1689–98), Intendant Jean Talon (1665–68, 1669–72), or Bishop François de Laval (1659–84) were capable of wielding power and influence beyond the limitations of their position. The level of political conflict also depended on the willingness of the central authorities to intervene and impose their will.

Louis XIV and Colbert were able to keep political dissent in check by eliminating the elected syndics inaugurated during the later stages of company rule. Any vestige of representative institutions was thenceforth excluded from the government of New France. The highly authoritarian and centralized nature of royal government was consistent with the prevailing doctrine that the king ruled by divine right. The lack of representative government in the form of popularly elected assemblies did not necessarily mean that despotism and tyranny prevailed. While the people could not publicly assemble on their own, the authorities could govern with due consideration to their interests and views. Colbert's instruction to Frontenac in 1672 clearly indicates the paternalistic spirit of royal government: "It is well that each speak for himself and none for all." Although government came from above rather than below and the power of the Crown was uncontested, the governor or intendant occasionally called public meetings to ascertain the views of the people on issues that affected the general interest. Moreover, King Louis XIV believed that he was required to govern in the interests of all of his subjects regardless of their wealth and social status and that human rights took precedence over property rights. The paternalistic absolutism of royal government was no substitute for democracy, but it represented a profound improvement over negligent company rule, and its administrative framework endured until the end of the French regime with little evidence of public discontent.

IMMIGRATION AND SETTLEMENT IN NEW FRANCE

Once Colbert had established the administrative framework of royal government, his major priority was to populate the colony. But before he could entice settlers to New France, he had to fortify the colony against the threat of Iroquois attack. In 1665 Alexandre de Prouville, marquis de Tracy, was dispatched to New France along with more than 1,000 regulars of the Carignan Salières regiment. The next year de Tracy led these distinguished soldiers in addition to 400 Canadian militia in an invasion of Iroquois country in present-day New York State. The Iroquois were so impressed by this massive display of force that they decided to make peace with the French in 1667. The peaceful 20–year interlude that followed allowed the colony to grow and the fur trade to expand.

Although the Carignan Salières were disbanded following the truce with the Iroquois, about 400 members of the regiment were persuaded to settle along the Richelieu River between the St. Lawrence River and Lake Champlain, the main Iroquois invasion route. Inspired by the military settlements of ancient Rome, Colbert arranged for another 400 discharged soldiers to be sent to Canada in the hope that they could be called upon to defend the frontier while increasing the farming population.

This scheme to combine defense and settlement was part of a more ambitious plan to populate the colony ably administered by Intendant Talon. Although private individuals and religious organizations had brought out small contingents of settlers in the two decades prior to his arrival in the colony in 1665, Talon realized that immigration on a more substantial and organized scale would be necessary if New France was to fulfill Colbert's mercantilist design. Settlers who could clear and farm the land were recruited, mostly from Normandy in northwestern France, by offers of free passage and land on easier terms than might be available to them in the homeland. When Talon conducted a census in 1666, he discovered that, out of a population of about 3,400, men outnumbered women by a ratio of at least three to one. To alleviate this shortage of marriageable women, Colbert sent over about 800 women with limited prospects at home—popularly known as *filles du roi* (daughters of the king)—to serve as wives for the settling soldiers and other eligible bachelors. Another source of immigrants were *engagés,* or indentured laborers, who were bound by a three-year contract to work for an established farmer in exchange for a wage. When their contractual obligations had been fulfilled, about 400 of these workers decided to stay in the colony and farm their own land.

By 1672, when Talon's term as intendant ended, approximately 4,000 men and women had been sent to New France at the Crown's expense, with the result that the population of the colony approached 10,000. Thereafter, government-subsidized emigration was reduced to a trickle in the wake of the outbreak of war with the Dutch

Republic, followed by a succession of other European conflicts that would continually divert France's attention away from its North American empire. In this regard, geography proved to be a major factor in determining France's lesser commitment to populating its overseas colonies than that of its chief European adversary. Great Britain was an island that could be readily defended by a strong navy without need of a substantial standing army. In addition to requiring a strong navy to compete with the English, France had to maintain a large standing army to defend its frontiers against surrounding land powers, most of which were potentially hostile. Therefore, England could afford to permit a large-scale emigration of surplus population to its American colonies, whereas France feared a shortage of vital human resources for military purposes.

With the decline of immigration, New France had to rely on natural population growth. To this end, early marriages and large families were encouraged by royal decree. In particular, an edict of 1669 established a comprehensive system of rewards and punishments to induce young women to be married by 16 years of age and young men by the age of 20. The government also provided for substantial gifts of money to couples with 10 or more children, a forerunner to modern family allowance provisions. Indeed, a high birthrate, although partially offset by a high infant mortality rate, was largely responsible for the rise in the population of New France to about 15,000 by the year 1700 and to more than 60,000 by 1760. Certainly, this number was modest in comparison to the 1.5 million people who inhabited the English colonies to the south by the mid-18th century. Nevertheless, the initiatives of Colbert and Talon had ensured the survival of the 300-mile strip of settlement hugging the St. Lawrence shore between Quebec and Montreal.

The growth of settlement and the increasing interest in farming raised concerns about the availability and efficient distribution of land. The Company of New France had succeeded in transplanting the French system of land distribution and landholding to New France but had failed to achieve the desired results of advancing colonization. Under the seigneurial system of tenure, all land belonged to the king who customarily granted tracts to influential nobility as a reward for favors or in return for military support. The noble landholder, or *seigneur*, in turn, divided the land into smaller parcels, serviced it, and distributed it to peasant farmers or *censitaires* in exchange for yearly rents, military service, and due respect and obedience. In New France, the Crown granted seigneurial rights as a general term of the fur-trading monopoly. In granting seigneurial rights to the Company of New France in 1627, the Crown specified obligations with respect to colonization. The company, in turn, granted more than 50 seigneuries in 1633–34, but the landholders proved to be more interested in obtaining title to large tracts than in clearing and settling them.

To make seigneurialism work in the Canadian frontier required state intervention and some modifications to the system. Under royal government, supervision of the seigneurial system was assigned to Intendant Talon, who upon his arrival sought to eliminate land speculation by specifying that land had to be settled and cultivated. He also initiated the policy of limiting the size of seigneuries to prevent the rise of a class of large landowners who might challenge royal authority. To reinforce this intention, the Crown issued the Edicts of Marly in 1711, stipulating that unoccupied seigneuries would revert back to the Crown. The power of the seigneur was further checked by the fact that the *censitaires* owed military service to the Crown as members of the militia led by captains chosen from among their ranks. Unlike his counterpart in France whose power was enhanced by his authority to raise his own army to offer in service to the king, the seigneur in New France had no military authority over his *censitaires*, thereby limiting his status to little more than a glorified land settlement agent.

This wood engraving by artist John Walker (1831–98) depicts Quebec ca. 1640. The strategic location of Canada's first permanent settlement on the heights overlooking the St. Lawrence River enabled the garrison to withstand numerous attempts to capture it.

Whereas in France the seigneurial system sustained a hierarchical social structure in which a wealthy land-owning class thrived on a dependent and often oppressed peasantry, in New France the intendant vigilantly enforced the mutual rights and obligations of the seigneurial participants. The seigneur's primary obligation to the Crown was to settle tenants on the land, to arrange for its cultivation, and to defend the seigneury in times of attack. The Crown granted the seigneury in perpetuity to the seigneur and his descendants, provided that these obligations were fulfilled. If the seigneur chose to sell his holding, the purchaser had to pay the *quint* (equivalent to one-fifth of the selling price) to the Crown. The seigneur was expected to maintain a responsibly occupied manor house as the administrative center for the seigneury, to build a flour mill for use by the *censitaires*, and to provide for a lower court to settle minor disputes that might arise between tenants. He could not refuse a land grant to any genuine applicant.

In exchange for the use of the land, the *censitaires* were obligated to pay the seigneur a specified annual rent or *cens et rentes*, customarily equivalent to about one-tenth of their annual income and payable partly in money and partly in produce. The *censitaires* also had to build their own houses, clear the land granted them, pay the *banalité* (equivalent to one-fourteenth of the flour that they ground at the seigneur's grist mill), perform the *droit de corvée* or contracted work for the seigneur (usually three days per year) and for the Crown (one or two days per year), and to maintain the portion of road that passed through their farms. While a *censitaire*'s holding customarily passed to his sons by inheritance, if he did choose to sell it, the purchaser had to pay the *lods et ventes* (equivalent to one-twelfth of the selling price) to the seigneur.

If either the seigneurs or the *censitaires* failed to fulfill their respective obligations, the intendant could, and frequently did, revoke the royal grant. The apparent balance between the interests of the seigneur and *censitaire* that the intendant was consistently careful to maintain was not attributable to any egalitarian spirit but rather to the realities of the Canadian frontier. The shortage of settlers compared to the abundance of land in New France fostered a more accommodating relationship between *censitaire* and seigneur. With the wilderness close at hand promising freedom and fortune in the fur trade, the *censitaire* in New France had alternatives if life on the seigneury became unbearable. Unlike his counterpart in France, he never became an oppressed serf of an impoverished peasantry. The seigneur realized that his right of tenure was dependent on the willingness of the *censitaire* to occupy his land, and therefore, he readily overlooked lapses in obligations and delinquencies in seigneurial dues. Although he enjoyed enhanced social status, the seigneur seldom became a member of an aristocratic or privileged class. A hierarchical social structure did emerge in New France, but the gap between classes was much narrower than it was in France.

The seigneurial system provided for a gradual but orderly growth of self-sufficient rural communities along the rivers of New France. By 1715 almost 200 seigneuries had been opened up along both sides of the St. Lawrence River from below Quebec to above Montreal. Because every settler desired land fronting the river for immediate access to transportation and fishing, farms took on a peculiar pattern of long rectangular strips that became narrower as successive generations divided their lots equally among the family's sons. Later in the century, as the front concessions filled, a second row of narrow strip farms stretched back from the first, with a roadway between the two. With the lower reaches of the Canadian Shield restricting northern settlement, a traveler following the St. Lawrence from Quebec to Montreal could see virtually all of New France.

Within the social organization of the seigneurial system, an agricultural economy was able to take root and eventually flourish, thereby reducing the dominance of the fur trade in the colonial economy. Indeed, Colbert and Talon believed that for the colony to prosper and fulfill the mercantilist design, it had to develop other resources for export besides beaver fur and become less dependent on French imports. Talon directed farmers to cultivate not only food crops but also nonfood crops like flax and hemp. He started a brewery, and the introduction of domestic animals opened up possibilities for local processing of leather, textiles, and dairy products. Talon foresaw that the forests could be exploited for lumber, potash, and tar. His construction of a shipyard laid the foundation for a more active shipbuilding industry at Quebec in the next century. He sought to open mines and to start an iron industry, although a lack of skilled labor and capital prevented the working of the iron deposits near St. Maurice until the 1730s. In the final analysis, few of the enterprises that Talon attempted to foster flourished after his departure from the colony in 1672. Talon's hopes to build up trade with the West Indies in lumber and fish met with limited success because of the difficulties of winter navigation along the St. Lawrence and the closer proximity of New England, where supplies were more readily and cheaply available. So, while New France gradually developed a thriving agricultural sector, the fur trade remained the heart of commercial life.

As Colbert and Talon were reviving the fortunes of the St. Lawrence colony, the prospect existed, albeit momentarily, that Acadia might benefit from royal paternalism upon its return to the French empire by the Treaty of Breda in 1667. Talon wanted to strengthen the defense and develop the resources of this neglected outpost in order to link it into the imperial trade with Quebec and the West Indies. In 1671 60 settlers were sent to Acadia to raise its population to 500. Although the colony was once again left to develop on its own by the following year, the population continued to grow to more than 800 by 1686, to over 1,100 by the year 1700, and to nearly 1,800 in 1714. The vast majority of the population farmed the fertile marshlands of the Annapolis Valley, the Minas Basin region at the head of the Bay of Fundy, and along the Chignecto Isthmus, which connects present-day Nova Scotia and New Brunswick. Port Royal remained the largest settlement, but small outlying communities emerged to the northeast during the 1670s and 1680s, including Beaubassin (now Amherst), Grand Pré (now Wolfville), and Cobequid (now Truro). Once again, English conquest interrupted the progress of the colony as Port Royal was captured and destroyed in 1690 but returned to France by the Treaty of Ryswick in 1697. It was becoming apparent that France did not care enough to defend Acadia and England had little wish to keep it.

Royal government also provided temporary assistance to the newly established French settlement in Newfoundland. Beginning in the early 1660s, the French settled the south shore of the Avalon Peninsula at Plaisance (now Placentia). The deep, ice-free harbor offered an excellent refuge for French ships and countered the English settlements along the eastern shore of the peninsula. The French government provided free passage and one year's financial support to encourage settlement in Plaisance. French fishermen at Plaisance maintained themselves largely by trading their catch to New England ships. But the colony languished after French assistance diminished in the early 1670s, and its population was never more than half the size of the English settlements.

THE CANADIEN COMMUNITY

By the middle of the 18th century, New France had evolved into a vigorous colony with a distinctively hierarchical and Catholic society. Already the colonists were referring to themselves as Canadiens, reflecting their consciousness of an identity unique from the French in France. The French officer Louis-Antoine de Bougainville, who came to Quebec in 1757, was struck by the apparent differences between the French and the Canadiens: "We seem to belong to another, even an enemy nation."

More than three-quarters of the Canadien population lived in compact village communities, farming their seigneurial plots along the St. Lawrence countryside. The seigneur was the natural leader of the community, enjoying considerable respect and social prestige even though he was not wealthy and usually had to work the land as hard as his tenants did. The government attached esteem to this position because seigneurs were so essential to colonization. The church also honored the seigneur with a special pew as well as a privileged role in religious processions, festivals, and other observances. Although he was not a member of a privileged aristocracy as was the noble in France, the seigneur was regarded by his tenants as a man of rank and influence whose advice they could readily seek.

Despite the sharp social distinction that existed between the seigneur and his tenants, the economic gap was often modest. As an independent, self-reliant farmer, the *censitaires* enjoyed a better standard of living and much more personal freedom than did their peasant counterparts in France. They were assured of as much land as they could cultivate in return for seigneurial dues that amounted to little more than 10 percent of their annual income from the land, and they paid no taxes to the government. Because of the favorable position of the *censitaires* in New France, it became increasingly common to refer to them as *habitants* (inhabitants) rather than peasants, which they regarded as a derogatory term. If the habitants were dissatisfied with their seigneurial leadership, they could turn for support and guidance to the captain of militia, who was chosen from among their ranks to be responsible for the organization and training of the local militia and for supervising the royal corvée. Indeed, the habitants' main struggle was not against the treatment that they received from their social "betters" but rather with the limited amount of fertile soil and the difficult climate of New France, which similarly challenged their seigneurial masters.

By 1760 nearly one-quarter of the population lived in the three major centers of Quebec, Trois-Rivières, and Montreal. Quebec, the capital of Canada and all of New France, was a political and cultural center with a population of about 8,000. Montreal, with a population of about 4,500, was supplanting Quebec as the commercial center of the colony by virtue of its strategic location at the hub of three major water routes into the interior of the continent. While the commercial transactions were made in Montreal, Quebec had become a warehouse center for the fur trade. Trois-Rivières, with a population of about 800, had become a farm service center for the surrounding countryside. The inhabitants of these urban centers included government officials, military personnel, merchants, fur traders, and skilled artisans such as carpenters and bricklayers.

The most senior government and military officials and the wealthiest merchants of Quebec and Montreal formed a small, powerful ruling elite, known as the "beaver aristocracy." The common interest of this group with strong metropolitan connections was the wealth and control of the fur trade. In the colony, members of the "beaver aristocracy" dominated the Sovereign Council or were closely associated with the governor or intendant, thereby wielding considerable influence and power. They sought to enhance their social rankings by becoming seigneurs over substantial tracts of land. Seigneurialism offered opportunities for lesser nobles, successful merchants, and retired military officers to enjoy the aura of nobility even though proprietorship of a seigneury did not bestow nobility. Unlike their English bourgeois counterparts who sought to become more economically prosperous, the more ambitious entrepreneurial class of New France was preoccupied with gaining entry into the ranks of the nobility or holding high office. Bourgeois commercial values did not prevail in New France. Wealth was sought not for reinvestment in commercial expansion but rather to enable the leading merchants to emulate the life of the French aristocracy. In Canada, it was much easier than it was in France for an ambitious person to adopt the values and attitudes of the nobility and to gain recognition as such. Indeed, a Canadian of humble origin could make his fortune in the fur trade, acquire a seigneury, and hope to move up the social ladder.

Living beyond the towns and countryside were a few hundred coureurs de bois who readily adapted to the Canadian wilderness, trading with the Natives and extending the frontiers of New France. The state frowned on them for trading illegally, selling liquor to the Natives, and generally defying authority when they visited the colony. The church objected to their free-spirited behavior and the bad example that their drinking, gambling, and carousing set for the impressionable youth in the settlement. These renegade fur traders invariably felt more at ease with the way of life of the Native people, and through intermarriage they produced the Métis nationality.

With the growth of settlement came the need for parish priests who would reside in the community and minister regularly to the spiritual and social needs of the Canadiens. But in the first two decades of royal government, the Catholic Church was distracted in its mission by clashes with civil authority and rivalry among the religious orders. The powerful Jesuits and Bishop Laval objected to the Crown's view that the church was an instrument in achieving its mercantilist designs. Like the Jesuits, Bishop Laval believed in the ultramontane perspective that the Catholic Church was directly responsible solely to the pope in Rome.

Laval's desire to subordinate all other groups in the colony to Jesuit authority produced widespread friction. The other clergy resented the Jesuits' seemingly fanatical supervision over all social and intellectual matters; the merchants objected to their interference with the fur trade; civil authorities were affronted by the attempts of Laval and the Jesuits to dictate various policies on the grounds that they affected faith and morals. When the bishop demanded that the royal government impose a tithe to support the church amounting to one-thirteenth of all the produce of the land, the farmers protested so vigorously that the amount was reduced to one-twenty-sixth of their wheat only. Consequently, the Crown had to provide an annual subsidy to the clergy to cover expenses that exceeded the amount of the tithe collected. Reflecting the opposing gallican view that the church was subject to the rule of the French Crown, Talon sought to offset the power of Laval and the Jesuits by bringing the Recollets back to New France in 1669. They joined the Sulpicians, who came to Montreal in 1657 and eventually became Frontenac's preferred religious order to neutralize Jesuit power. After the strong-willed Laval retired in 1684, relations between the civil and ecclesiastical powers became more tempered, and the bishops tacitly acquiesced to an interpretation of their spiritual authority that avoided serious clashes between church and state.

One of Laval's most enduring contributions to the colony was the recruitment and fostering of a Canadien clergy in response to the colony's chronic shortage of priests. To train Canadiens for the priesthood, in 1663 he founded the Grand Séminaire in Quebec, which eventually evolved into Laval University, the first institution of higher education in Canada. The seminary served as a base for the development of a close-knit and disciplined community of parish priests. By 1760 the colony was served by about 100 parish priests who, with the assistance of 30 Sulpicians, 25 Jesuits, 24 Recollets, and more than 200 nuns belonging to six religious communities, were actively engaged in the organization and operation of schools, hospitals, and charitable institutions. The close connection between religion and education may account for the lack of any Canadien literary tradition. The colony had no public library, printing press, newspaper, or other organ of public opinion. While the church did not encourage freedom of thought or the development of learning apart from its own teachings, the colonists do not appear to have demanded otherwise.

Through the evolution of the parish system, the church reinforced its position of spiritual and social leadership within the community. The parish priest increasingly gained the respect of the habitants as a man of Canadian background who understood their problems and who could advise and protect them in times of need. Moreover, as settlement grew, the church was able to take advantage of successive grants of land by the Crown to supplement the shortage of income from the collection of the tithe. By the mid-18th century, the church held over one-quarter of the land in the colony, and more than one-third of the population lived on church seigneuries. This substantial source of revenue enabled the church to become less dependent on royal subsidies and to carry out its social functions more effectively. In this way, the parish church vied with the seigneurial manor as the center around which the life of each community revolved.

The society and government of mid-18th-century New France was characterized by a distinction between metropolitan French and Canadien interests. The metropolitan group, consisting of the larger fur traders and seigneurs as well as higher civil, military, and religious officials, derived its power from connections with France. This ruling elite was committed to colonial development that enhanced their investment in the fur trade or at least did not interfere with the progress of the colony's leading staple export. The Canadiens, led by successful but less affluent seigneurs and merchants along with the parish priests, were committed to local development of a thriving agricultural community. While the metropolitan interests would prove to be fleeting agents of French imperialism, the Canadiens would remain to perpetuate the legacy of New France even after the impending British "conquest."

CHAPTER 5

CLASHING EMPIRES
AND FRONTIERS

The advent of royal government in 1663 not only gave rise to agricultural settlement along the St. Lawrence but also revived the sagging fortunes of the fur trade and promoted its transcontinental expansion. For nearly a century thereafter, a small contingent of adventurous fur traders, explorers, and missionaries carved a vast empire out of the North American wilderness. By the late 17th century, the westward expansion of the French fur-trading frontier led to military confrontation with the English empire. So long as the battle for control of the North American frontier was primarily a clash of rival fur-trading enterprises, then the French, with their strategic advantage of the St. Lawrence–Great Lakes transport system, could defend their empire. But by the mid-18th century, the French fur-trading frontier was on a collision course with the American settlement frontier, with the result that the clash of empires would not be settled on the battlefield so much as on the balance sheet. In the final showdown, the willingness of the British taxpayer to protect the valuable thirteen colonies exceeded the desire of the French taxpayer to support what the philosopher Voltaire referred to as "quelques arpents de neige" ("a few acres of snow").

THE EXPANDING FUR TRADE FRONTIER

In 1663 Pierre-Esprit Radisson and Médard Chouart Des Groseilliers were forced to surrender three-fifths of their fur cargo for the previous two years in lieu of fine and dues to the Company of New France for trading illegally in the country north of Lake Superior. Furious at this miscarriage of French justice, Radisson and Groseilliers offered their services to the English Crown and secured financial backing for a voyage that eventually landed in James Bay in 1669. The abundant furs yielded by the expedition convinced a group of London-based investors to form the chartered Company of Adventurers of England trading into Hudson's Bay, better known as the Hudson's Bay Company, on May 2, 1670. The French government would have much reason to regret the establishment of such an enduring and formidable adversary to the north of New France. Already in 1664, New Amsterdam had been captured from the Dutch, and now New York was added to New England, Virginia, Maryland, and the Carolinas to represent the English challenge to the south.

Although Colbert aimed to transform New France into a compact, settled colony, he also realized that France had to respond by outflanking the English challengers. Therefore, the intervention of royal government gave impetus to the expansion of the fur trade by subduing the Iroquois threat on the St. Lawrence–Great Lakes frontier and by encouraging exploration deeper into the interior of the continent. Colbert supported French expansion to the West in order to forestall English traders from interfering with the fur trade and to discover a western route to an ice-free winter port to serve Canada. In 1671 Jean Talon sent Jean-Baptiste Saint-Lusson to the Jesuit mission at Sault Ste. Marie to lay formal claim to the western lands of the Ottawas. In the following year, Jesuit Father Charles Albanel traveled from Tadoussac along the Saguenay River, portaged to the Rupert River, and reached James Bay in order to verify rumors about the English-sponsored exploits of Radisson and Groseilliers.

French expansion westward became even more aggressive after Governor Comte de Frontenac arrived in 1672. Immediately, he sent Louis Joliet, the Canadian-born explorer, and Father Jacques Marquette to locate the Mississippi River and to discover where it led. In 1673 Joliet and Marquette made their way from Lake Michigan to the Mississippi and followed its southward course for 600 miles until they reached the Arkansas River, far enough to determine that the mighty river emptied into the Gulf of Mexico rather than the Atlantic or Pacific Oceans. Adamant that the agricultural colony in the St. Lawrence Valley existed merely as a base to serve the fur trade, Frontenac acted in defiance of Colbert's orders by building Fort Frontenac (now Kingston) at the eastern end of Lake Ontario in 1673. With this trading post in the heart of Iroquois country, Frontenac was boldly sending a message that the French fur-trading empire would not be confined to the now-exhausted St. Lawrence region. The Iroquois, already preoccupied with their war with the neighboring Andastes and Mohegan peoples, realized the wisdom of not challenging the French at this time. Frontenac's main opposition came from the Montreal merchants who feared that the new post would drain business away from their emerging commercial center.

Frontenac then manipulated Colbert into allowing the construction of Fort Niagara at the western end of Lake Ontario in 1676 and a chain of posts at the foot of Lake Michigan and on the Illinois and Mississippi Rivers by 1680. Two years later, Frontenac's chief trading associate, René-Robert Cavelier de La Salle, reached the mouth of the Mississippi River, which he claimed for France. Frontenac and La Salle looked forward to the possibility of shipping furs to France by way of the Gulf of Mexico, thereby opening up a western commercial empire independent of New France. However, La Salle's effort to start a colony at the mouth of the Mississippi River failed and resulted in his murder at the hands of a mutinous crew in 1687.

While Frontenac was preoccupied with southwest expansion, the Montreal merchants were proceeding northwest in the mid-1670s with the building of Fort Michilimackinac at the junction of Lakes Michigan and Huron, which became a launching point for the fur trade along the upper Mississippi and beyond Lake Superior. By 1684 Daniel Greysolon, Sieur du Lhut, had established posts at Kaministiquia (Fort William) and Lake Nipigon, north of Lake Superior. Five years later, Jacques de Noyon reached Lake of the Woods, west of Lake Superior. To the north, the French Compagnie de la Baie du Nord was formed in 1682 to wage war against the posts of the Hudson's Bay Company. Military raids led by Charles de Troyes and Pierre Le Moyne d'Iberville wreaked havoc on the English posts from 1686 to 1697, but the Hudson's Bay Company tenaciously resisted. Thus, by pushing north, west, and south, establishing key posts where possible, France appeared committed to an imperialist struggle for the control of the continent.

The Iroquois and their English allies could no longer afford to respond passively to French imperialist design. In 1680 the Iroquois renewed their bid to gain control of the western fur trade by launching an assault on the Illinois country, and the French were once more confronted with the need to support their Native allies. When the Iroquois entered into a formal alliance with the English at Albany, New York, in 1684, it was clear that Native warfare would henceforth involve rival European powers in hostilities. French military invasions of Iroquois country in 1684 and 1687 led to an English-aided retaliatory attack on the French settlement at Lachine (above Montreal) in 1689. Frontenac strengthened the garrisons of the posts before launching a massive military campaign against the Iroquois that culminated in their defeat in 1696. By the end of the century, prolonged warfare and disease had taken their toll on the Iroquois, and they made peace with the French and 13 western tribes in 1701. This peace treaty secured Iroquois neutrality in any future colonial war between France and England and marked the end of the great Iroquois resistance to French westward expansion. With a significant French presence in the American West, the two imperial powers would find themselves locked into a clash of expansionist ambitions to supplement traditional differences in Europe.

COLONIAL FRONTIER RIVALRIES

Friction between New France and the thirteen colonies was primarily the outcome of trade competition on the American frontier. The outbreak of war between Catholic, feudal France and Protestant, democratic England, the leading imperial powers in Europe, merely offered their North American colonial communities opportunities to renew locally based hostilities. Throughout the 17th century, French and English entrepreneurs and administrators struggled to control the extensive North Atlantic fisheries and the lucrative fur trade. The fur trade, in particular, entangled its European participants in traditional Native conflicts as they sought to gain the upper hand in the competition between the St. Lawrence–Great Lakes and the Hudson-Mohawk commercial arteries. In the 18th century, however, the thirteen colonies, emerging from their confined area along the Atlantic seaboard, collided with the forces of French expansionism that were determined to preserve the western frontier for the fur trade.

The outcome of any conflict between the French and English colonies in North America should have been a foregone conclusion, judging by surface comparisons. The population of the thirteen colonies was 25 times larger than that of New France. The English colonies together had a diversified economy built on a solid agricultural base and supplemented by commerce, shipping, and an embryonic manufacturing sector. The French colonies still relied upon the fur trade as agriculture did not allow more than a subsistence living. The compact English colonies hugging the Atlantic seaboard were more readily defensible than was the far-flung French empire with frontiers extending upwards of 2,000 miles into the continental interior and nearly the same distance from north to south.

That the French empire in North America survived for over a century and a half in the shadow of a mightier English colonial presence to the south and a resourceful corporate competitor to the north can be attributed primarily to divisiveness among the Anglo-American colonies arising from differences in origin, religion, or economic interests. For example, Massachusetts and Virginia were long-time economic rivals, as were most of the New England colonies with New York and Pennsylvania. Some of the colonies were thoroughly indifferent to the issues that sustained the imperial conflict. The people of Pennsylvania, Virginia, Maryland, and the Carolinas believed that the Appalachian Mountain ranges to the west shielded them from French attack. Only the fur traders of New York with eyes on the St. Lawrence trading network and the Massachusetts merchant fleets interested in expanding their North Atlantic shipping prospects actively participated in the colonial struggle against the French. Even in New York, which bordered on New France, descendants of the original Dutch settlers living in the northern part of the colony had little inclination to support a struggle that they saw as beneficial only to the Albany merchants or the king of England. In the final analysis, whereas the fur trade was the backbone of the Canadian economy and well worth fighting for, it was, on the whole, a relatively marginal enterprise in the Anglo-American colonies, generally not worth risking one's life or property in its defense.

Furthermore, the St. Lawrence colony was naturally well-situated to ward off an English intrusion. The wisdom of Champlain's selection of Quebec as an effective military base for garrisoning and defending the St. Lawrence colony from an attack by sea was proven on several occasions. Upstream, a network of forts on the Richelieu River and the southern end of Lake Champlain blocked English access to the St. Lawrence via the Hudson-Mohawk waterway. Even the American frontier itself worked in favor of the French colony as the heavily forested Appalachian Mountain chain offered additional protection from a direct assault from the south. Forest warfare tended to favor the French who were more skillful at guerrilla tactics derived from decades of fighting the Iroquois. French forces were bolstered by adventurous coureurs de bois and their Algonquian allies were particularly adept at hit-and-run border raids against English settlements. In their attempts at retaliation, the English benefited from Iroquois support in the 1680s and 1690s. But after the peace treaty of 1701, most tribes remained neutral or began to view the encroaching American settler as the chief threat to their traditional way of life.

When roused to action, English colonial forces tended to rely on their maritime strength to strike at the military heart of New France. In 1690, the year after the outbreak of King William's War in Europe, a New England naval expedition led by Sir

William Phips set out to capture both Port Royal and Quebec. Although Port Royal had scarcely 1,000 settlers who were more concerned with tilling their farms than with expansionist designs, the English saw Acadia as a base from which France might seek to control the north Atlantic fisheries and to develop a competing trade with the West Indies. Port Royal was also a haven from which privateers operated in times of war to prey on New England shipping. When the French recruited the Abenaki, Malecite, and Micmac for frontier raids on New England settlements, the necessity to remove the Acadian threat became more imperative. An invasion force of 700 New Englanders easily overpowered a garrison of about 100 French troops and destroyed Port Royal. Launching an attack on Quebec, the Phips' expedition arrived too late in the season and had to cut short its massive assault to avoid the risk of entrapment in the St. Lawrence ice. Further plans to attack Quebec fell through for lack of help from England, and Port Royal was returned to France by the Treaty of Ryswick in 1697.

By the end of King William's War, France was already in the process of revising its strategic interests in its North American empire. The huge glut of furs in the warehouses of France had dramatically reduced the economic benefit of the Canadian beaver trade. But rather than retreat from the Great Lakes and Mississippi Valley, as some French government officials were urging, King Louis XIV and his minister of marine Louis Phélypeaux de Pontchartrain decided to maintain the western posts for political reasons. Henceforth, the western posts became necessary to keep the Natives within the French alliance, which was in turn vital for preventing Anglo-American expansion into the West. Accordingly, d'Iberville was instructed to establish a colony, which he called Louisiana, near the mouth of the Mississippi River in 1699. The establishment of New Orleans as their main base in Louisiana in 1718 was designed to consolidate French control over the lower Mississippi Valley and thereby halt the advance of the English into the southwest. To maintain French control of the upper Great Lakes region and thus block English access to the northwest, Antoine de la Mothe de Cadillac fulfilled royal orders to build a new settlement, known as Détroit (the straits), at the narrows between Lakes Erie and Huron in 1701. The existing French fur-trading posts in the Mississippi Valley and the Great Lakes basin would be fortified, and where required, new ones would be constructed. From Acadia on the north Atlantic coast, up the St. Lawrence River through the Great Lakes, and down the Mississippi River to the Gulf of Mexico, a cordon was to be drawn at the rear of the rapidly growing English colonies to contain them between the Atlantic Ocean and the Allegheny Mountains. In essence, the struggle on the American frontier had been transformed from a competition between colonial trading interests to a clash of expansive European empires.

EUROPEAN WARFARE ON THE AMERICAN FRONTIER

The outbreak of the European War of the Spanish Succession in 1702 offered yet another occasion for the resumption of hostilities in North America. Again Acadia became a primary target, especially after a French-Abenaki alliance endeavored to halt the northward advance of New Englanders into their territory on the Maine–New Brunswick frontier. The Acadians resisted repeated attacks by seafaring raiders from New England until 1710, when an English-supported naval force of 3,400 men and 36 ships under the command of Colonel Francis Nicholson easily captured Port Royal. To make the English conquest complete, Port Royal was renamed Annapolis Royal, and Acadia became known as the province of Nova Scotia, never again to return to the French empire.

England attempted a similar decisive strike against Quebec in 1711 by providing 5,300 of the 6,500-man naval fleet commanded by Sir Hovenden Walker. Another 2,300 colonial troops were dispatched by land via the Lake Champlain route to mount an assault on Quebec from the west. Quebec appeared doomed in the wake of an invasion force equivalent to about one-half the population of the entire St. Lawrence colony. But nature intervened as part of the English fleet ran aground in fog and gales at the mouth of the St. Lawrence. On news of this disaster, the attack by way of Lake Champlain was abandoned.

French-English colonial conflict also spilled over into the resident fisheries of the Avalon Peninsula of Newfoundland. In 1696 d'Iberville attacked the English settlements around St. John's, killing 200 people and taking 700 prisoners. The following year, the English retaliated with a naval expedition of 2,000 men that recaptured all of the settlements. Plaisance was the base for additional French raids on English settlements in 1705 and 1709. The Treaty of Utrecht, which ended hostilities in 1713, resulted in the French surrender of Acadia and their recognition of English claims to Newfoundland and Hudson Bay. Foreshadowing future imperial decisions, France was willing to sacrifice these North American possessions to make concessions for losses in Europe.

While mainland Nova Scotia was lost to the English, the French held on to Cape Breton Island, where by 1720 they had built the massive stone fortress and naval base known as Louisbourg. Designed to be an impregnable symbol of French sea power—the Gibraltar of North America—Louisbourg was strategically located on the northeastern tip of the island, guarding the entrance to the St. Lawrence. Over the next quarter-century, Louisbourg became not only a launching point for the French navy and privateers to disrupt New England fishing and trading fleets but also a thriving entrepôt for trade with the West Indies. Its construction signified France's renewed commitment to strengthening its North American empire in order to contain its imperial rival along the Atlantic seaboard.

To extend French control deeper into the interior of the continent, imperial authorities collaborated with colonial fur-trading interests eager to outflank the Hudson's Bay Company in the northwest. By the 1720s an active fur trade centered around Kaministiquia (now Thunder Bay) and Lake Nipigon. At the same time, the French government showed a revived interest in the search for a route to the Pacific. In 1730 Pierre Gaulthier de Varennes et de La Vérendrye, commander of the fur-trading post at Kaministiquia, offered to establish a post on Lake Winnipeg and to conduct explorations for a western sea from this base at no expense to the Crown. Supported by wealthy Montreal merchants, La Vérendrye aimed to build a chain of posts to serve as fur-trading and supply depots, closer to and more accessible for the local Natives than the remote English posts along Hudson Bay. Accordingly, from 1731 to 1734, La Vérendrye, accompanied by his three sons, built Fort St. Pierre on Rainy Lake, Fort St. Charles on Lake of the Woods, and Fort Maurepas where the Red River empties into Lake Winnipeg. In 1738 they added Fort Rouge near present-day Winnipeg and Fort la Reine at the present site of Portage la Prairie. From their base at Fort la Reine, the La Vérendryes went on to establish Fort Dauphin on Lake Manitoba and Forts Bourbon and Paskoya (The Pas) near the Saskatchewan River from 1741 to 1743. Their search for the western sea also took them southwestwardly to the Black Hills of South Dakota in 1742–43, and they may have even reached the foothills of the Rocky Mountains. In 1751 Boucher de Niverville traveled west on the Saskatchewan River and built Fort Jonquière, near the present site of Calgary. Thus, the French empire in North America had reached its western limits.

In expanding further into the northwest and in constructing the mighty naval base at Louisbourg, the French had taken advantage of over three decades of relative peace in Europe and North America. The outbreak of the War of the Austrian Succession in 1740 once again allowed the imperial powers of Europe to renew hostilities and to extend them to their North American empires. The New England colonies were especially concerned about Louisbourg's threat to colonial trade and shipping. Governor William Shirley of Massachusetts organized a force of 4,000 colonial militia that sailed for Louisbourg in 1745 under the command of William Pepperell. The Royal Navy supplied a squadron of ships under the command of Commodore Peter Warren to prevent reinforcements and supplies from France from reaching the beleaguered fortress. A garrison of 2,000 French militia and civilians endured six weeks of bombardment and blockades before surrendering. Louisbourg's fall revealed the limitations of French power in North America and cleared the way for an assault on Quebec. France valued Louisbourg enough to dispatch a naval expedition of 7,000 men to recapture the fortress in 1746, but the fleet was plagued by troubled seas and never succeeded in launching a counterattack. During the peace treaty negotiations at Aix-la-Chapelle, in 1748, France again manifested its concern by sacrificing its conquests in the Austrian Netherlands along with the city of Madras in India to regain Louisbourg.

The Treaty of Aix-la-Chapelle proved to be more a truce than a lasting peace, and both imperial rivals strengthened themselves for the inevitable renewal of hostilities. France endeavored not only to reinforce Louisbourg and the garrison at the mouth of the Saint John River but also to build Fort Beauséjour (near present-day Sackville, New Brunswick) on the Chignecto Isthmus in 1750. As New Englanders increasingly regarded the decision to return Louisbourg to France as evidence of a willingness to sacrifice colonial interests for imperial consideration, England sought to consolidate its position in Nova Scotia. To counterbalance Louisbourg, the imperial authority established Halifax on Chebucto Bay in 1749. Not only was Halifax meant to replace Annapolis Royal as the chief naval base and administrative center of Nova Scotia, it was also to become a substantial Protestant settlement to offset the original French Catholic Acadian population. To bolster the defense of Nova Scotia, the English also built Fort Lawrence on the Isthmus of Chignecto just as the French were completing nearby Fort Beauséjour.

Seeking to make the Acadians into completely trustworthy subjects, the governor of Nova Scotia, Edward Cornwallis, commanded them to swear an oath of unconditional allegiance to the British Crown in 1749. Despite threats of deportation, the Acadians generally ignored the governor's ultimatum. Already preoccupied with establishing Halifax, Governor Cornwallis decided against risking further complications by pressing for an immediate decision on the expulsion of the Acadians.

Another ominous challenge to the French empire in North America was the formation of the Ohio Land Company in 1748. This Virginia-based enterprise secured a British Crown land grant of one-half million acres with the intention of bringing English settlers into the fertile Ohio Valley. The battle lines were now drawn between two divergent and incompatible forces vying for control of the continental interior. The French sought to preserve the forest for the indigenous population and the fur trade, while the English hoped to deliver the area to the axe of the pioneer farmer.

In 1749 France laid a formal claim to the Ohio Valley as an expedition under Céloron de Blainville planted lead plates bearing the French coat of arms throughout the region to symbolize imperial possession. To check English advances into the area, the French built a chain of forts from Lake Erie to the forks of the Ohio River, where Fort Duquesne was situated in 1754. The reaction to this advance in the thirteen colonies was largely indifferent. For example, Pennsylvania was not concerned that some of its land was occupied by the French; New York expressed doubt that the French were intruding on English soil. Only Virginia, where the leading investors in the Ohio Company lived, was roused to action. In 1754 the governor of Virginia sent Major George Washington with some 300 men to expel the French, but this first English effort to gain control of the Ohio Valley was decisively repulsed at Great Meadows. This frontier clash proved to be the spark that ignited the final conflict over North America. Although Britain and France would remain ostensibly at peace in Europe for two more years, they were simultaneously motivated to devote unprecedented military support to their embattled colonies.

THE FINAL SHOWDOWN FOR NEW FRANCE

In 1755 both France and Britain sent large military expeditions to North America. While the French force of 3,000 soldiers under General Ludwig August Dieskau eventually landed in Quebec, the English force of 1,000 regulars under General Edward Braddock joined 1,500 colonial militia for an assault on Fort Duquesne. A contingent of 250 French soldiers and 600 Native allies ambushed the oncoming army and proceeded to demonstrate its superiority at forest warfare. Braddock was killed and his army destroyed. Two other English attacks on French strong points in the St. Lawrence Valley ended in stalemate because much of the fighting was waged in the forest. The only early English success came at Fort Beauséjour. The discovery of some 300 Acadians serving in arms among the French garrison prompted an English reaction that led directly to the tragic expulsion of the entire Acadian population.

The persistent refusal of the Acadians to take the oath of allegiance to the British Crown was not viewed as a serious security threat in the four decades after the Treaty of Utrecht. The Acadian population, which had grown to over 12,000 by 1755, was content to carry on its peaceful existence of farming, fishing, hunting, and trading. The produce from their fertile farms found a ready market in both the English and the French garrisons, and sometimes even in New England. The Acadians had no special loyalty to France, which had continually neglected them, nor were they disturbed by British rule. They were even prepared to pledge loyalty to Britain, but they did not want to commit to military service against France. While the British government was averse to presiding over the wholesale deportation of a long-settled people, Governor Colonel Charles Lawrence refused to accept the notion of Acadian neutrality. Given the state of war, he argued that a disloyal Acadian population could pose a serious threat to the new English settlements in Nova Scotia. He further contended that the mere threat of deportation would be sufficient to persuade the Acadians to conform and that at worst it would be necessary to take action against some recalcitrants as proof of his resolve. The Acadians, for their part, had reason to believe that their continued resistance would have no more serious consequences than it had over the past four decades. Unfortunately, both sides miscalculated, and in the general hysteria that followed Braddock's defeat in the Ohio Valley, the process of uprooting this passive people from the Annapolis Valley began in earnest in August 1755.

The expulsion of the Acadians was brutal and disorganized. Soldiers forced the Acadians from their homes and held them captive until they could be herded onto ships, which dispersed them to France, England, and various parts of the French and British empires. An estimated 7,000 were evacuated in 1755–56 while another 2,000 to 3,000 were deported by the time the policy was officially ended in 1762. While the expulsion destroyed Acadian society as a whole, the fate of individuals and groups of Acadians is difficult to track. Perhaps one-quarter to one-third died in the evacuation or resettlement process, victims of shipwrecks, diseases, and shortages of food and water. Countless families were split up and never reunited. An estimated 2,000 Acadians fled to Île Saint-Jean (Prince Edward Island); another 1,500 escaped to the St. Lawrence Valley; others made their way to the French islands of St. Pierre and Miquelon off the coast of Newfoundland; and 2,000 to 3,000 apparently ended up in Louisiana, where today there are more than 1 million descendants of the Acadians who have become known as "Cajuns." After the British government granted permission for Acadians to resettle in Nova Scotia in 1764, an estimated 3,000 returned, even though their land had been claimed by recently arrived New Englanders. Whatever their ultimate fate, the Acadians stand as tragic victims of the ruthless ambitions of two powerful European empires.

Meanwhile, the outbreak of the Seven Years' War in Europe in 1756 escalated the clash of empires in North America. The contrasting imperial strategies for this global conflict would shape the course and outcome of North American warfare. France focused on securing victories in continental Europe, while New France fought an essentially defensive war in North America. As in the past, France expected to be in a position to negotiate major colonial concessions in the final peace treaty. On the other hand, Britain planned to fight the war in Europe to a stalemate and gain the upper hand by cutting France off from its overseas empire. This difference in military commitment to the North American front would prove to be decisive in determining the outcome.

General Louis Joseph, marquis de Montcalm, who replaced General Dieskau as the commander of the French and Canadian forces in North America in 1756, confronted the challenge of having to wage war with limited human resources and supplies. The 3,000 regulars that France had sent out at the outset of hostilities represented an impressive start, but unfortunately he could expect no more than 2,000 reinforcements for the duration of the war. Although Montcalm could also rely on a colonial militia estimated at upwards of 10,000 men, they were also needed on the farms to produce food, which was always in short supply. While the Native warriors overwhelmingly supported the French cause and were fierce fighters, they were difficult to control and tended to have their own battle agendas.

Because of the constant manpower dilemma, Montcalm decided to focus on the defense of the St. Lawrence Valley in order to protect Montreal and Quebec against an English invasion. By capturing Fort Oswego, the main English entry to the Great Lakes, Montcalm further protected the upper St. Lawrence region in 1756. He also safeguarded the Lake Champlain–Richelieu River route to New France by capturing Fort William Henry. Typically, these initial victories were achieved through wilderness warfare tactics at which both the French militia and the Natives were proficient. However, Montcalm's refusal to give sufficient attention to defending the western posts raised the ire of Governor Philippe de Rigaud, marquis de Vaudreuil, and Intendant François Bigot, whose primary interest lay in the fur trade. Although Montcalm won this power struggle, the division within the colonial administration would inevitably add to his future military woes.

The French also benefited from the early ineffectiveness of the English military campaign. But in 1758 the tide of battle began to turn in the English favor when Prime Minister William Pitt reorganized the army and committed upwards of 20,000 regular soldiers to support approximately 25,000 colonial troops in order to wage a European-style battle. Moreover, Pitt devised a grand strategy that assigned a more prominent role to the superior Royal Navy. By focusing on crushing French maritime power, England could gain control of the sea lanes, thereby sealing the doom of New France. The Royal Navy blockade of Canada allowed the English to obtain reinforcements and supplies while depriving New France of imperial aid. As a result, New France faced overwhelming odds of nearly three to one in ships, four to one in soldiers, and 10 to one in financial commitment. Indeed, when Montcalm requested more military aid from France, he was informed that the king could not commit forces and resources comparable to those available to the English colonies.

Pitt's new military direction, however, did not yield immediate results as Sir James Abercrombie unsuccessfully led a massive English assault on Fort Carillon (also known as Fort Ticonderoga), which Vaudreuil had built three years earlier at the northern end of Lake George to block a northward advance on the St. Lawrence Valley via the Richelieu River–Lake Champlain route. Deciding to concentrate his force of about 3,500 men in the path of the most direct overland route to New France, Montcalm defeated an English army of 15,000. The French victory came at the expense of lightly guarded Fort Frontenac, which was easily captured and destroyed by a smaller English detachment led by Colonel John Bradstreet. Consequently, with its lines of communication to New France effectively cut off, the French garrison at Fort Duquesne had no choice but to destroy the outpost and to retreat in the face of the approaching English army. With the abandonment of Fort Duquesne, which the English renamed Pittsburgh after their prime minister, the Ohio Valley was under English control. In the meantime, the English fleet effectively blockaded Louisbourg, enabling the army of 13,000 troops led by General Jeffrey Amherst to capture the fortress with a garrison of little more than 3,000 after a siege of seven weeks. The fall of the French bastion guarding the entrance to the St. Lawrence cleared the way for a direct assault on Quebec, although the lengthy French resistance did succeed in scuttling English plans for an invasion before the onset of winter.

The military campaign of 1759 featured a full-scale French retreat to concentrate on the defense of the heart of New France, the Montreal-Quebec corridor. While Fort Niagara succumbed to English attack, the French preferred to burn the recently built Fort Rouillé (present-day Toronto) to the ground rather than have it fall into enemy hands. Thus, the French lost control of the Great Lakes region, and the abandonment of the posts along the Richelieu River–Lake Champlain route set the stage for a last-ditch stand at the stronghold of Quebec.

The English invasion force of 13,500 troops commanded by General James Wolfe held Quebec under siege for three months. Situated on the north shore of the St. Lawrence, Quebec was protected to the west by a line of steep cliffs and to the east by Montcalm's well-planned defenses that blocked every attack. As winter was approaching, Wolfe was faced with the possibility of having to withdraw from Quebec. In a desperate move to land his army, Wolfe found a small cove, Anse au Foulon, from which a narrow path led up the steep 200-foot-high cliffs. The French had left this area lightly guarded, believing it impossible for an invasion force to climb such heights. On the evening of September 12, Wolfe gambled, and by daybreak, he had succeeded in leading 4,500 troops onto the Plains of Abraham, a field outside the western walls of the fortress.

As soon as he discovered Wolfe's successful approach, Montcalm decided to mount an immediate counterattack to drive the English from the heights before they could bring up all their forces. The decisive battle for North American supremacy lasted less than half an hour and featured dubious military strategy highlighted by the deaths of both commanders—certainly an uncommon occurrence in the course of 18th-century warfare. Ultimately, the well-trained and disciplined British regulars triumphed over a French force that depended on Canadiens, untrained for European-style fighting in line.

The loss of Quebec was a major blow to the French, although they still controlled the St. Lawrence Valley. While the British fleet departed the St. Lawrence to avoid being frozen in for the winter, a sizable garrison stayed behind to guard the captured fortress, under the command of General James Murray. After a difficult winter, marked by shortages of food and an outbreak of scurvy, the English found themselves under siege by a French force from Montreal under Chevalier François-Gaston de Lévis, which arrived in the spring of 1760 to liberate Quebec. Ultimate victory at Quebec would be determined by the nationality of the first ship to sail up the St. Lawrence with the spring thaw. As it turned out, British sea power had dealt a fatal blow to the French navy off the western coast of France in November 1759. Accordingly, when English ships arrived first at Quebec in May 1760, the fate of New France was sealed. The final, anticlimactic chapter of the battle for Canada unfolded in Montreal where 2,000 French soldiers confronted 17,000 British and American troops. After the capitulation of Montreal on September 8, 1760, Canada passed into British hands.

The Seven Years' War in Europe would not end for three more years. Unquestionably, Britain had triumphed on the battlefield because it was more willing to commit

An oil painting by Adam Sherriff Scott (1887–1980) depicts the French regime giving way to the British regime in a ceremonial military transfer of power at Montreal in 1760.

vital resources to defend its North American empire, one built on the settlement frontier rather than on the fur-trading frontier. France's priorities clearly resided in Europe and in other colonies than New France. But as past experience had demonstrated, victory on the battlefield was not necessarily decisive in determining the final fate of a conquered colony. New France, particularly Acadia, had been previously captured in war and returned in peace. While politicians and diplomats negotiated the spoils of victory and defeat in Europe, the people of New France felt a sense of both hope and fear. They hoped that France would reconsider its low assessment of its North American colony. But they also feared that they would suffer the same fate as their colonial confrères in Acadia scarcely five years before. In 1763, the French-Canadian people would find their hopes dashed but their fears appeased.

PART THREE

THE BRITISH NORTH AMERICAN COLONIES 1760–1867

CHAPTER 6

THE CHALLENGE
OF IMPERIAL RULE
IN BRITISH NORTH
AMERICA

Until the middle of the 18th century, British interest in North America focused overwhelmingly on the thirteen colonies along the Atlantic seaboard. Although the fur-trading territory of the Hudson's Bay Company, the fisheries of Newfoundland, the recently captured French colony of Acadia, and the newly established naval base at Halifax, Nova Scotia, were included within the British Empire, these outlying areas paled in significance to the well-endowed American colonies, which contained a population about one-third the size of England's. The military conquest of New France in 1759–60, confirmed by France's surrender in the Treaty of Paris in 1763, certainly gave Britain a greater stake in the northerly reaches of the American frontier. But the challenges and complications of governing a people of different language, religion, customs, and culture not only led to resentment between and within the French and English communities of the St. Lawrence colony, renamed the Province of Quebec, but also fanned the flames of rebellion in the thirteen colonies, thus shattering the short-lived imperial unity of North America. The division of the continent as agreed upon in the Treaty of Versailles, which ended the American Revolutionary War in 1783, opened the way for two nations, one immediately and the other eventually, to be created out of British North America.

THE ROOTS OF ENGLISH CANADA

When Humphrey Gilbert arrived in 1583 to claim Newfoundland as an English colony, he found fishing vessels from various western European nations operating in St. John's harbor and settlers scattered throughout the surrounding countryside. When it became clear that the English claim to the Avalon Peninsula did not deter international fishing fleets, the imperial authorities actively encouraged the establishment of permanent settlement as a means of exerting greater control over the fisheries. In 1610 the London and Bristol Company sent John Guy with 40 men to start Newfoundland's first official colony at Cupids on Conception Bay. The company believed that residents would have the advantage of occupying the best fishing locations before the migratory fishermen arrived. Opposition from migratory fishermen and the area's lack of agricultural potential rendered the colony unsustainable. Lord Baltimore also attempted to establish a colony at Ferryland, south of St. John's, in 1621, but the harshness of the winters prompted him to turn his efforts toward Maryland in 1629. Although five more English colonial enterprises had failed by 1661, some settlers invariably stayed behind, with the result that the island had more than 500 permanent residents living in about 40 communities scattered along the eastern coast from Cape Bonavista to Trepassey. By 1680 the population had risen to about 2,000 with the arrival of people from the West Country of England, who came out as passengers on migratory fishing ships and decided to stay. Potato famines in the 1720s and 1730s drove thousands of Irish across the Atlantic to seek refuge in Newfoundland. Consequently, the population of the island reached 10,000 by the middle of the 18th century. But the determination of commercial fishing interests to restrict settlement succeeded in keeping the population below 20,000 by end of the century.

The growth of settlement eventually led to a modification of long-standing imperial policy toward the government of Newfoundland. Throughout the 17th and 18th centuries, Britain remained reluctant to promote organized government in Newfoundland because it valued the island as a fishing station and a naval base rather than as a colony. By the First Western Charter of 1634, the English government officially recognized the customary "fishing admiral system" of administration by which the captain of the first ship in port each spring had authority over the island, provided that he had the arms and manpower to enforce his control. The inevitable problem with this system was that the admirals stayed for only a few months of the year and had varying interests and capacities when it came to maintaining law and order. After contemplating the prospect of removing the colonists, the English government passed the Newfoundland Act in 1699, affirming the rights and authority of the fishing admirals but recognizing permanent settlement so long as it did not encroach upon the domain of the migratory fishermen. Colonial administration improved somewhat in 1729, when the imperial authorities appointed the naval officer in charge of the convoy escorting the fishing fleet to the island to serve as governor and commander in chief during the summer months. The naval governor was responsible for appointing resident justices of the peace to substitute for him during the winter. That this naval regime lasted for nearly a century further reflected the limited British commitment to the development of Newfoundland as a colony.

The deficiencies of law and order adversely affected not only the English settlers but also the native Beothuk population of Newfoundland. As the fishing industry and settlement extended along the eastern and southern coasts, the Beothuk preferred to withdraw into the interior. Limited access to their long-standing coastal fishing and hunting sites led to severe food shortages. Beothuk efforts to access these coastal areas often resulted in violent clashes with the fishermen and settlers, who felt unrestrained by legal sanctions. Those Beothuk who did not fall victim to starvation and English brutality succumbed to tuberculosis, resulting in the death of the last known Beothuk survivor in 1829.

Meanwhile, in the northwestern reaches of the North American continent, English rule was sustained by the Hudson's Bay Company. The founding charter of 1670 granted company control over all lands draining into Hudson Bay, a vast domain called Rupert's Land whose limits were unknown at the time but which actually included much of the western prairie and northern subarctic regions. The company was interested only in maintaining its fur-trading monopoly, and thus it made no effort to settle the barren lands around Hudson Bay. Unlike its St. Lawrence and Hudson River rivals to the south, the company did not have to worry about encroaching settlement or unlicensed private traders. Even when French traders sought to invade company domain, they faced a perilous and costly overland voyage from Montreal to Hudson Bay and back before they could ship their furs to Paris via the St. Lawrence River. By comparison, the Hudson's Bay Company traders benefited from the shorter and more direct sea voyage to London and ready access to cheaper and better quality English trade goods, which the Native traders preferred.

The limited competition enabled the company to maintain a policy of "sitting by the bay," as Cree and Assiniboine middlemen brought furs from the interior to the posts established at the mouths of rivers emptying into Hudson Bay. Only twice in its first century of operation did the company venture inland to reinforce its trade linkages with the Native tribes in the face of French competition. Henry Kelsey became the first European to reach the western prairies in 1690–91, while Anthony Henday reached the foothills of the Rockies in 1754. After each expedition, the company decided not to establish costly trading posts in the interior. Consequently, Rupert's Land remained unexplored and unoccupied until the arrival of the St. Lawrence traders in the 1770s.

The British government took a more active interest in colonizing the Province of Nova Scotia in hopes of overwhelming the French population of Acadia. Accompanying the founding of the naval base at Halifax in 1749 was the first systematic British effort to promote immigration to Canada. Governor Edward Cornwallis brought about 2,000 immigrants from Britain and New England to settle in Halifax, and within two years they were joined by some 1,500 "foreign Protestants," mostly of German origin, who settled in nearby Lunenburg.

After the expulsion of the Acadians in 1755, imperial authorities launched a special campaign inviting loyal Protestants from New England to claim the vacated French farmland around the Bay of Fundy. To attract more New Englanders, Britain granted Nova Scotia an elected assembly in 1758, the first official representative government in Canada. The result was a steady flow of New England farmers and fishermen during the 1760s, with settlement focusing in the Annapolis Valley, the Saint John River valley, the Isthmus of Chignecto, and the southeastern mainland coast. In 1764 the British government allowed Acadians to return, provided that they were dispersed throughout Nova Scotia. Hundreds of them settled around the Bay of Chaleur on the border between present-day Quebec and New Brunswick and along the lower Saint John River valley. Among the British immigrants arriving in the 1760s and 1770s were some 2,000 settlers from Ulster in Northern Ireland and several hundred Scottish Highlanders who, displaced by the enclosure movement at home, acquired land on Cape Breton Island and the new colony of St. John's Island.

Formerly the French colony of Île-St-Jean, St. John's Island (later Prince Edward Island) had been ceded to Britain by the Treaty of Paris in 1763. In 1767 the British government had granted all of the land on the island to 67 military officers and other Crown favorites on the condition that they settle their 20,000-acre holdings. Most of these landlords remained absentees who neglected to fulfill their colonizing obligations. The establishment of the island as a separate colony in 1769 and the granting of representative government in 1773 only served to protect the interests of the absentee landlords. As a result, the colony continued to struggle with vast areas of undeveloped land as absentee landlords refused to sell their land or to grant titles to those who attempted to settle on their own initiative.

Maritime settlement continued to focus on peninsular Nova Scotia, which on the eve of the American Revolution had a population approaching 20,000, the majority of whom were New Englanders. However, the northward flow of American migration had subsided by the end of the 1760s in the wake of the opening of the Ohio-Mississippi Valley to settlement. A constant impediment to Maritime development would be a limited agricultural potential that rendered the region much less attractive to settlers than the vast, fertile western interior frontier.

CONQUEST AND CONCILIATION IN THE BRITISH PROVINCE OF QUEBEC

While the Maritime Provinces were being populated predominantly by English-speaking people and governed by representative institutions, the conquered French colony along the St. Lawrence River was evolving in an uncertain and unique direction. The fall of New France presented British imperial authorities with the awkward responsibility of ruling over the subjects of its traditional European rival and the greatest threat to its growing North American empire. In the final analysis, the controlled response of both conquerors and conquered at this critical turning point in North American history lay the foundation for the bicultural character of the future Canadian nation.

When British commander in chief General Jeffrey Amherst proclaimed on September 22, 1760, that the conquered colony in the St. Lawrence Valley would be ruled by the occupying military forces, the French-speaking population of scarcely 65,000 had ample reason to be fearful about the prospects of cultural survival within an English-speaking American empire of more than 1.5 million people. Not only was the memory of the Acadian expulsion still vivid, but the ravages of war had taken their toll on the struggling French colony. Much of the town of Quebec lay in ruins, and many of the farms in the surrounding countryside had been devastated by the invaders. Commerce, notably the fur trade, suffered from the severance of economic ties with France, while agriculture had been neglected to the extent that seed was lacking for the next harvest. The hasty retreat to France of some 2,000 members of the colonial elite, including royal administrators, military officers, and the leading merchants and landholders, cast an ominous shadow over the future development of the Canadien community.

Even more precarious was the future of the Catholic Church in the wake of the death of the bishop of Quebec, Henri-Marie de Pontbriand, three months prior to the fall of New France. Without the appointment of a successor, new clergy could not be ordained; and the fact that the Catholic Church had been outlawed in Britain meant that it could no longer count on financial and legal support from the government. Certainly the refusal of the military rulers to guarantee the survival of French laws, customs, and institutions under the terms of surrender posed an imminent threat to Canadien society.

However, initial prospects did not conform to eventual reality. The interim military regime maintained the traditional administrative division of the colony into the three districts of Quebec, Trois-Rivières, and Montreal, each headed by a military governor responsible to General Amherst, who was headquartered in New York. The terms of surrender offered transportation to France within 18 months for the relatively few who wanted to leave, while the majority who chose to stay were guaranteed the free exercise of their Catholic religion and the security of their property rights. Furthermore, the governors—General James Murray in Quebec, General Ralph Burton in Trois-Rivières, and General Thomas Gage in Montreal—did not disturb the seigneurial system, nor did they interfere with the collection of the church tithe. Although judicial power rested with the military courts, they drew on the precedents of the French regime and relied on French clerks and attorneys, in addition to using the captains of militia as local magistrates. Moreover, the presence of British troops as a cash-paying market for local products and services stimulated a revival of economic life. Within a year, the military governors had restored agriculture, stabilized currency, and regulated supplies and prices.

The moderation and tolerance of the British military regime was a pragmatic response to the prevailing uncertainty over both the progress of the continuing war in Europe and the ultimate fate of the colony. Accordingly, the chief concern of the interim administrators was to avoid institutional change or interference with the normal way of life to an extent that would make their task of governing the overwhelming Canadien majority more difficult. Furthermore, unlike the situation in the much smaller colony of Acadia, there was no nearby French base to provoke popular resistance to the British conquerors. The transfer of power and the process of readjustment were rendered easier by the willingness of the Canadiens to accept the circumstances under which they had to persevere. Tired of the turmoil of recurring warfare, people were chiefly concerned with a speedy and permanent return to a normal, peaceful life. The vast majority of farmers, small merchants, seigneurs, and clergy had never been to France and thus preferred to remain in the land of their birth. Any feelings that they might harbor for France were more likely based on resentment of the imperial power's apparent abandonment of the colony and the indifference of the metropolitan population to the fall of New France.

Indeed, France's disinterest in its North American empire was confirmed in the final negotiations leading to the Treaty of Paris, which formally ended the Seven Years' War in February 1763. The unflattering fact was that, in dividing up the spoils of war, both France and Britain preferred the tiny West Indian sugar island of Guadeloupe over the vast territory of Canada, whose resource value was considered to be limited to the fur trade. In the final analysis, Britain chose to retain Canada for strategic reasons. Not only would keeping Canada remove the threat of France from North America, but also the colony along the St. Lawrence River could serve as a convenient military base in the event that the rumblings of political discontent in the thirteen colonies erupted into armed insurrection. Thus, by the terms of the Treaty of Paris, France gave up all claims to North America, including transferring Louisiana to Spain and Île-St-Jean to Britain, in return for being allowed to maintain the islands of St. Pierre and Miquelon as unfortified fishing stations off the southeastern coast of Newfoundland.

But before it could implement a plan to replace military rule with civilian government in the St. Lawrence colony, Britain had to deal with the growing unrest led by Pontiac, the Ottawa chief from the Detroit region, who by May 1763 had organized a powerful alliance of western tribes to resist encroaching English settlement in the upper Mississippi and Ohio River valleys. The western tribes were also upset with the English policy of negotiating treaties or outright purchases for Native land, in contrast to the French practice of making annual payments of ammunition and gifts in exchange for fur-trading rights. Hopeful of reviving its alliance with the French, Pontiac's confederacy attacked British garrisons and frontier settlements and succeeded in capturing every post west of Niagara, with the exception of Detroit. Nevertheless, with the growing realization that French military support was not forthcoming and with the revival of traditional intertribal rivalries, Pontiac's confederacy disintegrated and was eventually crushed by British military expeditions by late 1764.

Pontiac's uprising significantly influenced evolving British policy for governing the new British province of Quebec established by a royal proclamation issued in October 1763. To pacify the western tribes, the proclamation prohibited settlement of the land west of the Allegheny Mountains and restricted trade in the interior only to licensed traders. The justification for this early British recognition of aboriginal rights was that land for settlement was abundantly available to the north of the thirteen colonies, in Nova Scotia and Quebec. Without a substantial British military presence in the interior, however, this policy was unenforceable as thousands of defiant settlers, speculators, and traders from the thirteen colonies continued to trek across the Appalachian Mountains in search of fertile land and new business opportunities in the Ohio-Mississippi Valley. Indeed, this attempted restriction of American enterprise contributed to the growing resentment toward British imperial policies that would lead to rebellion a little over a decade later.

The Proclamation of 1763 assumed that the French Catholics of Quebec would inevitably be assimilated by a massive influx of English Protestants from the south. To that end, the first constitution of Canada under British rule promised "the enjoyment of the benefit of the laws of our realm of England," including representative institutions to which American colonists had become accustomed. However, the anticipated northward migration did not materialize, as the St. Lawrence Valley proved less enticing than the Ohio-Mississippi Valley. Only a few hundred merchants from Britain and the thirteen colonies were attracted to Quebec, initially by the opportunity to supply the needs of the invading army and eventually to fill the void left by the departing French fur traders. In effect, the so-called Conquest transferred Canada's commercial dependence from Paris to London, with the result that English-speaking merchants were better connected to assume economic leadership in Quebec than were their remaining French counterparts. The rise of an English commercial elite to a position of dominance would henceforth be a source of recurring conflict in Quebec politics and society.

After the military regime officially gave way to civil government in August 1764, the first governor of Quebec, General James Murray, sought to minimize potential cultural conflict by modifying the terms of the Proclamation that he considered to be inapplicable to the existing situation. Appointed by the British Crown, the governor was to rule the province with the assistance of an appointed legislative council until an elected assembly could be established. However, because the laws of England specifically prohibited

Catholics from holding office, Governor Murray had difficulty finding enough qualified people to serve in his administration. He was particularly reluctant to establish an elected assembly in which fewer than 500 English Protestants would control the destiny of well over 70,000 French Catholics. Murray soon realized that the Proclamation undermined the functioning of the judicial system by replacing the French Catholic captains

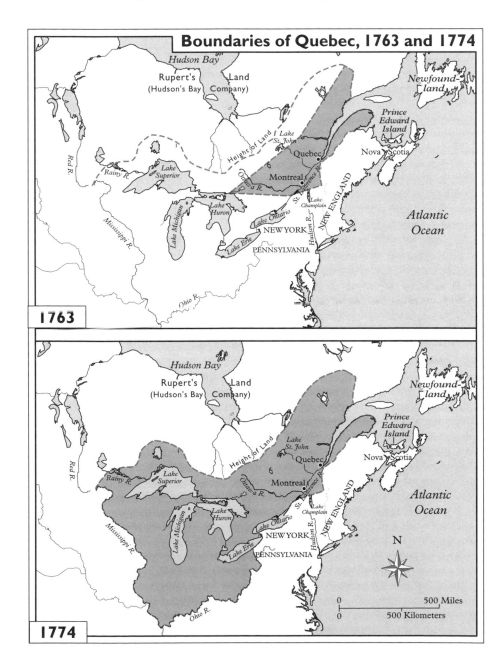

Boundaries of Quebec, 1763 and 1774

of militia as local magistrates with English Protestant justices of the peace and bailiffs who in most instances knew little about English law, let alone French law. So, to maintain order, he improvised by retaining French civil law in certain cases and by allowing Catholics to serve as lawyers and jurors.

While the Proclamation did not interfere with seigneurial land tenure or freedom of worship, it was ambiguous about the extent of these rights within the colony, and it certainly did not address the urgent need to appoint a new bishop for Quebec. Despite his initial distrust of the clergy and his preference to strengthen the Protestant religion in the colony, Murray pragmatically concluded that the support of the church was vital to communicate with and to secure the loyalty of the population. Therefore, he persuaded the British government to accept the authority of the pope in Rome to select Jean Olivier Briand as the new bishop of Quebec in 1766.

Governor Murray's implementation of the Proclamation may have endeared him to the traditional leaders of the French community—the clergy and the seigneurs—but in the process he outraged many of the English-speaking merchants. At the root of this intracultural conflict was a fundamental clash of values that was becoming more pronounced in British society as the 18th century progressed. As a high-ranking soldier and a gentleman, Murray tended to embrace aristocratic values that enabled him to appreciate the more authoritarian and feudal nature of French Canadian society, with its traditional belief in obedience and deference to authority.

By contrast, he was suspicious of the English merchants, whom he branded "Licentious Fanaticks" [sic] for their dangerously "American" notions of freedom and democracy that he believed were designed to destroy French society and to undermine his authority as governor. Imbued with a modern spirit of economic individualism and capitalist enterprise, the English merchants viewed Murray as an embodiment of the despotic tendencies of imperialism that too often interfered with their commercial prospects for the province of Quebec. They were already disappointed that the Proclamation did not annex the Ohio-Mississippi Valley to Quebec and regarded the license system for trading in the western interior as an unwarranted cost that cut too deeply into their slim profit margins. This attempt by the British government to make western trade equally open to all colonial merchants proved too difficult to enforce and had to be abandoned in 1768. Added to this concern about excessive regulation of trade, the English merchants were outraged at Murray's deviation from the Proclamation in matters of law and government, particularly his constant refusal to fulfill the promise of representative government and his peculiar sympathy for the institutions of the conquered French society. The persistent clamor of the English merchants prompted the imperial authorities to replace Murray as governor in June 1766.

Ironically, early political conflict in Quebec did not feature the expected clash between the French and English cultures but rather a struggle between rival English classes somewhat comparable to the discord that was breeding a rebellious spirit in the thirteen colonies. In Quebec, mutual economic interests tended to serve as a basis for racial cooperation in the aftermath of the conquest. After taking over the bulk of the export and import trade from the departed French merchants, the English merchants opened up markets for Canadian timber and grain in Britain and the West Indies. To increase production, they also encouraged the Canadiens to become more efficient in their agricultural methods.

But perhaps the most dynamic harmony of culture and enterprise was manifested in the expansion of the St. Lawrence fur trade farther into the western interior. With their connections in Britain, the English merchants had lines of credit and a range of trade goods that far exceeded the capacity of their departed French predecessors. Although they could not compete with the assets of their English counterparts, the remaining French merchants possessed superior knowledge and technique when it came to organizing and conducting the western fur trade. Moreover, the adventurous Canadien voyageur skillfully negotiated the rivers and lakes in the western wilderness and knew how to deal effectively with the Native traders. Thus, in competition with other English merchants operating via the Hudson River and Hudson Bay, the partnership of English capital and French labor helped to make Montreal the strategic center of the western fur trade for more than a half-century after the conquest. Only as the French focused more on agriculture while the English remained in control of commerce would divergent views on social matters become more pronounced and interethnic political conflict loom larger.

Murray's successor, Sir Guy Carleton, arrived in Quebec determined to redress the grievances of the English merchants. But he, too, was a soldier with an aristocratic temperament, and he soon realized the wisdom of Murray's approach to colonial governance. He developed an appreciation for the orderly, feudal Canadien way of life and a disdain for the English commercial class, whom he too felt were imbued with "radical" American democratic tendencies. As the political discontent that led to revolution mounted in the south, Governor Carleton began to regard Quebec as a potentially strategic military base against disloyalty and violence in America. In 1767, Carleton challenged the demographic assumption of the Proclamation:

> The Europeans who migrate will never prefer the long inhospitable winters of Canada, to the more cheerful climate and more fruitful soil of His Majesty's southern provinces . . . so that, barring catastrophe shocking to think of, this country must, to the end of time, be peopled by the Canadian race.

Supporting Carleton's assertion, the French population of Quebec, as a result of the highest birthrate ever recorded by a people of European origin, exceeded 90,000 by the early 1770s, outnumbering the English by about 15 to 1. Furthermore, Carleton confidently predicted that by placating the traditional French leaders, the clergy and seigneurs, 18,000 men capable of bearing arms could be mobilized in Quebec.

To secure the loyalty and cooperation of the Canadien majority, the British Parliament decided to follow Carleton's advice by replacing the ill-conceived Proclamation of 1763 with the Quebec Act in 1774. The Quebec Act officially abandoned efforts to implement representative institutions, thereby resolving the dilemma of whether to place colonial government in the hands of the small English minority or the large French majority. Furthermore, the Quebec Act recognized the uniqueness of Canadien society by opening membership in the appointed legislative council to French Catholics, by guaranteeing the seigneurial system of land tenure and the collection of seigneurial dues, by legalizing the right of the church to collect tithes from all Catholics in the colony, and by restoring French civil law with regard to property while retaining English criminal law. In essence, assimilation gave way to accommodation as the grand design of British colonial administration, and henceforth, Quebec would be treated as a province unlike the others.

The Quebec Act also extended the frontiers of the Province of Quebec into the Great Lakes basin and the Ohio-Mississippi Valley, ostensibly to appease the St. Lawrence traders and merchants who appeared to be most capable of conducting the fur trade successfully while maintaining good relations with the western tribes. Moreover, including

CANADA'S FIRST CONSTITUTION

THE QUEBEC ACT
ANNO DECIMO QUARTO
GEORGII III. REGIS.
CAP. LXXXIII.

An Act for making more effectual Provision for the Government of the Province of Quebec in North America. . . .

And, for the more perfect Security and Ease of the Minds of the Inhabitants of the said Province, it is hereby declared, That His Majesty's Subjects, professing the Religion of the Church of Rome of and in the said Province of Quebec, may have, hold, and enjoy, the free Exercise of the Religion of the Church of Rome, subject to the King's Supremacy, declared and established by an Act, made in the First Year of the Reign of Queen Elizabeth, over all the Dominions and Countries which then did, or thereafter should belong, to the Imperial Crown of this Realm; and that the Clergy of the said Church may hold, receive, and enjoy, their accustomed Dues and Rights, with respect to such Persons only as shall profess the said Religion. . . .

And be it further enacted by the Authority aforesaid, That all His Majesty's Canadian Subjects, within the Province of Quebec, the religious Orders and Communities only excepted, may also hold and enjoy their Property and Possessions, together with all Customs and Usages relative thereto, and all other their Civil Rights, in as large, ample, and beneficial Manner, as if the said Proclamation, Commissions, Ordinances, and other Acts and Instruments, had not been made . . . and that in all Matters of Controversy, relative to Property and Civil Rights, Resort shall be had to the Laws of Canada, as the Rule for the Decision of the same; and all Causes that shall hereafter be instituted in any of the Courts of Justice, to be appointed within and for the said Province, by His Majesty, His Heirs and Successors, shall, with respect to such Property and Rights, be determined agreeably to the said Laws and Customs of Canada, until they shall be varied or altered by any Ordinances that shall, from Time to Time, be passed in the said Province by the Governor, Lieutenant Governor, or Commander in Chief, for the Time being, by and with the Advice and Consent of the Legislative Council of the same, to be appointed in Manner herein-after mentioned.

Provided always, That nothing in this Act contained shall extend, or be construed to extend, to any Lands that have been granted by His Majesty, or shall hereafter be granted by His Majesty, His Heirs and Successors, to be holden in free and common Soccage. . . .

the western territories within the boundaries of Quebec, with its authoritarian government and feudal-style landholding system, appeared intended to thwart the expansionist ambitions of the thirteen colonies, which were now defiantly speaking of independence. In fact, the Quebec Act became one of the tyrannical Intolerable Acts of British imperialism that triggered the American Revolution. Thus, in the process of trying to secure the loyalty of an "alien" northern colony, Carleton's vision intensified the disloyalty of the southern colonies, which King George III regarded as the "jewel" of the British Empire.

THE AMERICAN INVASION OF QUEBEC AND NOVA SCOTIA

By the outbreak of the Revolutionary War in 1775, American propaganda denouncing British tyranny, praising democracy, and inviting the people to join the fight for individual rights and liberties had circulated widely in Quebec. The revolutionary leaders hoped that a significant number of former French colonists would seize the opportunity to be liberated from their despotic conquerors. The merchants who had emigrated from the thirteen colonies might also welcome the prospect of reversing the Quebec Act, which denied them the basic democratic rights accorded all Englishmen and yet granted rights and privileges to French Catholics that far surpassed those enjoyed by Catholics in Britain. However, the appeals to traditional English liberties did not emotionally stir the French Catholic population, which was not about to sacrifice its majority status in Quebec for submergence in a hostile English Protestant continental environment. Indeed, French Catholics were well aware of British-American antipathy for the rights and privileges that the Quebec Act accorded them. Despite resentment of the political provisions of the Quebec Act, the English mercantile group responded favorably to its revision of the provincial boundaries to include the western interior. Most of the St. Lawrence merchants remained aware of their dependence on imperial markets, creditors, and supplies, without which they would be helpless in the face of American competition. In the final analysis, only a small minority of Quebec's French and English communities actively supported the American revolutionary movement.

On the other hand, the American invasion of Quebec in 1775 demonstrated that disinterest in the Revolution did not necessarily translate into loyalty for the imperial cause, as Governor Carleton had predicted. In order to prevent the British from following through on Carleton's expressed objective to use Quebec as a counterrevolutionary military base, General George Washington dispatched General Richard Montgomery to launch an invasion by way of Lake Champlain and the Richelieu River, while Benedict Arnold led an overland expedition through the Maine wilderness. Washington hoped first to seize Quebec before its defenses could be organized and then to withstand British efforts to recover their losses. Weakly defended Montreal fell before Montgomery's attack in November 1775, with Carleton narrowly escaping to Quebec. Following up on his victory, Montgomery joined Arnold for a New Year's Eve assault on the military stronghold of the province, during which the former was killed and latter wounded. Still, the American force of about 3,000 troops continued the siege, leaving Carleton increasingly pessimistic about the prospects of resisting the invaders with insufficient reinforcements.

When Carleton declared martial law and summoned the militia in both Montreal and Quebec, the French clergy and seigneurs, ecstatic over the legalization of their right to collect their respective tithes, urged the habitants to enlist in the militia in order to protect the rights and privileges guaranteed by the Quebec Act. For their part, the habitants resented the imposition of this form of taxation, which had not been officially enforced since the Conquest, so they felt as much interest in supporting the British defenders as they did the American invaders. Viewing the Revolution as an Anglo-Saxon family squabble, the vast majority of French Catholics maintained an attitude of determined neutrality. While the Revolution appeared to be progressing well for the Americans and they were willing to pay favorable prices in cash for supplies, the habitants appeared sympathetic to the republican cause. But as the long winter siege at Quebec dragged on, the tide of French Canadian public opinion turned against the invaders when they ran out of cash and either offered to pay for their provisions with paper money or refused to pay at all.

With a garrison that included about 1,000 local militia, a far cry from his original prediction, Carleton was able to hold on to Quebec until May 1776, when a fleet of British ships with 10,000 reinforcements sailed up the St. Lawrence and forced the ill-equipped and demoralized Americans to retreat. British sea power rescued Canada from falling into American hands, and in the process left unanswered the question of whether or not the colony could have resisted on its own. The extent of Canadien neutrality also raised questions about the wisdom of the Quebec Act. While the French Canadians did not fight for Britain, neither did they rebel against their conquerors when the opportunity arose. On the other hand, the Quebec Act had been designed to gain the active loyalty, not the passive neutrality, of the habitants.

Carleton was shocked to discover that he had miscalculated the ability of the seigneurs to rally their loyal tenants and the clergy to inspire their parishioners from the pulpit to defend the province. The apparent docility of the habitants about which both Murray and Carleton had marvelled was based less on a deferential and obedient demeanor than it was on an aversion to war and an indifference to the issues that were of greater concern to their political and social leaders. Indeed, the American Revolution turned out to be the first of many historical events that had the effect of revealing a divergence of political perspective within French Canadian society. Many of the habitants regarded those who had collaborated with the British as *vendus*—sellouts to the conquerors. Others considered the British to be the lesser of two evils and pointed to the guarantees of the Quebec Act and the growing overseas market for furs, grain, and timber as indicative of the advantages of cooperation with the imperial authority. This ambivalence would prompt many future Quebec leaders to miscalculate the sentiments of the people.

Like the French, the Native people had an ambivalent attitude toward what they perceived to be a family feud between the British and their American offspring. While the western tribes tended to favor the British, who had cultivated good relations since the defeat of Pontiac, the Iroquois Confederacy was divided. Six Nations chief Joseph Brant persuaded the Mohawk and some Seneca to support the British, but many Oneida and Tuscarora sided with the Americans. The Onondaga and Cayuga remained neutral until an American attack in 1779 drove them into the British fold. That both British and American recruiters enjoyed success among the Native people in the Montreal area is a further indication of the divided loyalties that characterized responses to the American Revolution.

Despite their strong economic, political, and cultural ties with their former homeland, the Nova Scotia "Yankees" had little inclination to support the revolutionary

1776 portrait of Mohawk Chief Joseph Brant, or Thayendanegea (1742?–1807), by English painter George Romney. The renowned leader of the Six Nations Iroquois was staunchly loyal to the British cause during the American Revolution.

cause in the southern colonies. A few hundred inhabitants along the vaguely defined Maine–Nova Scotia border, in the lower Saint John River valley, and the Chignecto-Cumberland region at the head of the Bay of Fundy openly supported former New Englander Jonathan Eddy in his unsuccessful attempt to capture Fort Cumberland (Fort Beauséjour during the French regime) in 1776. But for the most part, even Nova Scotians who had recently migrated from New England could not identify with American grievances against the British government. The closing of the western frontier did not affect a colony that had an abundance of empty land suitable for settlement. Neither were the recent impositions of imperial trade regulations and taxation embodied in such legislation as the Townshend Acts, the Stamp Act, and the Tea Act considered to be burdensome or oppressive to Nova Scotia commerce. In fact, the commercial connection with Britain and the presence of the imperial garrison and naval forces were vital to the pioneer economy of Nova Scotia. Even if dissension had existed, the settled coastal communities of the colony were too scattered and isolated to be mobilized into an effective resistance against constituted authority.

While the merchants operating from the royal naval base at Halifax remained a bastion of loyalty to Britain, Nova Scotians in outlying communities were as unresponsive to efforts to recruit colonial militia or to levy taxes for imperial defense as they were to the revolutionary cause. Reluctant to take up arms against family and friends whom they had left behind only a decade or two before, most colonists chose to remain neutral during the revolutionary conflict and, if they had the opportunity, to trade with both sides. Like the French in Quebec, the "neutral Yankees" of Nova Scotia, along with the Acadians and the local Micmac and Malecite, were aroused from their preoccupation with the daily struggle to survive only when their communities were directly raided by American privateers. With the formidable presence of the Royal Navy discouraging any massive American assault, Nova Scotia remained firmly entrenched within the British Empire at the end of the Revolutionary War.

A DISPUTED CONTINENTAL BOUNDARY

The American Revolution ended in 1783 with the Treaty of Versailles, recognizing the independence of the United States of America and the division of the North American continent. Ironically, having withstood the American military invasion, the province of Quebec and the future Canadian heartland almost did not survive the diplomacy surrounding the boundary settlement. Whereas the eastern boundary of Quebec was easily settled, the western territory remained a source of dispute, since Britain retained military control of the Ohio-Mississippi Valley and the United States was determined to acquire the land over which it had been willing to wage war with the world's leading imperial power.

Britain decided to adopt a conciliatory approach to the western boundary settlement for both strategic and economic reasons. The peace negotiations began in Paris in late 1782 while a cease-fire was in effect in North America but war between Britain and France continued in Europe. In fact, the need to wage war on two distant continents was a major reason why mighty Britain could not suppress the American Revolution. Ultimately, Britain did not want to alienate its former colonies to the extent of driving the newly formed United States into a continued alliance with France, thereby jeopardizing British hegemony in Europe. Moreover, public opinion in Britain was decidedly split between the advocates of continued imperial expansion and the emerging notions of "little Englandism." In 1776 English political economist Adam Smith argued in *The Wealth of Nations* that Britain's economic interests would be better served by shedding the mercantile system with its burden of colonies and by engaging in international free trade, which would bolster the development of an industrial economy. So, even if it could not politically control the new United States of America, Britain realized that, as the world's foremost industrial producer, it could continue to derive the benefits of close trade relations with a nation that represented a rapidly growing market for manufactured goods.

For these reasons, imperial negotiators seriously considered the initial demand of American negotiator Benjamin Franklin that Britain should surrender all of Canada as a gesture of friendship and goodwill toward the new republic. However, France, which had provided naval support for the Americans during the Revolutionary War, decided to support British claims to the Ohio Valley in order to confine the new republic to the Atlantic seaboard, surrounded by a powerful neighbor and dependent on French economic and military support. Consequently, Franklin was forced to offer a compromise settlement based on the southern boundary of Quebec as established by the Proclamation of 1763. This boundary, running along the 45th parallel between the St. Lawrence and Mississippi Rivers, would have enabled Britain to maintain the Province of Quebec but would also have effectively transferred the future southern Ontario heartland to the United States. More concerned about the uncertain course of warfare in Europe, Britain was prepared to concede this area, which the Proclamation had reserved for occupation by the Native tribes and which had few European settlers. But once again, world events intervened to alter the precarious fate of Canada. With a crucial military victory at Gibraltar suddenly turning the tide of European warfare in Britain's favor, imperial negotiators raised their demands in America to embrace the extensive western boundaries of the Quebec Act. After further compromise, both sides agreed on a western boundary for Quebec that followed the current line through the St. Lawrence River and the Great Lakes.

Although the Treaty of Versailles officially granted the land of the Ohio-Mississippi Valley to the United States in 1783, Britain refused to surrender strategically located military and trading posts in response to pressure from the St. Lawrence fur traders and the western Native tribes. Competing against the American traders from Albany, New York, the St. Lawrence fur traders wanted to delay the transfer of the region south of the Great Lakes in order to continue to exploit its lucrative albeit diminishing resources. In view of their support of the imperial cause during the Revolutionary War, the Native people expected Britain to reciprocate in their resistance to the relentless westward movement of the American settlement frontier. Realizing that they had handed over the western lands to the Americans without making provisions for the rights of the Native inhabitants, imperial authorities feared that abandoning the posts would infuriate their Native allies and incite them to seek vengeance by attacking the precarious settlements in the St. Lawrence Valley. Taking advantage of vague wording in the peace treaty and the failure of the United States to fulfill treaty obligations to restore Loyalist property, Britain decided to retain its western posts in the hope that the spread of American settlement could be checked and that the new nation would eventually disintegrate. The dispute dragged on until 1794, when a military expedition led by General Anthony Wayne decisively defeated the Ohio tribes at the Battle of Fallen Timbers and forced them to cede their lands to the United States. Already at war with France, Britain readily agreed to the terms of Jay's Treaty, which provided for the evacuation of the western posts by 1796 and the resolution of other outstanding differences, including the Loyalist claims and the rights of British fur traders in the West.

The departure of the American colonies from the British Empire also involved negotiations that established the St. Croix River as the official boundary between what would be the future state of Maine and the future province of New Brunswick and which renewed fishing rights in the Gulf of St. Lawrence and the inshore waters of Nova Scotia and Newfoundland. Even though the Americans had forfeited these rights by seceding from the empire, imperial authorities realized the practical difficulties and the potential conflict that would result from their continued exclusion. American fishermen were also allowed the right to continue to dry their catch along unsettled mainland coasts. Despite being addressed by the Treaty of Versailles, the international boundary and fishing rights would remain sources of dispute between the United States and the British North American colonies.

With the end of the American Revolution in 1783, Britain had lost its most stable and populous colonies, which had formed the pillars of the old mercantile system. Britain still retained a foothold on the North American continent, but the remnants that were left could not compensate for the loss of the thirteen colonies. The three remaining northern colonies, consisting of scarcely more than 40,000 English Protestants and over 110,000 French Catholics, were isolated from one another and were at a much more primitive stage of development than the lost colonies to the south. The resources of the remaining empire in North America were far less varied, and the opportunities for expansion there far less extensive. Indeed, the sugar islands of the West Indies and the colonial prospects unfolding in India offered far more promise. Moreover, imperial authorities could easily have been discouraged by the lack of loyalty that the remaining North American subjects manifested in the face of invading rebels, were it not for concern over the plight of the "Loyalist" American refugees who made their way to Quebec and Nova Scotia.

CHAPTER 7

THE EMERGENCE OF COLONIAL COMMUNITIES

The American Revolution profoundly altered the destinies of two nations in North America. Ironically, the event that gave birth to the United States of America also gave impetus to the creation of English Canada. The Loyalists as refugees of the American Revolution became the founders of two provinces, Ontario and New Brunswick; and the presence of the Loyalists as a group with a strong moral claim on Britain prompted the restructuring of government by the Constitutional Act, itself a reaction to the American Revolution. Without the Loyalist presence, land-hungry New Yorkers and Pennsylvanians would have poured into the unoccupied southern Ontario frontier beginning in the 1790s, and New Englanders would have moved into sparsely settled New Brunswick when the Maine frontier expanded in the 1830s. The Loyalist population of Upper Canada also proved to be a bastion of defense against American invasion during the War of 1812. If not for the devotion of the Loyalists to the imperial tie, would Britain have had as much incentive to defend Upper Canada, the French Catholic settlement along the St. Lawrence, or the scattered communities in peninsular Nova Scotia, particularly in view of the prevailing neutrality in the latter two colonies during the American Revolution?

While these possibilities remain within the realm of speculation, it is reasonable to credit the refugees of the American Revolution with serving a vital custodial role at a time when the destiny of Canada was precarious. Indeed, when the tide of British immigration began to flow after 1815, the Loyalist presence had ensured that an English Canada still existed to offer the settlers an alternative living environment.

THE COMING OF THE LOYALISTS

A prominent Revolutionary leader, Samuel Adams, speculated that one-third of the people of the thirteen colonies actively supported the Revolution, one-third remained neutral, and one-third actively supported Britain. The accuracy of this estimation has been difficult to ascertain, but it does point to the prevailing lack of unity in the embryonic stages of American nationhood. Upwards of 100,000 people suffered persecution and were forced into exile for supporting the imperial cause or for remaining neutral during the Revolution, and as many as one-half of those refugees escaped to British North America. The more influential Loyalists, including royal officials, wealthy merchants, landowners, and professionals, as well as high-ranking military officers, returned to Britain during or after the Revolutionary War to take advantage of the preferments that awaited them there. The vast majority of Loyalists, however, being of lesser means, either drifted to nearby British colonies or gathered in the imperial stronghold at New York, from which they were evacuated to other parts of the empire.

Nova Scotia, as the most accessible British colony by sea and one with an abundance of vacant land for settlement, was considered the most convenient destination for

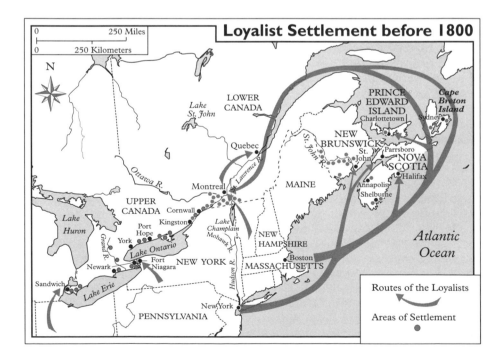

the 30,000 to 40,000 Loyalist refugees, who tended to come from the coastal towns. Almost half of the Loyalists were settled along the Saint John River valley, while most of the other half went to peninsular Nova Scotia. Small groups of Loyalists also settled in Cape Breton Island, Prince Edward Island, and Newfoundland. About half of the Loyalist immigrants came from New York or New Jersey, while the origin of the remainder was almost equally divided between New England and the southern states. Many of the approximately 3,000 black Loyalists who came to Nova Scotia had taken advantage of the British proclamation of 1779, which offered freedom to any slaves who left their American masters to support the British cause. Disappointed over the settlement prospects, nearly half of these black Loyalists had left Nova Scotia to join a free black colony in Sierra Leone by the early 1790s.

Indeed, disappointment was a prevailing sentiment as the sudden influx of a population that was almost double the size of the existing colony created difficulties for new and established settlers alike. For their devotion to the imperial cause, the Loyalists were promised land grants ranging from 100 acres for the head of a family, with an additional 50 acres for each member, to 1,000 acres for a military officer. Although poor crops, shortages of supplies, and delays in securing title to land contributed to early hardship, many of the Loyalists suffered from the reality of being former town dwellers unaccustomed to the challenges of pioneer life in Nova Scotia, with its marginal farmland and erratic climate. Despairing of the grueling life and limited resources of "Nova Scarcity," some Loyalists gave up the struggle and drifted back to the United States after tempers had subsided; others went to Britain or tried their luck in the new western province of Upper Canada.

Tension was further heightened by the rivalries that soon developed between Loyalist and existing settlers. Some Loyalists complained that the more desirable locations were already held by the earlier arrivals, while Loyalist leaders who had held official positions in the old colony demanded government posts in Nova Scotia. By virtue of their recent sacrifices, the Loyalists felt entitled to preferential treatment and were openly resentful of the "neutral Yankees," whom they suspected of disloyalty. To satisfy the Loyalists, the British government partitioned the colony in 1784 to create the new province of New Brunswick, composed mostly of Loyalists, which could serve as a buffer between peninsular Nova Scotia and the United States. The following year, the community of 3,500 people at the mouth of the Saint John River became the first incorporated city in what is now Canada. While Saint John was to be the economic heart of the new province, Thomas Carleton, the first governor of New Brunswick, selected Fredericton to be the provincial capital—not only to promote inland settlement but also to protect the garrison from a sudden American attack.

The several hundred Loyalists who settled St. John's Island (Prince Edward Island) did not fare as well as their New Brunswick counterparts. To attract Loyalist settlers, some absentee landlords promised grants of land with clear and secure title. However, after the Loyalists had settled and begun cultivating the land, the landlords were unwilling to grant them freeholder status. While many of the Loyalists left the island out of frustration, some stayed on as tenant farmers. Squatters and tenant farmers comprised the majority of the slightly more than 4,000 people who lived in the colony when it was renamed Prince Edward Island in 1799. The land question would continue to be a major source of conflict and a primary obstacle to Prince Edward Island's development for the next three-quarters of a century.

Upwards of 10,000 Loyalists made their way to Quebec, mainly from New York and New England by way of the Lake Champlain–Richelieu River route. Governor

Frederick Haldimand, who had succeeded Carleton in 1778, sought to avoid conflict with the French by arranging to settle some of the Loyalists along the sparsely populated southern shore of the St. Lawrence River. These settlements, later known as the Eastern Townships, laid the foundation for the English-speaking community in the Province of Quebec.

The majority of Loyalists, however, settled in the western frontier of the province well beyond the seigneurial lands. These western Loyalists arrived by land, mostly from the frontier districts of New York, Pennsylvania, and New England. They included members of loyal American regiments and their families; disbanded German, Swiss, and Dutch mercenaries who had fought in the British army; a small group of Quakers and Mennonites who had refused to bear arms due to religious conviction; aspiring frontier farmers; and Native Americans led by Chief Joseph Brant of the Six Nations Iroquois Confederacy. Since most of the western Loyalists were already familiar with the rigors of pioneer farming, they were better prepared for the backbreaking work of clearing the virgin forest, building crude shelters out of logs, planting their first crops, and coping with food shortages and severe winters. Despite the hardships of life in the wilderness, Quebec Loyalists were less inclined than Nova Scotians to consider returning to the United States or Britain because of the abundance of fertile land available to them.

To accommodate the initial wave of Loyalists, Governor Haldimand arranged for the purchase of land along the upper St. Lawrence River and eastern Lake Ontario as well as in the Niagara Peninsula from the Mississauga in 1783–84. Into these areas he relocated some 6,000 civilian refugees and former militia, granting them land on the same scale and terms as in Nova Scotia. Haldimand also reserved the Grand River valley for settlement by the majority of the 2,000 Iroquois Loyalists under Chief Brant. During the 1780s Loyalist settlements also spread along the northwestern shore of Lake Erie and up the Ottawa River.

As more successful Loyalists wrote back to friends and relatives in the United States about how they had been able to secure a grant of land merely by swearing allegiance to King George III, many aspiring American settlers who had taken little or no active part in the Revolution were prepared to denounce republicanism in return for a farm. For their part, imperial authorities were quite willing to grant land to new colonists renewing their old allegiance on the same terms as the original Loyalists. Within a few years, it was difficult to distinguish between those "United Empire" Loyalists who truly sought refuge in a British colony and those "Late Loyalists" who were attracted by the prospects of free land. The steady flow of American immigrants into the western frontier of the Province of Quebec during the 1780s and 1790s coincided with the natural expansion of settlement from the Atlantic seaboard into the interior. In their quest, land-hungry pioneers were inclined to be oblivious to national borders, with the result that the fertile upper St. Lawrence Valley and Great Lakes basin were regarded as a northward extension of the United States's western frontier. Late Loyalists soon outnumbered the original Loyalists as the population of western Quebec exceeded 20,000 by 1791.

THE CONSTITUTIONAL ACT OF 1791

Whether they had been actually driven from their homes because of their expressed loyalty to British rule or whether they were merely opportunistic land-seekers, the American immigrants expected to enjoy the constitutional and legal rights of British subjects.

But by providing for only seigneurial tenure and appointed legislators, the Quebec Act effectively denied them the rights to freehold land tenure and representative government to which they had become accustomed in the American colonies. Because they were more likely to be too occupied with the daily routines of farming and coping with the hardships of the wilderness to think about the problems of government, the overriding concern of American immigrants, once they had acquired, cleared, and cultivated their land, was to secure legal title. While the Loyalists were not about to relinquish their right to representative government, they tended to be less supportive of the democratic political aspirations of the British merchants of Quebec. For those settlers who had been victimized in their former homeland by excessive self-government, democracy raised memories of armed rebellion and mob violence.

The presence of a sizable contingent of English-speaking Protestants renewed the hope of the British merchants that the Quebec Act could be repealed and that the French would eventually be assimilated. Believing that they deserved political power commensurate with their contribution to the economic growth of the province, the English-speaking merchants of Quebec continued to demand an elected assembly. While the seigneurs were concerned that an assembly might tax land and make their tenants their political equals, the French mercantile and professional classes were becoming more favorable to the idea of an elective body over which the cultural majority could exert greater political influence. The stage was therefore set for political change in British North America.

Upon his return as governor in 1786, Carleton, now Lord Dorchester, was more receptive to English demands in view of the disappointing French response to the American invasion a decade previously. He appointed as his principal advisor and chief justice William Smith, a Loyalist from New York, to review the constitutional affairs of the colony. Smith's proposed union of all of British North America under a federal system of government in 1790 was prophetic, but the scheme was dismissed as impracticable by the imperial authorities, which considered the colonies to be too separated by distance and too divided in interests. In contrast to Smith's desire for a wider unity, the imperial authorities were convinced by their American experience to proceed in the opposite direction. Imperial authorities concluded that the American colonies had been allowed to grow too large and too strong; and most important, they had been allowed too much self-government. To prevent a similar occurrence in British North America, an imperial policy of "divide and rule" was adopted whereby colonies were to be kept small and dependent, thereby thwarting the rise of nationalism. The division of New Brunswick and Cape Breton Island from Nova Scotia in 1784 (Cape Breton Island was reunited with Nova Scotia in 1820) was further manifestation of this thinking. This imperial reorganization focused on averting what British officials perceived to be the principal constitutional weakness of the American colonies—the democratic elements of government had been allowed to prevail over the monarchical and aristocratic elements. A truly British constitution would maintain a balance between the interests of monarchy, aristocracy, and democracy.

Accordingly, the British Parliament passed the Constitutional Act in 1791, which provided for the division of Quebec into two distinct provinces. Beyond the farthest western seigneury, in the vicinity of where the Ottawa River meets the St. Lawrence River, the new province of Upper Canada was designed to accommodate the Loyalist immigrants. The remainder of the Province of Quebec was renamed Lower Canada and would continue to be governed under the terms of the Quebec Act with a few important

A watercolor by Phillip John Bainbridge depicting a buttonwood tree, 18 feet in circumference, in the bush near Chatham, Upper Canada, ca. 1840. The pioneer settlers faced the daunting task of clearing the primeval forest with only a primitive axe.

modifications. The provinces were given the option of maintaining French civil law or introducing English civil law, and naturally the first legislature of Upper Canada opted for the latter. Although the existing seigneurial system of Lower Canada was left untouched, the Constitutional Act did permit freehold tenure where desired. The rights of the Catholic Church under the Quebec Act were specifically reaffirmed. But the desire to strengthen Protestantism was reflected in provisions that assigned to the provincial government the right to collect tithes from Protestants and the obligation to set aside one-seventh of future land grants for the "support and maintenance of a Protestant clergy."

The Constitutional Act modified the Quebec Act most significantly in terms of the structure of government. Upper and Lower Canada were each to be governed by a lieutenant governor who was responsible to the governor general of all of British North America and who represented monarchical or executive authority. Because his tenure in office was short-term and because he knew relatively little about the province when he arrived, the lieutenant governor relied on the advice of leading citizens whom he appointed to the Executive Council, which functioned like the British cabinet. The lieutenant governor also appointed members to the Legislative Council, which served as the upper house or the aristocratic branch of government. An early draft of the constitutional bill intended to grant members of the Legislative Council hereditary titles was modelled after the British House of Lords. However, the thought of a pioneer nobility in the colonial backwoods was greeted with laughter when introduced to the British Parliament, with the result that the idea was discreetly dropped. Like the British upper house, the Legislative Council approved, amended, or rejected legislation passed by the democratic branch, the Legislative Assembly, the equivalent of the House of Commons in Britain. Even if the Legislative Council approved a measure passed by the popularly elected Legislative Assembly, it could still be subject to the veto of the governor and the British Crown. Such severe restrictions to self-government were designed to reduce the colonial assembly to little more than a debating society.

Nevertheless, in their effort to limit democracy, imperial authorities were no longer as willing to suppress representative government as they had been when conceiving and implementing the Quebec Act of 1774. Elected assemblies were deemed essential in order that the colonies might levy taxes to meet their own expenses. In an unsuccessful attempt to conciliate the rebellious American colonies, the British government had relinquished its power to raise revenue within any of its colonies in 1778. By 1791 the American revolutionary demand of "no taxation without representation" had become a common colonial expectation, and British taxpayers were more reluctant to bear the expensive burden of maintaining overseas colonies. But while conceding the practical necessities of democracy, imperial authorities further undermined the influence of the elected branch of government by setting aside one-seventh of all lands as Crown reserves. The revenues from the sale or lease of these lands were to be used to support the colonial administration, thereby making it less dependent on the taxation power of the Legislative Assembly.

The third British constitution in less than three decades, the Constitutional Act of 1791 finally captured the essential reality of the future Canadian identity. The Proclamation of 1763 had reflected the intention to assimilate the French culture and society into a uniform English Canada. The Quebec Act of 1774 had expressed the resignation to accommodate the French fact out of strategic necessity. The Constitutional Act recognized the coexistence of two ethnic communities, two languages, two cultures, and two sets of institutions within a British parliamentary system of government.

With the Constitution Act of 1791, the British government was confident that it had laid the foundation for the second British empire in North America, particularly by consolidating the loyalty of the English Protestant population and by encouraging further emigration from the United States. Underlying the act was the expectation that the political experiment of the southern republic would end in failure and that its people would either migrate to the northern colonies or demand the reinstatement of their country into the British Empire. Imperial authorities further believed that the Constitutional Act would sustain the loyalties of the French Canadians and perhaps even lead to their gradual assimilation, either into a growing English-speaking population or through their appreciation of the blessings of British institutions that would induce them to abandon their traditional way of life. Such considerations did not appear outlandish within the context of late 18th-century realities. Indeed, the appropriateness of the constitutional changes can be measured by the limited expressions of political discontent in British North America over the next three decades. That certain provisions of the Constitutional Act eventually gave rise to political friction was more attributable to the inevitable changes that subsequently occurred in colonial life.

THE CONSTITUTIONAL ACT OF 1791

ANNO TRICESIMO PRIMO

GEORGII III. REGIS.

CAP. XXXI.

An Act to repeal certain Parts of an Act, passed in the Fourteenth Year of His Majesty's Reign, intituled, An Act for making more effectual Provision for the Government of the Province of Quebec, in North America; and to make further Provision for the Government of the said Province. . . .

II. And whereas His Majesty has been pleased to signify, by His Message to both Houses of Parliament, His Royal Intention to divide His Province of Quebec into Two separate Provinces, to be called The Province of Upper Canada, and The Province of Lower Canada; be it enacted by the Authority aforesaid, That there shall be within each of the said Provinces respectively a Legislative Council, and an Assembly, to be severally composed and constituted in the Manner herein-after described; and that in each of the said Provinces respectively His Majesty, His Heirs or Successors, shall have Power, during the Continuance of this Act, by and with the Advice and Consent of the Legislative Council and Assembly of such Provinces respectively, to make Laws for the Peace, Welfare, and good Government thereof, such Laws not being repugnant to this Act; and that all such Laws, being passed by the Legislative Council and Assembly of either of the said Provinces respectively, and assented to by His Majesty, His Heirs or Successors, or assented to in his Majesty's Name, by such Person as His Majesty, His Heirs or Successors, shall from Time to Time appoint to be the Governor, or Lieutenant Governor, of such Province . . . shall be . . . valid and binding to all Intents and Purposes whatever, within the Province in which the same shall have been so passed. . . .

XLIII. And be it further enacted by the Authority aforesaid, That all Lands which shall be hereafter granted within the said Province of Upper Canada shall be granted in Free and Common Soccage, in like Manner as Lands are now holden in Free and Common Soccage, in that Part of Great Britain called England; and that in every Case where Lands shall be hereafter granted within the said Province of Lower Canada, and where the Grantee thereof shall desire the same to be granted in Free and Common Soccage, the same shall be so granted. . . .

AMERICAN IMMIGRATION AND THE WAR OF 1812 IN UPPER CANADA

The international boundary between the newly formed United States of America and the remaining British North American colonies established by the Treaty of Versailles in 1783 was virtually meaningless to many settlers of the North American frontier in the late 18th and early 19th centuries. In search of land that could provide a secure means of livelihood, people moved back and forth between American and British territory, often oblivious to notions of national sovereignty and loyalty. A sense of an American nationality was still in its infancy, and many citizens were apprehensive about the recent loss of their status as British subjects or about the prospects of life in the struggling new republic. While devotion to Britain may have prevailed among the first wave of Loyalists to arrive in Quebec and Nova Scotia, they were overwhelmingly outnumbered by the French and other American settlers whose political consciousness was limited by the arduous work of establishing farms and clearing new land. For the most part, nationalism was still tempered by realism in North American frontier life.

Within this context, the newest British North American province thrived as a haven for American immigrants during the two decades following the Constitutional Act. Because the peninsula of Upper Canada extended like a wedge into the westward path of land-seeking pioneers from New England, New York, and northwestern Pennsylvania, the American frontier movement naturally spilled over the northern border. While some imperial officials feared that American settlers would transport republicanism across the border, Upper Canada's first lieutenant governor, John Graves Simcoe, was certain that exposure to British institutions would remind the newcomers of the liberties and opportunities that they were missing outside of the empire. Simcoe's confidence was bolstered by the failure of the first federal constitution and widespread protests over high taxation in the United States. Moreover, the French Revolution of 1789 and the subsequent Reign of Terror seemed to offer evidence of the instability and corruption of a republican form of government.

From a practical standpoint, Simcoe also realized that American immigrants were the main hope for the rapid economic growth of the new province. With Britain once again embroiled in war with France, the prospects of transatlantic migration were limited. Accordingly, Simcoe launched an extensive advertising campaign in American newspapers praising the agricultural potential of Upper Canada, the almost nonexistent taxes, and the abundance of cheap land available on easy terms to any willing settler. He extended a special invitation to pacifist religious communities such as the Quakers, Mennonites, Dunkards, and Moravians by promising them exemption from military service. Simcoe was not so concerned with the "foreign" customs and beliefs of these largely German people as he was with their competence as farmers.

A recognition that wheat farming would become the basis for the province's growth and prosperity, in addition to his abhorrence for a "peculiar" American institution, prompted Simcoe to advocate the abolition of slavery. Not only were the several hundred black slaves who accompanied their masters to Upper Canada less essential to the northern wheat economy than they had been to the southern cotton economy, but they were also expensive to maintain throughout a longer and unproductive winter. As a result, the provincial legislature passed an act in 1797 that gradually abolished slavery by requiring

An early 19th-century homestead in the Upper Canadian wilderness is depicted in the publication Emigration: The British Farmer's Farm & Labourer's Guide to Ontario. *The first crops were usually planted among the stumps, which took years to be cleared from the land.*

that all children born to slaves be freed at 25 years of age and by prohibiting future importation of slaves into Upper Canada.

To open up more farmland in the interior and to facilitate the movement of troops in the event of an American attack, Simcoe ordered the military to construct two major roads extending from the new provincial capital of York (later Toronto), which he established in 1793. Yonge Street extending northward and Dundas Street extending westward would form the backbone of southern Ontario's modern highway system. Although Simcoe returned to England in 1796 where he lived until his death a decade later, his calculated efforts to attract immigrants from the south reaped dividends: by 1812 the population of Upper Canada approached 100,000, about three-quarters of whom were of American origin. For his vision of Upper Canada as an agrarian heartland and a favored destination for settlement more than for his zeal to create a replica of late 18th-century England in the wilderness, Simcoe deserves to be celebrated annually as the founder of the modern province of Ontario.

The anxiety and suspicion of Simcoe's successors concerning the future prospects of a province dominated by Americans under imperial rule intensified after the turn of the 19th century as strained diplomatic relations placed Britain and the United States on a collision course for a conflict that would be fought mostly north of the Great Lakes. With the outbreak of the War of 1812, the majority of the people of Upper Canada could conceive of no grievance that would prompt them to take up arms against their southern neighbors, with whom they were often linked by family ties or increasing economic intercourse. On the other hand, the horror of the upheaval and indignity that they had suffered at the hands of unyielding republicanism three decades earlier continued to haunt the core group of the Loyalists, whose influence remained strong within the provincial leadership.

The causes of the War of 1812 were related to unresolved issues dating back to the American Revolution. Although the British surrender of the western posts into American hands in accordance with Jay's Treaty in 1796 ushered in more than a decade of cordial relations between the two nations, it did not discourage St. Lawrence fur traders from competing against their American counterparts operating south of the Great Lakes. Moreover, the continued presence of the Canadian traders in the region gave impetus to renewed Native resistance to American western settlement. During the first decade of the 19th century, Tecumseh, the Shawnee chief, attempted to organize a Native confederacy to halt further American encroachment. Matters came to a head at the Battle of Tippecanoe in November 1811, during which Chief Tecumseh's forces were crushed and his alliance collapsed. Arguing that the Native resistance movement was bolstered by guns and ammunition from British or Canadian sources, western members of Congress clamored for war with Britain and an invasion of the British North American colonies in order to prevent future Native threats. The efforts of these so-called war hawks would not have been so successful without the background of hostility to Britain created by the maritime rights controversy in the north Atlantic.

The resumption of war between Britain and France under Emperor Napoleon Bonaparte in 1803 resulted in decrees of blockade and counterblockade that effectively denied freedom of the seas to neutral traders, notably the United States. British warships were aggressive not only in stopping and searching neutral vessels for cargoes bound for France but also in seizing suspected deserters from the Royal Navy aboard American ships. On occasion, sailors claiming American citizenship were seized and forced to serve on British ships, an indication that it was still difficult to distinguish the nationality of English-speaking people in the early 19th century. American indignation over such violations of national sovereignty led to a battle between the British ship *Leopard* and the Virginian vessel *Chesapeake*, which nearly precipitated war in 1807. Reluctant to take on British naval power, which had defeated Napoleon at Trafalgar two years earlier, President Thomas Jefferson opted to impose a trade embargo, the failure of which only served to aggravate the American war hawks. With Britain once again preoccupied with an intensified war against Napoleon in 1812, the Americans seized the opportunity to strike at a vulnerable empire.

The American appetite for war was whetted by the prospect that the conquest of British North America, which would open up the fertile land of Upper Canada for American occupancy and which would give the United States control of the St. Lawrence River, could be easily achieved. The colonial population of about half a million appeared hardly a match for eight million Americans, especially with Britain occupied with the intensified war against Napoleon in Europe. Besides, the poorly defended border could be readily crossed by an American army, which prompted former President Thomas Jefferson to assert that conquest of the northern territories was a "mere matter of marching." Confidence that the many recent American immigrants to Upper Canada would welcome the invading army as liberators was reflected in the proclamation that General William Hull issued to the citizens of Windsor in July 1812: "You will be emancipated from [British] tyranny and oppression and restored to the dignified station of freedom."

However, the American war effort was undermined by some questionable military strategy and a lack of national unity. American strategists correctly surmised that British sea power and New England's opposition to the war rendered futile an invasion of the Maritime Provinces. Indeed, the unlimited opportunities to trade with both sides without threat of invasion contributed to the prosperity of the Maritime Provinces during the war. In retrospect, the most effective strategy would have been to focus on cutting off supply lines between Montreal and Kingston. Instead, the Americans regarded a western attack on the Upper Canadian frontier starting from the Detroit River as the path of least resistance.

This dubious strategy, in addition to the superior leadership of British General Isaac Brock, offered hope for the defenders. Realizing that Britain was in no position to send reinforcements, General Brock had to rely on a force of less than 5,000 regular soldiers as the first line of defense. While he was able to secure alliances with the Native tribes, Brock had difficulty recruiting an Upper Canadian militia beyond the core group of Loyalists. He was particularly suspicious of the reliability and loyalty of recent American immigrants, many of whom were reluctant to fight against their former countrymen and some of whom were even inclined to desert to the invaders or to leave the battlefield to attend to their farms at harvest time. This precarious situation prompted Brock to adopt a defensive strategy that emphasized rapid and resolute offensive action.

With the help of fur traders and Native allies, Brock and his regulars captured the key western post of Michilimackinac, and for the duration of the war the American fur trade frontier remained in British hands. In 1812 Chief Tecumseh rallied hundreds of his warriors to the British cause and helped to defeat General Hull's forces at Detroit. The setbacks in the west prompted the Americans to launch an invasion of the Niagara Peninsula. Despite being vastly outnumbered, General Brock rallied a resistance force of 500 Iroquois, 1,000 British regulars, and 600 local militia to victory at the decisive Battle of Queenston Heights in October 1812. The victory was costly as General Brock was killed in action, but it dashed American hopes for an easy conquest and intensified opposition to the war, particularly in New England and the southern states.

In 1813 a second American invasion of the Niagara Peninsula succeeded in capturing York and burning the provincial parliament building but suffered defeats at the hands of British regulars at Stoney Creek and Iroquois forces at Beaver Dams. A third American invasion at Lundy's Lane was turned back in 1814, thereby leaving the Niagara frontier and the eastern part of the province firmly under British control. British successes in the Niagara region were offset by defeats in the west in 1813. American naval forces gained control of Lake Erie, thus forcing a British evacuation of Detroit. The American victory at Moraviantown on the Thames River solidified their hold on southwestern Upper Canada; the resultant death of Tecumseh, followed by the collapse of his confederacy, permanently removed any Native military threat in the lower Great Lakes region.

The Americans attempted to revise their ill-conceived strategy by launching a two-pronged attack on Montreal in late 1813. One column advancing north from Lake Champlain was turned back at Chateauguay by a combined force of British troops and French-Canadian militia under Colonel Charles de Salaberry, while the other column advancing by Lake Ontario was defeated by British regulars at Chrysler's Farm. The following summer, another American attack on Montreal also ended in failure. The active French resistance in 1813–14 contrasted markedly with the benign neutrality displayed in 1775.

The defeat of Napoleon and the cease-fire in Europe enabled Britain to dispatch 16,000 regular troops to North America and to launch a naval assault and blockade on the Atlantic seaboard, which turned the tide of the war in its favor in late 1814. Notably, Washington was captured and the capitol was burned in retaliation for the destruction of York in the previous year. In its subsequent restoration, the walls of the presidential mansion were whitewashed to hide the fire marks, and the building was thereafter called the White House. With the war at a virtual stalemate, with New England threatening secession, and with the revival of Napoleon imminent, both sides were anxious to negotiate an end to the war. The Treaty of Ghent, signed on Christmas Eve 1814, was an armistice that restored the prewar boundaries and scarcely addressed the issues that had instigated the conflict.

Nevertheless, this inconclusive outcome opened the way for a lasting peace between two North American partners as the sources of conflict soon disappeared. Maritime rights were no longer a concern with the end of the Napoleonic Wars in 1815. The progress of the American settlement frontier forced the Native tribes farther west, while the Canadian fur trade was more profitably conducted to the northwest. The Rush-Bagot Agreement of 1817 limited armed vessels on the Great Lakes to allow for police and protection against smuggling rather than the conduct of naval warfare. Furthermore, the Convention of 1818 identified the 49th parallel as the western boundary extending from Lake of the Woods, beyond the Great Lakes, to the Rocky Mountains, and further defined American fishing rights in Atlantic coastal waters. Although the fishing dispute would continue and the Maine–New Brunswick and Oregon Territory boundaries would not be resolved until later, a precedent for negotiated settlement and mutual accommodation was established between the United States and Britain that would ultimately foster an undefended border between two North American nations.

THE GREAT TRANSATLANTIC MIGRATION

The end of the War of 1812 in North America and the Napoleonic Wars in Europe marked a turning point in the flow of people to North America. Whether it was the British merchants replacing the French fur traders in Quebec, New Englanders moving to Nova Scotia, Loyalists fleeing the wrath of republicanism, or Late Loyalists satisfying their land hunger, the main flow of immigration to British North America had been overland from the thirteen colonies or the United States. While American immigration to the Maritime Provinces had ended with the influx of Loyalists in the 1780s, the steady flow into Upper Canada slowed to a trickle in the wake of the prevailing anti-American spirit after the War of 1812. Legislation prohibiting Americans from owning land until they had been residents for seven years certainly discouraged immigration to Upper Canada. The impact of this restriction is difficult to measure, since the American western frontier had already moved past Upper Canada and was focusing on the fertile lands of the Ohio-Mississippi Valley and beyond. The opening of the Erie Canal in 1825 and land routes south of the Great Lakes facilitated the movement of Americans across the Appalachian Mountains.

The natural decline of American immigration coincided with social and economic changes in Britain that stimulated the greatest transatlantic migration of English-speaking people to North America up to that time. The dangers of wartime travel and the constant need for troops during the American and French Revolutionary Wars as well as the Napoleonic Wars in Europe had limited the volume of overseas migration prior to 1815. The end of the Napoleonic Wars not only made overseas travel less dangerous and drastically reduced the military manpower requirements but also brought severe economic depression that aggravated the social and economic dislocation already arising from the Industrial Revolution in Britain.

As machines were replacing workers and factories were replacing small shops or cottage industries, the rapidly growing British cities were plagued by rising unemployment and working-class unrest. A changing agricultural economy impoverished small farmers and rural laborers, often driving them into the already troubled towns and cities. Notably, the spread of the enclosure movement in Scotland resulted in large landowners turning small farmers off their land because sheep- or cattle-raising generated more revenue than rent from tenant farmers. Similarly, subsistence farmers in Ireland were displaced because landowners preferred larger farm units that could be operated more profitably. The plight of the Irish became even more desperate in the 1840s with the failure of successive potato crops. As a result of a shortage of this staple of the Irish diet, hundreds of thousands of people faced starvation and death. Under such conditions immigration to North America became a viable alternative to poverty or starvation.

From the perspective of the British government, emigration became a strategy to rid the country of its surplus population, particularly the poor and unemployed who were a burden to the taxpayer and a potential danger to the state. In effect, the emigration of the poor to North America was viewed in comparable terms to the transportation of convicts to Australia. Initially, the British government assisted the exodus of unwanted people by offering free transportation, grants of land, and other provisions to help settle the immigrants. By the mid-1820s, however, the British government decided that aiding immigrants was too expensive and unnecessary, since charitable organizations and landowners anxious to rid their estates of impoverished tenants were offering assistance. But only a small minority of those who came to North America were sponsored or assisted, and the most destitute inhabitants of the British Isles could not afford the transatlantic passage. Therefore, most of the more than 5 million immigrants to North America from 1815 to the 1850s were hopeful and resourceful people willing to exhaust their own savings in order to escape unbearable or unpromising conditions at home.

While some immigrants could afford first-class accommodation, the vast majority had to endure an often treacherous, six-week Atlantic crossing in the steerage of crowded passenger ships or the dark and cramped hold of timber ships that had discharged their cargo in Britain and had filled up with human ballast for the return trip to North America. Under the British Passenger Acts, ships sailing to Quebec were allowed one adult or two children for every 12 square feet of steerage space, and each adult was allotted a sleeping space six feet in length but only 18 inches in width. Because of inadequate rations provided onboard ship, the immigrants had to carry their own food, which they cooked on stoves that often consisted of barrels lined with brick and covered with a grill. In addition to seasickness, dysentery and cholera—usually resulting from spoiled food and a lack of clean water and air—were common ailments that plagued the immigrants, sometimes with deadly consequences.

The peak immigration years were marked by outbreaks of plague. In 1832, cholera transmitted from Europe by immigrants to Quebec killed 1,500 people, including local residents, in a single month. In 1847, the famine-ridden Irish carried typhus that spread to other passengers by the filthy conditions below the decks of ships. Of the nearly 90,000 immigrants who sailed to Quebec in 1847, the peak year for transatlantic migration, over 10,000 died in passage or in the quarantine hospitals to which the diseased were dispatched upon their arrival.

If the immigrants arrived safely in Halifax, Quebec, or Montreal, they still faced a long, uncomfortable journey to the interior where, if they were fortunate enough to be able to afford to purchase land, they faced the backbreaking work of clearing the forest, building a home out of logs, and cultivating their farms. Thousands of immigrant farmers, experiencing the hardship and isolation of a pioneer's life in the wilderness, abandoned their farms for employment in the towns and villages or found work in lumber camps or in canal and railway construction. A considerable proportion of the newcomers to British North America immediately or eventually preferred to settle in the United States, attracted by higher wages in the eastern cities and an abundance of cheap land in the Midwest. Although few among the slightly more than 1 million immigrants who did choose to stay in British North America from 1815 to the mid-1850s had the resources or affiliations to rise to positions of leadership in business and politics, they provided the numbers and the labor that transformed the Canadian social and economic landscape.

While British immigrants to the United States were absorbed into an already large population, those who arrived in Canada virtually overwhelmed the small English-speaking communities and dramatically altered the cultural balance among the English, French, and Native communities. Whereas the French-speaking settlers represented slightly more than one-half of the approximately 600,000 inhabitants of British North America in 1815, they comprised less than one-third of the population of nearly 3 million by 1860. Correspondingly, the proportion of Native peoples was reduced from approximately one-fifth to less than one-twentieth of the total colonial population. The impact of the mass immigration is further reflected in the changing demography of the various colonies.

By 1840 about 40,000 Highland Scots had arrived in Nova Scotia to form a third group of English-speaking settlers, following the pre-Revolution New Englanders and the Loyalists. The steady flow of immigrants increased the population of Nova Scotia from approximately 80,000 in 1815 to over 300,000 by the early 1850s. A substantial number of Scots also went to Prince Edward Island, helping to raise the population of the province from less than 20,000 in 1820 to about 70,000 by 1850. New Brunswick was the destination for an estimated 60,000 immigrants, two-thirds of whom were southern Irish who settled mostly in the fertile Saint John River valley and on the Gulf of St. Lawrence shore. As a result, the population grew from about 75,000 in 1825 to more than 200,000 by 1850. Newfoundland only marginally shared in the great transatlantic migration of Britons as its population increased from 40,000 in 1815 to 80,000 in 1850. On the whole, through their sheer numbers, the new arrivals reduced the Loyalist character of the Maritime Provinces and challenged the Loyalist domination of colonial society and politics.

In Lower Canada, British immigrants enlarged the English-speaking communities in Montreal, Quebec City, and the Eastern Townships. By 1840, the English-speaking community of Lower Canada numbered about 160,000, almost one-quarter of the total provincial population. Montreal's population of 40,000 was equally divided between the two cultures. In the Eastern Townships, the British American Land Company, formed in 1833, was endeavoring to settle its 800,000-acre holdings with British immigrants, and Sherbrooke, the location of the company's headquarters, was emerging as an Anglo-dominated commercial center for the region. After 1840, however, comparatively few British immigrants were attracted to the Eastern Townships, and a wave of French colonization swept into the region. The persistence of seigneurial land tenure and French hostility to mass Anglo-Saxon immigration were serious deterrents to the spread of the English-speaking community in other areas of the province. Indeed, the growth in the population of Lower Canada from 330,000 in 1815 to 890,000 in 1851 was mainly attributable to the continuing high birthrate within the French-speaking community, rather than to the arrival of British immigrants.

The overwhelming majority of British immigrants settled in Upper Canada where large areas of fertile land were available, particularly in the central and western interior of the province. Unfortunately for the prospective settlers, this land was often difficult to acquire or access. Large tracts were set aside as Crown and clergy reserves or held for speculation by members of the government or their cronies. The lack of suitable roads into the interior also made it difficult for immigrants to open up new stretches of land far removed from the established settlements. Much of the impetus for opening up the Upper Canadian settlement frontier came from enterprising individuals and private land companies, which secured large tracts of land from the provincial government at bargain prices in exchange for their promise to bring out settlers and to provide roads, schools, and other local services. When the new settlers could earn enough money from the sale of surplus crops, they could then purchase their holdings from the land company. Peter Robinson brought some 3,000 southern Irish to the Peterborough area halfway between Toronto and Kingston in 1823 and 1825. Colonel Thomas Talbot settled over 30,000 immigrants on the 500,000 acres that he secured along the north shore of Lake Erie. He ruled over his domain like a feudal lord and honored himself by naming the main center of the Talbot settlement St. Thomas. But the most ambitious of all the settlement agents was the Canada Land Company. In 1826, under the direction of John Galt, it began to settle the 2.5 million acres of the Huron Tract extending from Lake Huron to near the western end of Lake Ontario. Not only did the Canada Land Company settle and service its holdings, it also spread information about the Canadas in Europe and the British Isles and ensured that immigrants arriving at Quebec were transported directly to Upper Canada, rather than drifting to the United States. As a result of these settlement schemes, the population of Upper Canada soared from about 100,000 in 1815 to 952,000 by 1851.

The great migration to British North America had run its course by the mid-1850s. With the prime agricultural land of Upper and Lower Canada completely settled, transatlantic immigrants were attracted by opportunities in the American Far West in the second half of the 19th century. Furthermore, the gold rush to Australia and the onset of Victorian prosperity in Britain turned the tide of emigration toward the overseas Pacific colonies. Not until the end of the century would immigration again be a major factor in Canadian population and economic growth. Nevertheless, the great transatlantic migration of British subjects following upon the northward continental movement of American people enabled the British North American colonies to move out of their pioneer stage of development.

CHAPTER 8

THE EXPANDING COLONIAL ECONOMY

In addition to the growth of population, the influx of American and British immigrants dramatically altered the nature and scope of economic development in the British North American colonies during the first half of the 19th century. The British North American economy at the turn of the century was still dominated by the cod fisheries in the Atlantic Provinces and the beaver fur trade, which the St. Lawrence commercial interests based in Montreal conducted principally northwest of the Great Lakes. In their relentless competition with the Hudson's Bay Company, the St. Lawrence traders extended the fur trade frontier to its transcontinental limits before the decline in fur resources and the beginnings of western settlement forced them to relinquish the trade to their archrivals in 1821. Thereafter, the St. Lawrence commercial empire focused on the expanding agrarian frontiers of Upper Canada and the American midwest. The Maritime Provinces benefited from the increased imperial demand for timber that spawned colonial shipbuilding and shipping activity, but their limited agricultural potential and the passing of the golden age of the wooden sailing ship were already sowing the seeds of regional economic disparity.

THE CLASH OF THE GREAT COMPANIES

While Upper and Lower Canada were developing their settlement frontiers based on agriculture and struggling with the War of 1812, the dynamic St. Lawrence commercial interests operating out of Montreal were extending their fur-trading empire across the continent. Although the capture of Michilimackinac during the War of 1812 enabled the St. Lawrence merchants to regain temporary control of their old fur-trading realm south of the Great Lakes, their hopes were ultimately dashed when the Treaty of Ghent returned the western frontier to the United States in 1814. Indeed, the treaty merely confirmed the inevitable, as the Canadian southwest trade was doomed by the steady advance of American settlement. But even as the southwest trade was winding down, various St. Lawrence "pedlars" were pursuing opportunities to expand the fur trade northwest of the Great Lakes beyond the limits reached by their French predecessors.

By setting up posts on the Saskatchewan and Assiniboine Rivers in order to bargain directly with the Native trappers, the St. Lawrence traders incited the Hudson's Bay Company to reciprocate. To keep pace with its rivals, the English-based company dispatched Samuel Hearne into the western interior, whereupon he discovered the Coppermine River and Great Slave Lake during his journey of 1771–72. Two years later, the Hudson's Bay Company officially deviated from its long-standing policy of confining its trading posts to the shores of Hudson Bay. The establishment of the company's first inland post, Cumberland House on the Saskatchewan River northwest of Lake Winnipeg, in turn, prompted the St. Lawrence traders to push even farther inland. Notably, Peter Pond, a Connecticut-born veteran of the southwest fur trade who joined forces with St. Lawrence interests, journeyed to the Athabaska River (in northern Alberta) in 1778. Competition meant continuous expansion as the rivals endeavored to outflank each other in their quest to reach new Native suppliers and new areas to exploit.

The increasingly long and costly trek from Montreal to the fur-rich Athabaska regions and beyond demanded more extensive and permanent organization backed by substantial amounts of capital. Moreover, the St. Lawrence traders soon realized that continued competition amongst themselves would undermine their prospects for success against the Hudson's Bay Company, which enjoyed the geographic advantage of a more direct and less costly water route to the heart of the continent. Consequently, by the early 1780s, Montreal-based entrepreneurs were consolidating their capital and resources to participate in cooperative ventures out of which emerged an ongoing partnership known as the North West Company. While the new company continued to rely on French traders and voyageurs, its management was dominated by an exclusive group of English-speaking (notably Scottish) merchants because their Canadien counterparts lacked the capital to join the corporate ranks.

The formation of the North West Company did not completely eliminate independent competition within the St. Lawrence fur trade. Indeed, the most serious threat to the North West Company came in 1800, when a group of discontented partners joined forces with southwest traders who were forced to turn their attention to the northwest after the British surrendered the western posts to the Americans. The ruinous competition of the New North West Company or XY Company forced yet another reorganization of the St. Lawrence fur trade in 1804 as the two Montreal-based rivals merged under the renewed auspices of the North West Company to pursue the rivalry with the Hudson's Bay Company.

The North West Company sought to overcome the geographical advantage of the Hudson's Bay Company by building up a great water and portage transport system across the continent. Large freight-canoes filled with trade goods and supplies traveled regularly from Montreal to Fort William (now Thunder Bay) at the head of the Great Lakes. Here the "wintering" partners, who resided permanently at the interior posts, arrived in their smaller canoes to meet the Montreal partners and to exchange the furs collected from the western tribes for a seasonal cargo of eastern goods and supplies. Furthermore, in the contest between the trading systems of the St. Lawrence River and Hudson Bay, the North West Company benefited from organizational flexibility, stressing the individuality, self-reliance, and bargaining skills of the traders. North West Company traders were inclined to be more enterprising because they were profit-sharing partners with greater decision-making powers than the salaried Hudson's Bay Company servants who rivaled them. Consequently, the North West Company's volume of trade was approximately six times greater than that of the Hudson's Bay Company by the turn of the 19th century.

The North West Company also proved to be the more prolific agent of exploration and discovery. The quest to expand the fur-trading frontier beyond the northern and western reaches of the Hudson's Bay Company led Alexander Mackenzie to the shores of the Arctic Ocean (via the river that bears his name) in 1789 and of the Pacific Ocean (via the Peace River) in 1793. Mackenzie's journeys reflected the hope that a navigable water route to the Pacific Ocean would give the North West Company the same geographic advantage that the Hudson's Bay Company enjoyed. The Pacific route as an exit for furs and an entrance for trade goods would thus replace the long and costly canoe and portage trek across the continent. With similar visions, Simon Fraser—who explored the river that bears his name in 1808—and David Thompson—who surveyed the entire Columbia River system from 1807 to 1811—were other notable North West Company employees who opened up the far western reaches of the continent. The exploits of Fraser and Thompson helped to stave off the competition of the American Fur Trade Company, owned by John Jacob Astor, who established Fort Astoria at the mouth of the Columbia River in 1811 but was forced to sell the post to the North West Company three years later. In laying claim to what is now British Columbia, the North West Company completed the transcontinental expansion of the fur trade and foreshadowed the developmental course of the future Canadian nation.

However, as the fur trade extended to the northern and western limits of the continent, the dynamism of the North West Company could no longer be sustained. Without new resource frontiers to exploit, the company's organization was unable to adapt to static or declining trade. The practice of dividing the profits annually among the partners prevented the building up of financial reserves for bad times, while decentralized authority could not impose the necessary control and discipline to adapt to changing market conditions. By contrast, the more conservative Hudson's Bay Company responded more effectively to economic duress. As a joint-stock company with limited liability and registered on the London Stock Exchange, the Hudson's Bay Company maintained the confidence of the Bank of England, and thus could mobilize financial resources that enabled it to sustain losses over an extended period. Moreover, a highly centralized structure enabled the company to modify its administrative methods and employment policies to place greater reliance on the initiative, judgment, and bargaining ability of the individual trader, ironically drawing heavily on the practices of its chief adversary. But above all, the company benefited from its strategic position on Hudson Bay and its reluctance to incur the burdensome cost of building and maintaining inland posts to compete with its more expansionist rival.

The final collapse of the St. Lawrence fur trade empire in the northwest was precipitated by a familiar enemy—the encroaching settlement frontier. The seeds of western settlement were sown by Thomas Douglas, earl of Selkirk, who endeavored to provide a haven for Irish and Highland Scottish peasants dispossessed from their land by the enclosure movement by settling them in British North America. After enjoying modest success with settlements on Prince Edward Island and in Upper Canada, Lord Selkirk turned his attention to the fertile Red River Valley, situated within the bounds of Rupert's Land as stipulated in the Hudson's Bay Company charter of 1670. Selkirk's motives extended beyond philanthropy when he purchased controlling interest in the financially struggling Hudson's Bay Company and secured 116,000 square miles of land in what is now southern Manitoba and the northern reaches of Minnesota and North Dakota. In 1812 the first settlers arrived in the small colony centered at the forks of the Red and Assiniboine Rivers, where the city of Winnipeg now stands. Lying across the main North West Company transport and supply lines between Fort William and the far west, the Red River colony was viewed as nothing more than a Hudson's Bay Company plot to destroy the St. Lawrence fur trade. Antagonism between fur traders and settlers culminated in a North West Company attack at Seven Oaks in 1816 during which Governor Robert Semple and 20 Red River colonists were killed. In retaliation, Selkirk hired former Swiss soldiers to capture Fort William. For the next few years, the warring companies remained mired in expensive litigation in the Canadian and British courts as each charged the other with unlawful activities. These legal struggles, in addition to his determination to maintain the Red River colony, cost Lord Selkirk his fortune and his health before he died in 1820.

On the brink of financial ruin, both companies decided to end their trade war and to join forces in 1821. The merger of the North West Company with the Hudson's Bay Company was not so much a victory for the latter as it was a consolidation of the fur trade whose economic realities dictated operating from Hudson Bay rather than from the St. Lawrence River. Nevertheless, the clash between the great fur-trading companies not only dominated life northwest of the Great Lakes in the late 18th and early 19th centuries but also had the effect of keeping the vast region within the British and Canadian sphere of influence. In exploring the entire northwest to the Pacific and Arctic shores, the traders of the North West Company were, in effect, the first agents of transcontinental expansion, and the subsequent development of the Canadian nation followed their course. In establishing the Red River colony as the first permanent settlement northwest of the Great Lakes, and by preserving the region for continued exploitation of fur resources in the face of American encroachment after 1821, the Hudson's Bay Company served as an agent of the British Empire until, nearly half a century later, the new Canadian nation was willing and able to take control.

THE REVIVAL OF THE ST. LAWRENCE COMMERCIAL EMPIRE

With the end of the St. Lawrence route as the main artery of the fur trade in 1821, the economically powerful Montreal merchant community sought new commercial horizons. Many of the St. Lawrence merchants were already turning their attention to new staples, timber, and grain, which reinforced commercial ties with Great Britain. At first the timber trade was a by-product of farming, since settlers had to clear the forest before cultivating the land. But when the Napoleonic Wars jeopardized Britain's supply of timber from the

Baltic countries in the late 18th and early 19th centuries, the rich pine and oak forests of the Ottawa and St. Lawrence valleys became so vital to sustain the Royal Navy that British North American timber was granted preferential treatment in the imperial market. After the war, the growing cities of industrial Britain continued to have an insatiable appetite for colonial lumber to build homes and factories.

As the forest receded before the advance of settlement, wheat was produced from the land that had been cleared. While the French Canadian farms of Lower Canada grew grain crops principally for domestic consumption, the newly cleared land of Upper Canada produced a surplus of wheat for sale in the British market. During the Napoleonic Wars, the occasional interruption of supplies from the Baltic countries and a series of bad harvests in Britain increased the imperial demand for Upper Canadian wheat. By the 1820s, increased demand for food to feed an expanding urban population led the imperial government to modify the Corn Laws, which placed duties on grain imports into Britain in order to protect domestic agriculture. As a result, grain from British North America was given preference in the form of lower duties in the imperial market, thereby making colonial imports cheaper than foreign supplies.

These British timber and grain preferences, in addition to the fact that the St. Lawrence–Great Lakes system of waterways was still the shortest and most natural route between Europe and the interior of the North American continent, offered enterprising Montreal merchants an opportunity to restore the commercial empire that had been lost with the end of the fur trade. They sought to become the brokers supplying British manufactured goods to the growing settlements in Upper Canada and the American midwest and shipping their agricultural products to Europe. If the St. Lawrence could remain the main water highway of trade between two continents, Montreal could emerge as the commercial metropolis of North America ahead of New York, Philadelphia, Boston, and other aspiring American Atlantic ports.

This goal appeared realistic in the early 1820s as Montreal, with a population exceeding 20,000, had surpassed Quebec as the leading city in British North America. First incorporated as a city along with Quebec in 1832, Montreal became the center of a major wholesale forwarding business that developed readily out of the earlier operations of the big fur trade supply houses. The establishment of the Bank of Montreal as Canada's first bank in 1817 began the city's long reign as the financial center of British North America and eventually of the future Canadian nation. Montreal's chief urban rival, Quebec City, with a population of 15,000 by the early 1820s, had grown somewhat more slowly as a provincial capital, an imperial military base, a shipbuilding center, the main St. Lawrence port of entry, and the main entrepôt for the timber trade of the St. Lawrence and Ottawa valleys.

The Montreal merchants and their associates were convinced that the achievement of their commercial aspirations depended on the improvement of navigation along the St. Lawrence–Great Lakes route. The advent of the steamship certainly made transportation more comfortable and efficient. As early as 1809 the steamer *Accommodation* had been launched at Montreal to cruise the St. Lawrence River, and by 1816 the first Canadian steamship, the *Frontenac*, appeared on the Great Lakes. However, the steady flow of traffic along the St. Lawrence–Great Lakes route was broken by the thunderous Niagara Falls between Lakes Erie and Ontario, long stretches of rapids west of Montreal, and the shallows between Montreal and Quebec. The need to tranship cargoes at these points could only be overcome through the construction of canals.

But for canal construction to proceed effectively, two political obstacles had to be overcome. First, jurisdiction over the St. Lawrence route was divided between Upper and Lower Canada. Neither province separately could command the credit rating in the international capital market that a single provincial legislative body controlling the entire revenues of the St. Lawrence economy could reasonably have expected to attain. Moreover, such a massive public works project required agreement upon a uniform policy and an administrative framework that was virtually impossible to achieve within the context of divided provincial jurisdiction. Second, political opposition to the construction of canals pitted the commercial interests of both provinces against the agrarian interests, which saw a greater need for public expenditures on the construction of roads to open up the backcountry. Ethnic conflict further complicated matters in Lower Canada as the agrarian interests were overwhelmingly French while the commercial interests were predominantly English. In the hopes of overcoming this impasse, the imperial government, influenced by the Montreal merchant community, proposed a legislative union of Upper and Lower Canada in 1822 but dropped the idea in the face of widespread agrarian opposition within both provinces.

The improvement of the St. Lawrence route became even more urgent after the completion of the Erie Canal in 1825. By linking the Hudson River with Buffalo on Lake Erie, the Erie Canal gave New York merchants a route for western trade that was cheaper to access than the unimproved St. Lawrence. Even the wheat farmers in the western part of Upper Canada could take advantage of the building of the Erie Canal to ship their produce by way of New York when market conditions were favorable. The Montreal merchants did manage to secure provincial funding to complete the first canal around the Lachine rapids in 1825, while William Hamilton Merritt persuaded the Upper Canadian legislature to support the building of the first Welland Canal to bypass Niagara Falls in 1829. In 1832 the Rideau Canal was opened, linking Lake Ontario at Kingston with the Ottawa River, thereby allowing sailing vessels to avoid the rapids of the upper St. Lawrence. The British government financed this alternate water route in the event of an American seizure of the St. Lawrence. Further improvements to the St. Lawrence route were still required if it was to remain competitive with the Hudson route for the trade of both the American Midwest and Upper Canada. The Hudson route had the advantage of leading to New York, which was an ice-free port open all year round, whereas the St. Lawrence route leading to Montreal and Quebec was closed for nearly half the year.

The political debate over public funding for the improvement of the St. Lawrence system raged throughout the 1830s and was not resolved until after the imperial government reunited Upper and Lower Canada into a single provincial jurisdiction in 1841. By 1848 a chain of first-class canals had been constructed around the rapids above Montreal, and the shallows west of Quebec City had been deepened, thereby allowing ships to sail by the St. Lawrence from the Atlantic Ocean to the upper Great Lakes. Although the St. Lawrence–Great Lakes system was still not deep enough to accommodate ocean-going vessels, it was efficient enough to rival the Hudson-Erie route and to enable Montreal to compete with New York as the major exporting and importing center for the North American continent. A new commercial empire based on agriculture and settlement enabled Montreal to extend its lead as British North America's richest and largest city, with a population of 57,000 in 1851. Its rival Quebec had in the process become an even bigger lumber port with a population of 42,000 by 1851.

Contributing to Montreal's rise as the commercial metropolis of British North America in the first half of the 19th century was the development of urban communities within the Upper Canadian hinterland. Established as a military outpost to guard the eastern end of Lake Ontario upon the arrival of the Loyalists in 1784, Kingston thrived as a transhipment point between lake and river transport on the St. Lawrence route. During the War of 1812, Kingston was the defensive stronghold of the province and the largest town in Upper Canada with a population of about 2,000. The construction of the Rideau Canal reinforced commercial links with Montreal and made Kingston a strategic choice to serve as the first capital of the united Province of Canada in the early 1840s. However, the lack of a sizable hinterland along with the improvement of the St. Lawrence to allow more through traffic reduced Kingston to a local market and service center of 11,000 inhabitants by mid-century. At the other end of the Rideau Canal along the Ottawa River emerged Bytown in 1826. A thriving inland lumber center of 8,000 people, Bytown became the city of Ottawa in 1854.

Spurred on by the influx of British immigrants and the rise of commercial agriculture after the War of 1812, the population of the provincial capital, the town of York, grew from scarcely 1,200 in 1820 to slightly over 9,000 when it was incorporated as the city of Toronto in 1834. Toronto's strategic location on the St. Lawrence–Great Lakes transport route was complemented by its access to the improved Hudson-Erie route and to the American railway system. Consequently, Toronto became not only a wholesale and retail center for a rapidly expanding agricultural hinterland but also a transhipment point for Upper Canadian as well as American midwestern wheat and flour headed for Britain via New York or Montreal. By 1850 Toronto, with a population of 30,000, was beginning to rival Montreal for metropolitan dominance of British North America, and later the Canadian nation. Links with Toronto helped nearby Hamilton grow into a significant marketing center and lake port with a population of 14,000 by mid-century.

Urban development in Upper Canada, however, was limited by inadequate inland transportation. Because early roads were often little more than dirt trails or paths cut into the wilderness, settlement for most of the first half of the 19th century remained confined to areas fronting the Great Lakes and the St. Lawrence River or along Yonge and Dundas Streets. However, as more immigrants arrived from the 1820s onward, the improvement of existing roads and the construction of new ones to connect the interior with the coastal settlements became a constant source of political controversy. Corduroy roads consisting of logs laid side by side on a bed of dirt were an improvement when they were new. But they would deteriorate quickly, particularly with inclement weather, and they made for a bumpy ride at best. As late as 1837, an Englishwoman remarked that it took her stagecoach well over three hours to travel a stretch of seven miles on the "highway" from Hamilton to London. In fact, London was the only significant inland center, boasting a population of about 10,000 when it was incorporated as a city in 1855. The poor state or absence of roads added to the arduousness and loneliness of life in the backcountry of Upper Canada until the dawning of the railway age in the 1850s.

Despite the completion of the St. Lawrence canal system and the growth of the Upper Canadian settlement frontier, Montreal's aspiration to become the continent's dominant commercial metropolis ultimately rested on a precarious foundation of public policy that was beyond its control. In particular, a combination of free trade in the United States and a protected market in Britain permitted British manufactured goods imported by way of Montreal to flow into the markets of the American Midwest, while American grain and other products entering Canada shared in the preferences that Britain extended to colonial products, and thus had the advantage over exports from American ports. Although the American government was moving in a protectionist direction after 1815, substantial tariff increases were checked by the opposition of the southern states.

Artist Charles William Jeffreys (1869–1951) depicts the slow and treacherous pace of inland transportation in the first half of the 19th century as a result of the appalling state of roads, which were often impassable after heavy rain.

An even more ominous sign of pending trouble for the Montreal merchants was the ongoing debate in Britain from the 1820s to the mid-1840s between the defenders of mercantilism and the advocates of free trade. The restrictions of the old colonial system, which had fostered the growth of British commerce, now appeared as obstacles to industrial expansion. As the world's leading producers, British manufacturers demanded the removal of all barriers to trade. Canadian commercial interests were worried when the preferential duty on timber was lowered in 1842, but they were relieved in the following year when the imperial Parliament passed the Canada Corn Act, which increased the British preference on flour imported from Canada. As a result, the act encouraged wheat from the American West to be milled in Canada for shipment to Britain.

However, the hopes of the Montreal merchants were dashed in 1846 when the impact of the disastrous Irish famine caused by the spread of potato blight brought the imperial government to the decisive step of repealing the Corn Laws. Ending the preference on colonial grain was justified on the grounds that quantities of cheap food were immediately needed to avert the threat of mass starvation in Ireland. But the subsequent reductions in the timber preference and the end of the Navigation Laws in 1849 signaled the systematic dismantling of the old colonial system. As the world's unchallenged industrial power, Britain could extend its imperial dominance, in effect, to most of the Western world, which eagerly demanded manufactured goods and willingly offered raw materials in return. Under these circumstances, Britain no longer needed to bear the expensive burden of defending and administering distant colonies that were already clamoring for self-government.

The loss of imperial grain preference was a serious blow to milling and transportation interests along the St. Lawrence route. Their plight was compounded by the Drawback Acts of 1845–46, which allowed free passage of Canadian exports and imports through American ports. Thus, while the British shift to free trade reduced the incentive for Americans to use the St. Lawrence route, the American legislation was luring Canadian trade from Montreal to New York. In their shock at this apparent abandonment by Britain, confirmed politically by the granting of responsible (self-) government to Nova Scotia and the Province of Canada, some prominent Montreal merchants, such as William Molson and John Redpath, signed the Annexation Manifesto of 1849. This document advocated the severance of all ties with Britain and the annexation of Canada by the United States. The Annexation Manifesto was overwhelmingly rejected by popular opinion, and the Montreal businessmen who signed it soon regretted that they had acted so rashly. The ambitions of the old St. Lawrence commercial empire were no longer feasible, but new opportunities for transcontinental economic expansion were already emerging for the second half of the 19th century.

COMMERCIAL DEVELOPMENT IN THE ATLANTIC PROVINCES

Meanwhile, the Atlantic Provinces were developing in relative isolation and in a different direction from their western colonial neighbors. With a limited amount of fertile land to offer, the Atlantic Provinces relied on the sea and the forest for their economic development. Newfoundland grew slowly, continuing to depend on its cod fishery supplemented by salmon fishing and seal hunting. As Britain gradually came to treat Newfoundland as a colony rather than as a large fishing station for summer fishermen, St. John's emerged as the main administrative center on the island. The town's excellent harbor, sheltered behind a line of rocky hills that protected it from the open Atlantic, enabled the town to become a strategic base of defense as well as a leading Atlantic fishing entrepôt with a population exceeding 8,000 by the early 1820s. The importance of St. John's continued to grow as it officially became the provincial capital when Newfoundland was granted representative government in 1832. The merchants and shipowners of St. John's financed the island's fishing trade and acted as suppliers of capital and manufactured goods to the outports.

In the immediate post–American Revolution era, Nova Scotia hoped to capitalize on the departure of the New England colonies from the empire by replacing them as a supplier of codfish and lumber for the sugar islands of the British West Indies. The British Navigation Acts, which decreed that imperial commerce should be reserved for imperial ships, initially protected maritime shipping from American competition in the British West Indies. Nova Scotia shipping also benefited from the bad relations between Britain and the United States leading up to the War of 1812, which further cut down American competition in the protected imperial markets. However, when relations between Britain and the United States improved after 1815, Nova Scotia could not sustain its strategic advantage in the West Indian trade because it was unable to supply foodstuffs other than fish.

The forests of New Brunswick, however, supplied the timber for the development of the Nova Scotia shipbuilding industry to complement its inshore fisheries. The "Bluenose" shipbuilders of Nova Scotia became world renowned for their splendid clipper ships, which sailed throughout the globe and formed the backbone of one of the world's leading merchant fleets. As the wooden sailing vessel gave way to iron-hulled steamships, Nova Scotia led the way. *The Royal William* built by Samuel Cunard, the most famous of the Nova Scotia shipowners and a leading West Indian trader, was the first mainly steam-powered ship to cross the Atlantic Ocean in 1833. In 1840 Cunard inaugurated the first regular steamship service across the Atlantic. By reducing the transatlantic crossing to less than four weeks, steamship travel encouraged immigration and commercial development and reinforced imperial economic integration.

Nova Scotia's economic growth continued to focus on Halifax, which was incorporated as a city in 1841. The provincial capital and imperial garrison base developed into a major shipping center, particularly for the West Indian trade, largely because of its substantial and secure ice-free harbor, which was situated close to the major North Atlantic shipping lanes. Halifax also became a regional financial center when a group of local merchants founded the Halifax Banking Company in 1825 and the more enduring Bank of Nova Scotia in 1832. Although its population grew from 11,000 in 1817 to 20,000 in 1851, Halifax's lack of an economic hinterland would restrict its rise as a commercial metropolis.

Besides contributing to Nova Scotia's shipping and shipbuilding industry, the forests of New Brunswick, covering nearly 90 percent of its landscape, were the catalyst for that province's economic development during the first half of the 19th century. Boosted by imperial preference, New Brunswick's rich white pine timber stands produced vital ship masts for the Royal Navy during the Napoleonic Wars. Closely integrated with the timber trade was a shipbuilding industry that by mid-century was turning out over 100 wooden sailing vessels per year. The most famous New Brunswick ship was the *Marco Polo*, launched from the building yard of James Smith in 1851. It earned the title fastest ship in the world for cutting a week off the previous record for the round trip from England to Australia, completing the run in less than six months.

Saint John emerged as the principal timber port and shipbuilding center of the Maritimes because of its strategic location at the mouth of the Saint John River. Extending more than 400 miles into the interior of New Brunswick, the Saint John River gave the city access to and control over a substantial resource frontier. As a result, Saint John, with a population of 22,000 in 1851, was edging ahead of Halifax in the race to become the commercial metropolis of the Maritimes.

A dispute over timber rights in a 12,000 square mile area on the New Brunswick–Maine frontier precipitated a settlement of the eastern boundary between the United States and British North America, which had been only vaguely drawn north of the St. Croix River at the end of the American Revolution. In 1839 an armed clash nearly erupted between New Brunswick and Maine loggers over the right to cut in disputed territory at the mouth of the Aroostook River. Although the terms of the treaty that British envoy Lord Ashburton and American secretary of state Daniel Webster negotiated in 1842 were unsatisfactory to both sides, they succeeded in establishing an enduring boundary between New Brunswick and Maine.

The reduction of the imperial preference on colonial timber during the 1840s raised serious concerns among Maritime traders, particularly in New Brunswick, where forest products accounted for more than 80 percent of exports by mid-century. But while the timber trade to Britain began to decline in relative terms, new markets for sawn lumber were already opening up in the growing cities of the United States. This loosening of the imperial tie and reorientation to the North American market was helping to set the stage for eventual Maritime participation in a transcontinental economy.

The middle of the 19th century turned out to be the high tide of Maritime economic development. The dismantling of the British mercantile system and the impending replacement of the wooden sailing vessel with iron and steel steamships on the world's oceans were serious blows to Maritime economic fortunes. But the Achilles' heel of the

Atlantic economy continued to be its limited agricultural potential. Only in Prince Edward Island did agriculture thrive, while Nova Scotia's Annapolis valley and New Brunswick's Saint John River valley, although rich in farmland, could not sufficiently fulfill regional agricultural needs. In the final analysis, excessive reliance on highly volatile staples like fish and timber would leave the Atlantic Provinces vulnerable to extreme boom and slump cycles.

As the colonies of British North America emerged out of their pioneer stage of development by the middle of the 19th century, it was becoming evident that their commercial life could not continue to depend upon the production of staples for export to an imperial market. The rise of free trade in Britain induced the colonies to pursue continental markets. The growing prospects of a north-south flow of trade with the United States was pointing the way toward reciprocity. Moreover, the British North American provinces were beginning to realize that their continued growth would depend on the breakdown of isolation and a convergence of their diverse interests. But the achievement of east-west transcontinental economic integration would require new political structures oriented toward nationalism rather than colonialism.

CHAPTER 9

FROM OLIGARCHIC RULE TO RESPONSIBLE GOVERNMENT

The economic and population growth that the British North American colonies experienced after 1815 was accompanied by challenges to the system of government established in reaction to the American Revolution. To restrict the rise of democracy, the excess of which supposedly had induced the thirteen colonies to rebel, the imperial authority encouraged a form of representative government that allowed political control to rest in the hands of an elite group of appointed colonial officials. The movements for political reform that arose in opposition to oligarchic rule were strongest in the larger provinces of Upper and Lower Canada where the outbreak of rebellion in 1837 forced a reconsideration of imperial policy toward colonial governance. The union of the Canadas and responsible government advocated in Lord Durham's Report and achieved during the 1840s would prove to be a prelude for further colonial unity and political independence leading eventually to nationhood.

THE EMERGENCE OF COLONIAL GOVERNING ELITES

Colonial oligarchies in British North America were a product of both pioneer conditions and imperial design. In a society in which relatively few men had the education, means, and leisure needed to hold the leading positions of government, it was inevitable that a small core of executive and judicial officers should form around the governor to offer advice and to conduct the day-to-day responsibilities of public administration. While the governor was generally a capable and devoted servant of the Crown, he was almost always a short-term visitor who seldom came to know the province well enough to be a commanding or effective leader. Under such fleeting circumstances, the lifetime appointees to the Executive and Legislative Councils invariably became the force of stability and permanence within the colony upon whom the governor could depend.

For their part, the members of the colonial ruling elite were usually able and public-spirited citizens who came from a small number of well-established families, often of Loyalist origin, and who sincerely believed in the duty of the better class of people to rule. The core of the ruling elite, the Executive and Legislative councillors, were able to consolidate their power by filling government offices with and distributing political patronage to like-minded men. A large class of government officials such as judges, justices of the peace, customs collectors, and postmasters owed their appointments to their direct or indirect connections with the provincial governing elite. The ruling elite also cultivated close relations with business and professional leaders as well as the higher clergy of the Church of England.

Oligarchic power was further extended by conscious imperial efforts to limit the elected assembly's control over lawmaking and public finances. Laws passed by the Legislative Assembly could be revised by the Executive or Legislative Councils and vetoed by the governor or the Crown. Some of the main sources of government revenue, notably Crown and clergy reserves as well as customs duties, were not placed under the control of the Assembly, which meant that the appointed officials could function independently of the taxation power of the elected representatives of the people. In effect, early 19th-century colonial government was democratic to the extent that it was representative of, but certainly not responsible to, the popular will.

The most powerful and wealthiest of the colonial oligarchies was the Chateau Clique of Lower Canada. While an elite group of merchants and seigneurs had served on the council to advise the British governor in the three decades after the fall of New France, the ruling oligarchy that evolved into the Chateau Clique received its impetus from the Constitutional Act of 1791. By granting representative institutions, the act gave the French Catholic population, previously indifferent to democracy, a forum within which to develop its political power and sense of nationalism. In the first session of the newly created Assembly in 1792, the French majority demonstrated its ability and willingness to flex its legislative muscle by engineering not only the election of a French-speaking member as the official speaker but also the equal recognition of French and English as the official languages of the legislature. In a sharp reversal of roles, the once-democratic English-speaking merchants allied themselves with their former arch rival, the governor, by accepting appointments to the Legislative and Executive Councils. In this way, they were able to protect the interests of the St. Lawrence commercial empire against a predominantly agrarian French majority elected to the Legislative Assembly. Although a few leading French-speaking seigneurs and merchants were invited into the ruling elite, just as some English-speaking businessmen and farmers opposed oligarchic rule, the basic political division in Lower Canada remained along ethnic and religious lines.

The ruling oligarchy of Upper Canada, the Family Compact, was grounded in the tensions between Great Britain and the United States. Compact members were usually second-generation Loyalists or British immigrants who had arrived in the province prior to the end of the 18th century. Most of them had fought in defense of the province during the War of 1812 because of an unswerving devotion to the British Crown and a strong anti-American sentiment. To members of the Compact and their associates, the United States was a source of unsound ideas and institutions in the realm of government and religion, in addition to being a powerful economic competitor and military threat. Upper Canada could never realize its destiny unless its predominantly American population was constantly kept aware of the dangers arising out of the close proximity of the United States. Besides embracing the late-18th-century concept of a balanced constitution, Compact members also believed that the lack of loyalty among certain segments of the population during the War of 1812 could be attributed to the lack of an established church. Accordingly, Bishop John Strachan devised a plan for a provincial system of education under the direction of the Church of England of which the British Crown was the head. Although freedom of worship still prevailed, the Anglican tradition was publicly supported as the pillar of a stable society, as it was in Britain.

The Compact's strong sense of British nationality was based on an appreciation of the extent to which colonial survival and development depended upon continued economic and military support from Britain. Outside the empire, Upper Canada was a primitive and isolated outpost; but within the empire, the colony was part of the world's foremost political community. For this reason, the Compact feared that rising anti-imperialist sentiments in Britain might prevail and cast the province adrift in a republican sea. While the Family Compact's vision for Upper Canada may have been responsive to late 18th- and early 19th-century realities, its undemocratic approach to colonial rule and its inadequate response to the social and economic changes in the wake of massive British immigration in the 1820s and 1830s would raise serious challenges to oligarchic power.

The oligarchies of the Maritime Provinces were not as strongly entrenched as those of Upper and Lower Canada, with the result that the political conflicts of the 1820s and 1830s were not as sustained or intense. Oligarchic rule in the Maritimes was not complicated by Lower Canada's ethnic division between English and French, nor was a privileged governing class aroused to defend against dangerous American influences, since the Loyalists outnumbered the original New Englanders and the War of 1812 had only marginally affected the Atlantic region. Furthermore, the slower rate of growth compared to the Canadas raised fewer contentious issues relating to social and economic change prior to the 1840s.

In Nova Scotia, as in the other Maritime Provinces, the same group of officials sat in both the Executive and Legislative Councils. The ruling elite, known as the Council of Twelve, consisted mostly of Halifax merchants and bankers who dominated the economic and political life of the province. Opposition to the council arose over control of public revenues, particularly relating to the endowment of non-Anglican educational institutions. Beginning in the late 1820s, Joseph Howe used his newspaper to attack the economic and political power of the oligarchy and to expose the undue privileges that the Church of England enjoyed in religion and education. After being elected to the Assembly in 1836, he assumed the leadership of the reform movement, and in the following year, he succeeded in securing the separation of the Legislative and Executive Councils as well as the inclusion on the latter body of four members from the Assembly. For the next decade, he would continue his struggle to have the entire Executive Council selected from the Assembly.

The governing elite of New Brunswick originated from the group of Loyalist military officials and bureaucrats who had served Sir Guy Carleton during the evacuation of New York at the end of the American Revolution. While the colonial oligarchy consisted of wealthy landowners who presided over vast timber stands, the Assembly was dominated by rival timber merchants. Since members of both the appointed and elected bodies had common economic interests and an Anglican Loyalist background, provincial politics remained relatively stable. The separation of the Executive and Legislative Councils was achieved with little controversy in 1832. However, the following year, the oligarchy and the Assembly clashed over control of the revenue from timber duties imposed on the heavily forested Crown lands or from the sale thereof. With mediation from the Colonial Office, the issue was resolved in 1837 when control of Crown lands and their revenue was transferred to the Assembly in return for a permanent civil list—that is, payment of colonial administration, including the salaries of civil servants.

Land was also the major issue on Prince Edward Island, but political discontent was directed toward the absentee landlords living in England who withheld their large holdings from settlement. The local oligarchy actually supported the Assembly's petition to the imperial authorities to have these absentee holdings revert to Crown lands in 1838. Although this effort was unsuccessful, the separation of the Executive and Legislative Councils was achieved in 1839.

Newfoundland remained at a rudimentary stage of political development until 1825, when rule by naval admirals ended and Britain appointed the first civil governor, Sir Thomas Cochrane. British recognition of the island as a colony rather than merely a fishing base was further confirmed with the granting of representative government in 1832. Predictably, the Assembly immediately clashed with the recently formed Legislative Council over the control of public finances. Constant internal dissension—between English and Irish, between Protestants and Catholics, between merchants and fishermen, and between St. John's and the outports—forced the British government to suspend the provincial constitution in 1842. An integrated legislature consisting of 11 elected members and 10 Crown appointees assisted the governor in ruling the province until the two-chamber system was restored in 1848.

THE RISE OF FRENCH-CANADIAN NATIONALISM

In sharp contrast to the orderly and peaceful opposition to oligarchy in the Maritimes, the accumulation of political grievances in Lower and Upper Canada culminated in armed insurrection, which only served to stall the rising reform movements. In Lower Canada, political conflict leading ultimately to violence was intensified by passionate divisions between two peoples of different languages, religions, economic interests, and concepts of the provincial destiny. As early as 1801, Jacob Mountain, the Anglican Bishop of Quebec, attempted to subvert the Catholic Church by anglicizing the provincial system of education. Whereas his legislative efforts were strongly supported by the Chateau Clique, they were vehemently opposed by the French majority in the Assembly. Political antagonism reached new heights in 1805 over the thorny issue of raising funds for the construction and maintenance of public works. The government, supported by the merchants, proposed a land tax that would have been detrimental to small farmers, the vast majority of whom were French. Instead, the Assembly increased customs duties and instituted a sales tax, much to the chagrin of the English commercial elite. The bitterness surrounding this confrontation led to the founding of *Le Canadien*, an avowedly nationalist newspaper that advocated the preservation of French-Canadian rights and institutions and which became the voice of the newly formed Parti Canadien.

French-English relations further deteriorated during the infamous "reign of terror" of Sir James Craig, governor from 1807 to 1811. In addition to dissolving the Assembly on two occasions for disagreeing with him and seizing the press of *Le Canadien* and jailing its proprietors for their allegedly treasonous protests, Governor Craig recommended assimilation of the French through the union of Upper and Lower Canada as well as large-scale British immigration, subordination of the Catholic Church to the Church of England, and the abolition of representative government in the province. Although he was recalled by the British government, which was concerned with maintaining French loyalty on the eve of the War of 1812, Craig's actions and sentiments had further advanced the nationalist ambitions of the Parti Canadien.

The Parti Canadien was the political vehicle of the emerging French-Canadian professional elite of lawyers, notaries, doctors, and journalists based in the Lower Canadian countryside. This new middle class, espousing liberal, democratic, and ultimately republican ideals, aspired to replace the seigneurs as the leaders of French-Canadian society. The French-speaking seigneurs were increasingly being criticized for exploiting the habitants by charging higher rents and for collaborating with the English-speaking commercial elite in return for patronage and preferments. The rising professional elite was also critical of the Catholic Church for its apparent support of the imperialist rather than the nationalist cause. In essence, the French-Canadian professional elite were economic conservatives in their defense of traditional agriculture against the threat of commercial capitalism, but they were political radicals in their demand for greater provincial autonomy and, if necessary, separation from the empire.

The liberal nationalism of the Parti Canadien found its champion and embodiment in Louis Joseph Papineau, son of Joseph Papineau who had led the fight for the recognition of French as an official language in the first Assembly in 1792. A seigneur and lawyer, the younger Papineau possessed an oratorical prowess and a charismatic presence that made him an outstanding popular leader and gained him prominence in the Assembly. He assumed a leadership role in the Parti Canadien after he was elected Speaker of the Assembly in 1815. At this stage of his political career, Papineau was still a moderate nationalist who admired British parliamentary institutions and defended the traditional Catholic feudal society. He endeavored to work closely with a small group of English-speaking reformers led by Scotsman John Neilson, editor of the bilingual *Quebec Gazette*, as well as some Irish Catholic dissidents, in a common effort at constitutional change that would make representative government more effective in practice.

The parliamentary strategy that Papineau adopted in order to achieve this objective was to assert the Assembly's traditional power of the purse. Although the governor had certain revenues at his disposal, such as customs duties and proceeds from the sale or lease of Crown lands, he came to depend increasingly upon additional funds from the Assembly to meet the growing costs of government. The governor could command the spending of public funds, but British parliamentary tradition recognized the right of the Legislative Assembly to authorize government expenditure. Thus, Papineau hoped that by controlling all revenues and expenditures the Legislative Assembly would be in a stronger position to control the governor and his councils. This issue came to a head in 1819 when the Assembly refused to approve funds for government expenditures unless it was given full control over all revenue and expenditures. The Legislative Council then rejected the Assembly's budget but proposed to relinquish control of all revenues in return for a permanent civil list that would assure the salaries of the governor and his appointed officials. Unwilling to give up this vital power, the Assembly was only willing to approve a civil list on an annual basis.

Underlying the political division on this key issue, which dragged on year after year for more than a decade, were sharply divergent concepts of the society and economy of Lower Canada. The French-dominated Assembly sought to preserve a rural society in which public funds would be directed to building roads and other local improvements beneficial to an agrarian economy. The English-dominated oligarchy strove to expand international trade and to promote urban growth through public expenditures on canals and other improvements to the St. Lawrence system of waterways. The determination to limit commercial expansion and the domination of the English-speaking business community was also behind French-Canadian opposition to the proposed reunion of Upper and Lower Canada in 1822. Whereas the Montreal merchants encouraged the influx of British immigrants to develop their Upper Canadian hinterland and to offset French preponderance in the Assembly, French-Canadian leaders like Papineau were vehemently opposed to any migration that threatened to overwhelm their culture or fill up agricultural land reserved for future generations of habitants. Likewise, the passing of the Canada Tenures Act of 1825, which allowed landholders to change from seigneurial to freehold tenure, and the chartering of the British American Land Company, which acquired a substantial portion of the Eastern Townships, were viewed as serious threats to the survival of the French-Canadian culture.

By 1831 the imperial government agreed to transfer most of the revenues to the assembly without condition, and in a further conciliatory gesture, Papineau and Neilson were offered membership in the Executive Council. But the offer was refused as Papineau was no longer in a compromising mood, and his nationalist views had become more radical. The renaming of the Parti Canadien as the Parti Patriote in 1826 reflected a growing affinity for republicanism and American-style democracy. This tendency and the implied threat of separation from the British Empire, by force if necessary, were embodied in the Ninety-two Resolutions of Grievances that the Patriotes drew up under Papineau's guidance and which the Assembly adopted in 1834.

Papineau's radical rhetoric and the republican tone of the Ninety-two Resolutions alarmed the moderate reformers. Although support came from the radical followers of Wolfred and Robert Nelson, moderate English-speaking reformers led by John Neilson wanted change only within the context of British parliamentary democracy; therefore they broke with Papineau. Likewise, French-speaking moderates feared that Papineau was leading them to cultural annihilation by the American republic, while the clergy, aroused by the anticlericalism of the radicals, opposed the use of force against a constituted authority. Nevertheless, Papineau and his supporters scored a decisive victory in the provincial elections of 1834, in which the opponents of the resolutions, including Neilson, were soundly defeated.

Viewing the impending political crisis in Lower Canada as a low priority, the imperial government did not respond decisively until 1837, when the Colonial Office abandoned the policy of conciliation and Colonial Secretary Lord John Russell issued the Ten Resolutions for Lower Canada. The resolutions included a rejection of self-government and an elected Legislative Council as well as authorization for the governor to use local tax revenues to cover government expenditures without the approval of the Assembly. Despairing of the prospects for achieving reform by constitutional means, Papineau and his radical followers prepared for revolution.

THE REFORM MOVEMENT OF UPPER CANADA

Equally frustrated with oligarchic rule, the movement for political reform in Upper Canada was heading in a similar direction, although without the complications of ethnic tensions that plagued Lower Canada. The basic complaints against the Family Compact were that it ignored or suppressed public opinion, distributed patronage in a narrow and selfish way, directed economic development for the profit of its members and associates, and monopolized much of the public land for the advantage of one religious denomination. The political grievances that sustained reform opposition to oligarchy had elicited scattered and isolated rumblings of discontent prior to the War of 1812. But in the wake of the postwar population and economic growth, the expression of these grievances became more widespread and more organized.

The Family Compact was as apprehensive about the hundreds of thousands of British immigrants who came to Upper Canada in the 1820s and 1830s as it had been suspicious of the American settlers who arrived prior to the War of 1812. These newcomers from Britain who had migrated because they were unsuccessful at home and who knew nothing about the province hardly seemed to be the most reliable candidates for public patronage. Accordingly, the Compact continued to insist that the province was lacking in men with sufficient education and training and proven loyalty to the Crown to fill government posts, or to extend power beyond the exclusive circle of the ruling elite. But as British subjects, many of these newcomers from overseas felt entitled to certain rights, privileges, and opportunities within the developing colony and were not reluctant to say so.

Such an opportunist was Robert Gourlay, a Scottish immigrant driven to Upper Canada in 1817 by the collapse of his fortunes at home and by the aspiration to promote a grand emigration and land settlement scheme for fellow Britons. While traveling around the province to survey prospective land grants, he circulated a questionnaire asking settlers to identify factors that retarded the development of their area. His statistical study revealed widespread dissatisfaction over the large tracts of land that remained unsettled as clergy and Crown reserves. He was also critical of the Compact's control of the appointed Legislative Council and advocated more power for the elected Assembly. Although Gourlay was a congenital dissident who had little to contribute to the province, his prosecution and expulsion for seditious libel in 1819 proved to be a serious mistake for the Compact. For as the reform movement took shape, the "banished Briton" came to be regarded as a martyr who had been ruthlessly persecuted by an arrogant and unyielding oligarchy.

Another troublesome character in the eyes of the Compact was William Lyon Mackenzie, a fiery Scottish immigrant who arrived in 1820. In 1826, his vicious attacks on the ruling elite in his York-based newspaper, the *Colonial Advocate*, inspired some of the younger Compact members to ransack his office, destroy his printing presses, and throw his typesetting equipment into Lake Ontario. Mackenzie's successful civil suit against the perpetrators was hailed as a victory for freedom of speech, and the incident launched his political career as a leading reform agitator. Starting in 1828, he was elected to the Legislative Assembly four times, and on each occasion, he was expelled for his unruly behavior. Although Mackenzie became a popular spokesman for the reform cause, his questionable antics and growing radicalism tended to distract attention from more concrete political grievances.

As Gourlay's survey revealed, land policy was at the center of political discontent in Upper Canada. Not only was land an attraction for settlement but also, in a pioneer economy where cash was in short supply, land was used as a form of currency for rewarding those who had rendered service to or had a claim upon the government, such as the Loyalists, retired military and government officials, and surveyors. In particular, proceeds from the sale or lease of Crown lands had been used to finance the building and maintenance of public works projects such as roads and bridges, while the sale or lease of clergy reserves was designed to defray the costs of maintaining a Protestant clergy as well as building and maintaining churches and schools. However, by the mid-1820s vast parcels of strategically located land remained undeveloped, either in the hands of speculators or locked up in Crown and Clergy reserves.

To help resolve this problem, the provincial government sold off the remaining Crown lands in 1824 to the newly formed Canada Company in return for an annual payment amounting to nearly £350,000 over a 16-year period. This transaction proved to be economically viable as the Canada Company brought new vigor to land settlement, not only by attracting large numbers of settlers to the province but also by investing heavily in infrastructural improvements. From a political standpoint, however, the deal was objectionable because the added financial support it gave to the provincial government reduced the Family Compact's dependence on the Assembly. Thus, the rising reform movement in the Assembly had reason to oppose the government's arrangement with the Canada Company.

As in Lower Canada, the Upper Canadian Assembly was asserting more control over the appropriation of public revenues and expenditures. Even with the lucrative deal with the Canada Company, the growing scope of government activity required that the Family Compact cultivate the support of like-minded men in the Assembly in order to enhance its access to tax revenue. Therefore, by the 1830s provincial elections featured bitter struggles between the Tories and Reformers, each seeking to control the public purse. The Tories tended to share their Compact allies' interest in using public funds to improve water transportation for the benefit of the mercantile community, whereas the Reformers were more inclined to direct funds to build roads that could open up more farmland in the interior. On the whole, the Tories and the Family Compact were more likely to think along provincial lines of development while the Reformers were more concerned with local improvements.

Land policy intersected with the contentious issue of religious privilege when it came to the allocation of clergy reserves. By virtue of its connection with the Compact and as the established church in England, the Anglican Church initially claimed Exclusive control over income from the rent or sale of clergy reserves. Until the 1820s this revenue was so small that clergy reserves were hardly considered a contentious issue, other than the occasional complaint that they stood in the way of settlement and development. In 1827 Anglican leaders decided to press for the sale of clergy reserves to meet the competition from the Canada Company. Because of a legislative stipulation that lots hindering the progress of settlement be sold first, clergy reserves ceased to be an obstacle to settlement. However, they became a source of political discontent when other religious denominations began to press their claims for a share of the sales revenue, thereby intensifying the growing unrest over the favored position of the Anglican Church within the province.

Indeed, British immigration was in the process of changing the religious face of Upper Canada to the extent that by mid-century about half of the population was Methodist, and Presbyterians slightly outnumbered Anglicans. Fearing that the Church of England was losing its grip on the religious life of the province, Archbishop Strachan sought to place education under Anglican dominance by securing a charter in 1827 for a provincial university, King's College (which became the University of Toronto in 1850). Led by Reverend Egerton Ryerson, the Methodists launched a campaign against religious privilege: in 1826 they urged the secularization of clergy reserves, with the proceeds of their sale being devoted to public education; and in 1829 they founded Victoria University in Coburg, a thriving lakeport east of York. Inevitably, sectarian rivalry spilled over into the political arena, exacerbating existing divisions between Tories and Reformers.

The distinction between Upper Canadian Tories and Reformers was not always clear since they were not organized and disciplined political parties in the modern sense. Rather, Tories and Reformers were loosely knit associations or factions of like-minded men whose divergent interests might require them to disagree with their cohorts on a particular issue. Certainly, the Reformers were far from united. Moderates like Ryerson and Robert Baldwin, inspired by the British struggle over the Great Reform Bill of 1832, favored a government responsible to the Assembly. On the other hand, radicals like Mackenzie and John Rolph, influenced by the rise of Jacksonian democracy in the United States, demanded an elected Legislative Council. Mackenzie's enthusiasm for republicanism drove Ryerson and other Methodist reformers into the Tory camp in 1833.

The factional nature of Upper Canadian politics contributed to an apparent ambivalence among the voters, whose preferences generally swung like a pendulum between Reformers and Tories. While the Reformers could claim victory in the provincial elections of 1828 and 1834, the Tories swept back to power in the elections of 1830 and 1836, with the election of 1832 ending in a virtual stalemate. The Tory electoral triumph of 1836 featured active campaigning by Governor Sir Francis Bond Head, who appealed to the British tie and warned against the perils of American republicanism. The indignity of this defeat followed by the repudiation of reform embodied in Russell's Ten Resolutions incited Mackenzie and his radical supporters to follow the rebellious course of Papineau and the patriotes.

FROM REBELLION TO REUNION

Political unrest in the Canadas was aggravated by an economic depression that plagued the Western world in 1836–37. Declining exports and prices in the agricultural sector were accompanied by a series of crop failures that seriously diminished the purchasing power of both Upper and Lower Canadian farmers. The agrarian crisis was particularly acute in Lower Canada, where overpopulation and soil exhaustion led to the decline of wheat production for an export market and necessitated a shift to coarse grains and potatoes for subsistence consumption. Farmers under economic duress were inclined to be more receptive to revolutionary rhetoric.

In Lower Canada, mass meetings, fiery speeches, and outbursts in the press were signs of an emerging revolutionary spirit in the autumn of 1837. By late October, patriote leaders had called for a revolt, issued a declaration of independence, and devised plans for a march on Montreal. Fearing that an early November riot by French and English extremists would spread out of control, Papineau and his associates fled Montreal. Anxious authorities mistakenly assumed that the radical leaders had gone into the countryside to launch a rebellion and thus issued a warrant for their arrest. When a small detachment of troops arrived at St. Denis on November 23 to execute these orders, they were repulsed by armed patriotes, consisting mostly of young farmers. During this opening clash of the rebellion, Papineau fled to the United States. Two days later, a larger contingent of British troops put down an uprising at neighboring St. Charles, southeast of Montreal. The most serious confrontation occurred on December 14, as 2,000 troops crushed a rebel force of 500 led by Dr. Jean-Olivier Chénier at St. Eustache, north of Montreal. The only other fighting consisted of a poorly organized revolt southwest of Montreal, which was easily suppressed in November 1838. Altogether, about 300 patriotes and 25 defenders were killed in action during the entire Lower Canadian rebellion, and among the rebels, 12 were executed for treason and 58 were exiled to the British penal colony of Australia.

Meanwhile, in December 1837, Mackenzie seized the opportunity to overthrow the provincial government at Toronto (formerly York) when most of the troops guarding the capital were dispatched to Lower Canada. On December 5, about 500 men from the surrounding farming district gathered at Montgomery's Tavern (then on the northern outskirts of Toronto). Armed with rifles, staves, and pitchforks, they marched down Yonge Street, whereupon they confronted a small contingent of loyal volunteer militia. Mackenzie's front rank fired, then dropped to the ground to let the next rank fire over their heads. Thinking that the men in front of them had been shot down, the men in the back ranks fled in panic. Two days later, a force of 1,500 militia marched up to Montgomery's Tavern and dispersed the remaining rebels within 20 minutes. During this somewhat pathetic skirmish, one defender and two rebels were killed, and two of the latter were tried and executed for treason in the aftermath. The rebellion ended a few days later when equally disorganized Mackenzie sympathizers led by Dr. Charles Duncombe were easily dispersed in the western part of the province.

Duncombe escaped to the United States along with Mackenzie, who subsequently attempted several unsuccessful border raids with the support of Americans, some of whom were interested in liberating Canada from British tyranny while others had little more than a penchant for looting. This final act of desperation actually involved more fighting than the rebellion itself and caused some tension between Britain and the United States that briefly raised memories of the War of 1812. But the U.S. government, preoccupied with western settlement, was adamantly opposed to these attacks, and peace was restored along the border by the end of 1838.

The ill-conceived and ill-fated rebellions of 1837 were more a product of historical accident than political design. Less than two years after the insurrection in Lower Canada, Papineau admitted that the patriote leadership had drifted into rebellion: "I defy the government to contradict me when I assert that none of us had ever organized, desired, or even anticipated armed resistance." The Upper Canadian uprising was sustained by little more than Mackenzie's rash judgement and demagoguery. Although the greater bloodshed and longer duration suggest that the rebellion in Lower Canada had more popular support, still a relatively small number of people—perhaps 1 or 2 percent out of a total population of about one million in the two colonies—actually followed the radicals in their resort to violence. The overwhelming preference was for reform along constitutional lines and through British parliamentary institutions. From this standpoint, the rebellions did little to advance the cause of political reform, and indeed may have slowed its momentum.

The days of oligarchic rule were already numbered by the late 1830s, inasmuch as the appointed branch of government had lost most of its fiscal powers to the elected representatives. Furthermore, prior to the rebellions the Colonial Office was already instructing Canadian governors to abide as much as possible by the will of the Assembly and to avoid undue interference in local affairs. The motivation behind the increasing imperial willingness to defer to local authority would become more apparent in the next decade when Britain moved toward dismantling the old colonial system.

The rebellions of 1837 did force the British government to take more seriously the problems of colonial government in British North America. In 1838, Lord Durham, who had been prominent in the achievement of the Great Reform Bill of 1832 in Britain, was appointed governor general and lord high commissioner of British North America with sweeping authority to investigate the causes of the political turmoil in the Canadas. Durham spent only five months in Canada before he was forced to resign over his unauthorized decision to grant amnesty to most of the exiled Canadian rebels. Nevertheless, in 1839, he completed his famous (or infamous) *Report on the Affairs of British North America*, which, in spite of its investigative limitations and its biased perspective, became a provocative and influential analysis of the state of mid-19th-century Canadian government and society.

Durham devoted most of his investigative and analytical attention to the political problems of Lower Canada, since the rebellion there had been deemed serious enough to suspend the provincial constitution. He was surprised to find "two nations warring in the bosom of a single state . . . a struggle, not of principles, but of races." The political strife in the province, Durham surmised, was rooted in the unprogressive nature of French-Canadian customs and institutions, notably the religious and classical orientation of the education system, which left people ill-prepared to function in the bustling world of commerce and industry and easy prey to irresponsible demagogues. On the other hand, Durham was sympathetic to the English-speaking merchants of Montreal, viewing them as dynamic entrepreneurs concerned with the economic development of the province and exasperated by French opposition to progressive schemes such as the improvement of the St. Lawrence canal system and the promotion of British immigration.

Accordingly, he found considerable merit in the merchant-backed proposal of 1822 to reunite the provinces of Upper and Lower Canada. The combined English-speaking population of approximately 600,000 in the two provinces could politically overwhelm the French population of approximately 500,000, thereby clearing the way for economic progress and eventual cultural assimilation. For the same reasons, Durham was also attracted to the idea of a federation of all British North America, but he realized that this larger union would have to await the further development of transportation and communication links between Canada and the Maritime colonies.

Finding Durham's recommendation for a union of the Canadas to be compelling, the British Parliament passed the Act of Union in 1840. The United Province of Canada,

LORD DURHAM'S REPORT (1839)

In a Dispatch which I addressed to Your Majesty's Principal Secretary of State for the Colonies on the 9th of August last, I detailed, with great minuteness, the impressions which had been produced on my mind by the state of things which existed in Lower Canada: I acknowledged that the experience derived from my residence in the Province had completely changed my view of the relative influence of the causes which had been assigned for the existing disorders. I had not, indeed, been brought to believe that the institutions of Lower Canada were less defective than I had originally presumed them to be. From the peculiar circumstances in which I was placed, I was enabled to make such effectual observations as convinced me that there had existed in the constitution of the Province, in the balance of political powers, in the spirit and practice of administration in every department of the Government, defects that were quite sufficient to account for a great degree of mismanagement and dissatisfaction. The same observation had also impressed on me the conviction, that, for the peculiar and disastrous dissensions of this Province, there existed a far deeper and far more efficient cause, – a cause which penetrated beneath its political institutions into its social state, – a cause which no reform of constitution or laws, that should leave the elements of society unaltered, could remove; but which must be removed, ere any success could be expected in any attempt to remedy the many evils of this unhappy Province. I expected to find a contest between a government and a people: I found two nations warring in the bosom of a single state: I found a struggle, not of principles, but of races; and I perceived that it would be idle to attempt any amelioration of laws or institutions until we could first succeed in terminating the deadly animosity that now separates the inhabitants of Lower Canada into the hostile divisions of French and English.

which officially came into being in 1841, was to be governed in accordance with the basic provisions of the Constitutional Act of 1791: a governor-general advised by an Executive Council would preside over an appointed Legislative Council and an elected Legislative Assembly. Deviating from Durham's original intent to merge the two cultures into a single English-dominated community to facilitate the assimilation of the French, the Act of Union stipulated that representation in the legislature was to be distributed equally between two distinct sections to be known as Canada West and Canada East, corresponding with the former provinces of Upper and Lower Canada, respectively. Assigning the same number of legislative representatives to each section even though the population of Canada East outnumbered that of Canada West by nearly 200,000 was a deliberate but short-sighted effort to reinforce English political dominance over the French. The initial French outrage over this underrepresentation, in

119

addition to the Act of Union's provision for official English unilingualism, would iron-ically give way to a comparable English response slightly more than a decade later when the continuing influx of British immigration would propel the population of Canada West past that of Canada East.

THE EVOLUTION OF RESPONSIBLE GOVERNMENT

While immediately accepting the union of the Canadas, the British government did not respond as favorably to the other major recommendations of Durham's Report. Based chiefly on his consultation with Robert Baldwin, Durham concluded that the primary cause of political discontent in Upper Canada was a defective constitution that encouraged the monopolization of power by "a petty, corrupt, insolent Tory clique." To combat the irresponsible power of the Family Compact, Durham recommended a form of "responsi-ble government" in which the governor would "secure the cooperation of the assembly in his policy, by entrusting its administration to such men as could command a majority." As the leading colonial advocate of this reform, Baldwin wanted the doctrine of responsible government based on the British cabinet system, whereby the governor merely accepted policies put forward by his advisors in the Executive Council who were collectively respon-sible to the majority in the Assembly. Instead, Durham proposed that the governor initiate policy to be administered by executive councillors with majority support in the Assembly. Nevertheless, the clear intent of this recommendation was to place effective control over colonial affairs in the hands of the elected representatives.

To strengthen colonial self-government, Durham further recommended the separa-tion of local and imperial affairs. He pointed out that regular interference in colonial affairs in the past had tended to make the British government a party to local squabbles that could jeopardize or detract from more important imperial interests. Accordingly, intervention in colonial affairs should be confined to a relatively few matters of real imperial concern such as constitutional change, international relations, foreign trade, and the management of public lands. Durham was supremely confident that local self-government based on the principle of executive responsibility to the people would lead to greater loyalty to, rather than secession from, the empire.

While Lord Durham's Report effectively legitimized the doctrine of responsible gov-ernment as an integral part of a reformed British constitution, rather than an instrument of American republicanism, the imperial authority remained reluctant to incorporate the principle into colonial administration. Imperialism dictated that a colonial governor could not serve two masters—that is, follow the instructions of the colonial secretary in Britain while acting on the advice of executive councillors responsible to a local assembly. But imperial authorities were confident that colonial government could be made more respon-sive in practice without becoming fully responsible in principle.

When he succeeded Lord Durham in 1839, Charles Poulett Thompson, who became Lord Sydenham, was confronted with the challenge of exercising power with the majori-ty support of the elected colonial representatives without yielding his independent authority as governor. In the hope of silencing demands for responsible government, Sydenham deliberately set out to eliminate remaining vestiges of oligarchic rule by estab-lishing much of the pattern of British ministerial government in Canada. He organized a group of government departments, each headed by member of the Executive Council, who was also required to hold a seat in the Legislative Assembly. With the replacement of the old lifetime appointees by elected members, the Executive Council was becoming a veritable cabinet of ministers under the leadership of the governor, who was virtually his own prime minister. These ministers were not collectively responsible to the Assembly but rather individually to the governor who regarded his council only as a body of advisors and department heads to consult. Still, by adopting the practice of choosing ministers acceptable to the Assembly, Lord Sydenham had effectively advanced a step closer to the principle of responsible government.

To ensure a favorable majority in the Assembly, Lord Sydenham actively campaigned against French candidates in Canada East and Reformers in Canada West during the first provincial election of the United Province of Canada in 1841. A shrewd and unscrupulous political tactician, Sydenham gerrymandered riding boundaries, manipulated poll results, and intimidated voters in the open voting to secure victory for English-speaking candidates, particularly Tories who were opposed to responsible government out of fear that it would weaken imperial ties and their influence in the legislature. Consequently, he was able to form an Executive Council that excluded French Canadians and yet enjoyed majority support of the Assembly. Furthermore, Sydenham maintained his control over the newly elected legislature by adeptly exploiting the division within the French ranks. The radicals, on the one hand, wanted to repeal the union of the Canadas and saw responsible government as a means of perpetuating it. The moderate reformers, on the other hand, supported responsible government as a way of changing the assimilationist features of the union.

However, Sydenham's political manipulations were unintentionally encouraging the Reformers of Canada West, led by Baldwin and Francis Hincks, to join forces with the moderate French Reformers, led by Louis Lafontaine and Augustin-Norbert Morin, to achieve their common goal of responsible government. In September 1841, Sydenham died before he had to face the difficult political problem of maintaining majority support for the governor's policies in the wake of the growth of formal party lines in the Assembly. His successor, Sir Charles Bagot, realized during the legislative session of 1842 that an effective majority in the Assembly could only be achieved by cultivating political support on a group rather than on an individual basis. Accordingly, he departed from the imperial policy of excluding French elected representatives from the Executive Council by attempting to recruit Lafontaine, who led the largest single political grouping in the Assembly. Lafontaine agreed to join the Executive Council only if Baldwin was included in the new ministry. By including Baldwin and Lafontaine along with three other Reformers in the Executive Council, Bagot retained his independent authority as governor and averted formal recognition of responsible government. But by bestowing a measure of political power upon the emerging Reform coalition, he gave impetus to the modern Canadian party system, which in itself advanced the cause of responsible government.

The next step on the road to responsible government resulted from yet another governor's attempt to resist acceptance of the principle. In 1844 Sir Charles Metcalfe, who had succeeded Bagot as governor in the previous year, clashed with the Executive Council over the right of a responsible ministry to approve all official appointments. When the governor refused to surrender what he considered to be a prerogative of the Crown, the ministry resigned, supported by the Assembly in a vote of confidence. Metcalfe dissolved the Assembly, called an election, and campaigned against the disloyalty and patronage-mongering of the Reformers. While Metcalfe was successful in engineering the defeat of Baldwin and the Reformers in Canada West, Lafontaine remained firmly entrenched in

On the left, Robert Baldwin (1804–58), reform leader of Upper Canada, and on the right, Louis Lafontaine (1807–64), reform leader of Lower Canada, photographed by Albert Ferland. The architects of responsible government established the first of many French-English political alliances that would lead Canada toward nationhood and sustain it hereafter.

Canada East. To form a government, Metcalfe called upon William Henry Draper, leader of the moderate Tory majority in Canada West. For the next three years, the rudiments of the future Conservative Party struggled to maintain a precarious majority support in the Assembly. The Executive Council functioned practically as a cabinet with Draper as virtual prime minister whose advice the governor had to accept or else turn to the only viable alternative, a Reform alliance led by Lafontaine, which would insist on the complete submission of the governor to majority party rule.

The struggle for responsible government was finally determined by the course of events in Britain rather than in the colonies. The repeal of the Corn Laws in 1846 and the Navigation Laws in 1849 heralded the end of the old colonial system and ushered in the era of free trade in Britain. Now that colonial economic activity was no longer subject to imperial control, there seemed little reason to control political life, either.

The political consequences of free trade for the British North American colonies were first manifested in Nova Scotia, where Joseph Howe was leading a fight for responsible government that was less turbulent but no less persistent than in the Canadas. In November 1846, Colonial Secretary Lord Grey sent a dispatch to Governor John Harvey stating "that it is neither possible nor desirable to carry on the government of any of the provinces of British North America in opposition to the opinion of the inhabitants." Another dispatch in March 1847 specified that there was now no obstacle to the full and immediate adoption of the British cabinet system in the colonies. When Howe led the Reformers to electoral victory later that autumn and followed up with a motion of nonconfidence in the existing ministry in January 1848, the governor had no recourse but to summon him and his party to form the next government. Thus, Nova Scotia had the distinction of inaugurating the new order of responsible government in the British colonies.

Two months later, the principle was extended to the Province of Canada, although in reality responsible government may have arrived a little earlier. When Lord Elgin assumed the post of governor in January 1847, he placed himself at the disposal of the precarious Conservative majority in the Assembly, which was opposed to responsible government. In effect responsible government prevailed, since the governor was willing to abide by the wishes of the Executive Council without question. When the Reformers were swept back into power in the election of January 1848, the stage was set for the formation of the first unified one-party ministry under Baldwin and Lafontaine two months later. The first test of responsible government came with the passing of the Rebellion Losses Bill to compensate various Lower Canadians who had suffered financially as a result of the Rebellion of 1837. Lord Elgin's routine approval of the bill in April 1849, in accordance with the principles of responsible government, unleashed the fury of the Montreal Tories who regarded the measure as a flagrant endorsement of treason. Interpreting recent British policy in terms of economic and political abandonment as well as submission to French domination, several prominent and avowedly loyal English-speaking members of the Montreal business community not only participated in riots resulting in the burning of the House of Parliament but also signed the Annexation Manifesto of 1849 supporting union with the United States. This expression of despair proved to be futile as responsible government was extended to all North American colonies of the British Empire, including Prince Edward Island in 1851, New Brunswick in 1854, and Newfoundland in 1855.

The achievement of responsible government, in effect political independence from Britain, highlighted an essential difference between the two nations that would ultimately share the North American continent. Whereas the thirteen colonies had to liberate themselves from Britain through revolution, the British North American colonies gained their freedom through evolution. Unlike the United States, which emerged out of a bloody struggle against imperialism, the future nation of Canada was nudged, if not pushed, toward independence by the same imperial power that had attempted to block American liberty less than a century before. The union of the Canadas and the achievement of responsible government represented the first steps on the road to nationhood for the British North American colonies. The final and most formidable step would be unity of political will between the Canadian and Maritime Provinces.

CHAPTER 10

THE ROAD TO CONFEDERATION

By the middle of the 19th century, the United Province of Canada and the Maritime colonies remained separated by hundreds of miles of wilderness and had little in the way of communication and commercial relations with one another. Even more isolated and remote were the vast domains of the rugged Canadian Shield and the frigid Arctic to the north as well as the prairie wilderness and towering coastal mountain region to the west, all of which were sparsely populated by Native peoples and fur traders. Yet within a span of two decades, the far-flung British North American colonies came to the realization that their continued growth, indeed their survival in the shadow of a powerful and ambitious neighbor, would depend on the breakdown of isolation and a convergence of their diverse interests. The coming of the railway age made transcontinental transportation and communication linkage feasible. The British withdrawal as an imperial force in the upper half of the continent and the apparent willingness of the United States to take its place rendered intercolonial unity more urgent. The political breakdown of the union of the Canadas and the rise of a Maritime union movement offered the occasion for the reconstitution of the British North American colonies into a new nation to be known as the Dominion of Canada.

RECIPROCITY AND RAILWAYS

The advent of British free trade conspired with the onset of economic depression throughout the Western world to reduce exports via the St. Lawrence by about one-third in the late 1840s. This downturn in economic fortunes, coinciding with the granting of responsible government, no doubt accounted for the panic among the Montreal merchants who signed the Annexation Manifesto of 1849. But with the revival of the world economy in the following year, thoughts of finding new markets and prosperity through political union with the United States had all but disappeared in the Province of Canada.

In fact, closer economic integration of the Canadian and Maritime colonies with the United States was becoming possible without sacrificing recently gained political autonomy. Much of the decline in British demand for grain and timber by 1850 was being offset by the emergence of new markets, particularly for wheat, dairy products, and sawn lumber, in the rapidly growing cities of the American Midwest and the Atlantic seaboard. While this continental trade was not about to develop on the same scale as transatlantic commerce, which had returned to normal levels by the mid-1850s, it offered Canada and the Maritimes an alternative strategy for economic development beyond mere dependence on the imperial market. Commercial reciprocity with the United States, therefore, became a major priority of the Canadian government, and the idea was endorsed by the British government as a means of reducing colonial dependence.

Although the American border regions were more favorable to reciprocity and the midwestern states were interested in free access to the St. Lawrence route, on the whole, strong protectionist sentiment still had to be overcome, particularly in the northern states. Another impediment was the growing sectional conflict over slavery. As supporters of slavery, the southern states were apprehensive in the wake of northern assertions that reciprocity was a prelude to annexation, which in turn would lead to a preponderance of free states in the union. Eventually, British envoy Lord Elgin was able to assuage southern concerns by arguing that a Canada made prosperous by free trade was less likely to accept annexation to the United States. The interest of the United States in reciprocity was increased in 1852 by the threat of a naval clash with Britain over the extent of American rights to the inshore fisheries of the Maritime Provinces. The American desire to resolve the long-standing fisheries dispute combined with the Canadian demand for freer trade culminated in the Reciprocity Treaty of 1854.

The treaty, concluded for an initial period of 10 years, provided for the free exchange of natural (as opposed to manufactured) products between the United States and the British North American colonies, free navigation of the American-controlled Lake Michigan and the Canadian-controlled St. Lawrence River, and joint access to all coastal fisheries north of the 36th parallel. Over the next decade, trade between the two partners to this agreement trebled in value, and henceforth, a regional commerce of convenience, involving the midwestern and northern border states with the St. Lawrence–Great Lakes region, New England with the Maritimes, and eventually the American western states bordering the 49th parallel with their Canadian counterparts, characterized a growing continental economic integration. Although more than half of Canada's trade and almost two-thirds of Maritime commerce was still conducted with Britain, these colonies were enhancing their future economic options by maintaining a foothold in each of the imperial and continental markets.

Competitiveness in either the imperial or the continental market after 1850 depended on continued transportation improvement, as exemplified by the completion of the

St. Lawrence canal system. Although more economical and efficient to use than the Hudson-Erie route to New York, the St. Lawrence route through Montreal was closed by ice for nearly half the year. Moreover, during the 1840s, every major American port on the Atlantic seaboard, including New York, Philadelphia, Boston, and Baltimore, was connected to the interior by railroads. By contrast to over 9,000 miles of railway in the United States, little more than 60 miles of track had been laid in all of British North America by mid-century; but within a decade there would be over 2,000 miles of railways, mostly in the Province of Canada.

To gain access to an ice-free Atlantic port, a group of Montreal businessmen collaborated with railway promoters from Portland, Maine, in 1850 to build the St. Lawrence and Atlantic line. When completed in 1853, the St. Lawrence and Atlantic had the distinction of being the world's first international railway. The following year, the Great Western Railway, promoted by Allan MacNab, opened its main line from Hamilton to Windsor with the intention of extending westward to Detroit in order to link up with the Michigan Central system and eastward to Buffalo in order to connect with the New York railway network. Accordingly, the Great Western could channel a share of the American midwestern trade through Canada West by serving as a portage route from Chicago to New York. By 1855 the Northern Railway was completed from Toronto to Collingwood on Georgian Bay. By linking Lakes Ontario and Huron, the Northern line serviced the agrarian hinterland north of Toronto and opened up the prospect of a combined water and rail route to the upper Great Lakes and beyond.

Railway-building fever was also prevalent in the Maritimes, albeit to a lesser extent. With provincial government assistance, lines were built linking Halifax to Truro in Nova Scotia and Saint John to Shediac in New Brunswick by the late 1850s. These lines reflected the hope of Halifax and Saint John merchants to link their ice-free ports with the St. Lawrence transport system and thus tap into the traffic between the American Midwest and Europe. However, to build and operate railways in the Maritimes was more expensive than in Canada because of the greater distances from larger urban centers and the lack of a populated hinterland to generate local revenue from shipment and passenger traffic. For such reasons, Joseph Howe's proposal for an intercolonial link with Canada fell through in 1852.

The most ambitious scheme was the Montreal-based Grand Trunk Railway. Initiated in 1853, the Grand Trunk was a transprovincial line extending from Sarnia at the southwestern end of Canada West to Quebec City in Canada East. The failure to negotiate the intercolonial extension to Halifax prompted the Grand Trunk to purchase the St. Lawrence and Atlantic Railway, which offered access to the ice-free Atlantic port of Portland, Maine. When completed in 1859, the Grand Trunk was the longest railway line in the world—a continuous stretch of 1,100 miles, which was later extended westward to reach Chicago. Not surprisingly, this extraordinary enterprise was constantly plagued by financial difficulties, despite a considerable infusion of private capital from British investors and the generous support of the Canadian government. As construction progressed, the Grand Trunk Railway Company repeatedly appealed for more aid from the provincial government, which, in turn, had to borrow heavily to satisfy this urgent need.

The government felt obliged to bail out the struggling railway not only because the line was considered vital to future economic development but also because six of the Grand Trunk's 12 directors were members of the Canadian cabinet. Such conflicts of interest were commonplace in mid-19th-century politics. Sir Francis Hincks, who fought for responsible government alongside Robert Baldwin, was intimately involved with the

Grand Trunk while he was serving as prime minister. Likewise, George Étienne Cartier was a paid solicitor for the Grand Trunk before becoming prime minister. Alexander Galt, as president of the St. Lawrence and Atlantic, arranged the absorption of the railway by the Grand Trunk and went on to become a minister of finance. Sir Allan MacNab, a leading promoter of the Great Western Railway and a prime minister from 1854 to 1856, summed up the spirit of the age when he frankly admitted: "All my politics are railroads." Indeed, government support for railways tended to be a contentious political issue at this time because each legislator argued that the venture with which he was associated was more deserving of preferential treatment.

The perilous position that the Canadian government had assumed through its generous support for railways was revealed with the recurrence of world economic depression in 1857. Not only was the Canadian railway boom brought to an abrupt halt, but the financial position of the provincial government was severely compromised. More revenue had to be generated to ensure the completion of the Grand Trunk, to bail out other hardpressed railways, and to pay down mounting public debt that largely resulted from railway support. In an age before income tax, the major source of public revenue was derived from customs duties on imports. Since the Reciprocity Treaty prevented a tariff increase on natural products imported from the United States, Finance Minister Galt had little recourse but to raise the tariff on manufactured imports in 1859. In so doing, he established the connection between railways and tariffs that would become the cornerstone of future national economic strategy.

Although Galt insisted that the primary purpose of his tariff was to raise revenue, it also represented the first serious move in the direction of industrial, as opposed to agricultural, protection, thus reflecting the profound changes that the Canadian economy was experiencing in the wake of the railway boom. The railway encouraged the development of related industries such as engine foundries, locomotive shops, rolling mills, and ironworks. Along with canal-building and shipbuilding, railways also stimulated a variety of secondary industries: flour mills, sawmills, boot and shoe factories, textile shops, breweries and distilleries, and wagon and carriage manufacturers. This industrial growth led to the development of numerous towns, mainly along the railway lines, to service the prosperous agricultural hinterland. Railways, along with reciprocity, reinforced the links that Montreal and Toronto were developing with their hinterland regions. While Montreal remained the largest city and the dominant metropolis of British North America, Toronto was emerging as its chief rival by the end of the 1850s. This metropolitan rivalry would be intensified in the second half of the 19th century by the increasing relationship between railway development and industrial protection.

Quite apart from its long-range implications, the tariff increase of 1859 immediately provoked vigorous protests from Britain and the United States, the sources of most Canadian manufactured imports. British manufacturers complained that the tariff was a violation of the principle of free trade. But Galt argued that free trade meant that the colonies were free to direct their own economic policies in their best interests. This assertion of colonial fiscal autonomy from Britain was allowed to pass unchallenged by the imperial authority, thus signifying a growing willingness to surrender control over the external economic relations of British North America. Furthermore, American manufacturers claimed that the higher tariff on their products violated the spirit, if not the letter, of the Reciprocity Treaty. The prospect of increased exports of manufactures to Canada had been a significant inducement for American acceptance of free trade. With this advantage removed, reciprocity no longer seemed an attractive proposition, and the demand increased for the treaty to be terminated at the first opportunity. The victory of the protectionist North in the Civil War would destroy the delicate regional balance in American politics that had made agreement on the treaty possible. Although formal cancellation of the treaty would not occur until 1866, the end was already a certainty many years before.

Despite government support on a large scale, the Grand Trunk was completed too late and was too costly to achieve its main purpose of redirecting American midwestern trade down the St. Lawrence to Europe. Capturing the growing traffic within Canada itself was not enough to prevent the Grand Trunk from bankruptcy with a deficit of $13 million by 1861. With Britain more firmly committed than ever to free trade and with the Americans obviously souring on reciprocity, Canadian business and political leaders turned their attention to another developmental prospect made possible by the advent of the railroad. The railroad offered a means of surmounting the great barrier posed by the Canadian Shield, beyond which lay a vast settlement frontier stretching to the Pacific and under British control. Railway links to the Maritimes and to the Pacific could set the stage for a revival of the transcontinental empire of the St. Lawrence based on interprovincial trade.

THE CHANGING PROSPECTS OF THE WEST

For nearly three decades after its merger with the North West Company in 1821, the revitalized Hudson's Bay Company ruled virtually unchallenged over the vast domain of Rupert's Land, extending from the upper Great Lakes to the Arctic and Pacific Oceans. Sir George Simpson presided over the realm like a despot, defending the company's chartered right to monopolize trade and governing the widely scattered posts with military-like discipline. He assiduously maintained the traditional priorities of the fur trade—efficiency of operation, maximization of profits, and discouragement of settlement. Aside from the nomadic encampments of the Native people, the only permanent settlement in the Hudson's Bay Company domain continued to be Lord Selkirk's colony along the Red River.

During the 1820s the Selkirk colony consisted of about 500 settlers situated along both banks of the river. Another 500 Métis were settled at Pembina to the south, where the Red River intersects with the 49th parallel. In 1834 the Selkirk heirs abandoned their interest in the settlement and sold it back to the Hudson's Bay Company, which organized it as the District of Assiniboia under a governor and an appointed council. By the late 1840s, the French-speaking Métis, situated mostly south and west of the forks of the Red and Assiniboine Rivers, comprised about half of the colony's population of 6,000. The Métis subsisted largely on the buffalo hunt, some small-scale farming, and seasonal labor for the Hudson's Bay Company. To the north, along the Red River toward Lake Winnipeg, lived the descendants of English-speaking fur traders and their wives along with the original Selkirk settlers. Despite their common native bond, the English-speaking settlers, many of whom were retired or active Hudson's Bay Company employees, did not mix a great deal with the French-speaking Métis.

A source of cultural division was the Hudson's Bay Company's tight control over the settlement, which the Métis increasingly resented. The company's claim that it had a monopoly over selling goods to the colonists and trading with the local Natives was decisively tested in 1849 when Pierre-Guillaume Sayer, a Métis trader, was charged with illegally trafficking in furs. Although the court found Sayers guilty based on the evidence, the judge decided to impose no sentence, no doubt influenced by a force of up to 300 armed Métis gathered outside the courthouse. Not only did this case signify the triumph of free trade over the Hudson's Bay Company monopoly, it also demonstrated that the Métis were the most cohesive community and the most powerful military force in the Red River colony. In 1851 Métis military supremacy in the region was further demonstrated with their decisive victory over the Sioux at the Battle of Grand Coteau in North Dakota, thus ending a decade of intense border conflict. Indeed, the presence of the Métis along with the Hudson's Bay Company was a deterrent to the northward progress of the American settlement frontier.

By the mid-19th century, the days of Hudson's Bay Company rule in the West were numbered amid growing American and Canadian interest in the region as an agrarian settlement frontier. Minnesota considered the Red River colony to be within its natural orbit of transportation and communication. The building of a wagon road to St. Paul in the early 1850s was followed by the inauguration of steamship service along the Red River in 1859. Upon the achievement of statehood in 1858, the Minnesota legislature passed a resolution in favor of the annexation of the Red River district.

A few Canadians who had recently arrived in the colony urged the Canadian government to take decisive action to ward off the expansionist threat from the south. Canadian interest in the Northwest was aroused by the findings of two distinct expeditions in 1857— a British-sponsored exploration led by John Palliser and a Canadian-based scientific inquiry conducted by Henry Youle Hind. Contrary to opinions rendered by fur traders and previous visitors to the Northwest, both expeditions reported on outstanding possibilities for agriculture, particularly in the Red River and North Saskatchewan River valleys. This news was especially welcomed in Canada West, where most of the good farmland was already occupied. But whereas the Canadians still had to overcome formidable geographical, economic, and political barriers before they could secure control over the vast northwestern frontier, Minnesota interests had direct and unimpeded access to the region along with a railway link from St. Paul to the Atlantic Coast. Indeed, by the early 1860s, the British Northwest appeared destined to become another Oregon.

The Convention of 1818 had placed the Oregon Territory, situated on the Pacific coast between California and the southern tip of the Alaska panhandle, under joint British and American occupation. In practical terms, however, the Hudson's Bay Company inherited control of Oregon from the North West Company in 1821 and maintained its fur-trading monopoly almost unchallenged for two decades. By the early 1840s the American western frontier was expanding across the Rockies to the Pacific slope, and the familiar conflict between the fur trade and settlement was extended to the southern half of the Oregon Territory. The Hudson's Bay Company, realizing its helplessness to stem the tide of settlement, aimed to contain its interests north of the Columbia River in the emerging dispute with the Americans. Although President James Polk came into office in 1845 with an electoral promise to fight for all of Oregon up to the Russian border ("54° 40' or fight"), the outbreak of war with Mexico over California made the Americans more amenable to compromise. The Oregon Treaty signed in 1846 extended the international boundary along the 49th parallel to the Pacific but left all of Vancouver Island in British hands. With this settlement, coming on the heels of the Maine–New Brunswick boundary settlement, the process of negotiating the southern boundary of the future Dominion of Canada was complete.

In an attempt to forestall the movement of Oregon settlers north of the new boundary, the British government established a Crown colony on Vancouver Island in 1849 and handed it over to the Hudson's Bay Company to promote settlement. The company had already established a major fur-trading post on the southern tip of the island in 1843, and the discovery of coal on the east coast led to the founding of Nanaimo in 1852. But by the mid-1850s, the company had exerted little effort to add to the population of approximately 1,000 on Vancouver Island and 200 on the mainland, in addition to upwards of 60,000 Native people in the region.

The discovery of gold in the Fraser River valley in 1858, just as the boom in California was subsiding, brought a rush of some 25,000 fortune-seekers into the region. Concerned about an American threat to British sovereignty and the danger of a clash with the Native peoples, James Douglas, governor of Vancouver Island and chief administrator of the Hudson's Bay Company, responded decisively by asserting his authority over the mainland. The imperial authority then established a separate Crown colony of British Columbia on the mainland, with Douglas as governor. When the gold rush moved into the Caribou region in the early 1860s, Douglas arranged for the construction of a 400-mile road along the Fraser Canyon to open up the southern interior. The gold rush soon ended and most of the Americans departed, leaving both Vancouver Island and British Columbia so economically depressed that the two colonies decided to unite in 1866.

The northward advance of the American western frontier gave every indication that the Red River colony and British Columbia would eventually go the way of the Oregon Territory. After serving as an agent of the British Empire for nearly half a century, the Hudson's Bay Company was no longer able or willing to resist the mounting pressure of settlement. More interested in pursuing the fur trade in the northern forests of Rupert's Land, the company was willing to sell the fertile southern plains by the early 1860s, but Canada would not yet agree to pay for land that it claimed as its own and which it could not yet settle in the absence of any system of communication. While Canada aspired to build the vital transportation linkages to develop and defend the British Northwest, the province remained politically paralyzed by persistent sectional and racial discontent.

CANADIAN SECTIONALISM AND POLITICAL DEADLOCK

Sectional division was an inherent feature of the ill-conceived union of the Canadas in 1841. The provision for equal sectional representation in the Act of Union, instead of accelerating the planned assimilation of the French, created a quasi-federal system of government that enabled Canada East to retain its distinctive laws, religion, language, and culture dating back to the Quebec Act of 1774. Within the sectionalized provincial legislature, the French were able to counter the assimilationist goals of union and emerge as a powerful force by consistently voting as a solid political bloc, in contrast to the divisive tendencies within the English-speaking political alignments. The high tide of political unity in the Province of Canada was reached with the formation of the Baldwin-Lafontaine Reform coalition, which brought together the majority political groups of the English and French cultural communities in 1848. The success of the Baldwin-Lafontaine administration in achieving responsible government demonstrated the practical desirability of forming a cabinet based on the principles of dual premiership and double majority. However, these principles would prove to be unworkable in the wake of the heated sectional and racial antagonism of the 1850s.

Ironically, after serving as a rallying point, the achievement of responsible government became a source of renewed political division. Whereas Baldwin and Lafontaine viewed responsible government as a constitutional end in itself, English and French radical reformers regarded it as a means to achieve further political change. Urged on by the return of Mackenzie and Papineau from political exile, the radicals demanded the full application of American-style democracy with its penchant for elective institutions. Furthermore, liberal attacks on the Catholic Church in Europe during the revolutions of 1848–49 inspired the radicals to advocate the separation of church and state. This resurgent radicalism eroded the strength of the reform coalition, and the retirement of Baldwin and Lafontaine from politics in 1851 unleashed new forces of factionalism in both sections of the province.

In Canada West, political radicalism found its most vocal expression in the "Clear Grit" movement, which derived its main support from the rapidly growing agrarian hinterland west of Toronto. In pressing for more democracy, the Clear Grits focused their attention on the emerging issue of representation by population. The census of 1851–52 (the first decennial census in Canadian history) revealed that the population of Canada West for the first time surpassed that of Canada East by 952,000 to 890,000; by 1861 the gap had widened as Canada West had 1.4 million inhabitants compared to 1.1 million for Canada East. Now it was Canada West's turn to complain about the unfairness of the union, and the Clear Grits led the charge. The Clear Grits also took the lead in the demand for the secularization of clergy reserves. A decade previously, Lord Sydenham had arranged for the proceeds from the sale of clergy reserves to be divided among the leading churches, with the Anglican Church still being favored. The insistence of the Clear Grits that these funds be used to support a public education system became the basis for a final settlement of this issue in 1854.

On the issue of separation of church and state, the Clear Grits had a potent ally in George Brown, owner of the Toronto *Globe*, the most influential Canadian newspaper. A staunch Presbyterian, Brown entered politics as a moderate reformer in 1851 to campaign against Anglican privileges. Brown and the Clear Grits became severely agitated over the passage of the Common Schools Acts of 1853 and 1855, which established a system of state-supported Catholic schools for Canada West on the strength of French votes in Canada East. Outraged at this apparent French domination of the union, Brown decided to support the Clear Grits in their demand for representation by population. Despite this support for "rep by pop," Brown remained devoted to the British constitution and the imperial connection, strongly opposing the Clear Grits's preference for American-style democracy. Brown and the Clear Grits also found common ground in their opposition to government financial support for the Montreal-based Grand Trunk Railway. Nevertheless, he strongly disagreed with those Clear Grits who advocated the dissolution of the union of the Canadas to remedy the political underrepresentation of the western section. As a businessman, Brown believed in the unity of the St. Lawrence economy, and his objection to the Grand Trunk was that it promoted the interests of Montreal over those of Toronto. He regarded the Northern Railway project, which served the interests of Toronto's rising business community, as being more deserving of public support.

Indeed, while the Montreal promoters of the Grand Trunk Railway were engaged in a futile attempt to capture the trade of the American Midwest, Brown and the Clear Grits were turning their attention to the prospects of developing the British Northwest. The desire of the Clear Grits to access a new agrarian frontier merged with the interests of Brown and the Northern Railway promoters to make Toronto the entrepôt of trade between the British Northwest and either London (England) or New York. In 1857 Brown persuaded the Clear Grits to drop their interest in American democratic ideas and dissolution of the union of the Canadas and to join forces with his own supporters of moderate reform to pursue the annexation of the British Northwest to Canada West and representation by population within the context of a British parliamentary system. This new Reform coalition emerged as the strongest political grouping in Canada West and would become the basis of the future Liberal Party.

The chief opposition to Brown and the Clear Grits in the realigned politics of Canada West was a new alliance consisting of Baldwin reform supporters led by Francis Hincks and moderate Tory or Conservative followers of William Draper under the direction of Kingston lawyer John A. Macdonald. Tending to draw its electoral support from districts east of Toronto, this political grouping not only objected to Clear Grit radicalism but also shared an affinity for business development and railway-building. A special interest in the Grand Trunk Railway and St. Lawrence commercial development enabled Hincks and Macdonald to cultivate new allies within the English-speaking business community of Canada East, where political alignments were also shifting dramatically.

After the achievement of responsible government, the French reformers who followed Lafontaine did not fragment to the same extent as did Baldwin supporters in Canada West. A small group of radicals, known as the Parti Rouge (the Red Party), under the leadership of A. A. Dorion, sought to revive the traditions of Papineau's Parti Patriote. Inspired by republicanism in the United States and France, the Rouges were the leading supporters of the Annexation Manifesto of 1849, which temporarily cast them in a strange alliance with some disgruntled members of the Montreal English-speaking business elite. Advocating dissolution of the Union of the Canadas while attacking the British connection, Rouges nationalists could be considered the forerunners of the Quebec separatist movement. They were also highly critical of the close links between government and business, focusing particularly on dealings with the Grand Trunk Railway. Their persistent anticlerical outbursts upset the Catholic Church and invariably alienated many of the French voters whose electoral tendencies were influenced from the pulpit. Consequently, unlike their western radical counterparts, the Rouges never succeeded in becoming a political force in Canada East.

The politics of Canada East continued to be dominated by the moderate French reform bloc, which by the early 1850s was known as the Parti Bleu (the Blue Party) under the leadership of George Étienne Cartier. Wishing to conserve their favorable position within the union in the face of resurgent radicalism, the Bleus reached a unique accommodation with English-speaking Tories from both sections of the province. For this accord to work, the St. Lawrence Tories had to accept the survival of the French Catholic society that they had formerly condemned as disloyal and had long sought to assimilate. Likewise, the French had to shed their resistance to English commercial enterprise, and their support for the abolition of the obsolete seigneurial system in 1854 epitomized their growing reconciliation with modern capitalism. Despite forming the largest political bloc in the united provincial legislature, the Bleus needed Tory support to form a majority government and thus to pass legislation that would protect French cultural rights. For their part, the Tories, who represented a minority in both sections of the legislature, needed French support to carry out their railway schemes for the St. Lawrence route. Both the Bleus and the English-speaking Tories also agreed that their respective interests could best be served by opposing representation by population. Following the election of 1854, which confirmed the disintegration of the old Baldwin-Lafontaine Reform alliance, Macdonald and Cartier officially engineered the formation of a Liberal-Conservative coalition ministry that eventually evolved into the Conservative Party.

The realignment of political forces during the 1850s was achieved at the expense of government stability. A persistent difficulty was the inability of any governing political group or party to maintain majority support from both sections. The Conservatives under Cartier and Macdonald were dominant in Canada East but could not attract more than a minority of voters in Canada West. The alliance of Brown and the Clear Grits, which was becoming increasingly known as the Liberal Reformers, held a solid majority of electoral support in Canada West but could not sustain more than a loose coalition with Dorion's Rouges, which were in the distinct minority in Canada East. For example, a Brown-Dorion ministry lasted scarcely three days in 1858. Complicating the political picture in a time when party lines were still somewhat blurred was the prevalence of independent legislative members, or "loose fish," whose loyalties would shift with the winds of special concessions and privileges. This precarious balance of political forces left government at the mercy of shifting allegiances and opinions on an issue-by-issue basis, with the result that the four provincial elections from 1854 to 1864 produced no less than 10 short-lived government ministries.

The persistent sectional conflict, which rendered the Canadian union virtually unworkable, motivated a search for alternatives other than the mere dissolution advocated by the more radical elements among the Clear Grits and the Rouges. To restore a stronger measure of separation between Canada West and Canada East, Rouges leader Dorion first proposed to the Legislative Assembly a full application of the federal principle to the existing union in 1856. Under a federal union, matters of local concern would be addressed by legislatures ruled by each sectional majority, while matters relating to the whole province would be handled by a general parliament based on representation by population. In 1858 Galt convinced Macdonald and Cartier to pursue a federal union of all the British North American colonies in order to facilitate the building of an intercolonial railway connecting Canada with the Maritime colonies via the Grand Trunk. In the following year, George Brown persuaded his Clear Grit allies to abandon their dissolutionist tendencies and accept a federal union of the Canadas under representation by population in anticipation that Canada West would dominate such an arrangement through its annexation of the Northwest. The British government was mostly unresponsive to such proposals because they appeared to be factional initiatives that did not yet have widespread support in all the colonies.

Thus, by the early 1860s, the convergence of several problems—political and sectional deadlock within Canada, the financial burden of railway-building, the growing urgency of western expansion, imminent commercial upheaval likely to follow the abrogation of the Reciprocity Treaty, and the troublesome question of defense in the wake of the British military withdrawal from North America and the revival of annexationist sentiment in the United States during the Civil War—was driving the Province of Canada not only to reconsider the legislative union of 1841 but also to develop its relationship with neighboring British North American colonies. The solution pointed to some form of federal union involving all the British North American provinces, and as the largest province and the one most seriously affected by these concerns, Canada would have to assume the initiative to persuade its reluctant neighbors to become partners in a great national experiment.

TOWARD A RELUCTANT PARTNERSHIP

Political deadlock in the Canadian legislature reached a climax in June 1864 with the defeat of the fourth ministry in a span of three years. Averting the prospect of a third election in as many years, Brown agreed to join Macdonald and Cartier to form the Great Coalition.

This historic alliance brought together the leaders of the largest political blocs from each section—Brown in Canada West and Cartier in Canada East—with the master political strategist of the era, Macdonald, to form a powerful governing force that had the capacity to end more than a decade of sectional deadlock and to fulfill the ambitions of the Province of Canada. The coalition government resolved to work toward achieving a federal union of all the British North American colonies and, if this effort failed, to settle for a federation of the two Canadas with a provision to include the West. The first course of action represented the Conservative proposal made by Galt in 1858, while the alternative embodied the plan devised by Brown and the Clear Grit Reformers in 1859.

At Brown's insistence, the coalition agreed that the new federation in whatever form it ultimately took would be governed on the basis of representation by population. Despite long-standing and vigorous objection, Cartier conceded the principle of representation primarily because he believed that under federalism the French language and religious and legal rights could be protected by a French-controlled provincial government. In fact, Cartier won over those who might have been tempted to support Dorion by arguing that federation would give French Canadians their own government with the power to legislate over matters that would ensure cultural survival and local development. Although he did not express it in those precise terms, Cartier appealed to notions of French Canada as a distinct society originally embodied in the Quebec Act of 1774. Besides, Cartier realized that, within a larger federation involving the Maritimes and the West, the French-Canadian propensity to vote as a cultural bloc would be advantageous in contrast to the diverse regional and political interests of the English-speaking provinces.

For Macdonald and his English-speaking followers, the new federation ensured the unity of the St. Lawrence economy and opened up prospects for its expansion. Macdonald's Conservatives had been more interested in a scheme encompassing union with the Maritimes and the building of the vital Intercolonial Railway link, whereas Brown's Liberals were more focused on western expansion. But recently, the Grand Trunk Railway supporters had developed a more profound interest in the prospects of British northwestern rather than American midwestern expansion. In 1861 Edward Watkin, representing the major British investors in the Grand Trunk, investigated the company's "organized mess" and reported that for the railway to pay off in the long run it would have to be extended eastward and westward to become a transcontinental line carrying trade from the Atlantic to the Pacific. Thus, the vision of Canada as an entrepôt of trade between Europe and the interior of North America was replaced by an even more grandiose dream of Canada as the commercial intermediary between Europe and Asia.

To follow up on this recommendation, Watkin organized other Grand Trunk investors to purchase a controlling interest in the Hudson's Bay Company in 1863, with the intention of opening up its western lands so that construction of the railway linking Canada to the Pacific could soon begin. However, a sectionally divided Canada remained unwilling and indeed unable to meet the asking price to acquire the Hudson's Bay Company domain and to support the building of a railway across the western plains and the Rocky Mountains. While the formation of the Great Coalition of 1864 was a step in the right direction, only a larger union of British North American colonies could command sufficient credit in the international financial markets to undertake such an ambitious scheme of transcontinental expansion.

The possibilities of a transcontinental railway network to link a united British North America aroused the interest of the imperial authority for defensive reasons. Opening the West to Canada and building a Pacific railway connection to transport settlers and

The architects of the Great Coalition, which made Confederation possible: John A. Macdonald (1815–91), Canada's first prime minister after Confederation (upper left), as photographed by the Notman Studio (Ottawa) in 1872; George Étienne Cartier (1814–73), who led Quebec into Confederation (upper right); and George Brown (1818–80), the owner of the influential Globe *newspaper, who envisioned Confederation as the key to western expansion.*

soldiers might save the region from advancing American settlement. An intercolonial railway would help to alleviate the dangerous weakness revealed during the so-called Trent Affair of 1861. In the early stages of the American Civil War, the North suspected Britain of being sympathetic to the South because it was a vital source of cotton for the British textile industry. Anglo-American tension reached its height when a Northern warship intercepted the British steamer *Trent* on the high seas and forcibly removed two southern agents on their way to England to generate more support for their cause. Indignant over this violation of freedom of the seas and anticipating war, Britain dispatched more than 10,000 reinforcements to defend Canada in the event of an American attack. The American government recognized the folly of fighting with the leading world power in the midst of its own Civil War and expeditiously freed the envoys, thereby ending the military crisis. Nevertheless, when the British troops arrived, the St. Lawrence was already frozen over, and the only railway link to Canada was on American soil through Portland, Maine, via the old St. Lawrence and Atlantic line that had been absorbed by the Grand Trunk. The need to undertake a winter trek overland in sleighs through New Brunswick demonstrated the strategic value of the proposed intercolonial railway and prompted the British government to reconsider its commitment to colonial defense.

Besides being a financial burden that the free traders wanted to eliminate, colonial defense was a potential source of embarrassment if ever Britain was to suffer defeat at the hands of the United States because it could not adequately protect its North American interests. Britain, therefore, began to exert strong pressure for a union of the British North American colonies so that they could assume more of the burden of defending themselves against the United States. For this reason, above all, the imperial authorities welcomed the formation of the Great Coalition and its initiative to negotiate a union with the Maritime colonies.

Nova Scotia, New Brunswick, and Prince Edward Island were already planning a meeting to discuss the prospects of a Maritime union. Accordingly, a delegation from the Province of Canada attended a meeting at Charlottetown, Prince Edward Island, in September 1864 to propose a federal union of British North America. Sufficient progress was made at the Charlottetown Conference to warrant postponement of the Maritime union discussion until after another meeting with the Canadians the following month at Quebec City. Over a period of slightly more than two weeks, the Quebec Conference proved to be decisive in drawing up 72 resolutions that laid the foundation for a new national constitution.

The first principle of unity was federalism. The Maritime and French-Canadian delegates insisted on a federal union so that their respective identities would not be submerged. Mindful that the Civil War in the United States was about to enter its fourth brutal year, the Canadian and Maritime delegates agreed on a strong central government to avoid the apparent mistakes of the United States Constitution in giving the states too much power. In contrast, the new central government was granted residual powers—that is, all powers not specifically assigned to the provinces. In addition, the power of disallowance gave the central authority the right to reject provincial laws of which it did not approve. The central government would consist of an elected body based on representation by population and an appointed body based on equal regional representation. The smaller Maritime Provinces saw the appointed branch of government as a means of offsetting their numerical weakness in the elected branch. Because it would assume all existing provincial debts and the cost of building the intercolonial railway along with such major expenditures as administration and defense, the central government was allowed unlimited taxing powers, including the collection of direct and indirect taxes such as customs and excise duties, which were among the main sources of revenue at that time. The provinces were restricted to levying only direct taxes but were to be compensated for the cost of education, roads, and other local responsibilities with an annual subsidy from the central government amounting to 80 cents per capita. The provinces could raise additional revenue by selling their natural resources, such as public lands, minerals, and waterpower.

The Canadian and Maritime delegates adjourned the Quebec Conference with the understanding that they would not risk subjecting the draft constitution to popular approval. Instead, they decided to follow the British procedure of ratification by provincial legislatures. In essence, the aversion to direct democracy was based on the concern that the people might not share the vision of their political leaders.

The Quebec Resolutions were debated in the Legislative Assembly of the United Province of Canada in February 1865. Relatively little criticism was expressed by members from the western section. In Canada East, however, the Rouges led by Dorion strongly opposed the resolutions, arguing that a true "confederation" was based on the supremacy of local over central authority, that such a monumental scheme should be subject to electoral approval, and that the proposed union was merely "a Grand Trunk job." The final vote taken in early March appeared decisive: 91 in favor and 33 opposed. But the vote among the French-Canadian members present was considerably closer: 27 in favor and 21 opposed. Thus, French Canada embraced nationhood, but with some serious reservations.

Support for the Quebec Resolutions in the Atlantic Provinces was even more precarious than it was in French Canada. Prince Edward Island rejected Confederation outright because it did nothing to resolve the long-standing absentee landlord issue; it left the tiny province with little, if any, power in the central Parliament; and it offered a railway link with Canada that was of little interest to the inhabitants. Newfoundland was completely indifferent to the idea of uniting with distant Canada, since most of the island's population and economic activity were focused on the far eastern coast and therefore oriented toward Britain. In Nova Scotia, Premier Charles Tupper's attempts to gain support for Confederation were countered by Joseph Howe, who argued that the province would be more likely to keep its identity and to enjoy more prosperity by remaining within a great empire than by joining a dubious experiment in nationhood. Not only did Tupper avoid Howe's challenge to call an election on the issue, he did not even dare to bring the Quebec Resolutions to a vote in the provincial legislature. Indeed, Confederation could have proceeded without the support of any of these three provinces, although the involvement of Nova Scotia was considered more highly desirable.

Without the support of New Brunswick, however, the Confederation scheme embodied in the Quebec Resolutions would have disintegrated, principally because a railway connection to an ice-free winter port had to pass through the province whether the terminal was Halifax or Saint John. Premier Leonard Tilley succumbed to pressure to call an election on the issue of Confederation. His opponent, A. J. Smith, pointed out that New Brunswick's trade flowed in a north-south rather than an east-west direction, particularly since the Reciprocity Treaty of 1854. Therefore, he proposed a provincial railway that linked up with Maine as a more viable alternative to the intercolonial railway. In the election campaign of March 1865, the pro-Confederation forces under Tilley were soundly defeated, thereby leaving the plan for nationhood in serious jeopardy.

At this critical juncture, the renewal of the American threat proved to be a convenient factor in turning the tide in favor of Confederation. The end of the American Civil War in the spring of 1865 raised concern that the victorious Union army, then the largest in the world, would be free to turn its aggression toward Canada as a measure of retaliation against Britain. In fact, some of its discharged soldiers were recruited by the Fenian Brotherhood, a fanatical republican Irish group dedicated to capturing the British North American colonies and using them as ransom to negotiate with the British government for the liberation of Ireland. Although the Fenian raids of New Brunswick in April 1866 and of the Niagara frontier of Canada West less than two months later featured only sporadic fighting,

JOHN A. MACDONALD SPEAKS IN THE CANADIAN LEGISLATURE ABOUT THE NEED FOR A FEDERAL UNION OF BRITISH NORTH AMERICA

The . . . only means of solution for our difficulties was the junction of the provinces either in a Federal or a Legislative union. Now, as regards the comparative advantages of a Legislative and a Federal union, I have never hesitated to state my own opinions. I have again and again stated in the House, that, if practicable, I thought a Legislative union would be preferable. (Hear, hear.) I have always contended that if we could agree to have one government and one parliament, legislating for the whole of these peoples, it would be the best, the cheapest, the most vigorous, and the strongest system of government we could adopt. (Hear, hear.) But, on looking at the subject in the Conference, and discussing the matter as we did, most unreservedly, and with a desire to arrive at a satisfactory conclusion, we found that such a system was impracticable. In the first place, it would not meet the assent of the people of Lower Canada, because they felt that in their peculiar position—being in a minority, with a different language, nationality and religion from the majority,—in case of a junction with the other provinces, their institutions and their laws might be assailed, and their ancestral associations, on which they prided themselves, attacked and prejudiced; it was found that any proposition which involved the absorption of the individuality of Lower Canada—if I may use the expression—would not be received with favor by her people. We found too, that though their people speak the same language and enjoy the same system of law as the people of Upper Canada, a system founded on the common law of England, there was as great a disinclination on the part of the various Maritime Provinces to lose their individuality, as separate political organizations, as we observed in the case of Lower Canada herself. (Hear, hear.) Therefore, we were forced to the conclusion that we must either abandon the idea of Union altogether, or devise a system of union in which the separate provincial organizations would be in some degree preserved. . . .

GEORGE ÉTIENNE CARTIER SPEAKS ABOUT HIS PREFERENCE FOR A BRITISH NORTH AMERICAN RATHER THAN A CANADIAN FEDERATION AND HIS VISION OF A NEW "POLITICAL NATIONALITY"

. . . representation by population, though unsuited for application as a governing principle as between the two provinces, would not involve the same objection if other partners were drawn in by a federation. In a struggle between two—one a weak, and the other a strong party—the weaker could not but be overcome; but if three parties were concerned, the stronger would not have the same advantage; as when it was seen by the third that there was too much strength on one side, the third would club with the weaker combatant to resist the big fighter. (Cheers and laughter.). . . .

The question for us to ask ourselves was this: Shall we be content to remain separate—shall we be content to maintain a mere provincial existence, when, by combining together, we could become a great nation? . . . Now, when we were united together, if union were attained, we would form a political nationality with which neither the national origin, nor the religion of any individual, would interfere. It was lamented by some that we had this diversity of races, and hopes were expressed that this distinctive feature would cease. . . . We could not do away with the distinctions of race. We could not legislate for the disappearance of the French Canadians from American soil, but British and French Canadians alike could appreciate and understand their position relative to each other. They were placed like great families beside each other, and their contact produced a healthy spirit of emulation. It was a benefit rather than otherwise that we had a diversity of races. . . .

they intensified fears of an American invasion that were already fueled by the revival of annexationist sentiment directed toward Canada and the British Northwest. In December 1865 the United States Congress had further undermined relations with British North America by legislating the end of the Reciprocity Treaty, to become effective March 1866.

The Fenian threat, coupled with the collapse of Premier Smith's railway link with Maine in the wake of the demise of reciprocity, gave New Brunswick Governor Arthur Gordon the opportunity to maneuver the anti-Confederation administration out of office. In the subsequent election campaign, Tilley benefited from the generous financial support of the Canadian government and the Grand Trunk Railway to sweep back into power. He then successfully engineered the Quebec Resolutions through the provincial legislature in time to join his Canadian colleagues at the London Conference to finalize the Confederation agreement in December 1866. Tilley's victory also enabled Tupper to get support from the Nova Scotia legislature to send delegates to the London conference.

GEORGE BROWN (WHO FORMED
THE GREAT COALITION WITH MACDONALD AND CARTIER)
EXPLAINS HIS SUPPORT FOR CONFEDERATION

Mr. Speaker, I go heartily for the union, because it will throw down the barriers of trade and give us the control of a market of four millions of people. (Hear, hear.) What one thing has contributed so much to the wondrous material progress of the United States as the free passage of their products from one State to another? What has tended so much to the rapid advance of all branches of their industry, as the vast extent of their home market, creating an unlimited demand for all the commodities of daily use, and stimulating the energy and ingenuity of producers? . . . But here, sir, is a proposal which is to add, in one day, near a million of souls to our population—to add valuable territories to our domain, and secure to us all the advantages of a large and profitable commerce, now existing. And because some of us would have liked certain of the little details otherwise arranged, we are to hesitate in accepting this alliance! (Hear, hear.). . . .

Sir, the future destiny of these great provinces may be affected by the decision we are about to give to an extent which at this moment we may be unable to estimate—but assuredly the welfare for many years of four millions of people hangs on our decision. (Hear, hear.) Shall we then rise equal to the occasion?—shall we approach this discussion without partisanship, and free from every personal feeling but the earnest resolution to discharge conscientiously the duty which an overruling Providence has placed upon us? Sir, it may be that some among us will live to see the day when, as the result of this measure, a great and powerful people may have grown up in these lands—when the boundless forests all around us shall have given way to smiling fields and thriving towns—and when one united government, under the British flag, shall extend from shore to shore.

At the London Conference, the Quebec Resolutions were only slightly modified to include protection for existing separate school rights; increased provincial subsidies; the designation of the union as a "confederation" rather than a "federation"; the renaming of Canada East and Canada West as Quebec and Ontario, respectively; and changing the name of the new nation from the Kingdom of Canada to the Dominion of Canada. Even while the terms of Confederation were being finalized in London, Joseph Howe appealed to British officials in London to reject the union on the grounds that it was being forced against the popular will. The British government ignored him, and the British North America Act passed through Parliament without much notice in March 1867. Indeed, Howe's Nova Scotia delegates commented bitterly on the limited attention devoted to the act in the House of Commons compared to the vigor with which the members participated in the debate on a new dog tax immediately afterward. On July 1, 1867, the colonial age of British North America came to an end, and the provinces of Nova Scotia, New Brunswick, Quebec, and Ontario officially united to form a new nation known as the Dominion of Canada.

Confederation was effectively a marriage of economic and political convenience between partners who had little desire to live together but could not afford to live apart. The reluctance with which the British North American colonies entered into their national partnership foreshadowed the persistence of the regional and cultural discontent that would characterize Canada's development in the last third of the 19th century and throughout the 20th century. Despite the precarious foundation of unity, Canada would manage not only to survive as an independent nation in the shadow of a mighty southern neighbor but also to fulfill the transcontinental ambitions expressed in its motto, adopted from Psalm 72: *A Mari Usque Ad Mare*—"From Sea to Sea."

PART FOUR

THE FOUNDATIONS OF CANADIAN NATIONHOOD 1867–1931

CHAPTER 11

NATION-BUILDING ASPIRATIONS AND STRATEGIES

In 1867 the new Dominion of Canada rested on a precarious foundation of nationhood. The British North America Act established a federal constitution uniting only four provinces—New Brunswick, Nova Scotia, Ontario, and Quebec—with a total population of less than 3.5 million, more than three-quarters of which was concentrated in the St. Lawrence Valley and the Great Lakes basin. Fearing American expansionism, the federal government led by Sir John A. Macdonald, Canada's first prime minister, moved decisively to acquire the North-West Territories from the Hudson's Bay Company and to persuade British Columbia and Prince Edward Island to join Confederation. Although Canada had become a transcontinental nation by 1873, its growth—indeed its survival—would depend on the development of a viable economic strategy that could maintain the fragile union of widely dispersed and divergent provinces. The hopes and aspirations of the struggling nation would ultimately rest on Macdonald's National Policy, which consisted of a protective industrial tariff, a transcontinental railway system, and the settlement of the West.

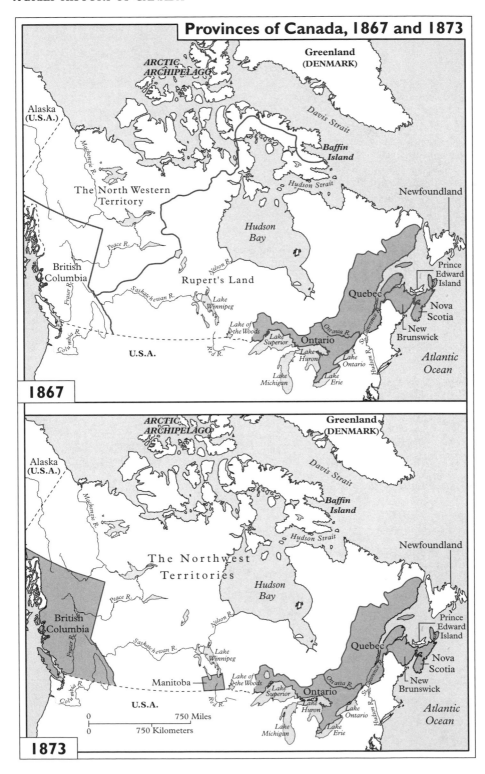

Provinces of Canada, 1867 and 1873

1867

1873

A BRITISH AMERICAN CONSTITUTION

Consistent with the basic character of the new nation, the Canadian constitution was a unique blend of British and American influences. The British political heritage was reflected in the preamble to the British North America Act of 1867, which expressed a desire for "a Constitution similar in Principle to that of the United Kingdom" with its unwritten tradition of governance resting on accumulated prerogatives, conventions, customs, statutes, and judicial decisions responding to changing requirements of government and society. Moreover, the union of provinces into a national political structure was legally enacted by the authority of the imperial Parliament rather than being established by a compact between independent states, as in the American case. Thus, the power to alter the constitution remained in the hands of the imperial authority, although it would be used only at Canadian request.

The realities of the North American environment, however, required a fusion of British parliamentary governance with American-style federalism. Since Canada was to have the first federal structure of government within the British Empire, the architects of Confederation naturally looked for guidance to the United States Constitution. Accordingly, they opted to have most of the provisions for the distribution of powers between the federal and provincial governments specifically written into the British North America Act. In essence, many of the principles and practices embodied in Canada's original national constitution reflected both admiration for and reservations about the political institutions of the powerful neighbor to the south.

The interplay of British and American influences in general and the written and unwritten nature of the Canadian constitution in particular is glaringly apparent in the provisions for executive and legislative power. The British North America Act declared executive power "to continue . . . to be vested in the Queen." In affirming the principle of monarchy as a traditional source of authority and stability, the Canadian constitution rejected the American system of an elected chief executive officer (the president) in favor of a head of state who was above party politics. The Crown would be represented in Canada by the governor-general upon whom the act appeared to assign almost autocratic power to exert influence in Canadian affairs in the interests of the British monarchy. The governor-general represented the might and splendor of the empire to which Canada still belonged and thus was subject to British laws in matters of defense and foreign affairs. But in reality, the executive authority of the monarchy established in the written constitution was largely overridden by the unwritten British constitutional practice of responsible government in local affairs, which the colonies had achieved in the 1840s and 1850s. In matters not affecting the empire, executive power actually rested with the prime minister and the Cabinet (formerly known as the Executive Council), even though neither are mentioned in the British North America Act. As Canada gradually asserted its national autonomy from Britain, the power of the governor-general would eventually decline to mere symbolic value, while that of the prime minister would ironically assume a quasi-presidential role in the Canadian Parliament.

Legislative power rested with Parliament, which, like its namesake in Britain and like the Congress of the United States, was bicameral in nature. The upper house, known as the Senate, was designed to perform roles similar to both its American and British counterparts. Like its American namesake, the Canadian Senate was supposed to provide a form of equal regional representation to protect the interests of the smaller provinces. But whereas the American Senate was based on the equal representation of every state, the Canadian Senate strove for equal representation of regions, with Ontario and Quebec each having 24 members while the Maritime Provinces of Nova Scotia and New Brunswick each had 12. The principle of equal regional representation was continued as new provinces were added to the Dominion. In another departure from the American Senate, whose members were chosen for six-year terms of office, Canadian senators were appointed by the Crown for life. The Senate resembled the British House of Lords not only in its nonelective and lifetime membership but also in its requirement of a property qualification, which ensured that men of "substance" had a base of power to counter the democratically elected lower house, the House of Commons. In these ways and to the extent that it was expected to review and revise legislation passed by the House of Commons, the Senate was principally a continuation of the old colonial Legislative Council under a new name.

Modeled on its counterpart of the same name in Britain (as was the American congressional House of Representatives), the House of Commons was to continue as the chief lawmaking and taxation body in Parliament, as the colonial Legislative Assembly had done in the past. Representation in the House of Commons was based on population, with the Province of Quebec assigned a fixed number of 65 seats and the other provinces proportionately represented. The House of Commons turned out to be a much more powerful legislative body than the Senate because, in accordance with the established practice of the British parliamentary system, the executive authority of the prime minister and the Cabinet rested solely on the vote of confidence of the lower house and not the upper house. Despite the provisions of the British North America Act, the Senate never took seriously its role as defender of provincial rights; and as the fear of democracy subsided, the upper house lost its relevance as a bastion of property rights. Likewise, the progress of democracy eroded the power of the governor-general, "according to his Discretion," to withhold royal assent of legislation passed by Parliament. Although they possess the power in theory, neither the governor-general nor the Senate would dare to disregard the "will of the people" as expressed through the House of Commons. Indeed, the rise to prominence of the House of Commons in Canadian governance reflected the triumph of the unwritten over the written constitution.

The provinces had much the same structure of parliamentary government as the Dominion. While a lieutenant governor was appointed by the Dominion to represent the Crown in the province and to preside formally over the provincial parliaments or legislatures, executive authority practically resided in the prime ministers or premiers (as they became more commonly known), who governed according to the cabinet system. Unlike the federal parliament, all of the provincial legislatures eventually dropped their upper houses and adopted Ontario's single elected chamber structure in a symbolic triumph of democracy over privilege.

With no British precedent to serve as a guide, the relationship between the federal and provincial governments in Canada was largely influenced by American political principle and experience. Like the American federal Constitution established 80 years earlier, the British North America Act specified the distribution of powers between the federal and provincial governments and made the application of these provisions subject to judicial review. However, in reaction to the recent outbreak of the American Civil War, which British and Canadian political leaders believed was caused largely by the struggle over states' rights, the British North America Act departed deliberately and significantly from the American model of federalism by allocating sweeping powers to the central government while assigning only limited powers to the provincial governments.

THE BRITISH NORTH AMERICA ACT, 1867
(30 & 31 VICTORIA, C. 3)

An Act for the Union of Canada, Nova Scotia, and New Brunswick, and the Government thereof: and for Purposes connected therewith. [March 29, 1867.]

Whereas the Provinces of Canada, Nova Scotia, and New Brunswick, have expressed their desire to be federally united into one Dominion under the Crown of the United Kingdom of Great Britain and Ireland, with a Constitution similar in principle to that of the United Kingdom:

And whereas such a Union would conduce to the welfare of the Provinces and promote the interests of the British Empire . . .

Be it therefore enacted and declared by the Queen's most Excellent Majesty, by and with the advice and consent of the Lords Spiritual and Temporal, and Commons, in this present Parliament assembled, and by the authority of the same, as follows: . . .

II. UNION

3. It shall be lawful for the Queen, by and with the advice of Her Majesty's Most Honourable Privy Council, to declare by Proclamation that on and after a day herein appointed, not being more than six months after the passing of this Act, the Provinces of Canada, Nova Scotia, and New Brunswick shall form and be one Dominion under the name of Canada. . . .

6. The parts of the Province of Canada (as it exists at the passing of this Act) which formerly constituted respectively the Provinces of Upper Canada and Lower Canada shall be deemed to be severed, and shall form two separate Provinces. The part which formerly constituted the Province of Upper Canada shall constitute the Province of Ontario, and the part which formerly constituted the Province of Lower Canada shall constitute the Province of Quebec.

VI. DISTRIBUTION OF LEGISLATIVE POWERS
Powers of the Parliament

91. It shall be lawful for the Queen, by and with the advice and consent of the Senate and House of Commons, to make laws for the peace, order, and good government of Canada, in relation to all matters not coming within the classes of subjects by this Act assigned exclusively to the Legislatures of the Provinces. . . . [Twenty-nine specific powers and responsibilities are hereafter enumerated.]
Exclusive Powers of Provincial Legislatures

92. In each Province the Legislature may exclusively make laws in relation to matters coming within the [16] classes of subjects next hereinafter enumerated. . . .

Section 91 of the British North America Act enumerated 29 specific powers of the Dominion government, including jurisdiction over the armed forces, postal service, banking and currency, fisheries, criminal law, the regulation of trade and commerce, the right to raise revenue by direct or indirect taxation, in addition to the general authority "to make laws for the Peace, Order, and Good Government of Canada." Section 92 listed 16 specific powers of the provincial governments, including responsibility for property and civil rights, civil law, municipal government, licences, education, hospitals, charitable institutions, prisons, chartering of companies within the province, and the right to raise revenue by direct taxation, in addition to the general authority over "all matters of a merely local or private nature in the province." To avoid the apparent flaw in the federal system of the United States, which gave "residual" power to the state governments, the British North America Act granted the federal government authority over "all Matters not coming within the Classes of Subjects by this Act assigned exclusively to the Legislatures of the Provinces." Section 95 also strengthened the central government by assigning it "concurrent powers" with the provinces in matters relating to agriculture and immigration, with Dominion legislation prevailing in case of disputes. That the federal government was given the right to name the provincial lieutenant governors and to disallow provincial laws further reflects the intention of the original constitution to create a highly centralized state to which the provinces would be clearly subordinate.

The British North America Act also dealt with other matters such as provisions for the admission of new provinces, the building of the intercolonial railway within six months after union, and the financial terms on which Confederation should operate. The financial arrangements proved to be controversial because, in surrendering to the new national government their right to collect indirect taxes, and particularly to levy customs duties, the provinces lost their main source of revenue. In return, the federal government agreed to assume provincial debts and to pay the provinces an annual subsidy based on the size of their population. The transfer of funds between the federal and provincial governments would be a constant source of contention in Canadian politics.

While it provided the constitutional and political framework for Confederation, the British North America Act could by no means ensure the survival and growth of Canada as a nation. Certainly, the act created the chief instrument for national unity and expansion; the federal government situated in Ottawa. But unless the federal government could extend its jurisdiction over a vast territory beyond the small nucleus of four provinces, the central purpose of Confederation could never be realized.

THE TRANSCONTINENTAL DOMINION

The key strategic objective of Confederation—western expansion—was rendered more urgent by growing American interest in the annexation of the British Northwest, particularly in the aftermath of the purchase of Alaska from Russia in 1867. In the wake of the imminent threat of a peaceful American invasion, evidenced by the activity of Minnesota traders in the Red River colony and the construction of the Northern Pacific Railway linking St. Paul to the West Coast, Toronto business and political leaders continued to press the Canadian government to acquire the North-West Territories, which George Brown had made a major condition for joining the Great Coalition in 1864. With the support of the imperial authority, the Canadian government reached an agreement in 1869 to purchase Rupert's Land, an area 10 times the size of the new nation, from the

Hudson's Bay Company at a cost of $1.5 million. In addition, the company was allowed to retain 45,000 acres of land surrounding its posts and one-twentieth of the "fertile belt" along the North Saskatchewan River.

The Red River colonists resented the fact that they were not consulted about the terms of the transfer of Rupert's Land to Canada, which was to be completed officially on December 1, 1869. While some of the Red River inhabitants hoped eventually to establish a separate colony under British rule, most of them felt immediately uneasy about the agitation of a group of chauvinistic transplanted Ontario settlers who too eagerly anticipated Canadian rule. Particularly alarming was the unexpected appearance of Canadian land surveyors who divided the territory into square lots (standard in Ontario), oblivious to the existing tradition of strip lots that gave inhabitants access to river transport. Amid the impending influx of more English, Protestant settlers from Ontario, the 25,000 Native and 10,000 mixed-race inhabitants of Red River worried about preserving their lifestyle hunting buffalo on the plains. Slightly more numerous among the mixed-race settlers, the French-speaking Métis were also concerned about protecting their French culture and Catholic religion.

The Métis turned for leadership to Louis Riel who, although only 25 years of age, was a fluently bilingual and well-educated spokesman for the rights of the Red River settlers. Resistance to the Dominion government began in October 1869 when Riel and a group of his followers stopped land surveyors near the Red River and then prevented the new Canadian governor, William McDougall, from entering the colony early in anticipation of the official transfer from Hudson's Bay Company rule. Taking advantage of the political vacuum created by the withdrawal of Hudson's Bay Company rule and the delay in the transfer of the territory to Canadian rule, Riel set up a provisional government on December 8, 1869, not only to provide law and order for the colony but also to negotiate local grievances and demands with the Canadian government.

When a small group of Canadians challenged the authority of the provisional government by attempting to attack Fort Garry, the headquarters of the provisional government, Riel became determined to assert his control over the colony by prosecuting one of the more provocative and unruly Canadians, Thomas Scott, a young member of the vehemently anti-Catholic Loyal Orange Order of Ontario. In an improvised court-martial proceeding, Scott was found guilty of hostility toward the provisional government, abuse of prison guards, and inciting other prisoners to violence. For these offenses, Riel ordered him to be executed by firing squad. Despite the ambiguities over who ruled Rupert's Land, Riel clearly lacked the executive authority to assume responsibility for such an act of state violence. This monumental blunder, a product of Riel's political inexperience and emotional instability, in addition to the deep-seated cultural divisions within the young nation, unleashed a storm of anger in Ontario, where residents regarded Scott as a martyr and Riel as a traitor and murderer. By contrast, Quebec regarded Riel as a protector of French, Catholic rights and a distinctive way of life in the West against Anglo-Protestant encroachment.

Within this highly charged political atmosphere, Prime Minister Macdonald endeavored to maintain a spirit of compromise and conciliation as negotiations to secure Rupert's Land under Canadian control proceeded. While he refused to recognize the Red River delegates as agents of a legally constituted government, he did accept them as representatives of the people of Red River. Agreement was reached for the colony to enter the Dominion as a province and for Riel to relinquish his authority to a lieutenant governor to be appointed by the Canadian government. On May 12, 1870, the federal government passed the Manitoba Act, which embodied most of the demands of Riel's provisional government and confirmed that the Red

River settlement would become the Province of Manitoba effective July 15, 1870. The powers and responsibilities of the British North America Act applied to Canada's fifth province, except that, unlike the other four provinces, its public land remained under the control of the Dominion government as was that of the rest of the North-West Territories, which was to be governed by a federally appointed governor and council.

While Manitoba's entry into Confederation satisfied the Métis and the French Canadians of Quebec, Macdonald sought to placate Ontario by dispatching a military expedition of 1,200 men under General Garnet Wolseley to restore law and order in the North-West Territories. The three-month trek across the rugged Shield and through American territory revealed the precariousness of the Canadian hold on its frontier west of Lake Superior. Fearing punishment, Riel fled to the United States, leaving behind a mixed legacy. Although his leadership had compelled the Canadian government to recognize the existence of the Red River community, the tragedy of ethnic and religious antagonism that accompanied the establishment of Manitoba would have enduring repercussions for a culturally divided nation.

Canada's acquisition of the vast North-West Territories from the Hudson's Bay Company opened up the prospect for bringing the distant province of British Columbia into Confederation, thereby linking the Atlantic and Pacific coasts. Indeed, in an effort to overcome post–gold rush economic stagnation and geographical isolation, the legislature of British Columbia had passed a resolution favoring a union with Canada in 1867. Nothing came of it, however, since Hudson's Bay Company control of the prairies made such a political connection virtually impossible. A more viable option appeared to be annexation to the United States since the population on the mainland was dominated by Americans who had arrived during the recent gold rush, and many of them had developed strong commercial ties with the northwestern states. Not only was British Columbia's transportation and communication network well integrated with the Pacific coastal ports to the south but the completion of the American Union Pacific Railway line in 1869 provided the province with its first links to the Atlantic seaboard. By contrast, the province had no links with Canada and only limited contact with Britain by sea around the tip of South America.

Nevertheless, significant British political and military influences were working in Canada's favor. Despite pressure from the Hudson's Bay Company to maintain British Columbia as a Crown colony under a governor and representative government, Britain wanted to lessen its naval and administrative commitments on the Pacific coast without leaving the colony vulnerable to American expansionist ambitions. Accordingly, in 1869 the British government appointed former Newfoundland governor Anthony Musgrave to serve as governor of British Columbia with instructions to advance the pro-Confederation movement led by businessman John Robson and journalist William Alexander Smith (who had legally changed his name to Amor de Cosmos in 1854). Once the transfer of Rupert's Land from the Hudson's Bay Company to Canada was completed in 1870, Governor Musgrave appointed a delegation to negotiate union with Canada. To join Confederation, British Columbia demanded that Canada assume the colony's $1 million debt, implement responsible government, undertake a public works program, and complete a road linking the isolated region to the rest of the country. Negotiating on behalf of the Dominion government, George Étienne Cartier did not merely agree to these demands but also gave British Columbia control over Crown land within the province and promised the construction of a railroad linkage with Canada to be completed within 10 years. The ambitious promise of a railroad in particular silenced any talk of annexation, and British Columbia became Canada's sixth province on July 20, 1871.

With its transcontinental ambitions realized, Canada could focus more attention on luring the remaining Atlantic holdouts into Confederation. Despite hosting the original Confederation conference at Charlottetown in 1864, Prince Edward Island had rejected union with Canada because of its dissatisfaction with the proposed financial terms and its preference for the prospect of economic union with the United States. Prince Edward Island hoped to negotiate a reciprocity agreement with the United States in return for the continued right of American fishermen to operate in island waters. Fearing the possible loss of Prince Edward Island to the Americans, Prime Minister Macdonald in 1869 offered the province more generous financial terms than had been proposed five years previously, in addition to improved transportation and communication linkages with the mainland and assistance in buying out the remaining British absentee landowners who still dominated the island. Although the offer was not immediately accepted, by the early 1870s failure to negotiate a free trade agreement with the Americans, continued economic stagnation, and the threat of provincial bankruptcy as a result of overly ambitious railway-building schemes induced Prince Edward Island to reconsider. Thus, on July 1, 1873, Prince Edward Island became Canada's seventh province.

The transcontinental territorial expansion of the Dominion of Canada (excluding Newfoundland) was completed in July 1880 when Britain, which had claimed ownership of the Arctic archipelago by virtue of discovery and exploration, transferred the northern region to Canada. The scattered colonies of British North America had evolved into the second-largest nation in the world, and the challenge ahead for Canada was to unite politically, economically, and socially this vast domain extending from the Atlantic to the Pacific and to the Arctic Oceans.

THE EMERGENCE OF NATIONAL PARTY POLITICS

The establishment of a national constitution and territorial expansion across the continent profoundly changed the nature and scope of politics in the former British North American colonies. Whereas political life before Confederation had featured localized factionalism and minimal interaction between colonial administrations, the creation of a national government in 1867 focused politics on Ottawa and its relations to the provincial capitals. When chosen by Lord Monck, Canada's first governor-general, to serve as interim prime minister until the first national election could be held in the late summer of 1867, Macdonald expressed a desire for a truly national government unencumbered by partisan political division. Accordingly, his first Cabinet was a coalition of representatives from different regions, cultures, religions, and economic interests. Nevertheless, the politically crafty Macdonald could not resist the temptation to follow the long-standing political tradition of awarding the more powerful positions in the government and the federal bureaucracy to his supporters and favorites. So, as differing concepts of national development began to emerge, various political factions that existed prior to Confederation soon coalesced into two major parties—the Conservatives and the Liberals—with representation and organization throughout the nation.

During the first national election campaign of 1867, the nascent Conservative Party led by Macdonald was successful in presenting itself as the architect and defender of a highly centralized federal union which was essential to fulfil its ambitious plan of nation-building "from sea to sea." The promise to link British Columbia to Canada by a railway within 10 years reflected the Conservative devotion to transcontinental expansion expeditiously and at whatever cost. Macdonald understood that the key to accomplishing his nation-building goals and to sustaining Conservative hegemony was to consolidate the political partnership between the Anglo business community and the French-Canadian leaders, embodied in his enduring alliance with Cartier that had been instrumental in the achievement of Confederation. Macdonald continued to rely on Cartier as his chief political lieutenant until his death in 1873. Afterward, Macdonald turned to Hector Langevin and then Adolphe Chapleau to help deliver a solid bloc of Quebec seats into the Conservative fold. The partnership of Macdonald and Cartier began a political convention that has generally continued to the present: a prime minister, whether English-speaking or French-speaking, collaborates with a lieutenant who represents the other major linguistic group in order to ensure broad-based support for the governing party.

Meanwhile, the opposition Liberal Party was emerging out of a loosely knit collection of discontented provincial reform remnants rallying around George Brown, who had left the Great Coalition with Macdonald and Cartier once Confederation became a certainty. Brown's narrow defeat in the wake of dubious Conservative election tactics in 1867 resulted in his resignation as Liberal leader and his eventual replacement by Alexander Mackenzie. Mackenzie lacked the dynamism of Brown or Macdonald to unite his party; moreover, the Liberals remained only tenuously connected to one another by a common antipathy toward the Conservatives and their nation-building strategy, rather than by a common philosophy or policy platform. Besides launching persistent attacks on alleged government corruption and waste, Mackenzie's Liberals came to stand for a more gradual and fiscally conservative course of transcontinental expansion and support for more provincial rights. Indeed, the narrow Liberal defeat at the hands of the Conservatives in the second general election in 1872 reflected the ambivalence and uncertainty of the Canadian people regarding the appropriate course of national development.

Macdonald's Conservatives were reelected on the promise to build a railway to the Pacific. Since the estimated $100 million cost of the railway link to the Pacific was considered beyond the resources of public enterprise, the Canadian government offered a subsidy of $30 million and 50 million acres of primarily western land to any private company that could undertake this ambitious project. In the ensuing competition for the railway-building charter, the Montreal-based Canadian Pacific Railway Company emerged victorious over Toronto interests, which not only accused the government of regional favoritism but also charged that its bidding rival was financially controlled by the Northern Pacific Railway Company in the United States. Even more serious allegations emerged in 1873 that the favored Montreal group, headed by steamship magnate Sir Hugh Allan, had contributed over $300,000 to the Conservative Party's reelection campaign of the previous year, with Macdonald and Cartier being the chief beneficiaries. As the incriminating evidence of financial kickbacks mounted and Conservative support in Parliament wavered, Macdonald and his Cabinet resigned rather than risk defeat by a motion of nonconfidence in the government. In accordance with parliamentary convention, the governor-general called upon Mackenzie as leader of the opposition to form a new government, the first Liberal administration in the young nation's history. Capitalizing on the public outrage over the so-called Pacific Scandal, Prime Minister Mackenzie dissolved Parliament and led his Liberal Party to a decisive victory in the election of 1874.

From the outset, the Mackenzie government was plagued by continuing internal party dissension and a coinciding worldwide economic depression. Even in power, the Liberals functioned more like a coalition of factions upholding regional interests than like a national political party with a transcontinental vision. Emphasizing the financial hardships arising from the depression of 1873, Mackenzie postponed the contracted railway to the Pacific in favor of building the line in sections to link with major Canadian waterways and American tracks. Whereas the Conservative strategy was to collaborate with the business community to build a complete east-west line in advance of settlement, the more cautious and economy-minded Liberals approached railway construction as a public enterprise to be undertaken only where settlement warranted. Thus, the Intercolonial Railway was completed to Halifax in 1876, while short lines were built running eastward from Winnipeg and westward from Lake Superior, connected in between by the Dawson Road and water routes that required some 70 portages. Responding to British Columbia's secession threats, the Mackenzie government immediately built a section of railway linking the Pacific Coast to the interior mountains and linked the province to eastern Canada by a telegraph line and a wagon road. This policy was particularly appealing to Ontario, which was far more interested in expansion into the North-West Territories than into the more remote Pacific region.

Liberal economic hopes also rested on a renewal of the Reciprocity Treaty of 1854, allowing the free trade of natural products between the United States and Canada. Having attacked Macdonald for his failure to secure reciprocity, the Liberal government sent Senator George Brown to Washington to negotiate a trade agreement in 1874. However, strong protectionist sentiment in the U.S. Senate rejected reciprocity, leaving the Liberals without a viable commercial policy. In the face of mounting financial difficulties, the free trade Liberals resorted to cutting government expenses and raising tariffs in order to generate sufficient revenue.

Although its economic policies were a failure, the Liberal administration took advantage of public reaction to the Pacific Scandal to achieve political and constitutional reforms that advanced Canadian democracy and nationhood. In order to minimize corruption and voting irregularities, the secret ballot was introduced, election dates and procedures were standardized across the country, candidates were required to record election expenses, and taverns were closed on election day. Other efforts at democratization included the elimination of dual representation, which had hitherto allowed a politician to represent simultaneously a federal and a provincial parliamentary seat; and the extension of the franchise effectively to all males (except for Native peoples), whether they held property or not. In 1875, Minister of Justice Edward Blake established the Supreme Court of Canada to review Canadian laws and to reduce appeals from the Canadian courts to the Judicial Committee of the Privy Council in Britain. The Judicial Committee continued to be the court of final appeal for nearly three-quarters of a century. Furthermore, Blake engineered the withdrawal of the governor-general's power to disallow legislation without consulting the Canadian Parliament, thereby reducing him to an executive figurehead before the prime minister and the Cabinet. Although the Liberal reforms expanded Canada's powers of self-government, they were overshadowed by economic policies that failed to unite and strengthen the nation.

THE NATIONAL POLICY

Widespread disenchantment with the Liberals renewed Conservative prospects for returning to power. But Macdonald realized that he would have to offer voters an appealing alternative to secure victory in the election of 1878. Macdonald succeeded in capturing the public imagination with the Conservative Party platform—called the National Policy, consisting of a protective tariff to stimulate Canadian industry, the completion of a transcontinental railway network, and the settlement of the West. Although the three strategic objectives of the National Policy originated prior to Confederation, Macdonald seized the opportunity to package them into an integrated nation-building scheme with a patriotic name. Indeed, the National Policy would remain the fundamental strategy of Canadian economic development for more than half a century.

Macdonald reasoned that if the United States would not agree to reciprocity of trade, then Canada would counter with "reciprocity of tariffs." Accordingly, the National Policy was officially inaugurated in 1879 when the Macdonald government raised customs duties on a wide range of manufactured and agricultural imports to unprecedented levels in a deliberate effort to encourage Canadians to buy domestic over foreign products. By increasing the cost of imports by as much as 35 percent, higher tariffs enabled Canadian manufacturers, mostly concentrated in the emerging industrial centers around Montreal and Toronto, to become more competitive with their much larger counterparts in the United States and Britain. Besides boosting infant domestic industry, higher tariffs encouraged foreign capital investment, especially by inducing American companies to establish branch plants in Canada in order to surmount the tariff barrier. Whereas future generations would lament Canada's precarious dependence on foreign investment, Canadians in the late 19th century welcomed American branch plants as a source of tax revenue for government and factory jobs for people who were increasingly opting for or considering immigration to the United States.

However, higher tariffs also made the cost of buying manufactured goods in Canada more expensive, particularly for farmers who exported most of their products and thus could not benefit from the higher prices in the Canadian market. Adding to the suffering of farmers was the tendency for their exports to be undermined in foreign markets by retaliatory tariffs. For the most part, farmers found little consolation in the claim that protecting domestic industry would eventually expand the market for their products in Canada and would enable them to enjoy the benefits of the nation's greater wealth and prosperity. The National Policy would remain a source of agrarian discontent in Canada.

With the passing of the cyclical depression and the revival of world trade in the late 1870s, the most immediate impact of the higher customs duties was to increase government revenue, which had hitherto been the primary purpose of Canadian tariff policy. While Alexander Galt's tariffs of 1858–59 were responsive to the demands of embryonic Canadian industry, his policy was more urgently motivated by the need to raise revenue to bail out government-supported railway enterprises. Two decades later, the link between tariffs and railways was renewed with greater emphasis in Macdonald's National Policy. The building of a transcontinental railway was essential to unite the country physically, to fulfill the promise made to British Columbia, to mobilize military forces to defend Canadian territory, and to develop an independent and interdependent national economy based on an exchange of western agriculture and eastern industry.

More favorable economic conditions encouraged a private syndicate of investors led by George Stephen, president of the Bank of Montreal; Donald Smith, governor of the Hudson's Bay Company; and J. J. Hill, an American railway promoter, to reconstitute the Canadian Pacific Railway Company (CPR) in 1880. Because British investors were reluctant to risk their capital in this ambitious railway project that reminded them of the losses of the Grand Trunk Railway, the CPR became for the most part a Canadian enterprise centered on Montreal. In a sense, the building of a transcontinental railway offered

Montreal the prospect of renewing its links with the vast fur-trading domain of the North West Company, and thereby reviving the old commercial empire of the St. Lawrence. The CPR also intensified the rivalry between Montreal and Toronto, which were vying for metropolitan dominance in Canada.

In return for building a railway from central Canada to the Pacific Coast within 10 years, the Canadian government granted the CPR the sections of line already completed (nearly 750 miles of track worth an estimated $31 million), a subsidy of $25 million, and 25 million acres of prime western land (which was eventually sold for more than $100 million). In addition, the CPR was granted a tax exemption on its construction materials and railway property, along with a 20-year monopoly of traffic in western Canada. This monopoly meant that no competing line could be built to the border to link up with American systems until the CPR's east-west traffic was well-established. The Liberal opposition vehemently attacked the Conservatives for this "act of insane recklessness" and for their unparalleled extravagance in awarding the CPR contract.

Certainly, the challenge of completing the longest railway line then existing in the world, spanning over 3,000 miles through such treacherous terrain as the rugged Canadian Shield and the towering Pacific mountain ranges, severely strained the financial and human resources of a nation of little more than 4 million people. By comparison, the United States had had a population of 40 million when it had completed its first transcontinental line two decades earlier. Nonetheless, the CPR project proceeded vigorously under the management of American engineer William Van Horne, who demonstrated his reputation for driving his construction crew as mercilessly as he drove himself. Van Horne was determined to build a superior quality railroad that would endure and to complete it at a mercurial pace in order to satisfy the demands of the investors and to ward off the competition of the North Pacific Railway, the American transcontinental line under construction to the south. Furthermore, the progress of construction was plagued by what Van Horne called "engineering impossibilities," including laying tracks along the sides of mountains, blasting tunnels through rocks, and bridging swift mountain rivers. Consequently, construction costs escalated well beyond the original estimates. When Stephen could not raise sufficient money from the sale of stock and from private capital, the CPR turned to the Canadian government for an additional $38.5 million in subsidies and $35 million in loans. CPR requests for more government support triggered such stormy debates in Parliament that by March 1885 even Prime Minister Macdonald despaired that his "national dream" had become a financial nightmare.

With the most difficult section through the Pacific mountains still to be completed and the CPR syndicate hovering on the brink of bankruptcy with little hope for further government assistance, Louis Riel ironically came to the rescue. In response to the outbreak of the North-West Rebellion, a military expedition was transported by the CPR from Ottawa to Winnipeg in six days, certainly a profound contrast to the three-month journey that the Wolseley expedition had to endure to quell the first Riel uprising in 1870. This spectacular demonstration of the value of the railway convinced the Canadian Parliament to allocate funds to complete the transcontinental line. On November 7, 1885, Donald Smith drove in the last spike of the transcontinental railway at the village of Craigellachie in the Selkirk Mountains of British Columbia to make Macdonald's national dream a reality. Nine days later, Macdonald's nemesis, Riel, was hanged in a Regina jail, likely unaware of the paradox that his act of treason in leading the North-West Rebellion had helped to unite the nation against which he fought.

With the completion of the CPR in 1885, following the implementation of the protective tariff policy in 1879, Macdonald's National Policy appeared to be taking shape as planned. The protective tariff was stimulating eastern industry, which not only could supply manufactured goods for western farmers but also could employ a growing urban population that would constantly need their agricultural produce. The railway could transport settlers and manufactures to the West and prairie agricultural products to eastern markets. But the realization of such an integrated national economy from coast to coast depended upon settlement of the West, the third strategic objective of the National Policy. Without a populated West, there would be limited east-west trade and thus insufficient traffic to sustain the CPR in which the Canadian government had invested so heavily.

The groundwork for western settlement was laid in the Manitoba Act of 1870, which stipulated that all ungranted land within the new province (as well as the remaining North-West Territories) was retained by the federal government to be administered "for the purposes of the Dominion." Following practices in the American West in order to appeal to prospective immigrants from there, the Canadian government divided land into townships of six square miles, and each township was further subdivided into 36 sections of one square mile or 640 acres. Once it had fulfilled its land grant commitments to the Hudson's Bay Company and the Canadian Pacific Railway Company, the government sought to encourage settlement by passing the Dominion Lands Act in 1872. The act provided each family or 21-year-old male a free grant of one quarter section (160 acres) in return for payment of a $10 registration fee, residence on the land for three years, cultivation of 30 acres, and the erection of a permanent dwelling. A settler who met these obligations qualified to purchase an adjoining quarter section at a reasonable price. The government was optimistic that its policy of free land grants would attract a multitude of western settlers whose presence would stimulate widespread commercial and industrial development.

To maintain law and order in the West, the Macdonald government on the eve of the Pacific Scandal organized the North-West Mounted Police (later the Royal North-West Mounted Police and now the Royal Canadian Mounted Police, or RCMP). Modeled after the Royal Irish Constabulary and the American cavalry, this federal police force of 300 men arrived in 1874 to establish a network of posts, including Fort Macleod, Fort Edmonton, Fort Calgary, and other strategic points throughout the North-West Territories. Dressed in their distinct bright scarlet tunics that reminded the Native peoples of the British redcoats whom they had long ago learned to trust, the Mounties patrolled an area the size of western Europe. They drove out American whiskey traders who had been exploiting the Natives, discouraged the tribes from fighting among themselves, and helped to preserve peaceful relations not only between Natives and settlers but also between ranchers and homesteaders. The Mounties were also instrumental generally in preparing the Native peoples for the dramatic changes in their lives resulting from the coming of white settlement and especially in assisting with the peaceful movement of various tribes onto the reservations.

The more orderly settlement of the Canadian West, in contrast to the violence and warfare that plagued the American western frontier, can also be attributed to a series of seven "Indian treaties" negotiated from 1871 to 1877. Adhering to the Royal Proclamation of 1763, which prohibited settlers from occupying territory that the Native peoples had not surrendered to the Crown, the Canadian government recognized that it had to negotiate treaties before settlement could proceed. The underlying objective of government policy was to relocate Natives on segregated reserves, to encourage them to adopt an agricultural way of life, and to convert them to Christianity in the hope that they would be assimilated into Canadian society. In accordance with these treaties, the federal government acquired

To mark the completion of the Canadian Pacific Railway, Donald Smith drives in the last spike at Craigellachie, British Columbia, on November 7, 1885. Overlooking Smith's right shoulder are W. C. Van Horne (left) and Sir Sandford Fleming (right), both instrumental in building the transcontinental line. Photographer: A. J. Ross, Calgary, Alberta.

legal control of Native ancestral land in northwestern Ontario and the western prairies in return for annuities, reserves, and freedom to hunt on Crown lands. Although both parties negotiated in good faith, differences in language, culture, and customs inevitably led to confusion over the nature and meaning of the treaties. Whereas the government maintained that it had purchased the land once and for all time, some Native leaders with no concept of property ownership believed that they had agreed to accept gifts in return for the temporary and mutual use of the land. Amid such fundamental misinterpretations and misunderstandings, aboriginal rights would emerge as a controversial issue in 20th-century Canadian politics.

To facilitate the assimilation of the Native peoples through the reserve system, the federal government passed the first Indian Act in 1876. The act and its subsequent amendments not only controlled all aspects of Native life but also viewed Native peoples as special wards of the state without the privileges of full citizenship. During the treaty negotiations, the government neglected to inform Native leaders of the degree to which this legislation would govern the lives of their people. In 1880 the federal government also established the Department of Indian Affairs with appointed agents who endeavored to promote "Canadianization" by suppressing such traditional practices as the Plains Indians' sun dance or the Pacific Coast Indians' potlatch. The department's chief vehicle for assimilation was enfranchisement, a legal process by which a person of good character, free of debt, and fluent in English or French agreed to relinquish Indian status and the right to live in the reserve community in return for full British citizenship, including the right to vote. Under this policy, Indian women who married non-Indians (whites, Métis, or Indians not governed by the Indian Act) automatically lost their Indian status under the Indian Act. In the final analysis, the aboriginal rights movement would gain momentum as the 20th century progressed because relatively few Indian men voluntarily chose to leave behind their reserves and be absorbed into the general society.

The concerted efforts by the federal government and the CPR to promote western settlement, which included an active campaign to recruit European immigrants as well as American homesteaders, fell short of expectations. The influx of young farmers from Ontario helped to increase the population of Manitoba from 25,000 in 1871 to 152,000 in 1891, while the remainder of the prairies attracted approximately 50,000 settlers during the same period. But these results paled by comparison to the millions of settlers who continued to pour into the American West where land was considered to be more desirable in terms of location and climate, even if more expensive to acquire. Furthermore, the recurring periods of depressions that afflicted the Western world from 1873 to 1896 were highlighted by declining commodity prices, which limited interest in the great prairie wheatlands of Canada.

The slow progress of western settlement seriously undermined the effectiveness of Macdonald's National Policy. Although the transcontinental railway was built, the east-west traffic was insufficient to warrant the huge public investment. While tariffs stimulated some industrial development in central Canada, the anticipated interprovincial trade did not materialize. Instead of promoting unity, the National Policy tended to provoke the divisive forces that were rising up to challenge Macdonald's concept of nationhood.

CHAPTER 12

THE CLASH OF NATIONALISMS AND THE RESURGENCE OF REGIONALISM

Despite Prime Minister Macdonald's formidable nation-building accomplishments, disappointment over the unfulfilled promises of Confederation was pervasive by the mid-1880s. Slow or uneven economic growth inspired alternative strategies to Macdonald's National Policy that urged closer ties with either Britain or the United States. But imperial federation and continental union proved to be expressions of nationalism that failed to capture the public imagination because they offered the prospect of a return to a form of colonialism or they could not accommodate Canada's regional or cultural diversities. Moreover, in the wake of growing resentment toward apparently inadequate or restrictive federal government policies, new allegiances to the fledgling nation could readily be subverted by enduring loyalties to the longer-established provinces or regions. The Maritimes and the West protested the domination of central Canada; Ontario challenged federal efforts to limit provincial power; and Quebec resorted to assertions of provincial autonomy in defense of a renewed cultural nationalism.

THE IMPERIALIST AND CONTINENTALIST ALTERNATIVES

The Canadian economy after Confederation continued to be dependent on the export market for natural resources, particularly grain, timber, and fish. Recurring slumps in world trade from 1873 to 1896 led to falling prices and contracting markets for these staple exports, which could not be offset by new agricultural prospects in the West and the growth of domestic industry in central Canada stimulated by the National Policy. Compounding the sense of economic failure was the more dynamic pace of development in the United States, where millions of European immigrants poured in to take advantage of a greater range of opportunity than Canada could offer. Likewise, discontented Canadians could not resist the lure of the southern republic as Maritimers joined the New England fishing fleets, French Canadians found employment in the mill towns of New England, Ontario farmers sought homesteads in the American West, and generally skilled industrial and railway workers found a demand for their services in cities along the Atlantic seaboard. While an estimated 1.2 million immigrants arrived in Canada from 1871 to 1891, over 1.5 million people left the country for the United States. During this period, a high rate of natural increase allowed the population of Canada to grow from 3.7 million to 4.8 million. Minuscule by American standards, this rate of population growth also lagged behind pre-Confederation levels.

In response to these troubling circumstances, some prominent English-speaking Protestants, fondly recalling the blessings of imperial trade preferences in the first half of the 19th century, contended that Canadian nationhood could be best served by reinforcement of the British connection that had loosened during the free trade era. The advocates of this perspective did not want to return to colonialism, but rather they were dedicated to securing Canadian political independence from the United States through economic, cultural, and military integration with the world's mightiest empire. This nationalist spirit was expressed as early as 1868 by the Canada First movement, which could have been more appropriately known as English Canada First or Ontario First. Its adherents envisaged a Canadian nationality invigorated not only by the struggle to overcome the northern climate and rugged landscape but also by a belief in the inherent superiority of the Anglo-Saxon race. Indeed, Canada Firsters supported the agitation against the Métis during the Red River uprising of 1869–70 and helped to provoke the reaction against French Catholics in Quebec that swept Ontario in the aftermath of Riel's execution of Thomas Scott. Although Canada First had disintegrated as a political movement by 1875, its divisive brand of nationalism, which pitted English-speaking Canadians against French-speaking Canadians and Natives against whites, would continue to flourish within the imperial unity movement of the 1880s.

Canadian interest in imperial unity corresponded with Britain's renewed commitment to its overseas empire in the last quarter of the 19th-century. The "little Englandism" of the mid-Victorian era, which had provided the impetus for Canadian nationhood, gave way to a new imperialism in response to the rise of Germany and the United States as viable challengers to Britain's economic and military supremacy. After British imperialists founded the Imperial Federation League in 1884, Canadian supporters of the movement formed a branch within three years. Imperialists on both sides of the Atlantic hoped that this consolidation of the British Empire on the basis of a centralized federation would open the way for mutual trade opportunities and military assistance, in addition to spreading the virtues of Anglo-Saxon civilization—the "white man's burden," according to Rudyard Kipling—to the "backward" societies of Asia, Africa, and the Pacific Islands. Pillars of the English-speaking Protestant community, like Colonel George Taylor Denison, a former Canada Firster who had fought against the Fenians and Louis Riel; Principal George Munro Grant of Queen's University in Kingston; George Parkin, who would serve as principal of Upper Canada College in Toronto; and Stephen Leacock, the renowned humorist, believed that the unity of the Anglo-Saxon race would enable Canada not only to enjoy economic prosperity and a greater sense of power in the world but also to overcome persistent ethnic tensions, provincialism, and the threat of American domination. While little of the imperialist agenda actually found its way into the realm of public policy, this nationalist sentiment would remain pervasive and influential, particularly in Ontario and the Maritimes, well into the 20th century.

That Britain would abandon free trade for a restored system of colonial preferences was never more than a dream of the more ardent imperialists in the late 19th century. A more realistic possibility was the renewal of reciprocity with the United States. After the United States cancelled the Reciprocity Treaty in 1866, the Canadian government made periodic overtures to revive the free trade agreement. The first opportunity came with the meeting of a Joint High Commission in Washington, D.C., convened in 1871 to settle outstanding disputes between the United States and Britain arising mainly out of the American Civil War. The United States demanded compensation for damage inflicted by southern ships, notably the *Alabama*, that were built in British ports. Moreover, the Americans wanted a restoration of the rights that they had lost with the end of the Reciprocity Treaty to fish in the territorial waters of the Maritime Provinces and Newfoundland and to use their ports freely. Britain and the United States were also engaged in a boundary dispute involving the possession of San Juan Island in the Portland Channel separating Vancouver Island from the mainland. Canada not only sought compensation for damages caused by the Fenian raids launched from American soil but also hoped to exchange the fishing rights for reciprocity.

Although Macdonald was appointed one of the British commissioners to represent Canadian interests, the other members of the imperial delegation were more concerned with restoring Britain's diplomatic relations with the United States. The resulting Treaty of Washington referred the *Alabama* claims and the San Juan Island dispute to international arbitration, which eventually settled both issues in favor of the United States. When the United States refused to deal with the Fenian claims, Britain decided to leave the matter out of the treaty and to compensate Canada instead. The treaty also gave the Americans the right to navigate freely on the St. Lawrence River in perpetuity and to fish in Canadian territorial waters for 10 years in return for a cash payment, which turned out to be $5.5 million. While Canada also received the right to navigate freely on Lake Michigan and three remote rivers in Alaska as well as free entry of Maritime fish into the American market, the much desired reciprocity agreement never materialized. Northern protectionist sentiment in the United States proved to be too strong, and the British negotiators did not want to risk the whole diplomatic accord by pressing further for reciprocity. Disappointed at Britain's willingness to sacrifice Canadian interests for the sake of American friendship, Macdonald reluctantly signed the treaty.

Nevertheless, the signing of the Treaty of Washington was an important moment in Canadian history in two respects. First, it marked the beginning of a series of events over the next six decades that would strengthen Canada's resolve to wrest control of its foreign policy from Britain. The appointment of the first Dominion high commissioner in 1880 to give Canada a greater voice in imperial policy was an outcome of the Treaty of Washington. Second, and of more immediate significance, Macdonald's signature on the treaty represented American diplomatic recognition of Canada as a distinct transcontinental nation in North America. Besides easing the tensions between Canada and the United States, the treaty established the principle of arbitration as a means of resolving international conflicts. This more cordial atmosphere enabled Britain to complete its military withdrawal from North America and rendered this prospect less perilous for Canada. For its part, the United States had to foresake its ambition to conquer Canada by force, but Britain's withdrawal from the continent increased American confidence in the prospect that its northern neighbor would eventually abandon its dubious experiment in nationhood and accept the natural triumph of American manifest destiny.

After they came close to securing reciprocity while in power in 1874, the Liberals in opposition continued their free trade crusade as an alternative to the National Policy, which was failing to stimulate external markets for staple producers—farmers, loggers, and fishermen—while the protective tariff on manufactured goods added to their costs of production. The majority of Liberals led by Edward Blake (who succeeded Mackenzie in 1880) favored a return to the Reciprocity Treaty of 1854, which was restricted to natural products. Even Macdonald's Conservatives agreed that such a policy of restricted reciprocity with the United States could be complementary to the National Policy. In 1887 Macdonald tried unsuccessfully to use the renegotiation of the fisheries clauses of the Treaty of Washington as an opportunity to renew reciprocity on the same basis as the treaty of 1854. However, if they were interested at all, the Americans preferred either unrestricted reciprocity, which involved the free exchange of manufactured goods in addition to natural products, or continental union, which would include not only the removal of all tariff barriers but also a sharing of internal revenue taxes and a common tariff policy against other countries. Richard Cartwright, former minister of finance in the Mackenzie administration during the 1870s, was the leading proponent of continental union within the Liberal Party. In *Canada and the Canadian Question*, a political tract for the election campaign of 1891, Goldwin Smith mounted an eloquent argument in support of continental union as the means to open up the natural north-south trade directions, to foster the unity of North America's Anglo-Saxon community, and to assimilate French Canadians. Macdonald, Blake, and other opponents countered that continental union was a prelude to political union and the loss of national independence.

In the general election of 1891, Wilfrid Laurier, who had succeeded Blake as Liberal leader four years earlier, campaigned for unrestricted reciprocity as a compromise to the positions of Blake and Cartwright. In leading the Conservative defense of the National Policy, Macdonald attempted to equate unrestricted reciprocity with annexation and the breakup of the British Empire. He appealed to imperialist sentiment with his popular campaign slogans: "The Old Flag, The Old Policy, The Old Leader" and "A British subject I was born, and a British subject I will die." Among the voters, the key issue of the election pitted staple producers, who supported the various manifestations of reciprocity, against the manufacturers, who favored continued industrial protectionism. The result was a Conservative victory by a narrow margin that reflected the divisions and uncertainties within the country. Three months after the election, Macdonald died at 76 years of age, leaving the nation that he was so instrumental in building over the previous quarter of a century to continue to debate whether its destiny lay in an imperialist, a continentalist, or an autonomous direction.

REGIONAL PROTEST AND PROVINCIAL RIGHTS

Macdonald also left behind a nation mired in the regional and cultural conflicts that had troubled his administration from the outset. The Maritime Provinces, which had been so reluctant to be part of Confederation, continually lamented the limited and inequitable benefits that political union conferred upon them. On July 1, 1867, many Maritime communities marked Confederation and the beginning of Canadian nationhood by flying flags at half-mast. Nova Scotians in particular resented the high-handed and undemocratic methods that had been used to impose Confederation on them. Accordingly, in the inaugural Dominion elections of 1867, Nova Scotia's voters seized the opportunity to elect opponents of Confederation to 18 of the 19 seats in the federal Parliament and 36 of the 38 seats in the provincial legislature. A resolution to repeal the union was subsequently introduced in the Nova Scotia legislature, and Joseph Howe led a delegation to London to appeal to the imperial authority to release the province from the "bondage" of Confederation. Since Britain wanted to reduce rather than increase its North American commitments, the Colonial Office refused even to meet with Howe, let alone consider his request to reintegrate Nova Scotia into the empire. While other anti-Confederation supporters favored either independence or annexation to the United States, Howe preferred to negotiate better terms for Nova Scotia within the federal union. In 1869, he agreed to Prime Minister Macdonald's offer of a position in the federal Cabinet and a larger annual subsidy for Nova Scotia. Some Nova Scotians were dismayed by Howe's conversion to Canadian federalism, and although the opposition to Confederation soon subsided, a legacy of resentment remained in the province. By yielding to Nova Scotia's demands, the federal government also set a precedent for the renegotiation of its future fiscal relations with the provinces.

By the 1880s anti-Confederation sentiment in Nova Scotia was intensified by the perception that the National Policy served the interests of central Canada at the expense of the Maritime Provinces. In reality, the Maritime economy was undergoing major structural changes that were unrelated to government policy. Maritime commerce, shipping, and shipbuilding suffered as the wooden sailing vessels gave way to iron-hulled steamships and as the West Indies trade declined in global importance. But because the adverse consequences of these changes became more evident in the wake of the recessions that recurred from 1873 to 1896, Maritimers tended to blame Confederation and the National Policy for their economic woes. They could point to the fact that the building of the Intercolonial Railway did not open up the markets of central Canada or bring western traffic to Atlantic ports. Furthermore, the protective tariffs of the National Policy not only failed to stimulate Maritime industry by comparison to central Canada but also incited Americans to retaliate by imposing higher duties on Maritime fish, leading to a devastating decline in the export market. When the ruling Conservative Party of Nova Scotia appealed to its federal counterpart in Ottawa for financial assistance in the early 1880s, Prime Minister Macdonald was too preoccupied with building the Canadian Pacific Railway.

In 1886 the Liberal administration of W. S. Fielding, which had come to power two years earlier on a wave of anti-Confederation sentiment, responded to further federal government refusal to negotiate better financial terms by introducing a resolution in the Nova Scotia legislature favoring the province's withdrawal from Confederation. Fielding also appealed to the other Maritime Provinces to secede in order to form an independent Maritime nation. If such a union proved to be unsuccessful, then Nova Scotia favored a return to its original status as a British colony. Both New Brunswick and

Prince Edward Island doubted the feasibility of Maritime union, and Nova Scotia's secession threats subsided when the federal government agreed to lower freight rates and to provide generous financial assistance for railway building in the province.

Meanwhile, Newfoundland stubbornly resisted union with the rest of Canada, despite a generous financial offer from the Dominion government and an active campaign waged by the supporters of Confederation in the province from 1865 to 1869. The provincial outlook was oriented toward the north Atlantic world, particularly Britain, and the island had little communication or economic connection with mainland Canada. Bolstered by the repeal movement in Nova Scotia, opponents of Confederation successfully argued during the provincial election of 1869 that union with Canada offered no tangible advantage to the island's fishing economy. Recurring slumps in the cod-fishing and seal-hunting industries in the 1870s and 1880s prompted Newfoundland to consider union with Canada and reciprocity with the United States as viable alternatives to British colonialism. Confederation prospects were further undermined when the Canadian government intervened to persuade the British government to veto a reciprocal trade agreement that the Newfoundland government had successfully negotiated with the United States in 1890. Even when Newfoundland reluctantly made overtures to join the Confederation in 1895, the Canadian government remained uncertain about the feasibility of assuming responsibility for such a financially hard-pressed province. Accordingly, talks broke down, and it would take more than half a century before Newfoundland and Canada would reach an agreement on Confederation.

Resentment toward Confederation as a manifestation of central Canadian imperialism was even stronger in the West. The Red River uprising led by Louis Riel represented not only the native Métis resolve to preserve their seminomadic way of life based on the buffalo hunt in the face of the advancing agricultural settlement frontier but also incipient western protest against eastern domination. After the Riel uprising and the creation of Manitoba, the federal government offered the Métis of the Red River region land grants of 240 acres in recognition of their status as descendants of the original inhabitants. Rather than contend with the growing number of agricultural settlers, mostly from Ontario, many of the Métis sold their land in Manitoba during the 1870s and moved northwest to the Saskatchewan River region, where they joined other compatriots who enjoyed the traditional way of life based on the river lot and the buffalo hunt. By the mid-1880s, however, both the Métis who departed for Saskatchewan and the agrarian settlers of Manitoba would have reason to be dissatisfied with the development policies of the federal government.

In Manitoba, discontent arose primarily over the CPR monopoly, which prohibited competitive railway lines from being built in the West until at least 1905. After the CPR established its freight rate schedule in 1883, western producers complained about having to pay shipping costs that were over three times more than those incurred by their counterparts in central or eastern Canada. To overcome the lack of transportation competition, which enabled the CPR to charge whatever the market would bear on the prairies, the Manitoba government chartered new railways that would link up with American lines. When the federal government repeatedly disallowed these provincial charters, Manitoba threatened to secure American financial and military support to build a railway from Winnipeg to the border. Accordingly, the federal government bought out the CPR monopoly in 1888 and decided not to block the construction of a new railway line operated by the American Northern Pacific Company. While the new railway line did not significantly lower freight rates, the incident did rally western support against the federal government.

The provision within the Manitoba Act that assigned ownership of provincial public lands to the Dominion government would also become a chronic source of federal-provincial conflict. Not only did Manitoba object to being deprived of the revenue derived from the sale or lease of its public land, but also ownership of these lands involved the federal government in a boundary dispute with Ontario. Prior to Confederation, neither the Hudson's Bay Company nor the province of Upper Canada had much interest in establishing the precise boundary between their respective holdings. But after the purchase of Rupert's Land from the Hudson's Bay Company in 1870, the governments of Canada and Ontario had two reasons to concern themselves with ownership of the 144,000 square miles of territory northwest of Lake Superior. Valuable timber and mineral rights were not only at stake but also opposing concepts of federal-provincial relations.

The distribution of powers outlined in the British North America Act was clearly designed to keep the provinces subordinate to the federal government. Macdonald's Conservatives sought to keep the provinces weak by invoking the power of disallowance whenever provincial legislation conflicted with federal enactments or generally interfered with the interests of the national government. The Liberal Party adopted the position that the federal government should resort to its power of disallowance only when the provinces exceeded their constitutional jurisdiction. The provincial governments countered with the argument that Confederation was a compact between the provinces and the Dominion whereby the provinces had voluntarily delegated certain powers to the federal government, which could be altered by mutual consent. Opponents of this "compact theory" of Confederation maintained that the British North America Act was a statute of a superior legislature rather than an agreement among provinces.

The strongest challenge to Macdonald's centralist views of Confederation fittingly came from Canada's most populated and affluent province. Oliver Mowat, the Liberal premier of Ontario from 1872 to 1896, like his predecessor Edward Blake, claimed that his province was a partner rather than a satellite of the federal government. Mowat saw in the Ontario-Manitoba boundary question an opportunity to reinforce the dominance of his province within the Confederation. When the federal government unilaterally awarded the disputed territory west of Thunder Bay to Lake of the Woods to Manitoba in 1881, Ontario appealed the decision to the Judicial Committee of the Privy Council, which ruled in the province's favor three years later.

In another landmark case, *Hodge v. The Queen*, the Judicial Committee in 1884 upheld Ontario's Act Respecting Licensing Duties, which the federal government had disallowed, because liquor licensing was a local matter and the provinces had full authority in their own realm of legal jurisdiction. Provincial power was further enhanced by yet another Ontario challenge over the role of the lieutenant governor as primarily a servant of the federal government. In 1892 the Judicial Committee ruled that the lieutenant governor as a representative of the Crown in Canada had the same relationship with the province as the governor-general had with the federal government. Ontario was also at the forefront of a series of Judicial Committee decisions, notably *Russell v. The Queen* in 1882 and the Local Prohibition case in 1896, which resulted in provincial power over property and civil rights taking supremacy over federal authority for peace, order, and good government. In effect, the Judicial Committee ruled that federal residuary power could exceed beyond the matters enumerated in Section 91 of the British North America Act only in times of extreme emergencies, thereby nullifying the centralizing intentions of Confederation.

Growing provincial power, however, did not translate into greater unity of the provinces, as demonstrated during the first Interprovincial Conference that convened at Quebec in 1887 to reconsider the basis of Confederation. The Conservative premiers of Prince Edward Island and British Columbia declined to attend, while four of the five premiers who did meet were Liberals. Dismissing the gathering as a Liberal Party conspiracy, Macdonald declined an invitation to send federal representatives. With few interests in common, the provinces were united only in attacking federal government policies. While Ontario and Quebec were divided by cultural sentiments, they were mutually suspicious of the smaller provinces' demand for more federal subsidies that invariably would mean higher taxation for central Canadians. Maritime complaints regarding tariffs or Manitoba's railway freight rate problems were also of little concern to Ontario and Quebec. Although it highlighted the lack of national unity after two decades of Confederation, the meeting was ultimately significant for inaugurating a new vehicle for political decision-making in Canada as interprovincial conferences evolved into federal-provincial conferences.

CULTURAL CONFLICT AND MINORITY RIGHTS

In Quebec, concern over provincial rights was complicated by the thorny question of minority rights. Quebec actively supported provincial rights as a strategy to preserve racial and religious privileges within the province but did not hesitate to call upon the federal government to nullify provincial measures that failed to protect the French minority in other provinces. The dilemma created by this position became apparent in 1871 when the New Brunswick government amended the Schools Act to introduce a non-sectarian system of education that would no longer provide public support for "separate" parish schools offering French language and Catholic religious instruction. Despite pressure from Acadian and Irish Catholics, the federal government refused to intervene on two grounds. First, while the British North America Act recognized denominational schools that had existed by law before Confederation, those in New Brunswick existed only by custom, and thus the new provincial act was not depriving Catholics of any legal rights. Second, the federal government was reluctant to intervene in education, a matter that was clearly under provincial jurisdiction according to the act. George Étienne Cartier and other Quebec political leaders agreed with Macdonald that federal intervention to alter existing provincial education laws would set a dangerous precedent.

The New Brunswick school dispute following upon the heels of the Red River uprising awakened the Quebec clergy to the fate of the growing population of French Catholics outside of the province. From the mid-19th to the early 20th century approximately 100,000 young French Canadians left Quebec every decade to seek more favorable economic opportunities either in the United States or elsewhere in Canada. In response to this exodus as well as to the imperialist and continentalist appeals for the unity of the Anglo-Saxon race, the ultramontane movement within the clergy sought to make Quebec the center of French Catholicism in North America, championing the cause of expatriates wherever they formed a community, holding their loyalty to the homeland, and occasionally attracting them back within its borders. The ultramontanes, therefore, believed that it was imperative to maintain the Catholic Church and the French language not only as instruments of cultural nationalism but also as barriers against the subversive ideas of Protestantism or modern secular thought. In their Programme catholique of 1871, the ultramontanes condemned the doctrine of separation of church and state, boldly claiming that the state was subordinate to the church and the pope was the supreme authority in civil and religious matters. The Programme catholique further declared that the Catholic Church had the right to intervene directly in politics and to brand as a sin a vote for a candidate who did not uphold the interests of religion as defined by the Quebec bishops. The lack of a dominant figure like Cartier to rally the forces of French Catholicism to the side of the Liberals, along with the anti-Catholic and anti-French attitude that prevailed within the Ontario wing of the party, drove the French clergy to support the Conservative Party despite the prominence of the Protestant extremist Orange Order within its ranks. While Macdonald appreciated the electoral value of this uneasy "holy" alliance, he and his party would have reason to regret this political fortune when the North-West Rebellion erupted in 1885.

Farther west along the Saskatchewan River, the Métis and the Native tribes were discovering that they could not escape the encroachment of agricultural settlement. Once again, the government system of square survey ignored the boundaries of the long and narrow river-lot farms and brought their titles into question. Once again, the federal government ignored the demands of the inhabitants for recognition of their land claims, for fulfilment of the Indian Treaty obligations, and for local self-government with representation in the national Parliament. And once again, the Métis, with the initial support of white settlers who were also upset over Ottawa's indifference to western grievances, turned to Louis Riel to lead their struggle against a government that apparently had learned little from the political turmoil 15 years previously.

Riel had lived in exile mostly in the United States since he fled Red River in 1870. He returned briefly to be elected and reelected to Parliament, and in 1874 he mysteriously managed to sign the members' register in Ottawa. In 1875 Riel was granted a general amnesty on the condition that he remain in exile for another five years. During his years in exile, Riel's religious obsessions caused him to spend time in a mental asylum, and he became convinced that God had chosen him to serve as "prophet of the New World." So, when approached to lead the western protest against an eastern-dominated national government in 1884, Riel believed that his divine mission was about to be fulfilled.

At first, Riel sought political change by peaceful means, helping to draft a petition demanding more generous treatment of Indians, more favorable land terms for both whites and Métis, local control of natural resources, lower tariffs, a railway to Hudson Bay as an alternative to the CPR, responsible government for the North-West Territories, and western representation in Ottawa. In the face of government inaction, Riel and his Métis followers grew increasingly impatient and adopted a more confrontational approach. As he had done at Red River 15 years earlier, Riel established a provisional government with himself as president in March 1885. This action and subsequent talk of violence alienated many of his white supporters, while Riel's growing religious fanaticism turned the Catholic Church against him.

Within an atmosphere of rising tensions, Riel's renewal of armed resistance against the Canadian government was ignited on March 26, 1885, by a clash at Duck Lake between a force of the Northwest Mounted Police (NWMP) and a band of Métis led by Gabriel Dumont, whom Riel had appointed as military commander of the resistance movement. Dumont's victory not only forced the NWMP to abandon Fort Carlton and retreat to Prince Albert but also encouraged Cree chiefs Poundmaker and Big Bear to mount Indian attacks at Battleford and Frog Lake, respectively. News of these skirmishes aroused the federal government to dispatch an expeditionary force of more than 5,000 troops to the West via the partially completed Canadian Pacific Railway. The speedy arrival of this force under the command of Major General Frederick Middleton highlighted the value of the transcontinental railway and helped to discourage a larger Indian uprising, thereby localizing the rebellion. After three weeks of fierce fighting, Riel was defeated and captured in the decisive battle at Batoche, the headquarters of his provisional government, on May 15, 1885. Dumont fled to the United States, while Poundmaker and Big Bear continued to resist briefly before surrendering.

Unlike his first uprising, which occurred within a political vacuum, Riel's second act of armed resistance was clearly a revolt against a constituted authority. The Canadian government proved to be far more decisive in suppressing the North-West Rebellion than in preventing its outbreak in the first place. The vast majority of Plains Indians who honored their treaty promises not to take up arms against the state were rewarded with gifts and supplies, while the relatively few who participated in the rebellion were dealt with harshly by the courts. In the subsequent trials, 125 Indians and Métis were prosecuted, and eight Indians were publicly hanged to demonstrate the government's determination to resist challenges to its authority. For his part in leading the rebellion, Riel was charged with treason and fought all of his lawyers' efforts to have him acquitted by reason of insanity. After one hour of jury deliberation, Riel was found guilty and was sentenced to execution by hanging.

In the process, the leader of western protest against eastern domination and the defender of Native rights against encroaching white "civilization" also became the catalyst for ethnic and religious passions that had been smoldering uneasily since the Red River uprising. English Protestant Ontario, still remembering him as the murderer of Thomas Scott and an obstacle to provincial aspirations to annex the West, demanded Riel's execution. On the other hand, French Catholic Quebec, hailing Riel as a defender of cultural and minority rights in the West, called upon the federal government to pardon him. Appeals for clemency came from all parts of Canada and the United States as well as from Britain and France. After several delays, including a legal appeal to the Judicial Committee of the Privy Council and further investigations of Riel's sanity, Macdonald concluded that "Riel must swing" in order to keep Ontario loyal to the Conservatives and to herald the triumph of Canadian law and order in the West. These motives were vital to the success of his National Policy. Bolstered by the support of his French-Canadian lieutenants, Hector Langevin and Adolphe Chapleau, Macdonald was willing to gamble that his party's strength in Quebec would hold firm. As it turned out, Riel's execution in November 1885 would profoundly transform the political landscape of Quebec.

Both Wilfrid Laurier, a rising federal Liberal politician, and Honoré Mercier, leader of the Quebec Liberal Party, seized the opportunity to capitalize on Riel's "martyrdom." Laurier declared at a mass rally attended by over 50,000 people on the Champs de Mars in Montreal: "If I had been on the banks of the Saskatchewan, I too would have shouldered a musket." Within two years, Laurier was leader of the federal Liberals, and a little over a decade later, he would become the first French-Canadian prime minister. At the same rally, Mercier condemned the federal Conservatives as the party of English Canada, and particularly of Ontario Protestant bigotry. Indeed, the demise of the Conservative Party in Quebec in the 1890s can be traced back to the bitterness aroused by Riel's execution.

Mercier endeavored to revive the long-standing Rouge notion, all but discredited by persistent ultramontane attacks during the 1870s, that only an autonomous Quebec government could adequately represent French-Canadian interests within the Confederation.

Mercier allied his Liberal supporters with dissident Conservatives to form the Parti National, which would emphasize French Canada first, reminiscent of the Canada First movement's focus on the interests of English Protestant Ontario. In the provincial election of 1886, Mercier led the Parti National to a narrow victory, and as premier of Quebec, he set out to win the confidence of the ultramontane clergy by cultivating his image as defender of the Catholic religion and French-Canadian rights. In 1888 the Quebec legislature passed the Jesuit Estates Act, which was primarily intended to compensate the Jesuit Order for property seized by the Crown after the British Conquest. To settle the rival claims of the Jesuits and the Catholic hierarchy in Quebec, the provincial government called upon the pope to arbitrate.

Predictably, Protestant Ontario, led by Conservative member of Parliament D'Alton McCarthy, objected vehemently to papal intervention in Canadian affairs and demanded that the federal government use its powers of disallowance. However, Macdonald refused to intervene in a provincial matter that would generate more ethnic and religious antagonism, so McCarthy's motion of disallowance was decisively defeated. With strong support from the Protestant Orange and Masonic Orders, McCarthy formed the Equal Rights Association, which advocated a Canadian nationality based on one language (English), one culture (British), and one faith (Protestantism). After being burned in effigy in Quebec for sacrificing Riel to the English Protestants, Macdonald found himself vilified in Ontario for conspiring with French Catholics.

To build up support for the Equal Rights Association, McCarthy took his anti-Catholic and anti-French campaign to Manitoba in 1889, where he urged the Liberal government of Thomas Greenway to abolish separate Catholic schools and French language rights, both of which had been guaranteed in the Manitoba Act of 1870. In

Louis Riel (1844–85; seated), surrounded by his Métis associates at Red River ca. 1869. Riel epitomized Canadian cultural division inasmuch as he was branded as a traitor and murderer in English Protestant Ontario but was celebrated as a patriot and martyr in French Catholic Quebec.

171

response to the rhetoric of McCarthy and the Equal Rights Association as well as to the steady decline in the size of the French Catholic community relative to the English Protestant population, the provincial legislature passed the Manitoba Schools Act in 1890. The act discontinued government financial support for separate schools in favor of a uniform, state-funded, secular education system administered by a newly created Department of Education. The same session of the legislature abolished French as an official language, contrary to Section 23 of the Manitoba Act.

Disappointed Catholics in French and English Canada urged the federal government to use its general power to disallow provincial legislation or its specific power to pass remedial legislation to protect minority education rights under Section 93 of the British North America Act. Macdonald adopted the same cautious strategy that had served him well in the New Brunswick school question of 1871. The Manitoba school question differed from the New Brunswick dispute in the sense that the federal government was being called upon to defend rights that were constitutionally guaranteed.

Nevertheless, Macdonald remained determined to avoid a federal-provincial clash over a volatile political issue that could inflict serious electoral damage on his party. His strategy was to let the courts decide. While the Supreme Court of Canada upheld the right of Catholics to have state-supported separate schools, the Judicial Committee of the Privy Council reversed this decision and ruled in favor of the Manitoba government's position. In another legal case, the Privy Council ruled that the federal government had the constitutional right to pass remedial legislation to protect minority rights, even though the Manitoba law had been ruled constitutionally valid.

When remedial legislation was finally introduced to Parliament in 1896, it fell victim to the disintegration of the ruling Conservatives, who had gone through four leadership changes in the five years since Macdonald's death. Macdonald's successors as prime minister—John J. Abbott (1891–92), John S. Thompson (1892–94), Mackenzie Bowell (1894–96), and Charles Tupper (1896)—were either unable or were not in office long enough to build a party consensus on the issue. In the end, the remedial bill was stalled by prolonged debate until the five-year term of Parliament expired. The Manitoba schools question thus became a major issue in the federal election of 1896. The divided and disorganized Conservatives expressed support for remedial legislation when campaigning in Quebec but denied that the bill would ever become law when campaigning in English-speaking Canada. The Liberals under the leadership of Wilfrid Laurier were able to shift the focus of the Manitoba schools question from minority rights to provincial rights. In this way, Laurier could challenge the political authority of the ultramontane Catholic clergy without appearing to abandon the interests of his native Quebec. In the final analysis, Quebec's historic shift from the Conservative to the Liberal fold was decisive in securing a narrow victory for Laurier, thus giving Canada its first French-speaking and Catholic prime minister.

Charles Tupper's defeat after slightly more than two months at the head of the Conservative government bestowed on him the ignoble distinction of serving the shortest term of any Canadian prime minister. More important, the general election of 1896 marked the end of the Conservative ascendancy in national politics, an era dominated by Sir John A. Macdonald. Laurier would emerge as the heir to Macdonald as a master strategist in the complex politics of cultural division, regional protest, and national unity. His 15-year reign as prime minister would be marked by a reversal of national economic fortunes, the rise of the Liberal political ascendancy, and the growing diversification of Canadian society, all trends that would continue throughout the 20th century.

CHAPTER 13

THE WHEAT BOOM AND NATIONAL EXPANSION

At the end of the 19th century, Prime Minister Wilfrid Laurier predicted: "The nineteenth century was the century of the United States, the twentieth century will be the century of Canada." Laurier's confidence was buoyed by the remarkable prosperity that Canada was enjoying since he came to power in 1896 and which it would continue to experience with only brief interruptions during the first three decades of the 20th century. As much as Laurier may have believed that his government's policies were responsible for the turnaround in Canada's fortunes, the reality was that Macdonald's National Policy was finally fulfilling its promise. Just as the National Policy had faltered because of the slow progress of western settlement, so it flourished in the wake of the extraordinary influx of immigrants to the prairies, which triggered the so-called wheat boom from 1896 to 1914. Accordingly, the late 19th-century pessimism and doubt about Canada's survival gave way to a new sense of optimism and confidence that inspired a greater interest in external relations. In the process, renewed controversies over contributions to imperial defense and commercial reciprocity with the United States led to the downfall of the Laurier government.

WESTERN SETTLEMENT AND THE TRIUMPH OF THE NATIONAL POLICY

The settlement of the Canadian West after 1896 was stimulated by the reversal of the same external factors that had previously been impediments. The revival of world trade was marked by a rise in the demand for agricultural products and other raw materials to supply the growing cities and factories in Britain and western Europe. The price of wheat, for example, quadrupled from 1891 to 1921, thereby making farming a more profitable venture. Furthermore, as the American western frontier reached the limits of its expansion by the end of the 19th century, the cheap and fertile land of the Canadian prairies became known as the "last, best west."

The prospect of developing the Canadian West was enhanced by improvements in agricultural techniques and technology that enabled settlers to cope with the natural limitations of climate. The application and refinement of "dry" farming techniques helped to overcome the relatively low rainfall of the prairies. The advent of the chilled steel plough facilitated cutting through the hard prairie sod, while improved harrows and seed drills as well as tractors and threshers made it possible to work large farms effectively. Perhaps the greatest advance was Marquis wheat, a high-yielding strain that could mature in less than 100 days, thereby reducing the hazards of a late spring or an early autumn frost and extending the farming frontier to the northern areas of Alberta and Saskatchewan. As a result, Canadian wheat exports increased from barely 2 million bushels in 1896 to over 150 million bushels in 1921.

As the wheatlands of western Canada became more attractive to settlers, the federal government embarked upon an ambitious immigration policy administered by Minister of the Interior Clifford Sifton, who had migrated from Ontario to Manitoba during the 1880s. Believing that agriculture was the backbone of the Canadian economy, Sifton organized vigorous publicity campaigns in Britain, the United States, and continental Europe promoting the unparalleled opportunities of farming in the "Wondrous West," as one of his many pamphlets was entitled. While government agents recruited immigrants with an offer of a quarter section (160 acres) of free land under the Dominion Lands policy, the Hudson's Bay Company and the Canadian Pacific Railway were willing to sell their favorably located holdings at reasonable prices because more people meant more business. The response was overwhelming as from 1896 to 1914 upwards of 2.5 million immigrants came to Canada, with about 1 million of them settling on the western prairies. Accordingly, Canada's population expanded from 4.8 million in 1891 to 8.8 million in 1921 while the population of the West, including Manitoba, the North-West Territories, and British Columbia, grew from little more than 250,000 to over 2 million during the same period.

In response to this growth, western settlers pressured the federal government to grant provincial status to the North-West Territories. Under federal jurisdiction, the North-West Territories had been politically organized under a governor and an appointed council in 1875. The region was granted representative government in 1888 and responsible government in 1897. Rejecting proposals to create one large province that might become too powerful, the federal government passed the Autonomy Bills to divide the North-West Territories into the provinces of Alberta and Saskatchewan in 1905. As in the case of Manitoba, the federal government retained ownership of the natural resources of the two new provinces in order to maintain control over their settlement and development in the critical formative stage. The northern boundary of the two provinces was established at the 60th parallel, the same as that of British Columbia, and the 110th meridian was chosen as the boundary between the two new provinces because it divided them into areas of roughly equal size. Together, the three Prairie Provinces would evolve into another strong regional interest to challenge the dominance of central Canada and the power of the federal government.

Western settlement was the catalyst for sustained national economic prosperity that ultimately seemed to justify Macdonald's National Policy. Relentless in attacking the National Policy as the source of regional discontent and Canada's economic ills while they were the Official Opposition, the Liberals wholeheartedly embraced the strategy after they came to power. The former advocates of free trade and reciprocity with the United States continued Macdonald's policy of tariff protection to stimulate domestic industry and east-west trade. The Liberal tariff policy of 1897 also extended Macdonald's idea of reciprocity of tariffs by offering lower customs duties to countries giving similarly favorable terms to Canada. Since Britain already adhered to such a policy, the Liberal tariff revision amount-ed to a measure of imperial preference that did not conflict with protectionist goals and yet appealed somewhat to both free trade and imperialist sentiments. As a result, Britain became the leading market for western grain in addition to other farm exports such as meat, dairy products, and fruit. Heavy British investment in Canadian development dur-ing the wheat boom period further strengthened relations between the two countries. Indeed, Laurier, like Macdonald, was committed to a national economic strategy that was transcontinental and transatlantic in scope.

The expansion of prairie settlement and east-west trade strained the facilities of the Canadian Pacific Railway. Rising western demand for lower freight rates and better ser-vice, especially to remote areas not linked to the CPR, convinced the Laurier govern-ment that another transcontinental line was necessary. By 1903 two powerful railway enterprises responded to offers of government support to compete with the CPR. The second-largest railway system in Canada, the Grand Trunk Railway, revived its earlier plan to extend its eastern-based line to the Pacific by undertaking to build the Grand Trunk Pacific from Winnipeg to Prince Rupert, some 550 miles up the coast from Van-couver. To open up the northern regions of Ontario and Quebec, the federal government agreed to construct the National Transcontinental from Winnipeg to Moncton and then to lease the new railway line to the Grand Trunk. Meanwhile, William Mackenzie and Donald Mann, who had built up the western-based Canadian Northern into the third-largest railway system in Canada, undertook to extend lines from Edmonton to Vancouver and from Port Arthur to Quebec City to fulfill their own transcontinental ambitions. The federal government tried to persuade the Grand Trunk and the Canadian Northern interests to join forces, but their mutual jealousies and conflicting ambitions stood in the way of any agreement. Indeed, the government could have forced a merger by making its support conditional upon a joint venture, but the optimism of the age induced even the normally pragmatic Laurier to assume that unlimited national expansion would enable Canada to sustain three transcontinental railways.

The completion of the two new transcontinental lines by 1915 added some 22,000 miles to the national railway system, thereby giving Canada the highest mileage per capi-ta of any country in the world. But the outbreak of World War I in the previous year cur-tailed the flow of immigration and slowed down the pace of national expansion. Not only did the three transcontinental railways find themselves involved in ruinous competition for a volume of traffic that was less than anticipated in the populated areas, but also the lines ran almost side by side through hundreds of miles of unproductive Shield wilderness and sparsely settled western communities. Further burdened by mismanagement and mounting debt, both the Grand Trunk Pacific and the Canadian Northern staggered into bankruptcy, and the Grand Trunk reneged on the agreement to assume the lease of the National Transcontinental.

The federal government could not afford to allow the railway companies to collapse because both taxpayers' money and the nation's reputation with international creditors were involved. A royal commission appointed in 1916 to investigate the railway problem recommended that the federal government take over the troubled lines. Over the next seven years, the Canadian Northern, the Grand Trunk Pacific, and the Grand Trunk were amalgamated with the National Transcontinental and the Intercolonial to form the state-owned Canadian National Railway (incorporated in 1919) to compete with the privately owned Canadian Pacific Railway (CPR). Despite the dubious financial legacy of the new transcontinental railways, their construction enhanced national prosperity, provided employment for many immigrants, and helped to uncover the previously remote or unknown northern resource frontier.

NEW RESOURCE FRONTIERS AND THE NEW INDUSTRIALISM

While the much-anticipated expansion of the western frontier was unfolding in accordance with the design of the National Policy, a new northern frontier was opening up to enhance the prospects of Canadian industrial development. Long the preserve of the fur trade, the Canadian Shield and the western Cordilleras became a treasury of minerals, timber, and hydroelectric power in the late 19th and early 20th centuries. As early as 1883, CPR construction crews blasting through the rugged terrain of northern Ontario discovered copper and nickel deposits in the vicinity of Sudbury. As refining processes, uses, and markets for the metal developed, Sudbury became the world's largest nickel producer. The building of the Temiskaming and Northern Ontario Railway led to the discovery of rich silver deposits around Cobalt north of Lake Nipissing in 1903 and touched off a mining boom that spread northward to Kirkland Lake and the Porcupine district. Railway construction through the Kootenay region of southeastern British Columbia also led to significant discoveries of gold, silver, copper, lead, and zinc. Although the economic importance of these mining operations was enduring, they did not capture the public imagination to the same extent as the Klondike gold rush of the late 1890s.

Fortune-seekers from all parts of the world flocked to the Klondike and Yukon River valleys to pan for gold starting in 1896. At the height of the gold rush in 1898, the previously unsettled subarctic frontier had a population of about 30,000, more than half of which was concentrated in the newly established town of Dawson. In the same year, the federal government created the Yukon Territory, administered by an appointed commissioner, in an effort to ward off the prospect of annexation to Alaska. Even if the economic significance of the Klondike strike was somewhat exaggerated and short-lived, the tales of sudden riches, heroic and tragic exploits, and the rowdiness and lawlessness of the mining frontier were immortalized through popular fiction and folklore, notably the poetic verses of Robert W. Service.

Perhaps less romantic than the mining booms, the exploitation of forest and water resources was just as vital to national development. The Douglas fir, spruce, and cedar stands of British Columbia along with the white pine forests of Ontario satisfied construction demands on the treeless prairies as well as in the growing cities and towns of central Canada and the United States. British Columbia's forests also supplied lumber to Asia. In addition, the softwood forest wealth of the Cordilleras and the Shield was a valuable source of pulpwood for the development of the pulp and paper industry, which made Canada one of the world's leading exporters of newsprint. Furthermore, the fast flowing rivers of the Shield and Cordilleras could readily be harnessed as sources of hydroelectric power, replacing coal in the booming factories of central Canada as well as in the evolving mining and pulp and paper industries. The age of electricity under public ownership and control was ushered in by the creation of the Ontario Hydro-Electric Power Commission (now Ontario Hydro) in 1906 to distribute and eventually to produce this vital source of energy.

Western settlement and the opening of the northern resource frontier stimulated industrial expansion, particularly in central Canada. As the National Policy had intended, a growing agricultural population in the West increased the demand for eastern manufactured goods, thereby giving rise to agricultural implements works, iron and steel foundries, machine shops, railway yards, textile mills, boot and shoe factories, and numerous smaller manufacturing enterprises that supplied consumer goods. By keeping out lower-priced foreign manufactured goods, the high tariff policies of the federal government received much credit for protecting existing industries and encouraging the creation of new enterprises. To climb the tariff wall, large American industrial firms opened branches in Canada, and the governments of Ontario and Quebec aggressively urged them on by offering bonuses, subsidies, and guarantees to locate new plants within their borders. Canadian industrial enterprises became increasingly attractive to foreign investors, especially from the United States and Great Britain. Much of the over $600 million of American capital that flowed into Canada from 1900 to 1913 was earmarked for mining and the pulp and paper industry, while British investors contributed nearly $1.8 billion, mostly in railway building, business development, and the construction of urban infrastructure. As a result, the gross value of Canadian manufactured products quadrupled from 1891 to 1916.

Expanding markets offered greater opportunities for mass production and necessitated larger sources of capital, which in turn led to the growing concentration of Canadian industry and finance. Small, often family-owned manufacturing companies merged to form large corporations that were considered more efficient and competitive in an expanding market. Corporate conglomerates such as the Steel Company of Canada (Stelco), Dominion Steel, Algoma Steel, Canada Cement, Maple Leaf Milling, Dominion Textiles, Massey Harris, and Imperial Oil emerged in the early 20th century to dominate production and distribution within their respective industries. By limiting foreign competition, high tariff policies tended to encourage the rise of these monopolies, which aroused hostility from small business and farmers. Although the federal government responded by passing the Combines Investigation Act in 1910, this attempt to control the growth of monopolies was ineffective mainly because the laissez-faire-oriented public sector was reluctant to interfere with private enterprises that employed so many workers and paid substantial taxes.

The financial sector was also consolidating into powerful organizations as government regulation dating back to the Bank Act of 1871 favored the development of a centralized system of branch banking that, unlike the decentralized system in the United States, tended to encourage the absorption of smaller and weaker banks by their larger and more stable competitors. Accordingly, the number of Canadian banks had decreased from 41 in 1886 to 22 in 1914. The three largest Canadian banks—the Bank of Montreal, the Montreal-based Royal Bank, and the Toronto-based Bank of Commerce—extended branches throughout the country and invested heavily in new industries.

Corresponding with the emergence of large corporations was the organization of skilled industrial workers into unions. Early labor unions were mutual aid societies rather than bargaining agents for their members. Not until 1872, after a successful strike of the Toronto Typographical Society against George Brown's *Globe* newspaper for a nine-hour day and six-day week, did the federal government pass the Trade Union Act, which recognized the right of registered unions to exist and to organize without fear of prosecution as illegal associations. On the other hand, an amendment to the Criminal Code passed at about the same time imposed severe penalties, including a prison sentence, for most forms of picketing and union pressure. In 1883 the Trades and Labour Congress of Canada (TLC) was formed as the second-largest national union association, surpassed in membership numbers only by the American-based Knights of Labor. Soon after its formation, the TLC affiliated itself with Samuel Gompers's American Federation of Labor (AFL), while remnants of the Knights of Labor formed a craft union known as the Canadian Federation of Labour in 1902. Other localized unions, such as the Provincial Workmen's Association in the Maritimes, the Catholic unions in Quebec, and the radical American-based International Workers of the World (IWW), which enjoyed some success in the West, emerged to challenge the international unions.

Despite these initial efforts to organize industrial workers, division within the labor ranks and the hostility of employers and government slowed the growth of unions. The union movement was divided over whether workers should be organized by industry or by trade. The Knights of Labor and the IWW endeavored to develop working-class consciousness and political organization through industrial unionism. The AFL and TLC promoted trade unionism that refrained from partisan political activity in favor of using economic power in the form of strikes and boycotts to achieve immediate improvements in wages, working hours, and working conditions. By 1914, over 140,000 out of a total trade union membership of about 166,000 belonged to international unions, thus raising concerns about foreign influences within the labor movement among both supporters and opponents. Furthermore, scarcely one in 10 workers was unionized, and most unskilled or semiskilled workers as well as all female laborers remained unorganized.

Government demonstrated its growing awareness of labor's role in industrialized Canada through the establishment of the Royal Commission on the Relations of Labour and Capital in 1889, through its proclamation in 1894 of Labour Day (the first Monday in September) as a national holiday, through the creation of the Federal Department of Labour in 1900, and through passage of the Industrial Disputes Investigation Act in 1907. The Ontario government also introduced the Workmen's Compensation Act in 1914, and most provinces established their own departments of labor by the early 1920s. On the whole, however, government maintained a laissez-faire attitude that it should not interfere in the workplace, with the result that the Industrial Disputes Investigation Act became more an instrument to prevent strikes and lockouts from disrupting industry than to resolve labor disputes equitably.

Thus, in the late 19th and early 20th centuries, Canada underwent a veritable industrial revolution that would permanently alter the way in which people earned their livelihoods. Increasingly, the factory was replacing the farm as the embodiment of the workplace as many Canadians found the prospect of a steady wage to be more appealing than relying on the unpredictable forces of nature and world markets. However, workers would soon discover that their economic and social security was no less precarious within modern industrial life.

IMMIGRATION AND THE SEEDS
OF MULTICULTURALISM

Besides altering the political map and economic fortunes of the nation, the wave of immigration that helped to sustain the prairie wheat boom significantly diversified the cultural composition of Canadian society. In 1891 the Canadian population was 58 percent British, 30 percent French, and 12 percent "other." This distribution reflected a basic assumption underlying Canadian immigration policy that preference should be given to foreign peoples who could be readily assimilated into the existing population. Physical and cultural distance from Britain and the degree to which skin pigmentation conformed to that of white Anglo-Saxons were the essential criteria by which the assimilation potential of immigrants was measured.

Naturally, the more than 1 million British immigrants who arrived from 1896 to 1914 were deemed to be most "desirable" or "preferred" by virtue of their language, religion, and customs. Still, British homesteaders who lacked farming experience had a difficult time adapting to a frontier environment. A notable example was the settlement established near Saskatoon by Reverend Isaac Barr, who proclaimed his "patriotic" intentions: "Let us take possession of Canada: Let our Cry be 'Canada for the British.'" However, most of his settlers were Londoners with no farming experience and little tolerance for pioneer hardships. The miserable failure of the Barr Colony acted as a deterrent to future British colonization schemes. Other British settlers who failed to adjust to rural life either drifted to the booming Prairie towns or left for the cities of the United States.

The nearly three-quarters of a million Americans who migrated to Canada during the wheat boom period were likewise desirable in terms of language and social customs, although their republican political ideas might be cause for some concern. Sifton was particularly interested in recruiting experienced pioneer farmers of the American West and in repatriating Canadians who had settled in the United States. However, American blacks were not welcome in Canada. While Canadian immigration agents highlighted the opportunities available to white settlers, they sought to discourage blacks by emphasizing the harshness of the climate and the loneliness of life on the western plains. The agents' efforts were apparently successful since less than 1,500 blacks immigrated to Canada during the first decade of the 20th century.

Sifton hoped to attract immigrants from northern and western Europe—Belgium, France, Germany, Holland, Scandinavia, and Switzerland—whom he regarded as easier to assimilate than the less desirable southern Europeans, including Armenians, Greeks, Italians, Jews, Portuguese, Spaniards, and Turks. The imperialist belief in the inherent superiority of the northern over the southern "races" was at its height in the early 20th century. Although the influx of the preferred northern and western Europeans turned out to be lower than anticipated, Sifton did express a special appreciation for the agricultural skills of eastern and central Europeans: "I think a stalwart peasant in a sheepskin coat, born on the soil, whose forefathers had been farmers for ten generations, with a stout wife, and a half-dozen children, is good quality." Through their experience on the land, Sifton was confident that these immigrants would eventually be "nationalized."

Of the nearly three-quarters of a million Europeans who arrived from 1896 to 1914, more than 100,000 were Ukrainians lured by the prospect of larger landholdings than were available to the peasantry in the Russian and Austro-Hungarian empires. Enthusiastically responding to the offer of *vilni zemli*, or free land, these industrious newcomers cleared and cultivated vast areas of prairie land and established tightly knit communities that retained many vestiges of their old world culture. They communicated in their own language, encouraged their children to wear their national dress, and worshiped in their distinctive Ukrainian Catholic and Orthodox churches with onion-shaped domes. Ukrainian cultural devotion aroused concern among Anglo Canadians such as social reformer J. S. Woodsworth, who in 1909 wrote about "how difficult is the problem of Canadianizing them" in his book *Strangers Within Our Gates*.

Other eastern European group settlement proved equally difficult to absorb. Religious persecution in their native Russia caused three pacifist sectarian groups—the Mennonites, the Doukhobors, and the Hutterites—to immigrate to western Canada on the promise from the federal government that they would be granted communal settlements, religious freedom, and exemption from military service. The German-speaking Mennonites were first to arrive, settling in the vicinity of Winnipeg during the 1870s. The success of the Mennonites encouraged immigration officials to offer special privileges to the Russian-speaking Doukhobors, who settled in the Prince Albert and Yorkton regions of Saskatchewan in 1899. However, their "strange ways" and several incidents of mass civil disobedience, including nude marches sensationalized in newspapers, aroused Anglo-Canadian hostility toward the Doukhobors. When they refused to swear an oath of allegiance to the Crown as a condition for gaining title to free land, they forfeited their holdings and relocated in the Kootenay region of British Columbia under the spiritual leadership of Peter Veregin in 1907. The German-speaking Hutterites lived in South Dakota until 1917, when wartime persecution forced them to resettle in southern Manitoba and southern Alberta. Assured of exemption from military service, they lived a simple communal life with their own schools and churches. The Hutterites prospered and expanded their farms rapidly, sometimes incurring the resentment and jealousy of their neighbors, who objected to their collective farming practices.

Sifton tolerated eastern European immigrants as good farmers, but he disapproved of southern Europeans because they tended to swell the ranks of the urban working class. In this regard, he faced considerable criticism from business interests who wanted Italians as cheap labor. However, labor unions were antagonistic toward unskilled Italian workers who, by accepting lower wages, took jobs away from union workers. The Jewish communities that formed in Montreal, Toronto, and Winnipeg after 1880 also incurred Anglo-Canadian displeasure for their unassimilable character, lack of agricultural experience, and industrious tendencies.

For the same reason, Asian immigrants were not welcome on the western prairies, but they were recruited as a source of diligent and cheap labor mainly for railway-building, fishing crews, and mining and lumber camps in British Columbia. Chinese immigrants first arrived during the gold-rush era from the late 1850s to the early 1860s, and another 15,000 were hired to work on the CPR in the 1880s. Unfortunately, Chinese workers were resented as unfair competition since they could readily be exploited by ruthless entrepreneurs. The provincial government imposed a head tax (payable upon entering the country), which reached $500 by 1903, to limit Asian immigration. Nevertheless, British Columbia's Asian population exceeded 10 percent by 1911. Opposition to Asian immigration reached a peak of frenzy in 1907 with the formation of the Asiatic

Exclusion League, which soon organized a protest march through Vancouver's China-town. In the ensuing riot, the mobs attacked Chinese residents and destroyed their property. British Columbians' insensitivity to Asian immigration was further demon-strated in 1914 when the provincial government refused to allow a shipload of prospec-tive immigrants from India to land in Vancouver. For two months, the ship anchored offshore, while the 400 predominantly Sikh passengers argued that they were British subjects and that many of them had professional qualifications. Ultimately, they were denied permission to land, and a Canadian naval vessel escorted the "alien" ship out to sea amid cries of "White Canada forever" and refrains of "Rule Britannia."

Canadian attitudes toward "foreigners" in the early 20th century were universally racist, inasmuch as the concept of a multicultural society still lay more than a half-century in the future. T. S. Sproule, a Conservative member of Parliament, proclaimed unabashedly and without much rebuttal: "Canada is today the dumping ground for the refuse of every country in the world." In *Strangers Within Our Gates*, Woodsworth spoke for many English-speaking Canadians when he warned: "If Canada is to become in a real sense a nation, if our people are to become one people, we must have one language." Anglo Canadians believed that the schools and churches had to "Canadianize" these newcomers, not only by teaching them English but also by inculcating British-Canadian beliefs in citizenship, democracy, and the Protestant work ethic.

The Anglo-Canadian perspective of education as an instrument of cultural assimila-tion and national unity further complicated attempts to resolve the schools question in the West. In 1897 Laurier concluded a compromise with Manitoba Premier Thomas Greenway that did not restore the state-supported separate school system but allowed religious instruction in the public schools for the last half hour of the day and bilingual teaching when 10 students in any school had a native language other than English. Because French no longer had the status of equality with English that it had been accorded under the Man-itoba Act of 1870, the Catholic hierarchy in Quebec accused Laurier of capitulating to the English-Canadian Protestants and appealed to the pope in Rome to intervene. Despite condemning the Manitoba School Act of 1890 and judging the Laurier-Greenway com-promise as unsatisfactory, the papacy agreed with Laurier that these terms were the best that Catholics could hope to obtain given their minority position in Manitoba.

Western opposition to separate denominational and linguistic schools reflected not only the prevailing cultural intolerance but also the declining influence of the French Catholic community since the Manitoba Act of 1870. Although thousands of French Canadians responded to the Catholic clergy's call to settle in the West during the 1880s, their numbers paled in comparison to English-speaking migrants. The Canadian West was simply too distant and remote compared to neighboring New England, which offered more employment opportunities in its factories and mills and which was already home to the majority of the more than 1 million French Canadians living in the United States by 1900. Furthermore, the Catholic clergy discouraged emigration from the province, preferring instead to encourage the colonization of northern Quebec.

A limited French Catholic presence and rising concerns about cultural homogene-ity of a growing population shaped the emerging schools question in the North-West Territories. The North-West Territories Act of 1875 allowed both Protestants and Catholics to establish schools and to share in public funds for education. The act also allowed the use of both English and French as languages of instruction. By the 1890s, however, French had been reduced to the language of instruction only in the early years of the declining Catholic school system. Bowing to pressure from Henri Bourassa, grandson of Louis-Joseph Papineau and emerging as the leading French-Canadian nationalist in Quebec, Laurier included an educational clause in the Autonomy Bills of 1905 restoring the original separate school system of the North-West Territories and incorporating it into the newly created provinces of Alberta and Saskatchewan. Widespread Anglo-Protestant protest, highlighted by Sifton's resignation, prompted Laurier to negotiate a compromise resolution similar to that achieved in the case of the Manitoba School Question. While Sifton felt uneasy enough about Laurier's handling of the issue to refuse to return to the Cabinet, Bourassa denounced the compromise as an infringement on rights previously enjoyed by French-Canadian Catholics in the West. He further argued that they should have the same rights that English Protestants in Quebec were granted at the time of Confederation. The controversy over western schools soon subsided as Bourassa and other French-Canadian nationalists essentially abandoned any hope of spreading their cultural influence to the West and focused on coping with the social and economic impact of urbanization and industrialization in Quebec. But the cultural bitterness incited by the schools questions would not be forgotten, especially as the controversy over Canada's imperial defense commitments further aroused nationalist passions in the general election of 1911.

EXTERNAL RELATIONS AND NATIONAL UNITY

The prosperity of the wheat boom era also prompted a reconsideration of Canada's national status in light of changing relations with Britain and the United States. Canada was a self-governing nation in the realm of domestic affairs, but it remained a colony in matters of international relations. Accordingly, the Dominion could only negotiate with other countries under the auspices of the British government, which conducted diplomatic relations for the empire as a whole. This continuing colonial status was not disputed at the time of Confederation because the new nation wanted to maintain the security of imperial defense, which appeared vital in the wake of Anglo-American tensions during the 1860s. The expectation was that, as in the colonial era, Britain would maintain an imperial garrison as the first line of defense and that the Canadian militia would supply auxiliary forces. In 1870, Prime Minister Macdonald surmised that, because of Canada's weakness in the face of an overtly expansionist southern neighbor, "It will be a century before we are strong enough to walk alone."

Obviously disagreeing with Macdonald, the British government decided to withdraw its garrisons from Canada in 1870–71, leaving the naval base at Halifax as the only British military presence. Disappointment over this decision was magnified by the Treaty of Washington in 1871, which demonstrated the precariousness of dependence on the imperial authority to act on Canada's behalf. The indignation over the apparent British willingness to sacrifice Canadian interests in order to maintain American friendship, however, was tempered by the realization that the struggling young Dominion was still heavily reliant on imperial economic and military support. Therefore, for the first three decades of nationhood, Canada was in the ambivalent position of wishing to maintain the security of the imperial tie while aspiring to greater control over national affairs.

The rise of imperialist sentiments during the 1880s and 1890s renewed British interest in closer relations with its self-governing colonies, of which Canada was the largest and oldest. Joseph Chamberlain, who was appointed colonial secretary in 1895, became the leading advocate of more centralized administration of the British Empire in order to enhance its strength and unity in world trade and defense. Certainly, the underlying assumptions of imperial unity—Anglo-Saxon superiority and identity with a glorious empire rather than an obscure colony—were appealing to many English-speaking Canadians. Moreover, the Canadian government actively participated in the Colonial Conferences associated with Queen Victoria's Golden Jubilee in 1887 and Diamond Jubilee in 1897, and Ottawa hosted another meeting of colonial premiers and British cabinet leaders in 1894. Laurier could also point to the measure of imperial preference included in his tariff policy of 1897 as a manifestation of Canada's willingness to play a key supporting role within a reconstituted British Empire. However, Canada was reluctant to undertake commitments that would ultimately compromise national independence. For this reason, Laurier rejected Chamberlain's proposals for an imperial council that would reduce Canada's legislative autonomy and for a specific financial pledge in support of the British navy.

Although Laurier recognized that when Britain was at war, Canada was legally obliged to follow, he was determined that Canada should be the sole judge of the commitment to be made to imperial defense. The outbreak of the Boer War in South Africa in 1899 brought the issue to a head. Chamberlain saw the clash between the British Cape Colony and the rebel Boers, descendants of the original Dutch settlers in the republics of Transvaal and the Orange Free State, as an opportunity to demonstrate to potential European adversaries that Britain could call upon military support and unity from its self-governing colonies. Canadian imperialists responded enthusiastically to the prospect of sending troops overseas to fight alongside British forces. The governor-general, Lord Minto, and the British-appointed commander of the Canadian militia, Major General Edward Hutton, assumed that Canada would heed the call to arms and had no difficulty enlisting English-speaking recruits.

While expressing sympathy for the British military effort, Laurier repudiated Minto and Hutton by insisting that the Canadian Parliament still had to decide on the nature and extent of the nation's commitment to imperial defense. Laurier was acutely aware of the imminent problem of national unity aroused by the Boer War. French Canadians were opposed to participation in a distant imperial war that posed no apparent threat to Canadian security. Prime Minister Macdonald had used this same argument to reject a British request for Canadian troops to participate in a military expedition to the Sudan in 1885. Furthermore, French Canadians tended to identify with the Boers' struggle for liberation from their imperial oppressors. In response to imperialist accusations of disloyalty to Britain, French Canadians insisted that they were merely affirming a truly Canadian nationalism.

The Laurier government compromised by sending a voluntary force of 1,000 men to serve under the British command, stipulating that this decision should not be "construed as a precedent for future action." By the end of the Boer War in 1902, another 6,300 Canadians had volunteered under private auspices or through direct recruitment on behalf of the British government. Laurier's policy was attacked by English imperialists as an abdication of Canadian responsibility and by French nationalists as submission to British pressure. Bourassa resigned his parliamentary seat in protest and became Laurier's leading nationalist adversary in French Canada. The passionate rhetoric on both sides eventually ran its course, and the controversy did not prevent Laurier from achieving a decisive victory in the national election of 1900. Nevertheless, the Boer War controversy gave the first indication that Canada's involvement on the world stage would be an additional source of internal cultural conflict.

During the Colonial Conference of 1902, Laurier continued to oppose Chamberlain's plan for greater imperial unity in defense and government and to press for the revival of imperial trade preferences as an alternative to a proposed customs union. Although Laurier agreed to regular Canadian participation in further meetings to be known as Imperial Conferences convened at four-year intervals, he was concerned that such consultation with Britain on foreign affairs would involve Canada in implied commitments without commensurate influence over decisions. For the Imperial Conferences to be truly consultative, Laurier believed, Canada should be granted greater control over its foreign relations. But Britain resolutely refused to impair the unity of imperial diplomacy. The liability of diplomatic subordination for Canada once again became apparent during the Alaska boundary dispute.

The Klondike gold rush precipitated a dispute over the boundary between Canada and Alaska, which had never been clearly established when the United States purchased the territory from Russia in 1867. While the major goldfields were definitely within Canadian territory, access to them from the Pacific Ocean was not as certain. At the center of the dispute was control over the main entrance to the Yukon and the Klondike River district, the port of Skagway and the inlet leading to it known as Lynn Canal, both located in the panhandle or coastal strip. The boundary claims of both countries included Skagway and the head of the Lynn Canal, thereby allowing them to control the lucrative trade generated by the gold rush. In the wake of U.S. president Theodore Roosevelt's threat to send in American troops, the dispute dragged on until 1903 when it was referred to a joint commission of six officials. While Roosevelt appointed three representatives who had publicly opposed any compromise, the British government appointed two Canadians and the Lord Chief Justice of England, Lord Alverston. As was the case with the Treaty of Washington, Britain appeared to put Anglo-American friendship ahead of the Canadian claims inasmuch as Lord Alverston voted with the U.S. members of the commission. Thus, the Alaska boundary dispute revived anti-American sentiments and demonstrated Canada's need to control its own external relations.

The establishment of a Department of External Relations and an International Joint Commission in 1909 were noteworthy, albeit limited, steps in that direction. While the responsibility for policy-making remained with the British Foreign Office, the new department assumed some of the administrative functions relating to the Canadian government's growing relations with other countries, principally Britain and the United States. Designed to facilitate direct Canadian-American negotiations on mutual problems, the commission consisted of three Canadian representatives, appointed by the Crown on the recommendation of the Canadian government, in addition to the three American delegates. The responsibilities of the commission included the international waterways, boundaries, and any other matter raised by the governments of the two countries. The absence of a British delegate among the Canadian contingent represented a significant departure from the bodies that had negotiated the Treaty of Washington and the Alaska boundary dispute.

Canada's relations with Britain and the United States became the focus of the national election of 1911. Imperial relations were complicated by the escalating rivalry for European naval supremacy between Britain and Germany. As the threat of war mounted, Britain renewed its appeal for colonial contributions to the imperial naval fleet. Instead of a direct contribution of money to the Royal Navy over which Canada would have no influence, Laurier preferred to build a distinctly Canadian naval force. Accordingly, in 1910 he introduced the Naval Service Bill to establish a naval college to

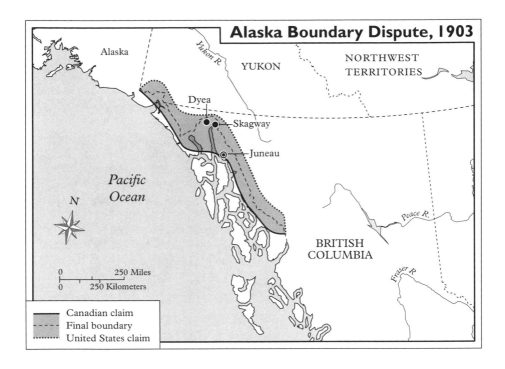

train officers and a Canadian navy consisting of five cruisers and six destroyers that could be placed under British command in the event of war.

What Laurier thought would be a suitable compromise for a controversial national and international issue turned out to satisfy neither the imperialists nor the French-Canadian nationalists. While the imperial-minded Conservatives favored the development of a national naval force in the long run, they ridiculed the "tin pot navy" as a disgrace to Canada's role within the empire and called for an immediate response that included a direct financial contribution to the British fleet as it prepared for war. At the same time, Bourassa led the French-Canadian opposition to the bill on the grounds that the proposed Canadian navy would only encourage British militarism, which would inevitably draw Canada into European conflicts. Although the intense opposition from both sides did not prevent the comfortable Liberal majority in Parliament from easily passing the bill, the controversy would come back to haunt Laurier in the national election of the following year.

Further dividing the nation was the renewed controversy over reciprocity with the United States, a policy that had been the goal of the Canadian government since the termination of the original agreement in 1866. Responding to yet another American rejection of reciprocity in 1897, Laurier boldly declared: "There will be no more pilgrimages to Washington." The subsequent economic boom, which redeemed the high-tariff National Policy, rendered reciprocity less urgent than it had appeared in the last third of the 19th century. By 1910, however, the United States had become more interested in free trade with Canada, partly in response to the growing north-south trade fueled by the opening of the northern resource frontier. The settlement of the long-standing fisheries dispute by the International Court that same year had also helped to build goodwill between the two North American neighbors. When the American government formally offered to negotiate reciprocity, Laurier saw an opportunity to appease western agrarian agitation against national economic policies.

Western farmers had been especially persistent in their demands for lower freight rates and tariffs. The Laurier Liberals attempted to address the former grievance through the Crow's Nest Pass agreement of 1897, in which the federal government awarded the CPR a subsidy to build a branch line to Nelson, British Columbia, in return for lowering freight rates between the West and central Canada. As far as the tariff was concerned, farmers resented having to buy their agricultural implements and other manufactured goods in a closed protected market and to sell their wheat in an open competitive market. To exert pressure on government, the farmers organized various provincial or regional Grain Growers' Associations and in 1909 formed the Canadian Council of Agriculture. The coun-

Wilfred Laurier (1841–1919) was Canada's first French-Canadian prime minister. His service as prime minister from 1896 to 1911 remains the longest unbroken tenure in office.

cil's demand for tariff reform convinced Laurier that he could make significant political gains by balancing the National Policy with reciprocity.

Early in 1911, the Canadian and American governments concluded a trade agreement that in effect renewed the Reciprocity Treaty of 1854. The proposal provided for the free entry of Canadian natural products into the United States, while American manufacturers benefited from a lower Canadian tariff. The two countries agreed to implement free trade through concurrent legislation rather than by a treaty so that Canada could avoid seeking British approval. But while reciprocity passed through the U. S. Congress, the agreement encountered vigorous opposition in the Canadian Parliament. A group of Liberals led by Clifford Sifton abandoned Laurier and sided with the Conservatives, who feared that the achievement of reciprocity would prolong the 15-year Liberal ascendancy. Outside of Parliament, the Canadian Manufacturers Association along with powerful railway, banking, and commercial interests that were ardent supporters of the National Policy waged an emotional campaign that associated reciprocity with disloyalty to the imperial tie, the threat of American annexation, and the lingering bitterness over the Alaska boundary dispute. The Canadian opponents of reciprocity were helped by the rhetoric of American supporters of the agreement such as the speaker of the House of Representatives who proclaimed: "I am for it, because I hope to see the day when the American flag will float over every square foot of the British North American possessions clear to the North Pole."

Thus, Laurier became trapped in a nationalist cross fire during the national election campaign of 1911. In Ontario, Laurier was branded as a continentalist amid the Conservatives' rallying cry, "No Truck or Trade with the Yankees"; he also incurred the imperialist wrath over his handling of the naval controversy. Yet in Quebec, Laurier was accused of being too much of an imperialist for his authorship of the Naval Service Bill. As the Liberals went down to defeat at the hands of the Conservatives led by Robert Borden, it became apparent that Laurier was an unwitting victim of the prosperity of the age and an evolving sense of nationalism. The east-west trading system of the National Policy was working effectively, thereby rendering interest in north-south traffic less pressing. Moreover, the question of Canada's survival was giving way to an assertion of national confidence that was increasingly suspicious of foreign domination and entanglements. Canada's stature within the international community would be put to the test with the outbreak of World War I.

CHAPTER 14

THE CONFIRMATION
OF NATIONHOOD

Canada made an impressive debut on the world stage during World War I. The outstanding performance of Canadian soldiers on the battlefields of Europe and the continued expansion of the national economy in support of the war effort further advanced the cause of Dominion autonomy. On the other hand, national unity suffered in the wake of the conscription crisis of 1917, which sparked a clash of nationalisms between the English and French cultural communities and altered the course of Canadian electoral politics. During the mostly prosperous 1920s, the balance of the Canadian economy clearly shifted from agriculture to industry with the further expansion of manufacturing and the northern resource frontier. The uneven distribution of the benefits of post-war growth and prosperity, however, contributed to the revival of regional discontent expressed through the Winnipeg General Strike of 1919 and the rise of the western Progressive Party and the Maritime rights movement. Determined to shape a distinct sense of Canadianism that was free of imperialism and sensitive to continentalism, the Liberals under Mackenzie King continued the quest for national autonomy and the reconstitution of the British Empire into a Commonwealth of Nations, ultimately achieved by the Statute of Westminster in 1931.

THE GREAT WAR

As Europe drifted toward war, the Borden administration was faced with the same question of imperial defense that had contributed to Wilfrid Laurier's defeat. Convinced that a military crisis existed overseas, Prime Minister Robert Borden introduced a new Naval Aid Bill in 1912 that abandoned Laurier's plan for a Canadian navy in favor of an emergency contribution of $35 million to cover the cost of three battleships to be built and equipped in Britain. Apart from this emergency aid, Borden expected that any permanent defense measures would be contingent upon a greater Canadian voice in deciding imperial foreign policy. Despite strong opposition in Quebec, Borden's Naval Bill passed the House of Commons, only to be blocked by the Liberal-dominated Senate in 1913. But before the naval question could be settled, the long-anticipated war erupted in Europe.

When Britain declared war in response to Germany's invasion of neutral Belgium in August 1914, Canada, as part of the empire, was automatically at war. Initially, support for the war effort was virtually unanimous as both English and French Canada recognized that the defeat of Britain and France by Germany would severely jeopardize Canadian growth and security. Few Canadians questioned the recruitment propaganda and newspaper reports that depicted the war in terms of a struggle between democracy and tyranny. Without opposition, Parliament passed the War Measures Act, which gave the federal government broad emergency powers to suspend civil liberties and to regulate any aspect of society or the economy deemed essential for the conduct of the war. The early enthusiasm for the war effort and the acceptance of sweeping state power was also based on the assumption that the war would be a short-lived skirmish resulting in a decisive Allied victory.

Within the first two months of the war, Canada's standing army of only 3,000 was reinforced by more than 30,000 volunteers to form the Canadian Expeditionary Force, which became the First Canadian Infantry Division. The First Division was thrust into unimagined trench warfare and had to withstand the first poisonous chlorine gas attacks outside the small Belgian town of Ypres in 1915. Ultimately, four divisions were organized into a distinct Canadian Corps that distinguished itself in battle after battle on the western front, notably the Somme in 1916 and Passchendaele and Vimy Ridge in 1917. The Canadian Corps was also instrumental in the final, successful Allied attack, especially during "Canada's hundred days" from August 4 to November 11, 1918, when troops broke through the fortified Hindenburg Line and pushed across the Belgian border to reach Mons on Armistice Day.

Thousands of other Canadians served with distinction in the British and Allied armies. Canadians were among the leading "aces" who engaged in man-to-man air combat in the service of the Royal Flying Corps, the forerunner of the Royal Air Force. For example, the legendary Billy Bishop was credited with shooting down 72 German fighters, earning him the coveted Victoria Cross, while Ray Brown reputedly shot down the notorious "Red Baron" von Richthofen. Canadians were engaged in the Atlantic Coastal Patrol, which evolved into the Royal Canadian Navy after the war. By the end of the war, some 625,000 Canadian men and women were mobilized for the armed forces, over two-thirds of whom served overseas. The toll of Canadian casualties included upwards of 60,000 killed in action (comparable to the losses suffered by the United States) and more than 200,000 wounded. The Canadian fighting effort was truly remarkable for a country of only 8 million people.

While the Canadian armed forces were distinguishing themselves on the battlefield, the civilian population on the home front was geared up for a level of war production that would have a profound and lasting effect on the national economy. With the extraordinary demand for food by European allies, the export of Canadian agricultural products, meat, and livestock soared beyond all expectations. The amount of prairie wheatland under cultivation almost doubled, while grain prices rose over 50 percent. The German blockade of the Baltic region increased the need for Canadian lumber and wood pulp. European munitions factories consumed more and more minerals, especially base metals such as copper, lead, zinc, and nickel, leading to the opening of new deposits and the development of new methods for processing low-grade ores. Under the pressure of war, Canada expanded its range of manufacturing output, particularly in the realm of heavy industry, including ammunition, weaponry, steel ships, and aircraft frames. With one-third of its manufacturing capacity absorbed in munitions production, Canada emerged from World War I as a major industrial state. The expansion of agriculture and industry so overwhelmed the east-west trading system that, for the moment, the building of three transcontinental railway networks appeared justified.

Organizing the nation's resources for wartime production required an unprecedented degree of government intervention in the economic and social spheres. Munitions production was brought under the direction of a Shell Committee established by the minister of the militia, Sir Sam Hughes. When Hughes was accused of corruption, patronage, and profiteering in 1915, the committee was replaced by the Imperial Munitions Board acting under the British Ministry of Munitions. As rising wartime demand led to shortages of basic commodities such as food and fuel and to price inflation—which increased the cost of living by about 50 percent from 1915 to 1918—the Canadian government was compelled to impose a system of rationing. Among the public agencies established to regulate the production, sale, distribution, and consumption of a variety of essential products and raw materials were the War Purchasing Commission and Munitions Resources Commission in 1915, the Cost of Living Commission in 1916, the Food Control Board and the Fuel Control Board in 1917, and the War Trade Board in 1918. Of enduring significance was the government effort to control wheat production and marketing through the formation of the Board of Grain Supervisors in 1917, which became the Canada Wheat Board in the following year. Likewise, the federal government's decision to take over major Canadian railways except for the CPR in 1916 was a prelude to the formation of the Canadian National Railway (CNR) system by 1920.

The most enduring intrusion of government into the lives of its citizens, however, resulted from the financial burdens imposed by World War I. The traditional sources of federal government revenue, customs duties on imports and the sale of bonds primarily in the London market, proved insufficient to conduct the war effort. Consequently, as a result of a sustained campaign appealing to patriotism, the government sold over $2 billion worth of "victory bonds" over the duration of the war. During the war, New York replaced London as the main market for Canadian securities. The federal government also invaded the field of direct taxation, which had hitherto been left to the provinces, with the imposition of a business profits tax in 1916 and the first national income tax in 1917. The federal government promised that its levy of 3 percent for a family earning more than $3,000 or an individual earning more than $1,500 was merely a temporary wartime measure.

Even more critical than the government's monetary requirements was the need for human resources. As the war progressed, Canada experienced a shortage of "manpower" not only to serve in the armed forces but also to work on farms and in factories and offices. So the country called upon its great reservoir of "womanpower." About 2,500 women made a significant contribution on the battlefront by serving in a nursing capacity in the Canadian Army Medical Corps; 56 women died while in the service of Canada. Women also served the country through voluntary organizations such as the Imperial Order of Daughters of the Empire (IODE), the Red Cross, the Young Women's Christian Association (YWCA), and the Canadian Patriotic Fund, incorporated by the federal government in 1914 to assist families of soldiers overseas. The demands of recruiting and war production created labor shortages that allowed women to enter the workforce to fill office positions and factory jobs previously held by men. Employers actually found it advantageous to employ women, not only because of their capabilities but also because they were paid less than half the wages that men earned. But labor unions objected to women joining their ranks because they were considered to be merely temporary, cheap workers. An important consequence of the active involvement of women in the war effort and the workforce was the extension of voting rights by federal and provincial legislation passed during and immediately following the war.

THE CONSCRIPTION CRISIS

The shortage of recruits for enlistment in military service jeopardized not only the war effort but also national unity. In his New Year's message for 1916, Prime Minister Borden promised that Canada would contribute 500,000 soldiers to the war effort, well over double the number of recruits who had already enlisted. But the drain on human resources resulting from brutal trench warfare on the European battlefield had already dampened enthusiasm for the war, which was reflected in the steadily dwindling monthly recruitment figures. Moreover, farm production and the expanding munitions industry competed with the armed forces for human resources. By the end of 1916, enlistments were still 70,000 short of Borden's goal, and controversy was brewing over relative contributions to the war effort. Rough estimates indicated that volunteers were nearly one-half British-born, about one-third native-born English-speaking Canadians, while French Canadians and non-Anglo-Saxon immigrants equally comprised the remainder of the recruits. Differential rates of enlistment intensified imperialist passions and prejudices, while provoking a renewed defensive nationalism within the French-Canadian community.

The reluctance of French Canadians to participate more actively in the war effort was partly related to their North American cultural outlook. Long cut off from their ancestral homeland, French Canadians did not share a strong emotional attachment to France or Britain. Canada was their homeland, and many French Canadians saw no reason to become entangled in Britain's imperialistic war. Moreover, French Canadians were discouraged by the superior attitude and uninformed prejudice of Minister of Militia and Defense Hughes, who presided over the recruitment, organization, and training of French-Canadian volunteers with little consideration for their distinct language and culture. Few French-speaking officers were appointed, particularly in the higher ranks, and the chief recruiting officer in Quebec was an English Protestant clergyman. Other than the Royal 22nd Battalion, better known as the "Vandoos," which served with distinction on the battlefield, no French-speaking regiments were formed, and English remained the sole language of the Canadian armed forces.

The question of language was aggravated by the revival of the separate schools controversy. On the eve of World War I, the substantial French-speaking population that had settled in northern and eastern Ontario near the Quebec border had built up a system of state-supported separate schools in which French was a major language of instruction. Opposition to French language schools arose from the Orange Order, which believed that the English language was essential to imperial unity, and from the Irish Catholics seeking to control the separate school system by favoring religious but not bilingual education. In 1913 Regulation 17 of the Ontario Department of Education made English the official language of education and restricted the use of French as the language of instruction to the first two years of elementary school while permitting French as a subject of study for one hour a day. French-Canadian outrage was most vehemently expressed by Henri Bourassa who compared Ontarians to the Germans, remarking that it was not necessary to go to Europe to fight tyranny, since the enemy lived next door. Reinforcing French-Canadian alienation, the Manitoba Education Act of 1916 overturned the bilingual clause of the Laurier-Greenway compromise by abolishing French as the language of instruction within the provincial school system. By then, Bourassa was openly condemning the war, and riots had erupted in the wake of recruitment efforts in some Quebec communities.

The anti-French sentiments expressed in the schools controversies and the recruit-ment campaigns were symptomatic of the prevailing climate of nativism and cultural repression fostered by wartime patriotism. The federal government used the War Mea-sures Act to control the movement of "enemy aliens," which meant that all German or Austro-Hungarian immigrants were viewed with suspicion and threatened with intern-ment; by the end of the war, 83,000 alleged German and Austrian sympathizers were interned in camps. Public antipathy toward Germany led to the town of Berlin, Ontario, being renamed Kitchener in 1917.

As Canadian casualties mounted overseas and the system of voluntary enlistments could not keep up with the demand for troop reinforcements, Borden concluded that conscription was imperative. The Military Service Act introduced in July 1917 made mil-itary service compulsory for all able-bodied British subjects from 20 to 45 years of age, with the exception of those in vital industries, those who were conscientious objectors, and those to whom service would pose "serious hardship." Prime Minister Borden hoped to avoid dividing the nation on the issue of compulsory service by forming a coalition gov-ernment with both Conservative and Liberals in his Cabinet. Laurier realized that to sup-port Borden might mean sacrificing Quebec to his rival, Bourassa, whereas to oppose conscription and a coalition government would risk alienating many English-speaking members of the Liberal Party. Laurier declined Borden's offer to form an alliance and decided to lead the campaign against conscription.

While opposition to conscription was most passionate and at times violent in Que-bec, farmers and industrial workers in English Canada had reason to object to compul-sory military service. Farmers who were already hard pressed for help were reluctant to sacrifice their sons into the armed forces, while workers saw military conscription as a prelude to compulsory industrial service that would limit their labor mobility and rights. Both groups demanded "conscription of wealth" in the form of higher taxes and govern-ment control of business to ensure that the entrepreneurs who were benefiting from a booming war economy made their sacrifices. Opposition also came from pacifist groups such as Quakers, Mennonites, and the Canadian Women's Peace Party. Nevertheless, the Military Service Act passed through Parliament on the strength of both Conservative and Liberal support but at the expense of national unity.

To enforce conscription, Borden proceeded with his plan to form a coalition gov-ernment and then to call a national election. While Laurier remained in opposition, a large contingent of English-speaking Liberals, particularly in Ontario and the West, followed Clifford Sifton to join Borden in a Union government in October 1917. In preparation for an election, the government passed the Military Voters Act, which extended the franchise to all men and women in the armed forces and denied it to conscientious objectors. Furthermore, the War Times Election Act gave the right to vote to the widows, wives, sisters, and adult daughters of Canadians serving overseas while disenfranchising citizens from enemy countries who had been naturalized since 1902. The rationale behind these legislative measures was that the enfranchised would be inclined to vote for the Conservatives while the disenfranchised had tended to vote for the Liberals. During the election campaign, Borden sought to secure more votes by promising to exempt farmers' sons from conscription. When the government reneged on this pledge after the election, thousands of farmers staged an angry demonstration in Ottawa, further indicating that opposition to compulsory military service extended beyond the French protest.

Bolstered by campaign rhetoric that claimed that voting for Laurier's fragmented Liberals amounted to support for Germany, Borden's Union government predictably carried every province but Quebec in the federal election of December 1917. That the Liberals won 62 out of 65 seats in Quebec but only 20 out of 140 in the rest of the country highlighted the depth of ethnic division between English and French Canada incited by conscription. The implementation of conscription triggered more protest demonstrations and riots in Quebec, including one in the provincial capital on Easter weekend of 1918 during which four people died. Ultimately, only about one-quarter of the 100,000 Canadian soldiers recruited through conscription reached the European front by the end of the war in November 1918. Thus, while the conscription crisis was short-lived in military terms, its political and social legacy would prove to be enduring.

NEW ECONOMIC DIRECTIONS IN THE ROARING TWENTIES

At the end of World War I, Canadians expected to reap the rewards of having fought so courageously to "make the world safe for democracy." However, their optimism was immediately dampened by the outbreak of the Spanish influenza epidemic of 1918–19, which killed some 21 million people worldwide, including 50,000 in Canada. Indeed, almost as many Canadians died from this "silent enemy," which was almost certainly brought back home by returning soldiers, as had been killed overseas during World War I. The epidemic, which overtaxed all medical facilities and personnel, brought not only death but also social and economic disruption. In an effort to control the spread of the disease, municipal and provincial governments closed all but necessary services and enacted laws to quarantine afflicted families and communities as well as to enforce the wearing of gauze masks in public. Business suffered from the lack of demand for products or the lack of healthy workers to meet production needs. The Canadian government responded to the crisis by establishing the Department of Health in 1919.

Canadians were further plagued by postwar economic instability. The renewed demand for consumer goods in the wake of the reabsorption of over half a million war veterans into civilian life raised the cost of living by 1919 to double the level it had been five years earlier. But as the demand for war supplies declined and wheat prices dropped by more than half, inflation gave way to recession in 1920. Looking upon the recession as an inevitable cyclical slump accentuated by the transition from wartime to peacetime production from which the free enterprise economy would naturally recover, the federal government responded by merely restricting immigration and inaugurating a program for assisting the provinces in the provision of relief to unemployed urban workers. The return of prosperity by 1923 seemed to confirm this laissez-faire faith in the unlimited prospects of the Canadian economy based upon the National Policy.

As in the past, wheat production figured prominently in the economic boom that prevailed for the remainder of the 1920s. War-ravaged Europe still needed food supplies, and postrevolution Russia was temporarily in decline as a grain-exporting nation. With prices recovering to within two-thirds of the wartime peak, western farmers extended the agrarian frontier into the semidesert regions of southwestern Saskatchewan and southeastern Alberta and as far north as the Peace River valley. The 1928 crop, which proved to be the largest on record, established Canada as the leading wheat-exporting nation in the world. Western farmers benefited from reduced railway freight rates that helped to make the price of Canadian wheat attractive in European countries. Indeed, the 1920s proved to be the high tide of Canadian railway transportation, not only because of the organization of the CNR system but also because the CNR and its private competitor, the CPR, spent over $700 million to build branch lines, improve passenger service, and modernize equipment. Although Canadian railways became renowned for their comfortable and luxurious passenger service, wheat shipments from western fields to eastern grain elevators and markets remained the backbone of the transcontinental system. This postwar wheat boom, however, would not be the economic catalyst that its prewar predecessor had been, primarily because Canadian farmers were increasingly competing with other wheat-growing countries, such as Argentina, Australia, and a rejuvenated Soviet Union, for a shrinking world market.

Furthermore, the Canadian government was no longer as committed to the centralized economic direction embodied in the National Policy. Indeed, by the 1920s the original purposes of Confederation had been achieved: a flood of settlers had filled the vacant lands of the West, a vast transcontinental transportation network was complete, and a protective tariff had stimulated a substantial manufacturing industry. Although immigration resumed in 1923, the federal government no longer undertook extensive advertising and recruitment campaigns. The age of free land grants had passed, and immigrants to the west had to purchase farms. Thousands of immigrants still came to complete the settlement of the western prairies during the 1920s, but the influx never reached the levels of the prewar wheat boom. The majority of the approximately 1 million immigrants who came to Canada during the decade tended to settle in the expanding urban centers, where they became part of the growing industrial workforce.

Postwar immigration continued the trend toward multiculturalism initiated by the prewar influx of non-British and non-French people. By 1931 the Canadian population was less than 52 percent British, a little over 28 percent French, and 20 percent "other." In other words, ethnic groups other than English and French had increased by three-quarters since the turn of the 20th century. These new ethnic groups were still a distinct minority, but they continued to raise concerns about the changing character of Canadian society.

The greatest developments in the postwar Canadian economy were not in wheat farming on the western prairies but in the extraction and processing of pulpwood, minerals, and hydroelectric power from the northern resource frontier. The ample softwood timber stands of the Canadian Shield and the Western Cordilleras sustained a pulp and paper industry that made Canada the world's leading exporter of newsprint by the end of the

1920s. With much of its own softwood timber stands depleted, the United States offered a lucrative market for Canadian newsprint to sustain its mass-produced daily newspapers, magazines, advertising copy, and cardboard packaging. At first, unprocessed pulpwood was converted into paper in American factories. But as the decade progressed, American entrepreneurs found that the availability of cheap hydroelectric power and good transportation facilities made it more economical to establish branch plant paper mills in Canada. Added incentives came from the provincial governments of Ontario, Quebec, and British Columbia, which strategically restricted the export of pulpwood, while providing a welcoming environment for the establishment of branch plants. By the end of the decade, three giant companies—International Paper Paper Co., Abitibi Paper Co., and Canadian Power and Paper Co.—controlled more than half the pulp production, and Americans owned and controlled more than one-third of Canada's pulp production.

The United States also needed Canadian base metals to produce consumer goods such as automobiles, radios, and electrical appliances. As prices for base metals such as copper, zinc, lead, and nickel rose high enough to encourage northern exploration and to reopen some mines with lower-grade ores, American capital was vital to finance purchases of complex and expensive mining equipment. Canada's greatest mining ventures during the 1920s included the gold and copper operations of Noranda Mines in Quebec; the copper and zinc operations of the Hudson Bay Mining and Smelting in Flin Flon, Manitoba; and the International Nickel Company of Canada (INCO) of Sudbury, Ontario, which controlled 90 percent of world nickel production. The discovery of oil and natural gas in the Turner Valley south of Calgary in 1914 heralded Alberta's future role as a major energy producer.

Mining and the pulp and paper industry stimulated and were stimulated by the development and use of hydroelectric power. The numerous rivers and lakes of the Canadian Shield were harnessed to produce cheap and efficient supplies of electricity for home lighting and for manufacturing goods such as appliances, automobile parts, and chemicals. Realizing the importance of hydroelectric power in the process of industrialization and urbanization, the provincial governments and the business community accepted public ownership as the most economical means of maintaining an efficient power supply.

In addition to the new staples, new technology relating to transportation and communication contributed to the prosperity and growth of the 1920s. The advent of the automobile and the industry that it spawned had a spectacular impact on the Canadian economy. By the end of the 1920s, more than 1.2 million automotive vehicles (cars, trucks, buses, and motorcycles) were in operation on Canadian roads, about triple the number at the beginning of the decade. About three-quarters of these vehicles were manufactured by branch plants of the "big three" American companies—Ford, Chrysler, and General Motors—which had absorbed most of their smaller Canadian competitors. The more automated American giants could make mass-produced and less expensive models, such as the popular Ford Model T, which sold for under $400. At such a reasonable price, the automobile evolved from a play toy of the rich into a necessity of life that one out of every two Canadian families owned.

The automobile revolutionized the Canadian landscape of the 1920s as the railway had done in the 1850s. Road-building became more important than ever, particularly in the cities, where asphalt-paved streets became more commonplace. By the end of the 1920s, Canada had more than 75,000 miles of roads, 10,000 miles of which were paved in asphalt. The automobile and better roads boosted the tourism industry by encouraging ownership of summer cottages and facilitating travel to northern vacation lands, particularly for Americans. By the end of the 1920s, some 4 million American visitors were spending over $300 million a year in Canada, as they enjoyed the unspoiled beauty of the vast natural landscape. Increased automobile travel also stimulated factories that manufactured tires and spare parts as well as service stations and petroleum refineries.

Aviation also expanded greatly in the 1920s as veteran World War I pilots, using surplus war planes, opened up the northern resource frontier. They flew geologists, prospectors, equipment, and minerals into remote areas, in addition to providing supplies and services for isolated settlements. Communications were also improved by the popularization of the telephone, originally invented in 1875 by Alexander Graham Bell, a Canadian. The greatest communications invention of the era, however, was the radio, which became the most popular entertainment medium. In 1920 Montreal radio station XWA (later CFCF) relayed the first scheduled broadcast in North America. The radio also accelerated the rise in popularity of spectator sports, highlighted by the first broadcast of *Hockey Night in Canada* by Foster Hewitt in 1923. Despite these pioneer efforts, more than three-quarters of the radio programs to which Canadians were listening by the end of the decade originated from the more powerful American border stations. This programming, along with the rising American film industry, was beginning to exert a pervasive influence on Canadian culture. In effect, while the hearts of Canadians were still closely tied to the British Empire, their minds were increasingly being Americanized.

The changing orientation of Canadian life mirrored the new direction of the Canadian economy. Unlike wheat, which moved from west to east for shipment to the British market, the new extractive staples, including minerals, pulpwood, and hydroelectric power, traveled more along north-to-south lines, since their main markets were in the United States. While Britain remained the chief market for the older products of farming and the forest, the new staple exports helped to make the United States Canada's leading trading partner by the early 1920s. Furthermore, whereas the expansion and settlement of the western agrarian frontier and its integration into a transcontinental and transatlantic economic framework had been directed almost exclusively by the federal government, the development of the northern resource frontier and its integration into a "continental" economy was largely driven by provincial governments. In effect, the "new continentalism" was further shifting the balance of power and responsibility from the federal to the provincial governments. The lack of a new national economic strategy, the rise of provincial power, and the uneven distribution of prosperity among regions contributed to the outburst of discontent directed toward the federal government and the two traditional political parties.

RENEWED REGIONAL PROTEST AND NEW POLITICAL CHALLENGERS

Postwar political unrest was complicated by conflicting demands and expectations that divided city from country and east from west. In the cities, industrial workers who had generally cooperated with government and business during the war responded to postwar inflation by staging a series of strikes in 1918 and 1919 to support their demands for better wages, working conditions, and job security. Buoyed by the doubling of union membership during the war, the labor movement, in typical Canadian fashion, remained divided over the most effective strategy for overcoming the power of big business. While the more conservative trade unions, which were dominant in eastern Canada, preferred strategic labor action to bolster collective bargaining rights, the industrial unions, which were stronger in the West, were adopting a more radical political course. Labor organizers from the Prairie Provinces and British Columbia, inspired by the supposed triumph of the working class over ruling capitalist oppression in the Russian Revolution of 1917, met in Calgary in March 1919 to form a branch of One Big Union (OBU), an offspring of the radical American-based International Workers of the World (IWW). Advocating the formation of a socialist state, which they believed would be more responsive to the needs of the working class, the delegates at the Calgary convention called for a general strike to take place simultaneously in many western cities and ultimately to spread across Canada. Their reasoning was that government and industry would inevitably be forced to capitulate when confronted with a complete withdrawal of the services of labor. Two months after the Calgary convention, the theory was put to the test in Winnipeg.

Metalworkers' and builders' unions in Winnipeg launched a strike that was supported by other unionized workers including police officers, firefighters, telephone and telegraph operators, and delivery personnel, virtually closing down the city. The predominantly British-born union leaders called for a total general strike and created a committee to regulate the activities of more than 30,000 strikers and to maintain essential services in the city. Comparing this strike committee with its apparent dictatorial powers to the Bolsheviks who had staged the Russian Revolution in 1917, Winnipeg business and political leaders countered by forming the Citizens' Committee of One Thousand to maintain public utilities during the strike. Despite the outbreak of sympathy strikes across the country, the six-week confrontation at Winnipeg was actually losing momentum and workers were drifting back to their jobs when Arthur Meighen, minister of justice and soon-to-be prime minister, ordered the Royal North-West Mounted Police to arrest the strike leaders. A few days later, the workers organized a protest demonstration in downtown Winnipeg during which violence erupted between police and strikers, resulting in one death and one serious injury. The infamous Bloody Saturday ended with the dispersal of workers and the establishment of military control of the city. The strike committee soon called off the strike without having achieved any of its goals.

In retrospect, the Winnipeg General Strike was hardly the Communist-inspired conspiracy to usurp Canadian democracy that government and business leaders feared, although the tendency of strike leaders to utter the idealistic rhetoric of the Russian Revolution without understanding or appreciating its autocratic outcomes distorted public perceptions of the nature of the labor movement. In fact, the Winnipeg General Strike was a major setback for the labor movement, as union membership declined by one-third to a low of a quarter-million by the mid-1920s. Throughout the decade, business sought to limit trade union effectiveness through wage cuts, industrial consolidation, and improved technology and managerial methods. In retaliation, workers staged a series of strikes, most of which ended in violence and total failure. Moreover, organized labor remained divided between the conservative Trades and Labor Congress (TLC,) which favored craft unions, and the All-Canadian Congress of Labour (ACCL), created in 1927 to promote industrial unionism. Labor, however, did make some inroads in Canadian politics as J. S. Woodsworth, one of the arrested leaders of the Winnipeg General Strike, was elected to the federal parliament in 1921, while three other arrested leaders were elected to the Manitoba legislature even though they were serving prison sentences at the time.

In addition to labor strife, the postwar period also featured renewed agrarian unrest. Long-standing dissatisfaction with high tariffs, freight rates, and interest rates on bank loans and mortgages led farmers in both eastern and western Canada to conclude that Liberal and Conservative government policies were too biased in favor of the interests of big business, particularly manufacturers and financial institutions. Influenced by the earlier Grange and Populist movements in the United States, Canadian farmers resorted to political organization on a national and a provincial basis in order to secure adequate government representation of agricultural interests.

In 1918 the Canadian Council of Agriculture, the national association of farmers organized eight years earlier, adopted a political program called the New National Policy, which included the following demands: tariff reduction, particularly on manufactured goods; higher taxes on profits and incomes rather than on land; public ownership of utilities in the realms of transportation and power; continuation of cooperative marketing strategies as embodied in the wartime Wheat Board; political reforms to enhance democracy, notably abolition of the Senate and direct legislation through such methods as the initiative and referendum; and social reforms like old-age pensions and mothers' allowances. Encouraged by the victory of the United Farmers of Ontario under the leadership of E. C. Drury in the provincial election of 1919, the Canadian Council of Agriculture launched the National Progressive Party in the following year. With Manitoba farmer Thomas A. Crerar as its leader and the New National Policy as its political platform, the Progressives became the most successful third party in the nation's history by winning 65 seats in rural Ontario and the Prairie Provinces in the federal election of 1921. By comparison, the incumbent Conservatives, led by Arthur Meighen, who had succeeded Borden in the previous year, were reduced to 50 seats, mostly in Ontario. Laurier's successor as Liberal leader, William Lyon Mackenzie King, grandson and namesake of the notorious leader of the Upper Canada Rebellion of 1837, formed a minority government by taking 116 out of 235 seats. The Liberals swept all 65 seats in Quebec, as Meighen suffered the wrath of French-Canadian voters for his role as author of the conscription bill four years earlier.

The electoral success of the Progressive Party, bolstered by the victories of the United Farmers of Alberta and the United Farmers of Manitoba in the provincial elections of 1921 and 1922, respectively, marked the pinnacle of agrarian political strength in Canada. But the challenge of preserving rural values and agricultural interests in an increasingly urban and industrial age would prove to be daunting. The United Farmers of Ontario were out of power by 1923, while the Progressive Party was bitterly divided from the outset over how most effectively to exert its newly won influence in the House of Commons. The moderate Manitoba wing of the party headed by Crerar believed that the Progressives should support the minority Liberal government in return for its pledge to make significant concessions to farmers. King convinced Crerar that, in their policy positions regarding tariffs, taxation, and social reform, Progressives were merely "Liberals in a hurry." The radical Alberta wing of the Progressive Party headed by Henry Wise Wood was opposed to engaging in party politics and advocated group government whereby farmers would cooperate with other interest groups to achieve mutual goals. As a result of this division in the ranks, the Progressives declined to serve as the Official Opposition, Crerar resigned as leader in 1922 to be replaced by Robert Forke, and the so-called "ginger group" led by Wise Wood had seceded from the party by 1924.

The fragmented Progressives could only manage to retain 24 seats in the federal election of 1925, while the Conservatives mounted a comeback and emerged with a plurality of 116 seats versus 101 for the Liberals. Since no party could command a majority of the 245 seats in the House of Commons, King asserted his constitutional right to continue to govern provided that he could retain the support of the Progressives. By lowering tariffs and introducing an old-age pensions scheme (which the Senate eventually rejected), King was able to keep the Progressives on the Liberal side for six months. But the postponement of the promised return of natural resources to the Prairie Provinces alienated the Progressives, and a customs scandal relating to liquor smuggling in the United States where Prohibition was in force resulted in a crisis of confidence in the Liberal administration. To avoid losing a decisive vote in the House of Commons, King exercised his constitutional right to ask Governor-General Julian Byng to dissolve Parliament and to call a new election. Byng responded by asserting his constitutional right to deny King's request and called upon Conservative leader Arthur Meighen to form a government. Unable to secure sufficient Progressive support, the Meighen administration was defeated by a motion of nonconfidence within three days to earn the distinction as the shortest government in national history.

The King-Byng constitutional crisis became a major issue in the federal election of 1926. To deflect attention away from the customs scandal, King took advantage of the prevailing interest in national autonomy, accusing the governor-general of attempting to perpetuate colonialism by refusing to take the advice of his elected representatives and charging Meighen with jeopardizing responsible government by taking power unconstitutionally. Regardless of the merits of his argument, King succeeded in leading the Liberals to a majority victory mostly at the expense of the disintegrating Progressives, who were reduced to nine parliamentary seats. Although Progressivism ceased to be a force in national politics as many of its moderates were absorbed into the Liberal Party, the agrarian movement remained active in western provincial politics, particularly in Alberta, where the United Farmers remained in power until 1935. Despite its short-lived national prominence, the Progressive Party deserves credit for pressuring the federal government into finally transferring control of natural resources to the three Prairie Provinces in 1930, thereby bringing down the curtain on the original National Policy.

While the Progressives were serving as the voice of agrarian protest in the West, the Maritime Rights movement was expressing that region's relative economic decline and its consequent disillusionment with the Confederation. When Nova Scotia and New Brunswick entered Confederation in 1867, they were assigned nearly one-fifth of the seats in the House of Commons. But by 1925, the parliamentary representation of the three Maritime Provinces, including Prince Edward Island, was reduced to one-eighth, largely as a result of regional depopulation. Workers and manufacturers had left for central Canada and the United States in search of better economic opportunities. Besides a chronic lack of natural resources, the region suffered from postwar economic change: the wartime boom at the ports of Halifax and Saint John had subsided, the decline of shipbuilding and railway construction reduced the demand for iron and steel, the conversion to hydroelectric power and oil limited the market for Cape Breton coal, lower tariffs no longer offered sufficient protection to Maritime industry, and the price of fish was steadily dropping as advances in refrigeration made meat a dietary staple.

The influential entrepreneurs and professionals who led the Maritime Rights movement encouraged the regional electorate to vote overwhelmingly against the governing party in the federal elections of 1921 and 1925. In particular, this amorphous movement demanded increased annual subsidies for the Maritime Provinces and greater tariff protection to revive the region's steel and coal industries. When the Liberals returned to power in 1926, King attempted to defuse the Maritime rights movement by establishing a royal commission under the direction of Sir Arthur Rae Duncan to investigate regional grievances. In its report in 1927, the Duncan Commission typically recommended increased federal subsidies for the Maritime Provinces and their struggling industries. The federal government did raise provincial subsidies, but any hope that it would undertake initiatives to promote regional development were dashed by the onset of the Great Depression.

THE ACHIEVEMENT
OF NATIONAL AUTONOMY

While national unity was being severely tested on the home front, Canada's distinguished performance on the battlefields of Europe during World War I was enhancing its stature within the world community of self-governing states. Canada entered the war clearly subordinate to the British government, which felt no obligation to consult its dominions about war strategy or even to keep them informed on developments in international relations. But as Britain became more reliant on military support from its self-governing colonies, it became increasingly difficult to ignore their demands for a greater voice in imperial affairs. For this reason, the British military command abandoned its original plan to absorb Canadian recruits and agreed to the formation of a distinct Canadian Corps. But the Canadian Corps remained under British command, which meant that the Canadian government had no share in the decisions relating to its deployment. Borden continued to press for "fuller information" and "consultation respecting general policy in war operations," but Canadian-born Colonial Secretary Bonar Law was "not able to see any way in which this could be practically done." The acute and urgent recruitment crisis that led to the decision to impose conscription in 1917 gave the British government a will to find a way.

To persuade them to intensify their war effort, the Dominion prime ministers were invited to join the British cabinet to form an Imperial War Cabinet that would be responsible for the general direction of war strategy and foreign policy. Furthermore, the Imperial War Conference, meeting simultaneously with the Imperial War Cabinet in 1917, passed Resolution XI recognizing the equality of the Dominions with one another and with Britain "as autonomous nations of an Imperial Commonwealth." About the same time, the Canadian Corps, following its success at Vimy Ridge, was placed under the command of General Arthur Currie, the first Canadian commander of the armed forces. Thus, Canada emerged from World War I with an ability to exert control over its armed forces and to exercise genuine influence in relevant matters of imperial foreign policy.

Canada's evolution from colony to nation was further advanced by the postwar peace settlement. The British government embarked upon the peacemaking process on the assumption that the allied great powers would play the major role, while the smaller states and the Dominions would be consulted only on matters directly affecting them. However, Borden insisted that Canada's significant contribution to the Allied war effort entitled it to separate representation at the peace conference in Versailles in 1919. Ultimately, the Dominions won the right to sign the Treaty of Versailles, and Borden also secured the right of the Canadian Parliament to approve the treaty prior to imperial ratification. In the continuing battle for independent national status, Canada won a seat on the new League of Nations and the International Labour Organization, despite the American objection that admission of the Dominions was advantageous to Britain. Yet Canada was adamant in its objection to a system of collective security proposed in Article

X of the League of Nations Covenant, which bound member nations to come to each other's aid in the event of foreign aggression against them. Although unsuccessful in modifying or eliminating the provision, which U.S. president Woodrow Wilson regarded as the cornerstone of the league, Canada clearly articulated an isolationist suspicion of European entanglements that would become the basis for North American foreign policy for the next two decades.

To reduce the possibility of being dragged into another European war, Canada continued to seek even greater autonomy within the British Empire during the 1920s. After greatly advancing the cause of Canadian autonomy over the previous nine years, Borden retired in 1920 and his successor, Meighen, maintained the same interest in the development of a common imperial foreign policy based on mutual and continuous consultation between Britain and the Dominions as free and equal partners of the Commonwealth.

When he came to power in 1921, Prime Minister King adopted a cautious approach to foreign policy in order to maintain national unity. He was keenly aware of the divisive effects of Canada's involvement in international affairs and the damage done to his political party before and during World War I. Consequently, he did not share the faith that Borden and Meighen had in the prospects that Canada could exert sufficient control over its foreign policy within a common imperial framework. Wishing to maintain the imperial tie but suspicious that Britain wanted only to use its self-governing colonies to enhance its own power, King was determined to free Canada from the last traces of colonial restraint and to complete its evolution toward full national status.

The difficulty of shaping a common imperial foreign policy became apparent during the Chanak crisis of 1922. When British troops stationed in Chanak, Turkey, to guard the neutral zone between the Mediterranean Sea and the Black Sea came under siege by Turkish nationalists, the imperial government appealed to the Dominions for reinforcements. King was upset that Canada had not been appropriately consulted about events in Turkey until they reached the crisis stage, and he remained unconvinced that becoming involved in this distant conflict was in Canada's interest. To the imperial request, he replied that "only Parliament could decide," and unfortunately for Britain, or perhaps fortunately for Canada, the House of Commons was not in session. By contrast, Opposition leader Meighen insisted that Canada should have responded: "Ready, aye, ready we stand by you." The crisis was soon resolved by the Treaty of Lausanne, which prompted King to declare that, because it had not been a party to this agreement, Canada would not be bound by it. In effect, Canada had succeeded in avoiding foreign entanglements and in discrediting the notion of a common imperial foreign policy.

The demise of imperial unity in diplomatic affairs was completed by the signing of the Halibut Treaty of 1923, an agreement between Canada and the United States relating to fishing rights on the Pacific coast. While negotiations were conducted entirely by Canadian minister of marines and fisheries Ernest Lapointe, the British ambassador in Washington expected to sign the treaty in keeping with imperial tradition. But the Canadian government insisted that Lapointe alone should sign the treaty, a decision the British government did not dispute. For the first time, Canada had assumed responsibility for concluding a formal treaty with a foreign power on its own behalf. The Imperial Conference later that year formally abandoned the idea of a common imperial foreign policy and affirmed the right of the Dominions to conclude treaties with foreign states. Canada's power to control its international relations would be confirmed in 1927 when Vincent Massey took up residence in Washington as the first Canadian-appointed foreign

THE STATUTE OF WESTMINSTER, 1931

AN ACT to give effect to certain resolutions passed by Imperial Conferences held in the years 1926 and 1930. [22 George V, Chapter 4]

11th December, 1931

WHEREAS the delegates to His Majesty's Governments in the United Kingdom, the Dominion of Canada, the Commonwealth of Australia, the Dominion of New Zealand, the Union of South Africa, the Irish Free State and Newfoundland, at Imperial Conferences holden at Westminster in the years of our Lord nineteen hundred and twenty-six and nineteen hundred and thirty did concur in making the declarations and resolutions set forth in the Reports of the said Conferences:

And whereas it is meet and proper to set out by way of preamble to this Act that, inasmuch as the Crown is the symbol of the free association of the members of the British Commonwealth of Nations, and as they are united by a common allegiance to the Crown. . . .

NOW, THEREFORE, BE IT ENACTED by the King's Most Excellent Majesty, by and with the advice and consent of the Lords Spiritual and Temporal, and Commons, in this present Parliament assembled, and by the authority of the same, as follows: — . . .

2. 1. The Colonial Laws Validity Act, 1865, shall not apply to any law made after the commencement of this Act by the Parliament of a Dominion. 2. No law and no provision of any law made after the commencement of this Act by the Parliament of a Dominion shall be void or inoperative on the ground that it is repugnant to the law of England, or to the provisions of any existing or future Act of Parliament of the United Kingdom . . . and the powers of the Parliament of a Dominion shall include the power to repeal or amend any such Act, order, rule or regulation in so far as the same is part of the law of the Dominion.

3. It is hereby declared and enacted that the Parliament of a Dominion has full power to make laws having extra-territorial operation.

4. No Act of Parliament of the United Kingdom passed after the commencement of this Act shall extend or be deemed to extend, to a Dominion as part of the law of that Dominion, unless it is expressly declared in that Act that that Dominion has requested, and consented to, the enactment thereof. . . .

minister, and the United States reciprocated by opening a legation in Ottawa. Other countries soon followed suit in accepting Canada as fully self-governing in matters of trade and other international affairs.

The changing relationship between Britain and its Dominions was officially recognized in the Balfour Report signed at the Imperial Conference of 1926. The report proclaimed the Dominions to be "autonomous communities within the British Empire, equal in status, in no way subordinate to one another in any aspect of their domestic or external affairs, though united by a common allegiance to the Crown, and freely associated as members of the British Commonwealth of Nations." In addition to defining the status of the Dominions, the Balfour Report clarified the basis of their equal partnership with Britain through several recommendations that were legalized by the Statute of Westminster, enacted by the British Parliament in 1931. The governor-general was no longer an official of the British government but merely the representative of the Crown. Henceforth, communication between the governments of Britain and Canada would be direct rather than through the governor-general. In 1928 Britain appointed a high commissioner to reside in Canada for the purpose of facilitating contacts between the two governments and in recognition of the new equal Commonwealth relationship. No longer could a British law override a colonial law, and the Dominions could alter any imperial law in force within their borders. The British Parliament still retained the power to amend the Canadian constitution, the British North America Act of 1867, but only at Canada's request and only until the Canadian Parliament agreed on an amendment process. The Judicial Committee of the Privy Council remained the final court of appeal, but again, this arrangement rested on the consent of the Dominion.

Besides officially recognizing the existence of the British Commonwealth of Nations in place of the old British Empire, the Statute of Westminster, signed into law on December 11, 1931, was a veritable declaration of Canadian independence, completing a process of nationhood begun in 1867. Canada was now principally responsible for its destiny not only within its national boundaries but also within the international realm. Growth in international stature, however, would not necessarily mean a desire to assume greater responsibility in foreign relations, as Canada's isolationist stance during the 1930s would demonstrate.

CHAPTER 15

A SOCIETY TRANSFORMED

Sustained economic prosperity and industrial growth from 1896 to 1929 transformed Canada into a predominantly urban society. This reality was confirmed by the national census of 1931, which recorded that 53.7 percent of the Canadian population lived in incorporated cities, towns, and villages (as the term "urban" was then defined), compared to 19.6 percent in the first national census 60 years earlier. The Canadian response to this transition from rural to urban life in the late 19th and early 20th centuries was somewhat ambivalent. Optimists hailed the emerging city as a physical embodiment of human progress in business and technology, as well as a vibrant milieu for cultural and artistic achievement. Pessimists, on the other hand, lamented the demise of the rustic lifestyle in the wake of rural depopulation and feared the debilitating influences of the "evil city," where the ills of modern society were so concentrated and highly visible. Widespread concern over the impact of urbanization and industrialization spawned a "reform" impulse that featured a conflicting array of pragmatic and idealistic visions about the future direction of Canadian society and government. Consequently, the so-called reformers tended to enjoy limited success, but their crusades prompted a reconsideration of the role of the state in the social and economic lives of its citizens.

THE GROWTH OF CITIES

The rural character of Canada at the time of Confederation was highlighted in the national census of 1871, which indicated that less than 10 percent of the population lived in the nine cities and towns with more than 10,000 inhabitants. Only Montreal (107,000), Quebec City (60,000), and Toronto (56,000) could be considered urban centers of significant size. Initially, urbanization focused on Montreal and Toronto, the chief beneficiaries of the National Policy. The building of the CPR in the 1880s reinforced Montreal's position as the hub of the national transportation network, the leading manufacturing center, the headquarters of the important banking and financial institutions, and Canada's dominant commercial metropolis. Accordingly, Montreal's population increased from 155,000 in 1881 to 220,000 in 1891. At the same time, Toronto's population grew even more impressively—from 86,000 to 181,000—thanks largely to the rise in the number of manufacturing firms in the city from 932 to 2,401. Although urban development was more widespread during the first three decades of the 20th century, Montreal and Toronto further extended their metropolitan dominance by taking advantage of an abundance of cheap immigrant labor and natural resources from the Canadian Shield. The head offices of most resource enterprises were located in Montreal and Toronto, thereby stretching their hinterlands deeper into the northern frontier. Hydroelectric power was also a catalyst for the expansion of urban services and infrastructure, notably streetcar transport and street lighting. By 1931, Montreal maintained its status as the country's largest city, with a population of nearly 819,000 as compared to more than 631,000 for Toronto.

Nevertheless, Toronto enjoyed the benefits of a more expansive urban hinterland than did its metropolitan rival. With the advent of automobiles and improved roads after the turn of the 20th century, the farming districts on the outskirts of the city were transformed into an expanding suburban frontier, particularly after World War I. The population of the suburban communities that would later amalgamate with the city to form Metropolitan Toronto approached 200,000 by 1931. Curiously, five of the 12 Toronto suburbs were still classified as rural communities in the national census of 1931 because they were incorporated as townships rather than as cities, towns, or villages. York Township had a population of more than 55,000; East York Township over 35,000; and the townships of Scarborough, North York, and Etobicoke each exceeded 20,000.

Southwestern Ontario also felt the urbanizing effects of being within Toronto's hinterland. Hamilton became a major steel-producing center with a population that increased from 49,000 in 1891 to more than 155,000 in 1931. During the same period, two manufacturing centers emerged in the southwest part of the province: London, which grew from 32,000 to 71,000, and Windsor, which grew from 10,000 to 63,000. Several other budding manufacturing centers, such as Kitchener, Brantford, and St. Catharines had evolved from small towns to mid-size cities with a population in the range of 25,000–30,000 by 1931. The national capital, Ottawa, which grew from 44,000 in 1891 to 127,000 in 1931, represented a sizable market for manufactured goods within both the Toronto and Montreal orbits. Urbanization was even spreading to northern Ontario in the wake of the development of the resource frontier. Fort William and Port Arthur (both amalgamated in 1970 to form the city of Thunder Bay), along with Sault Ste. Marie and Sudbury, each of which had fewer than 2,500 inhabitants prior to the turn of the 20th century, had become thriving service centers with populations of 20,000 to 25,000 by 1931.

In Quebec, the only major industrial center outside of the Montreal area was the provincial capital, Quebec City, the population of which grew from 63,000 in 1891 to more than

130,000 in 1931. The Montreal suburbs of Verdun and Outremont went from farming communities of fewer than 2,000 in 1901 to substantial centers of more than 60,000 and nearly 30,000 inhabitants, respectively, by 1931, while Westmount's population rose from 9,000 to 24,000. Benefiting from its location halfway between Montreal and Quebec City, the service center of Trois-Rivières expanded from 10,000 in 1901 to 35,000 in 1931. During the same period, Hull, one of the main centers of the pulp and paper industry located across the Ottawa River from the nation's capital, and Sherbrooke, a small textile center in the Eastern Townships, more than doubled in population size, to approach 30,000.

The proliferation of smaller towns and villages throughout the southern Quebec countryside reflected the continuing ambivalence of French-speaking Catholics toward industrialization and urbanization. Ultramontane Catholic nationalism tended to stress to its parishioners the special legitimacy of rural and agrarian life in contrast to the corruption and immorality of the urban and industrial world. In the factories of the city, the church hierarchy argued, French Canadians were merely common laborers subject to the dictates of English-speaking masters and their Protestant work ethic. But in the countryside, according to Jules-Paul Tardivel, editor of the newspaper La Vérité, the noble French-Canadian farmer, with the help of his large family, was master of his fate, which was shaped by the bounty of the land and other natural forces. Accordingly, the church-dominated school system continued to emphasize religious and classical studies rather than technical or scientific education. A minority viewpoint shared by French-Canadian business leaders and some progressive Catholic clergy recognized the limited supply of fertile land in the St. Lawrence Valley and encouraged industrialization and urbanization as a means to stem the tide of emigration to the cities and factories of the United States.

Industrialization and urbanization in the West was related to settlement of the agrarian frontier and the expansion of the transcontinental railway network. Winnipeg's strategic location as the eastern gateway to the West made it the major distribution point for the Prairie grain trade and the site of one of the world's largest rail yards. As a result, Winnipeg's population expanded from 25,000 in 1891 to almost 219,000 in 1931. Not settled until the 1880s and 1890s, the other four dominant Prairie cities evolved into significant commercial centers with clearly defined hinterlands by 1931. With a population of 53,000, Regina, the headquarters of the North-West Mounted Police and the capital of Saskatchewan, competed with Saskatoon, which had a population of 43,000, as the center of the provincial grain trade. Calgary, a CPR rail center of almost 84,000, serviced the ranching and farming country of southern Alberta, while Edmonton, the provincial capital with a population of over 79,000, presided over the expanding central farming districts and newly opened northern resource frontier of the province.

Vancouver benefited from its role as the Pacific gateway to the West to surpass Victoria, the provincial capital, as the commercial and financial center of British Columbia. Vancouver's population soared from 13,000 in 1891 to nearly 247,000 in 1931, while Victoria only grew from 17,000 to 39,000 over the same period. With its excellent harbor and as the western terminus of the CPR, Vancouver became the entrepôt of the Prairie grain trade, the coastal salmon fishing industry and lumber trade, and the Klondike gold-rush traffic. The opening of the Panama Canal in 1914, which put European markets within reach of Pacific coastal ports, along with the development of the resource frontier of the Cordilleras, would by the late 1920s propel Vancouver past Winnipeg as the premier city of the West and the third largest in Canada.

Industrialization and urbanization in the Maritime Provinces could not keep pace with developments in central and western Canada. The productive Cape Breton coal fields gave rise to a prosperous iron and steel industry by the early 1880s, while an abundance of fish and timber sustained regional processing operations. However, Maritime industry could not compete with its central Canadian rivals because of limited resources, a small population base, and distance from the continental interior where the economic center of gravity had shifted by the late 19th century. Consequently, Maritime cities grew at a slower rate than elsewhere until World War I. After enjoying a brief wartime boom as a result of their strategic location for military purposes, Maritime centers experienced little if any growth during the 1920s. As the terminus of the CPR, Halifax experienced a modest rise in population from 38,000 in 1891 to 59,000 in 1931, while Saint John, which had been bypassed in favor of Moncton as a CPR station, gained less than 9,000 residents to bring its population to a little under 48,000. Ranked as the fourth- and fifth-largest cities in Canada at the time of Confederation, Halifax and Saint John had slipped to thirteenth and fifteenth place, respectively, by 1931. Only the coal-mining center of Sydney on Cape Breton Island showed signs of above average growth in population, from 2,500 in 1891 to 23,000 in 1931.

The trend toward greater urban concentration was reflected in the fact that by 1931 two out of five Canadians were living in the 69 cities and towns with a population exceeding 10,000 and the five suburban Toronto townships. Indeed, one in five Canadians lived in the seven cities with a population exceeding 100,000. As cities expanded and the population became more concentrated, politicians, planners, civil engineers, businessmen, health officials, journalists, and humanitarians became aware of the complex challenges confronting their communities, and they began to take an active interest in improving the quality of the urban environment.

CIVIC BOOSTERISM AND THE URBAN REFORM MOVEMENT

The Canadian response to the challenges of urban living in the late 19th and early 20th centuries was a combination of traditional civic "boosterism" and an activist "reform" impulse that was also prevalent in the United States and Britain. Often the interests of the boosters, who sought to maximize business opportunities and to enhance property values within their communities, blended well with the concerns of the so-called reformers, who endeavored to make their cities healthy, moral, and democratic. Whatever their motives and ambitions, these community-spirited citizens were determined to improve living conditions within their cities by planning the physical environment, regulating public utilities, restructuring municipal government, and promoting health, education, and social welfare.

Despite the prevailing laissez-faire attitude toward state intervention, economy-minded civic officials eventually came to equate greater public investment in urban services and infrastructure with efficient management and sound business practice. Certainly, the costly commitments related to the construction and maintenance of roads, including the rebuilding of urban street systems to make necessary changes in sidewalks, lighting, sewers, and water mains, were justified on this basis. The unsatisfactory and at times treacherous state of roads largely accounted for the obsession with railways in the second half of the century. The appearance of the automobile in the first decade of the 20th century accelerated the demand for concrete or asphalt paved roads because its fast-turning wheels tore through existing macadamized surfaces with even more disastrous effects than did horse-drawn wagons and carriages, while the bone-jarring ride on cedar block pavement had adverse effects on both vehicles and passengers. R. O. Wynne-Roberts, a noted civil engineer, expressed the perspective of many business-minded reformers across Canada in 1914 when he praised the asphalt paved road as a visible embodiment of civic progress and "a lucrative investment":

. . . Well-paved and clean streets . . . because they are seen by all . . . constitute a measure of successful administration, foresight, and judicious expenditure of ratepayers' money. The converse is equally true, for unsightly, dirty streets are powerful factors in the demoralization of people.

Concerned about shabby streets as well as the general appearance and efficiency of the modern city, engineers, architects, surveyors, and planners, inspired by the so-called City Beautiful and Garden City movements in the United States and Britain, endeavored to shape the physical character of Canadian cities to create a more attractive, humane, and orderly environment. City governments or citizens' groups commissioned planners such as Thomas Adams, the British town planner who was appointed to the federal Commission on Conservation in 1909, to design stately and finely landscaped civic buildings and squares, wide streets with treed boulevards, and a network of parks and playgrounds. Urban planning was concerned not only with the aesthetic appearance of the city but also with economic, health, and safety issues. In justifying the value of investing in parks and playgrounds, Adams noted in 1920:

. . . The increased value these open spaces give to adjacent land counter-balances the cost of acquiring them. . . .

The greatest benefit from the parks will, however, be derived from the increased health and, consequently, greater efficiency of the population. Parks are a better investment than hospitals and asylums, and if we do not spend money on the one we shall be compelled to spend it on the other in greater degree than is needed if we exercise proper judgement and foresight.

Thus, the interest in the physical development of the city environment corresponded with the concerns of child welfare advocates who believed that supervised parks and playgrounds would benefit less privileged children by keeping them off the traffic-laden streets and by combating the idleness that often led to delinquency and crime.

Health and safety also motivated the improvement of sewage and waste disposal. Open gutters laden with raw sewage were still commonplace even in the larger Canadian cities by the 1880s and 1890s. Only 10 percent of all buildings in Winnipeg, for example, were connected to closed sewers by 1889, and only one-third were connected as late as 1902. Even when the system of closed sewers was extended to all districts of the city, discharged effluent could still contaminate the local water supply and trigger periodic epidemics of typhoid fever. For example, typhoid epidemics took the life of nearly 200 people in the Toronto in 1892-93 and 133 in Winnipeg in 1904-05. Doctors, civil engineers, and social reformers found in such unfortunate incidents an opportunity to raise public consciousness about the value of health and sanitary regulations.

The late 19th- and early-20th century Canadian municipal scene was marked by heated debate over public versus private ownership of services that directly or indirectly affected the entire population of a city. Gradually, as the desire of franchise-holding utility companies for maximum profits clashed with the city's concern for efficient services, public ownership prevailed in the provision of water, electricity, and mass transit. Because water pollution was widely recognized as a public hazard, waterworks were among the first utilities subject to municipal improvement and control, with Montreal, Ottawa, and Toronto leading the way during the 1870s. An Edmonton councillor candidly admitted the rationale behind the establishment of a publicly owned hydroelectric power installation in his city as early as 1902: "Cheap power is essential in order to induce manufacturing establishments to locate in the City of Edmonton." Similar motives were behind the formation of Ottawa Hydro in 1905 and Toronto Hydro in 1911.

By the early 1890s Port Arthur's streetcar system had become the first in Canada to operate under municipal ownership primarily by default rather than by design. No private interests would risk undertaking the service, which civic authorities deemed essential if Port Arthur was to remain competitive in its rivalry with Fort William for commercial supremacy in the northwestern Ontario region. Public ownership also came in response to rejection by private capital in St. Thomas at the turn of the century. In a more lucrative market such as Toronto, public ownership was deemed desirable because private companies preferred to limit their operations to the more congested and therefore profitable downtown sections and balked at demands for expansion into the recently annexed and less populated suburban districts, where the service was urgently needed. Likewise, the movement for civic streetcars in thriving new western cities such as Edmonton and Calgary was fed by the real estate and commercial concerns of civic leaders rather than by any ideological considerations. Indeed, for Canadian cities, public ownership of utilities was a socialist means to achieve a capitalist end.

An editorial in *The Municipal World* (1905) entitled "Treat Municipal Government as Business" expressed the prevailing reform spirit regarding the structure of municipal government: "the modern city is a corporation or a huge business with many branches, most of which call for special aptitude and training." Beginning in the 1890s, urban reformers questioned the traditional structure of municipal government, which vested executive and legislative power in an elected mayor and council, on two grounds. First, the aldermen who sat on the council were vulnerable to corruption, patronage, and parochial or partisan interests associated with their particular wards or neighborhoods, and thus less inclined to address the welfare of the city at large. Second, the untrained aldermen were ill-equipped to deal with the multiplicity and complexity of the new urban problems with businesslike economy and efficiency.

Accordingly, new structures were inaugurated that would replace the part-time, amateur, partisan, or ward-dependent civic administrator with full-time, salaried, and autonomous professionals or specialists utilizing bureaucratic methods of scientific management. The drive for business government began with an assault on the ward system of elections. Some cities enlarged and reduced the number of wards, such as Toronto did in 1891. Other cities abolished them altogether in favor of election of councillors at large, as was the case in Saint John and Fredericton in 1894; in a number of Ontario centers, including Guelph, London, and St. Catharines after 1898; in Victoria in 1912; and in Calgary in 1913.

In order to separate legislative and executive authority, Toronto created a Board of Control in 1896 to carry out executive functions. Winnipeg adopted a Board of Control based on the Toronto model in 1906, as did Ottawa in 1908, Montreal in 1909, Hamilton in 1910, and London in 1914. Calgary established a similar form of executive body in 1908 but called it a commission. Upon its incorporation as a city in 1904, Edmonton opted to place executive authority in the hands of an appointed Board of Commissioners, which provided council with expert administrative guidance; within eight years Regina, Saskatoon, Prince Albert, and Red Deer had followed this lead. In many instances, council authority was further reduced by the creation of specialized boards or commissions, such as the Toronto Transportation Commission (TTC), with independent powers in a particular area of city government. Following the American example, Saint John in 1912 and Lethbridge in 1913 replaced their councils with commissioners elected at large. In a similar vein, Westmount in 1913 and Guelph in 1919 adopted an American-style city manager as chief executive officer, with the elected council being retained as the legislative body.

Whatever form it took, the goals of municipal reform were clear—to take vital areas of decision-making out of the hands of the corruptible and/or untrained neighborhood politicians and the general public and to place it in the hands of engineers and other experts who supposedly had the interests of the whole community in mind. Ironically, reform often took on an undemocratic quality, such as the restriction of voting rights and office-holding only to men of substantial property who obviously had a greater stake in citywide development. Often, these experts from the business and professional worlds were no less susceptible to corruption, patronage, and administrative misjudgment than were their amateurish predecessors.

SOCIAL AND MORAL REFORM MOVEMENTS

While civic boosters and business-minded urban reformers were preoccupied first and foremost with economic development and property values, another group of humanitarian reformers was more concerned about the potentially debilitating physical, moral, and social effects of urban concentration on the individual. Public health reformers were conducting vaccination campaigns to control smallpox and sanitation campaigns to clean up housing and streets and to sanitize water and milk supplies in major eastern cities in the late 19th century. An adherent of the sanitarian school of preventative medicine, Dr. William Canniff, upon his appointment as Toronto's first medical officer of health (MHO) in 1883, instituted regular annual inspections of homes, schools, factories, dairies, and slaughterhouses in order to discover and remove "nuisances" that were thought to cause disease. Dr. Charles Sheard, who became MHO in 1893, added a bacteriological approach to disease control by establishing a city laboratory to undertake periodic testing of the quality of the tap water, ice, milk, and food that Torontonians consumed. During his tenure as MHO from 1910 to 1929, Dr. Charles Hastings managed to convince civic authorities that a healthy and productive worker and taxpayer was "the most valuable asset" of a municipality and "that money used for public health work . . . gives them a larger return than any other investment." Somewhat prophetically, the year before the great influenza epidemic of 1918–19, he pointed out that the contamination of any class would lead to the infection of the rest of the community, since disease did not respect social standing.

Public education was already seen as an important stimulus to social and moral improvement by the late 19th century. One of the main objectives of educational reformers was to increase the years of formal attendance at school. In Ontario, for example, education was made compulsory and free for children up to 12 years of age in 1871 and up to 14 years of age in 1891. Influenced by Friedrich Froebel, a German educational philosopher, some reformers contended that education should also be made more child-oriented through the establishment of kindergartens for younger children. In 1883 James L. Hughes, a Toronto school inspector, and his future wife, Ada Marean, established the first Canadian public school kindergarten, and four years later Ontario formally incorporated kindergarten into the public school system. The Free Kindergarten Association in Winnipeg advocated the same for Manitoba, arguing that "the proper education of children during the first seven years of their lives [did] much to reduce poverty and crime in any community." The Adolescent Attendance Act of 1919, which raised the age of compulsory schooling to 16 years, proved to be a boon to secondary education in Ontario and was soon followed by similar legislation in the other provinces.

Educational reformers also endeavored to link the elementary schools with the public health and child welfare movements. The school was a logical place to conduct the campaign to inculcate personal hygiene practices that would contribute to the development of a healthier community because children were the parents and taxpayers of the future. After 1910 medical and dental inspection of schoolchildren by a public health nurse became a regular feature of the elementary system. A concern for the physical and moral outlook of children also led to an expansion of public libraries, as well as parks and recreational facilities. In 1882 the Ontario Legislature provided for the establishment of free libraries supported by a levy on local property taxes. British Columbia (1891), Manitoba (1899), Saskatchewan (1906), and Alberta (1907) soon followed Ontario's lead, while the Maritimes did not act until the 1930s and Quebec not until 1959. John J. Kelso, a leading child welfare reformer, founded the Children's Aid Society in 1891 and was active in closing reformatories and organizing playgrounds as an alternative outlet for children of poor families.

Other urban reformers were concerned about the proliferation of social ills that made the modern city a haven for slums, prostitution, and criminal activity. As they industrialized, cities tended to become more socially stratified. Electric streetcars and eventually automobiles enabled the more affluent members of society to reside in the suburban districts, where they could escape the congestion and pollution of the inner city. Because they were less able to afford transportation, the working-class groups, particularly new immigrants, tended to congregate in rental accommodation within the less attractive areas of the inner city.

Working-class life was consistently plagued by economic insecurity. Limited educational opportunities meant that workers were restricted to low-paying jobs from which they often faced the prospect of layoffs, particularly in winter or slow economic periods. In an age before government-funded social welfare programs, layoffs could mean months of subsistence without wages or alternative sources of income support. Illness, injury, or advancing age could also relegate workers and their families to prolonged poverty and destitution. Besides family and friends, the only recourse for inner-city residents experiencing economic misfortune was to seek charity from the various churches and private philanthropic organizations. In the late 19th century, local government in the larger cities, such as Toronto and Montreal, responded to pressure from private charitable organizations to provide them with financial assistance to service the growing number of impoverished citizens.

The willingness of organized religion to assume an active role in dealing with the social problems of urban life gave rise to the social gospel movement, which was prominent from the 1890s to the 1920s. The social gospel movement attracted members of all of the major Protestant denominations who shared a belief in environmental determinism. In essence, they believed that improvement in social conditions would lead to improvement in individual social behavior. Accordingly, social gospellers wanted churches to be concerned with social problems, such as prostitution, alcoholism, intolerable living and working conditions, and the plight of immigrants, rather than merely with such personal "sins" as sex, drunkenness, and negligence.

Early social gospel efforts to improve the quality of life for the downtrodden in Toronto included the founding of St. Andrew's Institute by Presbyterian minister Reverend D. J. Macdonnell in 1890 and the Fred Victor Mission by the Methodists with assistance from the Massey family in 1894. After the turn of the century, Sara Libby Carson started the Toronto and McGill University settlement houses, among a chain of such institutions established by the end of World War I to assist the destitute. In 1908 the Protestant denominations that embraced social gospel joined together to form the Moral and Social Reform Council, reorganized as the Social Service Council of Canada in 1912. Two years later, the council sponsored the first national congress on social problems.

Perhaps the most prominent social gospeller was J. S. Woodsworth, a Methodist minister and avowed socialist whose book *My Neighbour* (1911) was an impassioned plea for the reform of living conditions in Canada's cities. Woodsworth would go on to distinguish himself as a labor leader in the Winnipeg General Strike of 1919, and he would be instrumental in pressing for the first old-age pension legislation in 1927. He would become best known as the leader of the Cooperative Commonwealth Federation (CCF), a national political party established in 1932. Social gospel supporters also contributed to the passing of the Workmen's Compensation Act in Ontario in 1914, which established financial benefits for those who suffered injuries in the workplace, and the Manitoba Pensions Act in 1916, which provided a basic allowance to widowed, divorced, or deserted wives with children. Social gospellers were actively involved in other social and moral reform movements, including prohibition, women's suffrage, and urban reform. Besides preparing the way for the modern welfare system, social gospel is also credited with providing the impetus for the first sociology programs in Canadian universities.

The social and moral reform movements of the late 19th and early 20th centuries gave women an opportunity to become more actively involved outside the home. Until then, most women lived in domestic obscurity with no political or legal rights; their role was defined in terms of being wives and mothers serving the needs of their husbands and children. In her relatively short life span, the rural woman was confined to performing backbreaking labor on the family farm and enduring the hardships of many childbirths in an age before medicalized deliveries and birth control. Although the urban woman had a greater opportunity to find work outside the home, she was usually hired as a domestic or as cheap and unskilled factory labor. Educational opportunities were customarily limited to females from affluent families, who could then aspire to become teachers or to marry well. While industrialization and urbanization did little to improve the lot of working-class women, their middle-class cohorts came to believe that they could reform society through their "natural" nurturing instincts.

By the turn of the 20th century, local, provincial, and national women's organizations, such as the Women's Christian Temperance Union, the National Council of Women, the Young Women's Christian Association (YWCA), and the Dominion Women's Enfranchisement Association were emerging as influential agents of social change. Like their counterparts in Britain and the United States, women reformers in Canada fought for the right to vote. As early as 1876, Dr. Emily Stowe, who had been barred from medical school in Canada because she was a woman, launched the Toronto Women's Literary Club, which was renamed the Toronto Women's Suffrage Society in 1883 and the Dominion Women's Enfranchisement Association in 1889. Besides campaigning for basic voting rights, women reformers were active in the prohibition movement, which waged war against the evils of liquor. The Woman's Christian Temperance Union, formed in 1874, identified "demon drink" as the leading cause of domestic violence and divorce, in addition to inefficiency and underproductivity in the workplace. Thus, prohibitionists called upon the power of the state to outlaw the sale of alcoholic beverages.

The suffrage movement gained support during World War I as women's groups were able to point to the catastrophic overseas conflict as evidence of male aggression that would be tempered if women had the right to vote and the opportunity to rule. The contributions and sacrifices of women working in the munitions factories and offices, serving as nurses in the armed forces, and supporting their families while their husbands were fighting overseas was compelling testimony that they deserved to participate fully in political life. Led by Nellie McClung, women in the four western provinces won the right to vote in provincial elections in 1916, and within six years, all of the other provinces followed suit with the exception of Quebec, which waited until 1940. The federal government extended voting rights to women in war service or those whose fathers, husbands, or sons were serving overseas during the controversial conscription election of 1917. Finally, on January 1, 1919, all non-Native women over 21 years of age were granted the right to vote in federal elections. In 1920 Edith Rogers of Manitoba became the first woman to be elected to a provincial legislature, while in the following year, Agnes Macphail, running for the Progressive Party, became the first woman to be elected to the Canadian Parliament. The climax of the struggle for legal rights came in the famous Persons Case of 1929. The Alberta provincial court and the Supreme Court of Canada had maintained that five Alberta women, including McClung, did not qualify for a Senate appointment because they were not "persons" in the legal sense. In overruling both courts, the Judicial Committee of the Privy Council called the exclusion of women from public office "a relic of days more barbarous than ours."

Prohibitionists also gained support during the war as they urged government to "remove a greater enemy than the Hun from our midst." Although prohibition was successful in the three Prairie Provinces during the war, opposition from the returning soldiers undermined the further success of the crusade. By the end of the 1920s, the provinces had opted to sell liquor in government-regulated outlets. With the waning of prohibition and the success of the women's suffrage movement, the various reform movements lost their momentum during the 1920s. But those reformers who advocated a more active role of the state in the social and economic lives of its citizens would reemerge during the Great Depression of the 1930s and World War II to help prepare the way for the rise of the welfare state.

THE EMERGENCE OF NATIONAL CULTURE

The expanding cities and towns became the locus for the development of Canadian culture after Confederation. Cultural development in the colonial period was essentially derivative as successive waves of immigrants transplanted their interest in European literature, art, and music to their frontier environment. The proliferation of local newspapers starting in the early 19th century represented the earliest expression of a "Canadian" culture. The first Canadian to gain an international reputation in the literary world was Judge Thomas Haliburton, whose series of 22 satirical essays about Maritime life and politics appeared in Joseph Howe's newspaper *Novascotian* before being published in book form as *The Clock Maker* in 1836. As many as 80 editions of *The Clock Maker* were printed during the 19th century. Also important were the journals of travelers, explorers, and settlers, which fascinated European audiences who were curious about the unique North American wilderness. Samuel Hearne, Alexander Mackenzie, David Thompson, and Alexander Henry recounted their adventures in the western fur trade in the late 18th and early 19th centuries, while William Dunlop, Catherine Parr Trail, Anna Jameson, and Susanna Moodie romanticized the hardships of Upper Canadian pioneer life from the 1820s to the 1850s. The majestic landscape of the Canadian wilderness also inspired two of the more well-known mid-19th century artists: Cornelius Krieghoff, a German immigrant, captured the charm and quaintness of Quebec rural life through his colorful paintings, while Paul Kane, an Irish immigrant residing in Toronto, portrayed Native life in the northwest before the encroachment of the settlement frontier.

After Confederation, an emerging sense of nationalism, initially promoted by the Canada First movement, inspired a more vigorous and diverse expression of a distinctly Canadian culture through music, art, literature, and even sports. In 1880 the lieutenant governor of Quebec asked Calixa Lavallée, then considered to be one of Canada's greatest musicians, to compose a patriotic song for the celebration of St. Jean Baptiste Day (June 24), now recognized as the province's "national" holiday. Within a few days, Lavallée composed the music while Adolphe-Basile Routhier, a justice of the Quebec Superior Court, wrote the lyrics to "O Canada." The Quebec press proclaimed: "At last we have a truly French-Canadian National Song." "O Canada" was not performed in English until 1901, and exactly a century after its original composition, the song was officially adopted as Canada's national anthem. A more popular song in English Canada at the turn of the 20th century was "The Maple Leaf Forever," originally written in 1867 as a poem by Toronto school principal Alexander Muir. By the late 19th century, almost all Canadian cities had choir-singing groups, while Montreal, Quebec City, and Toronto developed symphony orchestras and opera companies. Canadian music received a further boost when the University of Toronto's faculty of music opened in 1919, and Vincent Massey founded the Hart House String Quartet housed at the university from 1924 onward. The advent of the radio and the phonograph, which brought music directly into Canadian homes, would expand the audience for Canadian productions by the 1920s.

The Canadian government established an early precedent for supporting national cultural development through the active involvement of British governor-generals and lieutenant governors who regularly hosted and attended important social functions, in addition to encouraging the purchase and display of the works of Canadian artists. For example, Lord Dufferin and the Marquis of Lorne both helped to establish the Royal Canadian Academy of the Arts in 1880, the predecessor to the National Gallery of Canada. The first president of the academy, Lucius O'Brien, and other members, such as Homer Watson, Daniel Fowler, and John Fraser, were recognized as being among the leading landscape painters of the time and were the precursors of the better-known Group of Seven. Also significant in the late 19th and early 20th centuries was a group of Canadian artists trained in Paris, the art capital of the world. Besides Watson, this group included William Brymmer, Robert Harris, Percy Woodstock, George Reid, and Paul Peel, perhaps the best-known Canadian painter in Europe. Quebec produced a talented coterie of artists, including the French-speaking Napoleon Bourassa, Louis-Philippe Hébert, and Ozias Leduc along with the English-speaking James Wilson Morrice and Maurice Cullen. The Newfoundland-born Cullen would be an inspiration to A. Y. Jackson, who became a member of the internationally renowned Group of Seven.

Jackson, Frank Carmichael, Lawren Harris, Franz Johnston, Arthur Lismer, J.E.H. MacDonald, and F. H. Varley officially formed the Group of Seven in 1920. (Tom Thomson was an associate of and an inspiration to members of the group, but he had drowned in a canoe accident in Algonquin Park in 1917.) The Group of Seven depicted the Canadian North as the mythical embodiment of the national spirit, in the way that the West was in the American tradition. The North countered the influence of the South not only in terms of the United States but also in terms of urban and industrial development undermining the national spirit within Canada. Even after disbanding in the early 1930s, the influence of the group endured, and its body of work continues to be celebrated as a summit of Canadian artistic achievement. A contemporary of the Group of Seven who found inspiration in its art was Emily Carr. Her art focused on the natural wonders of British Columbia before she turned to literary pursuits later in life. David Milne did not enjoy the attention in Canada that the Group of Seven received, but he was recognized in the United States and was highly acclaimed by succeeding generations of artists.

The main literary achievements in the late 19th century were in the realm of poetry. Charles G. D. Roberts, Archibald Lampman, Bliss Carman, and Duncan Campbell Scott became known as the "Confederation Group" because of their romanticized efforts to capture the essence of the new Canadian nationality in nature. The imperialist nationalist sentiments reflected in their poetry were also expressed by Pauline Johnson, daughter of a Mohawk chief and his English wife. Also using her Mohawk name, Tekahionwake, and often dressing as a Native princess during her poetry readings, Johnson celebrated her Iroquois heritage while serving as a cultural ambassador for Canada in her travels throughout Britain and the United States. By the 1920s, the imperialist themes had been replaced by a more realistic and unsentimental view of Canadian life as expressed in the poetry of E. J. Pratt at the University of Toronto and a group of McGill University poets, including F. R. Scott, A.J.M. Smith, A. M. Klein, and Leo Kennedy, who endorsed the modernist movement.

In Quebec, the poetry of Octave Crémazie and Louis Frechette expressed a patriotic concern for *la survivance* of the French-Canadian nationality in the late 19th century. Crémazie's romantic verse commemorated the past glory of Quebec under the French empire as did Frechette's, which also alluded to current injustices in the wake of the hanging of Louis Riel. With the founding of a school at the turn of the century called the Ecole littéraire de Montréal in 1895, Quebec poets began to depart from their romantic and patriotic themes in favor of a more somber, humanistic outlook. Perhaps the most dynamic member of the school at the turn of the century was Emile Nelligan, who produced 170 poems by the time he was 20 years of age before suffering an emotional breakdown that confined him to a mental institution for the last four decades of his life. His poetry is still widely read in Quebec, where he continues to enjoy legendary status.

Corresponding with the rise of free public libraries, writers of novels and short stories also came into prominence in the late 19th and early 20th centuries. The themes of nationalism and imperialism pervaded novels such as William Kirby's *The Golden Dog* (1877), Gilbert Parker's *The Seats of the Mighty* (1898), and Sara Jeannette Duncan's *The Imperialist* (1904). After the turn of the 20th century, novels were inspired by Canada's regional diversity. For example, Charles Gordon (writing under the pseudonym of Ralph Connor) romantically depicted the adventure and physical challenge of settlement in the West in *The Sky Pilot* (1899) and *The Foreigner* (1909); Lucy Maud Montgomery's *Ann of Green Gables* (1908) conveyed the charms of Prince Edward Island to an international audience; and Stephen Leacock's *Sunshine Sketches of a Little Town* (1912) satirically captured

Pauline Johnson, or Tekahionwake (1861–1913), daughter of a Mohawk chief and his English wife, was one of the most celebrated poets of her era.

small-town Ontario life. Mazo de la Roche's romantic depiction of rural Ontario life in *Jalna* (1927) sold upwards of 100,000 copies, prompting 16 sequels. Her work contrasted sharply with the brutal realism of Frederick Phillip Grove's *Settlers of the Marsh* (1925), which explored the inner psychic tension of a Norwegian settler on the Prairies. By far the most famous French-Canadian novel was Louis Hemon's *Maria Chapdelaine* (1913), written in the tradition of rural idealism. The heroine, Maria, must choose between two suitors, one promising the material advantages of life in the United States, the other remaining dedicated to the spiritual benefits of the Quebec countryside. In deciding to remain true to the traditional French-Canadian values of agrarianism, Catholicism, and family, Maria was defying the early 20th-century realities of urban and industrial Quebec.

Popular culture increasingly flourished in cities and towns after Confederation. In particular, sporting activities and events attracted a growing audience as the age of professionalization was inaugurated. The most internationally celebrated Canadian athlete of the late 19th century was Toronto's Ned Hanlon, who in 1880 won the professional rowing Championship of the World. Canada's first world champion held on to his rowing title for the next four years. Other notable Canadian athletes to achieve such distinction were Tommy Burns (born Noah Brusso), who was the world heavyweight boxing champion from 1906 to 1908, and Six Nations Native Tom Longboat, who won the World Professional Marathon Championship in 1909.

Canada's national sport in the 19th century was undoubtedly the traditional Native game of lacrosse. When it was formed in 1867, the National Lacrosse Association, the first sports organization in Canada, adopted as its motto—"Our country, our game." As lacrosse declined in popularity, ice hockey, which was first played in Montreal in 1875, would emerge as the national game by World War I. The Amateur Hockey Association of Canada was formed in 1886 as the first national organization, while the Ontario Hockey Association (OHA) became the first provincial body in 1890. Governor-General Lord Stanley donated the coveted Stanley Cup to the national champions, the Montreal Amateur Athletic Association, in 1893. Within a decade, hockey was being played by professionals, leading to the formation in 1908 of the National Hockey Association (NHA), which was reorganized as the National Hockey League (NHL) in 1917. The popularity of the NHL was enhanced by the inauguration in 1923 of Foster Hewitt's radio broadcasts of Hockey Night in Canada, which (along with its French counterpart, *La Soirée de hockey*) became an enduring tradition, particularly with the later advent of television. Canada demonstrated its supremacy in amateur hockey by winning the gold medal at the 1924 Olympics and repeating the feat four years later. While professionals competed exclusively for the Stanley Cup after 1908, the Allen Cup and the Memorial Cup became emblematic of the amateur championship at the senior and junior levels respectively.

Although football was played as early as 1865 in Canada, it became recognized as a national sport only when Governor-General Earl Grey donated the cup that bears his name in 1909. Still, the British version of football, now known as soccer, tended to be more popular in the 19th century. During the 1870s, the distinctly American sport of baseball began to compete with the British game of cricket for popularity in Canada. While the sport became the national pastime in the United States, baseball was played only at an amateur level in Canada. In 1891 James Naismith, a Canadian physical education instructor at the School of Christian Workers in Springfield, Massachusetts, invented the game of basketball, which likewise would become a popular professional sport in the United States but would be played only at the amateur level in Canada. Nevertheless, the Edmonton Grads dominated women's basketball from 1915 to 1940, winning the world amateur championship four times. Although Scottish immigrants formed curling clubs in the early 19th century, the popularity of the sport was given a boost by the inauguration of a national competition for a trophy known as the Brier in 1927. This annual event also gave impetus to Canada's continued dominance in world curling competition.

By the 1920s, Canadian popular culture was becoming more Americanized through the importation of magazines, radio programming, and movies. American magazines such as the *Ladies' Home Journal, McCall's,* and the *Saturday Evening Post* were far outselling the leading Canadian mass-circulation magazine, *Maclean's* (published under that title since 1911). More than three-quarters of the radio programs to which Canadians listened came from the United States. In 1928, the Canadian government established a royal commission to review public broadcasting. The Aird Commission's report recommended that broadcasting become a public monopoly to ensure greater Canadian content and to help unite Canadians. American-produced movies from the Hollywood studios that came to dominate the North American film industry as the 1920s progressed also began to exert a profound influence on Canadian culture and lifestyle.

With the growing expression and recognition of a distinct national culture along with the unrelenting movement of people from the countryside to the city, the basic character of modern Canada was taking shape by 1930. The National Policy had fulfilled its objective of transforming Canada into an industrial nation. The seeds of multiculturalism had been sown amid the prevailing bicultural landscape. Canada had made an auspicious debut on the world stage, and its national stature was confirmed by the Statute of Westminster in 1931. In essence, the nation was ready to advance beyond its adolescent stage of development. But before it could continue its expansive course, Canada would have to endure a decade and a half of national economic crisis followed by international upheaval.

PART FIVE

AFFLUENCE AND ANXIETY IN THE MODERN ERA

CHAPTER 16

THE PERILS OF DEPRESSION AND WAR

The almost continuous growth and prosperity of the first three decades of the 20th century not only ensured Canada's survival as a nation but also transformed it into a modern urban and industrial society and an active participant in international affairs. Henceforth, Canada would be able to exert greater influence on the course of world development, and conversely, world events would have a more profound impact on the nation's destiny. The troublesome consequences of this reality became strikingly evident during the 1930s, when Canada and most of the Western world suffered through a severe and sustained economic crisis that has become known as the Great Depression. Then, during the first half of the 1940s, much of the world was again mobilized for a second great war that, like its forerunner a quarter of a century earlier, challenged Canadians and their government to make the most effective use of their fighting and productive capacities. In Canada, as in most countries, the Great Depression and World War II together caused a degree of political, social, and economic upheaval that dramatically altered the role of government in the lives of its citizens, and thus set the stage for the rise of the welfare state.

ECONOMIC CRISIS AND SOCIAL DISTRESS

The spectacular crash of the New York stock market that financially wiped out thousands of stock speculators in October 1929 signaled the start of an economic crisis of unprecedented magnitude and duration for North America. Unlike most European nations, which struggled in the wake of the social and economic dislocation caused by World War I, Canada and the United States were unprepared for the abrupt end to the boom and the optimism that they had enjoyed throughout much of the 1920s. Political and economic leaders in both countries correctly assumed that the great crash on Wall Street was symptomatic of declining business confidence. But they proved to be mistaken in their belief that this "cyclical" slump in the economy would be as short-lived as others had typically been over the past three decades or more. A misunderstanding of the multifaceted causes of the Great Depression led to ineffective government responses that only served to aggravate the economic and social distress of the numerous people who suffered or feared the loss of their jobs.

Indeed, the causes of the Great Depression were related to factors that were mostly beyond the control of the Canadian government and which revealed the extreme vulnerability of the Canadian economy to world market conditions. Because one-third of its gross national income was derived from exports, Canada suffered from a substantial decline in the demand for and the price of such primary products as grain, fish, newsprint, lumber, and mineral resources (with the exception of gold and nickel) in the markets of the United States and Europe. Prices for primary commodities dropped not only because of domestic overproduction and overcapacity but also because of the lower demand resulting from the rise of economic nationalism. The United States, Canada's largest customer, attempted to protect its own workers and farmers from foreign competition and to stimulate its domestic market by raising tariffs to historically high levels in 1930. European countries retaliated by raising their tariffs and further restricting imports, much to Canada's detriment.

The fall in wheat exports was particularly dramatic because of difficulties in selling the record-breaking 1928 and 1929 crops; stiff competition from Argentina, Australia, and Russia; and reduced purchases by European countries attempting to revive their own production through restrictions on food imports. By 1932 the price and volume of Canadian wheat exports had dropped to less than one-quarter of their predepression levels. The meager incomes of Prairie wheat farmers were further diminished by natural disasters, as drought in 1934 and again in 1937 parched the Prairie soil and scorching wind turned the landscape into a veritable desert. Some areas of southwestern Saskatchewan and southeastern Alberta experienced drought conditions throughout the decade, while grasshoppers and wheat rust further contributed to crop failures. Prairie wheat production plunged to a historic low in terms of yield per acre in 1937, when the total crop yield was less than one-third of the peak levels achieved in 1928. Agricultural incomes in the Prairies declined by as much as 75 percent, and numerous communities, including farmers, businesses, and governments, faced the threat of bankruptcy.

The repercussions of the decline in wheat exports were felt throughout the national economy. Railway revenues were drastically cut; industry suffered from the slumping sales of farm machinery and lower farm-purchasing power in general; and construction activity was curtailed, as was the demand for consumer products. The gross national product fell by 40 percent from 1929 to 1932. But the most tangible indicator of the severity of the depression was the rise of unemployment to a historic high of 32 percent

Drought conditions for much of the 1930s turned parts of the western prairies into a "dust bowl" as scorching winds blew the topsoil away and forced farmers to abandon their unproductive land. The typical dust storm was photographed at Pearce Airport west of Lethbridge, Alberta, in 1942.

of the national labor force in May 1933. Thereafter, the unemployment rate declined gradually but was still at 10 percent in 1939; only in 1941, as the Canadian war effort escalated, did unemployment return to its predepression levels. The unemployment problem was critical not only because of its magnitude and duration but also because of its largely urban context. When Canada had been predominantly rural and agrarian in nature, access to land to provide a subsistence living offered greater flexibility in times of economic distress. But with more than half of the population living in urban areas, the responsibility to deal with the consequences of unemployment and the accompanying social and economic distress shifted from the individual to community organizations, and ultimately to the government.

The initial government response to the economic crisis was misguided and inadequate. Prime Minister King resorted to the customary refrain of politicians everywhere—that prosperity was "just around the corner." Still wedded to the laissez-faire doctrines of 19th-century liberalism, most politicians and economists believed that a government's best course of action in difficult economic times was to do little more than balance the budget, maintain a sound currency, and adjust tariff policies. King continued to insist that relief for the unemployed was a local or provincial responsibility, although he reluctantly considered the possibility of federal assistance to the provinces. During a debate on the issue in the House of Commons, Prime Minister King responded angrily to criticism of his government's failure to provide sufficient unemployment relief by insisting that he would not give a "five cent piece" to provinces under Conservative administration. The statement would come back to haunt him in the election of 1930.

Conservative leader R. B. Bennett, a millionaire Calgary lawyer, not only exploited King's unfortunate statement but also promised to aid the provinces, to put the unemployed back to work, and to end the depression. In particular, he promised to "blast a way into world markets" by raising tariffs to protect Canadian industry, and he attacked the Liberals for their ineffective retaliation against the high tariff policy that the United States had recently adopted on Canadian imports. The voters found Bennett's rhetoric appealing and elected 138 Conservatives, while the Liberals were reduced to 87 seats and various independent groups took the other 20.

The Bennett administration immediately embarked upon the most extensive revision of the Canadian tariff system since the inauguration of the National Policy. The general tariff level was raised by almost 50 percent as most agricultural and industrial products were given added protection from foreign competition. Britain's abandonment of free trade in 1932 opened the way for negotiation of the imperial preference agreement that Laurier had proposed earlier. Although a trade accord was reached involving Canada, Britain, and the Commonwealth, the participants tended to allow tariff reductions only on those products that did not adversely affect their own economy. The success of this effort to revive the declining imperial market was limited, and worse still, the United States was incited to retaliate by further raising duties on Canadian imports. Canada's foreign trade dropped by two-thirds from 1929 to 1933, thereby discrediting Bennett's policy of economic nationalism as a way out of the depression.

On the whole, no coherent government plans emerged for dealing with rural distress or chronic urban unemployment. In addition to providing loans and grants to western provinces on the verge of bankruptcy, the Bennett government attempted to keep wheat prices from falling further by purchasing more than 200 million bushels before reestablishing the Wheat Board in 1935 to market grain abroad and to assure farmers a minimum price for their crops. The Bennett government also inaugurated a program to assume an increasing share of the financial burden of unemployment relief. From 1930 to 1937, the federal government spent more than $400 million (about 40 percent of the total cost) to assist the provinces and municipalities to fulfill their responsibility for providing unemployment relief. But little more than one-quarter of this federal relief outlay came during the downswing of the depression (1930–33) when unemployment was soaring and the need for assistance was critical. The bulk of this relief assistance consisted of direct payments to the unemployed, commonly referred to as "the dole," because public works programs were deemed too costly to administer. The Department of National Defence briefly operated relief camps (or "slave camps," as they became known), which provided work for some 20,000 unmarried unemployed men who were paid a wage of 20 cents per day. This experiment was abandoned in the wake of the so-called Regina Riot in 1935 when several hundred discontented camp workers participating in the "On to Ottawa Trek" to protest their inhumane treatment by the government clashed with a contingent of Royal Canadian Mounted Police. Government officials constantly feared that the unemployed masses might be influenced by communist propaganda.

The inadequate government response resulted in widespread human suffering, particularly for urban workers and Prairie farmers deprived of their livelihoods. Since Canada did not have an effective system for dispensing public welfare, many of the unemployed and destitute had to rely on private charity and the dole, a humiliating experience in a society that still believed that poverty was basically the consequence of personal failure. By 1934 more than 2 million Canadians (one-fifth of the national population) depended on public relief. When confronted with this stark reality, Bennett was more determined to cut the federal relief budget, complaining that people had become "more or less relief conscious, determined to get out of Government all they could." The meager public assistance that was available was administered in a haphazard manner and at a substandard level of subsistence by local authorities, which themselves were dependent

Some 1,800 unemployed ride the rails to participate in the "On to Ottawa Trek," halted at Regina in June 1935.

on federal and provincial grants to meet their relief obligations. Overwhelmed by the financial burden of unemployment and relief, many cities and towns across Canada went bankrupt and became subject to provincial supervision and control. In essence, municipal governments and their unemployed citizens were victimized by the failure of the federal and provincial authorities to recognize that mass unemployment and social welfare in a modern urban and industrial society required a far greater and more systematic commitment of state resources and administration.

The personal hardships of the depression decade were also evident in demographic trends. Canada's population increased from 10.4 million in 1931 to 11.5 million in 1941, the slowest growth rate since the 1880s. Young people were forced to postpone marrying and starting a family until times improved, with the result that by 1937 the birthrate had declined by more than 25 percent since the beginning of the decade. Canada was also a less welcoming place for immigrants during the depression as the number accepted dropped from 169,000 in 1929 to 12,000 in 1935 and never rose above 17,000 a year for the remainder of the decade. The prevailing fear was that immigrants would either take scarce jobs or end up on the relief rolls. With the Immigration Act providing for the deportation of immigrants on relief, the federal government returned an unprecedented 30,000 immigrants from 1930 to 1935, and even went so far as to deny refugee status to European Jews fleeing Nazi Germany. Not measurable by any statistic was the sense of economic insecurity that the Great Depression instilled in Canadians for generations to come.

THE POLITICS OF DISCONTENT

The Great Depression dramatically altered the Canadian political landscape and perceptions of the role of government in social and economic life. Disappointed with government responses to their plight, Canadians were willing to consider political alternatives that emerged at the federal and provincial levels. When the new political personalities, parties, and movements proved to be no more capable of remedying depression conditions, it became necessary to renew the relationship between the federal and provincial governments as a prelude to the building of the welfare state.

The demand for greater government intervention was most vigorously expressed by the Co-operative Commonwealth Federation (CCF), a coalition of farmer and labor groups formed in Calgary in 1932 under the leadership of an avowed socialist, J. S. Woodsworth. On the one hand, CCF was an extension of the old Progressive Party in the sense that it was backed by the United Farmers of Alberta and other western farmers' organizations. On the other hand, CCF resembled the British Labour Party with its belief in the British parliamentary system and a gradual, peaceful progress toward socialist goals. Despite embracing socialism, CCF had little inclination to associate with the emerging Canadian Communist Party led by Tim Buck.

The CCF platform, outlined in the Regina Manifesto in 1933, was influenced by a group of university intellectuals based in Toronto and Montreal who had already formed the League for Social Reconstruction to promote political education. The manifesto, which called for a "new social order," included such "radical" measures as centralized government planning, public control of financial institutions, nationalization of key industries, socialized public health services, security of land tenure for farmers, and a national labor code that included provisions for insurance covering illness, accident, old age, and unemployment. Deeply rooted in Prairie farm politics, especially those of Saskatchewan, the CCF also gained support among workers in the ports and mines of British Columbia and the factories of Ontario. But the party was unable to make any headway in Quebec, where the powerful Catholic Church vehemently opposed socialism, as it did communism.

In Alberta, evangelist William Aberhart used his weekly religious radio broadcasts to launch the Social Credit Party. Aberhart blamed the depression on international bankers and attributed the plight of Prairie farmers to "eastern" financial interests. He further believed that the basic flaw in the economic system lay in the inadequate distribution of purchasing power, which could be remedied through the payment of a "social dividend" amounting to $25 per month to every resident of Alberta. With this increased purchasing power, the people could buy the goods that they needed and thus stimulate production and put the unemployed back to work. The appeal of such a promise to an economically desperate population, combined with the religious fervor generated by the radio broadcasts, resulted in a landslide victory for Social Credit in the provincial election of 1935. But when the party attempted to put its theories into practice, its legislation was either disallowed by the federal government or ruled unconstitutional by the courts since monetary matters were under federal jurisdiction.

Prime Minister Bennett also faced a revolt within his own party in 1934. Minister of Trade and Commerce Harry H. Stevens chaired the Royal Commission on Price Spreads, which revealed unfair practices of big business with regard to corporate profits, consumer prices, and labor wages. When Bennett attempted to suppress his attacks on the iniquities of big business, Stevens resigned from the Cabinet. As the federal election of 1935 approached, Stevens formed the Reconstruction Party with a vague platform promising to "re-establish Canada's industrial, economic, and social life for the benefit of the great majority," notably the small business community.

Mounting opposition from within his party and from new political forces demanding decisive government action to deal with the depression prompted Bennett to launch a bold new program of economic and social reform under state control. Bennett had already demonstrated a willingness to extend the realm of government intervention by reviving the Wheat Board, increasing the federal share of the cost of old-age pensions from 50 to 75 percent, and expanding federal relief grants to the provinces. Furthermore, in 1932 the Canadian Broadcasting Commission, renamed the Canadian Broadcasting Corporation (CBC) in 1936, was established to give the federal government regulatory control over the whole field of radio broadcasting. The Bank of Canada was founded in 1934 as a federal government agency to regulate monetary policy and to control private banks. Nevertheless, Canadians were astounded to hear Bennett proclaim his intention to reform capitalism in a series of five national radio broadcasts in January 1935.

The style and substance of Bennett's policy announcements were reminiscent of the New Deal inaugurated by U.S. president Franklin Roosevelt two years earlier. The "Bennett New Deal" reforms included measures to improve farm credit and the marketing of natural products; legislation providing for a minimum wage, a 48-hour work week, unemployment insurance, social security, and health insurance; and laws to enforce fair trade practices, to regulate trusts, and to control business standards. Despite the merits of these reforms, many of which were immediately implemented, most Canadians regarded Bennett's transformation from a fiscal conservative to an advocate of state paternalism as mere political opportunism.

The New Deal legislation did not prevent voters from blaming Bennett for failing to end the depression as promised, with the result that the Conservatives were reduced to 39 seats, in the election of 1935, their worst performance up to that time. The Liberals, promising little more than the slogan "King or Chaos," swept back into power with an unprecedented 171 seats, even though their popular vote was less than it had been when they lost in 1930. Significant in 1935 was the performance of the new parties, which together attracted nearly one-quarter of the voters. While Stevens was the only Reconstruction candidate elected, his party eroded Conservative support by taking almost 10 percent of the popular vote. Likewise, the Social Credit Party under Aberhart undermined the Conservative vote in capturing 15 of its 17 seats in Alberta. The CCF won about 10 percent of the vote but only seven seats, which coupled with a disappointing showing in the Saskatchewan provincial election of 1934 prompted the party to moderate its socialist rhetoric and policies.

In the wake of depression conditions, the winds of political change were also blowing through the provinces. As Aberhart was leading Social Credit to power in Alberta, Maurice Duplessis was leaving the ranks of Quebec Conservatives to form a new French-Canadian nationalist party, Union Nationale. This latest nationalist movement reflected the ambivalent reaction to the progress of urbanization and industrialization in Quebec. On the one hand, the industrial revolution that Quebec experienced after World War I curtailed the migration of young French Canadians to the factory towns of New England. On the other hand, urban and industrial growth inevitably transformed many farmers into wage earners, a trend that was worrisome to the traditional French-Canadian leadership. The Catholic Church, in particular, was concerned that its hold on the people would diminish when they moved from rural parishes to urban centers where they would be exposed to such social and moral influences as trade unions, socialist ideas, and materialistic opportunities and expectations that might seriously threaten their faith. Duplessis championed clericalism and the traditional rural-agrarian idealism that still appealed in the small towns and countryside of Quebec.

Duplessis's brand of nationalism also took advantage of the heightened resentment during the depression toward the exploitation of the French-Canadian laborer by the "alien" English-owned corporations that increasingly dominated the Quebec economy. Skillfully portraying himself as a defender of provincial rights, Duplessis led Union Nationale to victory over the long-reigning and scandal-ridden Liberal administration of Louis-Alexandre Taschereau in the Quebec election of 1936. Duplessis welcomed American investors to develop the province's resource frontier and endeavored to serve their interests by suppressing the collective bargaining rights of trade unions. His notorious Padlock Law in 1937, allowing for the seizure and closure of any place used for "subversive" activity, was ostensibly directed at communists but was broadly interpreted to apply to any group disapproved by the church or the government. For nearly two decades (1936–39 and 1944–59), Duplessis would rule over Quebec like a benevolent dictator.

In Ontario, Mitchell Hepburn led the Liberals to victory in the election of 1934 on the strength of radical rhetoric to fight for "the dispossessed and oppressed" against the "big shots." Nonetheless, Hepburn appealed to dissatisfied taxpayers, particularly among the rural and mining interests, by cutting relief expenditures and fighting against organized labor. When the American-based Committee for Industrial Organization (CIO) organized a strike at the General Motors plant in Oshawa in 1937, Hepburn was determined to break the union. He feared that CIO success in Oshawa would encourage unionization in the northern Ontario mines. To break the strike, the premier formed his own police force, known irreverently as "Hepburn's Hussars" and "Sons-of-Mitches." Prime Minister King's refusal to send in RCMP reinforcements at Hepburn's request soured relations between the two Liberal leaders. Hepburn further alienated himself from the federal government with his propensity to champion provincial rights in matters relating to social policies and intergovernmental finances.

In British Columbia, another Liberal premier, T. Dufferin Pattullo, also became embroiled in a conflict with the federal wing of his party. After his election in 1933, Pattullo instituted a reform program, including extensive public works and social services, which eventually became known as the Little New Deal. His frustration with the limitations of provincial power regularly clashed with King's determination to control the "spendthrift" provinces regardless of their political allegiance.

Confrontation between the federal and provincial governments, which had been building since Confederation, was accentuated during the Great Depression by discrepancies between resources and responsibilities. The provinces had the constitutional power to deal with prevailing social problems, but they lacked the financial resources to do so because of their limited taxation power under the British North America Act. On the other hand, the federal government had the fiscal resources but not the constitutional authority to take decisive action in the realm of social welfare. Indeed, the Judicial Committee of the Privy Council ruled the minimum wage, maximum hours, social and unemployment insurance, and fair trade practices provisions of the Bennett New Deal to be unconstitutional because they fell within provincial rather than federal jurisdiction. In response to this situation, the federal government in 1937 appointed the Royal Commission on Dominion-Provincial Relations to reexamine "the economic and financial basis of Confederation and the distribution of legislative powers in the light of the economic and social developments of the last seventy years." Although the Rowell-Sirois Commission reported too late to affect the outcome of the Great Depression, its findings and recommendations would help to lay the foundation for the Canadian welfare state.

The recovery of the Canadian economy by the late 1930s was only peripherally influenced by government policy. The King government increased the amount of federal relief assistance to the provinces and, in response to a recommendation of the National Employment Commission in 1938, deliberately incorporated deficit financing into its recovery strategy. In so doing, the federal government was following the theories of British economist John Maynard Keynes, who argued that if private enterprise failed to produce full employment, then the state had to take the initiative to create jobs even if it meant incurring substantial budgetary deficits. For the next half-century, the Keynesian notion of an active public sector would supersede the laissez-faire priority of balancing the budget. The King administration also attempted to stimulate the economy by negotiating reciprocal trade agreements with the United States in 1935 and 1938, with the result that both countries lowered the duties on some of each other's imports. In 1937 the federal government extended the scope of national transportation and communication by launching Trans-Canada Airlines (the forerunner of Air Canada), which could fly from Montreal to Vancouver in 18 hours.

One of the legacies of the Great Depression was the unproven belief that if the government had intervened sooner and more decisively the economic crisis would have been moderated or terminated. Ultimately, the depression merely faded away amid the rising armament boom as another war loomed overseas. The sad irony was that only history's bloodiest and most destructive war was capable of subduing history's greatest economic crisis.

FROM ISOLATIONISM TO INTERNATIONAL CALAMITY

The economic crisis of the 1930s instilled in Canada a reluctance to exercise the right confirmed by the Statute of Westminster in 1931 to participate fully in international affairs. The prevailing spirit of economic nationalism throughout the world prompted Canada to be more concerned with protecting its own interests and avoiding costly entanglements overseas. The masses of unemployed workers and drought-ridden farmers at home were a more pressing priority than the misfortunes of people in foreign lands. Foreign relations inevitably affected national unity, as Quebec tended to reject the view that Canada was part of an integrated world community whose interests extended beyond national borders. Finally, Canada could not help but be influenced by the strong isolationist stance of its powerful neighbor and major trading partner, the United States. While the Bennett administration was hopeful of strengthening bonds with Britain and the Commonwealth, King was more realistic in his perspective that Canada was a North American nation geographically, economically, and militarily.

Canada's determination to limit its overseas commitments was evident in its response to Japan's invasion of Manchuria in 1931. Concerned about the potential loss of trade at a time of worsening depression, Canada refused to condemn this Japanese aggression against China and avoided taking sides in the subsequent conflicts between the two Asian countries, which would escalate into a major theater of international warfare in the following decade. When Italy's fascist dictator, Benito Mussolini, tried to revive the imperial glory of ancient Rome by invading the weak African nation of Ethiopia in 1935, Walter Riddell, Canada's delegate to the League of Nations, proposed oil sanctions against Italy as a punitive measure. Fearing a backlash in Quebec where sympathy for Catholic Italy was strong and wishing to avoid participation in armed struggles not directly related to Canadian interests, Prime Minister King declared that

Riddell's proposal was not the policy of the Canadian government. The subsequent decision to drop the proposed oil sanction demonstrated the league's indecisiveness in the face of a determined adversary. Mussolini's defiance of the league gave further encouragement to Nazi dictator Adolf Hitler, who orchestrated the German invasion of the Rhineland, Austria, and Czechoslovakia. In an effort to avoid war, Britain and France adopted a policy of appeasement that allowed Germany to expand into neighboring territory in the hopes that Hitler's imperial ambitions would soon be satisfied. Canada heartily supported appeasement because it appeared to be a way of avoiding overseas commitments. King even visited Hitler in 1937 and came away convinced that the German leader was more concerned about the spread of communism than in waging war with Britain and France.

King's faith in Hitler, like the policy of appeasement, proved to be misguided. On September 3, 1939, Britain and France declared war on Germany following its invasion of Poland. Unlike in 1914 when the British declaration of war automatically included its colonies and Dominions, Canada, as an autonomous member of the British Commonwealth of Nations, was determined to choose its own course of action. "Let Parliament decide," proclaimed King, as he clearly indicated that his government would vote to support Britain and would not resort to conscription, thereby appealing to both the English- and French-speaking communities. With Woodsworth as the only dissenting vote on pacifist grounds, Parliament approved the Canadian declaration of war, which came one week after that of Britain.

Asserting that Canada's declaration of war did not reflect the wishes of Quebec, Premier Duplessis called a provincial election. Four French-Canadian federal ministers led by Minister of Justice Ernest Lapointe threatened to resign, thereby leaving Quebec without representation in the federal Cabinet, if Union Nationale was returned to power. Quebec voters declared their unqualified support for the war effort by electing the Liberals under Adelard Godbout. Always looking for an opportunity to challenge the federal government, Premier Hepburn of Ontario abusively condemned King's conduct of the war to the point of prompting the prime minister to call a national election in March 1940. The Liberal victory by an increased majority convinced King to reject Conservative demands for a coalition government to formulate and implement war policy.

At the outset of World War II, Canada expected that its primary contribution would be the production of war supplies rather than the mobilization of armed forces, which were hitherto small in number. In late 1939, the Royal Canadian Air Force (RCAF) agreed to administer the British Commonwealth Air Training Plan, which eventually produced 130,000 aviators, more than half of whom were Canadian. Not only did this scheme have the advantage of being acceptable to French Canadians because it was based at home rather than abroad, but the nearly $1.3 billion that the Canadian government invested in it was a stimulus to the national economy. The hope that Britain and France could subdue Germany with Canadian material support was dashed by June 1940 when France fell and Italy entered the war on the German side. With the neutrality of the United States and the Soviet Union continuing until 1941, Canada stood as the next strongest nation to Britain in the fight against the German-Italian-Japanese Axis.

As they had during World War I, Canada's armed forces met the challenges of military service and all-out warfare with their customary courage, bravery, and fighting efficiency. The Canadian army, which expanded from 4,000 troops to almost 700,000 men and women under the command of General A. G. McNaughton, distinguished itself on several critical battlefronts: the defense of Hong Kong in 1941, the bold raid on the

French coast at Dieppe in 1942, the conquest of Sicily in 1943, the D day landing at Normandy as well as the capture of Rome and the Belgian port of Antwerp in 1944, and the liberation of the Netherlands before the final offensive against Germany in 1945. The Royal Canadian Navy, which expanded from 17 to 900 vessels and from 3,000 troops to a force of 100,000 men and 6,500 women, played a vital role in patrolling the sea lanes of the North Atlantic and guarding the approaches to the harbors of North America, in addition to contributing 110 battleships to the Allied landings in Normandy. The Canadian air force, which expanded from 4,000 to more than 200,000 men in both RCAF squadrons and RAF crews, fought in the Battle of Britain; participated in the nightly bombings of Germany; and flew over Malta (in North Africa), Italy, India, Burma, Alaska, and the Arctic. Altogether, about 1 million Canadians or more than one-twelfth of the national population saw military service at home or overseas during World War II. More than 40,000 Canadians were killed in the bloodbath that claimed as many as 60 million lives worldwide from 1939 to 1945.

The magnitude and duration of the war effort again brought the thorny question of conscription to the forefront of Canadian politics. From his experience during World War I, Prime Minister King was well aware of how divisive the issue of compulsory military service for overseas operations could be for the country and for his political party. For more than two years King was determined to keep his "no conscription" pledge, which had secured French-Canadian support for the war effort, despite the persistent demands of those English-speaking Canadians who had family members fighting overseas or who pointed to the British and American commitment to total war on the basis of national conscription. As pressure from public opinion and within his government mounted in 1942, King decided to consult the Canadian people by holding a national plebiscite that asked them if they would release the government from its anticonscription pledge. Predictably, Quebec voted 72 percent against while the rest of Canada voted 80 percent in favor. The result of the plebiscite freed King from his pledge and increased the demand for conscription in English Canada. But French Canada felt betrayed to the extent that a new political party, the Bloc Populaire, was formed with both Quebec and federal wings. While some Quebec nationalists viewed conscription in terms of English Canada's continued attempts to assimilate French-Canadian culture or of the federal government's violation of provincial rights, most French Canadians lacked enthusiasm for compulsory overseas service because they did not feel immediately concerned with the European conflict. They had been estranged from France for nearly two centuries and had no strong loyalty to Britain. Thus, the majority of French Canadians would have preferred Canada to remain neutral as the United States did until late 1941, but they did not oppose Canada's participation in the war on the basis of voluntary enlistment.

While King introduced legislation to make conscription possible, his position remained "not necessarily conscription but conscription if necessary." He further specified that conscription, if implemented, would be for home service only and that overseas service would be on a voluntary basis. The furor over conscription died down until late 1944 when Minister of Defense J. L. Ralston returned from a tour of Canadian forces in Europe to report that more reinforcements were needed to replace the higher than expected casualties in the Normandy fighting. When attempts to raise more volunteers failed, King had little choice but to agree to conscription for overseas service. Only 13,000 conscripts were sent overseas before the war in Europe ended in May 1945.

King and the Liberal Party escaped the second conscription crisis with far less political fallout than Robert Borden, Arthur Meighen, and the Conservatives had incurred in the aftermath of World War I. In contrast to the way in which Borden and Meighen had pushed the conscription agenda in the face of French-Canadian opposition in 1917, King had proceeded more cautiously and with greater sensitivity to the implications of the issue for national unity. So whereas the first conscription crisis effectively crippled the Conservatives in Quebec for much of the remainder of the 20th century, the Liberals were able to retain their French-Canadian support in winning the national election of 1945, albeit by a substantially reduced majority. Quebec preferred to take its frustration out on the provincial Liberals by returning Duplessis and the Union Nationale to power in 1944. The anticonscription Bloc Populaire was not a factor in either the provincial or the federal election and soon disappeared.

The cultural sensitivity to French Canadians that King and the Liberals demonstrated during the conscription controversy was not extended to other ethnic communities, however. In particular, members of ethnic groups whose homelands were at war with Canada faced harsh treatment from the government and a general public influenced by patriotic propaganda. Although no evidence of subversive activity was found, hundreds of Germans and Italians were interned in camps or detained in jails. The worst injustice was perpetrated against more than 20,000 Japanese living in British Columbia, many of whom were Canadian citizens. They were herded into camps in the interior of the province, and many of them had their property confiscated. More than four decades would pass before the federal government would acknowledge the mistreatment of Japanese Canadians and would offer an official apology and financial compensation. The prevailing climate of racial intolerance during World War II also blinded Canadians, and the rest of the world, to the Jewish Holocaust perpetrated by Nazi Germany.

The perils of war fostered a unity of the English-speaking world to an extent that Goldwin Smith would have appreciated a half-century earlier. The military, economic, political, and diplomatic collaboration of Canada, Britain, and the United States in a common effort against a common enemy reinforced the evolving concept of the "North Atlantic Triangle." In contrast to the situation during World War I, Canada did not have to struggle for recognition of national autonomy in its relationship with Britain. The progress of air transportation (Trans Canada Airlines began regular overseas flights in 1941) and radio communication encouraged continuous consultation between Canada and Britain, thereby

Mackenzie King (1874–1950), addressing the Canadian people on VE Day (May 8, 1945), served as prime minister for more than 22 years, the longest tenure in the British Empire.

negating the need for such institutions as the Imperial War Cabinet or Imperial Conferences. Some diehard imperialists still tried to revive the movement for imperial centralization or imperial unity, but these notions appeared anachronistic in view of Canada's increasingly close relations with the United States.

Growing economic ties were reinforced by common continental defense concerns. In 1940 Canada and the United States signed the Ogdensburg Agreement, which created the Permanent Joint Board on Defense to "consider in the broad sense the defense of the north half of the western hemisphere." The board planned joint Arctic defenses against a northern attack by air, and chains of Canadian-American air bases and radio posts were stretched across the Arctic wilderness. The Alaska Highway, extending 1,500 miles through the British Columbia and Yukon wilderness, was rendered urgent by Japanese presence off the coast of Alaska in 1942. At the same time, the Canol project, involving the building of a pipeline from the Norman oil wells in the Arctic reaches of the Mackenzie Valley to a refinery at Whitehorse, was undertaken to assure fuel supplies to Alaska. Canada and the United States also established extensive air bases in Newfoundland and Labrador to prevent the gateway to North America from falling into enemy hands. Besides these defensive arrangements, the Hyde Park Agreement of 1941 tied the Canadian and American economies even more closely together by encouraging joint planning of war production on a continental basis. These developments emphasized the extent to which the strategic interests and productive capacities of Canada and the United States were becoming integrated.

FEDERAL POWER AND STATE CONTROL

Coming on the heels of the Great Depression, which called for an extraordinary measure of state intervention in the economy, World War II further challenged Canadian government to make the most efficient use of national resources through even more systematic central planning and state control. In the process, the role of the Canadian government in economic and social life was permanently transformed, and the welfare state was inexorably launched.

As France succumbed to the German blitzkrieg (lightning war) in June 1940, the Canadian Parliament passed the National Resources Mobilization Act to organize the nation's productive capacity and human resources for an all-out war effort. Much of the regulatory power of the state was exercised by the newly created Department of Munitions and Supply (originally the War Supply Board) headed by Clarence D. Howe, who applied his extensive engineering knowledge and experience to run Canada's war production program with ruthless efficiency bordering on authoritarianism.

Howe oversaw the creation of new industries and the expansion of existing ones to produce vital war materials such as airplanes, tanks, battleships, minesweepers, radar equipment, artillery and ammunition, synthetic rubber and plastics, and aviation fuel. By the end of the war, Canadian manufacturing production had more than doubled, and the national industrial structure had become more comprehensive and diversified. Industrial expansion meant increased demand for natural resources, the allocation of which Howe's department also controlled. Consequently, hydroelectric power production expanded by half; forest production rose by two-thirds (including the doubling of pulpwood); and mineral production was up by one-fifth, with nickel, asbestos, and aluminum being in highest demand. Agricultural production, notably mixed and dairy farming as well as the raising of hogs, cattle, and sheep, increased by nearly half, although surplus wheat continued to be a problem with the loss of European markets.

To assure a steady supply of war materials, the production of nonessential consumer goods was curtailed. Sugar, tea, coffee, butter, meat, and gasoline, for example, were rationed through a system of government-issued coupons. The Department of Munitions and Supply was also responsible for mobilizing Canada's labor force for war production. The 400,000 unemployed at the outbreak of war were largely absorbed into war-related industries. Not only did Howe's department ensure that Canadian factories operated to full capacity, it also directly or indirectly employed more than 1 million workers. As during World War I, women were encouraged to enter the workforce in response to the general labor shortage created by the war. The shortage of workers was a boost to the union movement as its membership doubled to more than 700,000 during the war. Nevertheless, employers fiercely resisted union attempts to impose collective bargaining, and the federal government constantly intervened to prevent strikes that could adversely affect war production. In 1941 the War Time Prices and Trade Board was established to give the federal government authority to impose price and wage controls in order to prevent the spiraling inflation that had prevailed during World War I. But the freezing of wages proved to be a major cause of labor unrest and industrial disputes. Labor dissatisfaction and union efforts to ensure recognition contributed to a wave of strikes that resulted in 1 million working days lost in 1943.

Although the war eliminated unemployment and restored a degree of prosperity not experienced since the late 1920s, Canadians remained concerned, even fearful, about postwar economic and social security. The Royal Commission on Dominion-Provincial Relations proved to be instrumental in redefining the future role of Canadian government. Chaired by Newton Rowell, who was succeeded by Joseph Sirois after ill health forced him to retire, the commission produced a report in 1940 that proposed a revision of Confederation to stabilize provincial finances and to ensure that all Canadians received equal services. The federal government would assume the whole burden of unemployment relief and unemployment insurance as well as existing provincial debts. The provinces would "rent" to the federal government their right to collect income and corporation taxes as well as succession duties in return for "adjustment grants" that would replace the system of federal subsidies to the provinces agreed upon at the time of Confederation. Through this new system of adjustment grants based on financial need, the federal government would assist the provinces to administer a uniform standard of social and educational services.

Following the recommendation of the Rowell-Sirois Commission, the federal government, with provincial consent and after making the requisite amendment to the British North America Act, established the Unemployment Insurance Commission (UIC) Fund in 1940. Supported by compulsory contributions from both employees and employers, the UIC Fund would provide for those who might become temporarily unemployed. About half the work force was initially covered by this scheme. Prime Minister King became even more interested in social welfare measures when a public opinion poll in September 1943 indicated that the CCF had edged past the Liberals and Conservatives in popularity. The following year T. C. Douglas led the CCF to victory in the Saskatchewan provincial election. Clearly, the threat from the left could not be ignored. In response to a recommendation of the federal government's Committee on Reconstruction under the direction of Leonard Marsh, the King administration introduced the Family Allowance Act in 1944. The program to provide monthly payments of

$5 to $8 to help parents support their children became popularly known as the "baby bonus." King's strategy to draw support away from the CCF appeared to pay off in the federal election of 1945 as the party won 28 seats, four times more than in the previous election but not enough to deprive the Liberals of a majority government.

After the election, King convened the Dominion-Provincial Conference on Reconstruction to plan the reconversion of the national economy to peacetime conditions. King hoped to convince the provinces to continue the "temporary wartime expedient" to which they had agreed four years earlier whereby they were appropriately compensated for relinquishing to the federal government their authority to levy succession duties as well as income and corporation taxes. To maintain this arrangement, the federal government offered to increase grants, to pay part of the cost of a comprehensive health insurance plan and an old-age pension scheme, and to expand coverage of unemployment insurance. When Ontario, Quebec, and Alberta objected to the concentration of financial powers in the hands of the federal government, Ottawa resorted to making "tax rental" agreements with individual provinces. Viewing such arrangements as an infringement on provincial autonomy, Quebec insisted on operating its own income tax system. Despite numerous attempts over the next two decades, agreement on a common federal-provincial revenue-sharing scheme could not be reached.

Canada emerged from World War II a stronger nation in three respects. First, the nation had survived the worst economic crisis in its history and had set in motion the public institutions to protect the social and economic security of its citizens from being so threatened in the future. Second, Canada once again demonstrated that it was a formidable force in the international arena and was prepared to abandon its prewar isolationism to preserve world peace. Third, despite the recurring conscription crisis, national unity remained intact at the end of the war, and Canadians could focus on economic reconstruction and renewal rather than on political appeasement. Indeed, the stage was set for the remarkable postwar boom.

CHAPTER 17

AN EXPANDING NATION IN THE AGE OF AFFLUENCE

After suffering through a decade and a half of depression and war, Canada enjoyed a decade and a half of extraordinary economic and population growth after World War II. Expansion in the level of industrial production as well as in the exploitation of natural resources was accompanied by the so-called baby boom and a renewed tide of immigration that influenced virtually every aspect of national life. Internationally, Canada emerged from another outstanding war effort as a strategic "middle power" in a disturbingly bipolar world order. Canada's diplomatic challenge was to balance its growing prominence within the diminished yet influential British Commonwealth with its precarious position as a major trading partner and military ally of the powerful United States. Prosperity and international recognition, however, could not stem the tide of rampant regionalism as the provinces endeavored to renegotiate their relationships with the federal government with the coming of the welfare state.

THE POSTWAR BOOM

While Canada's economy had expanded and diversified during World War II, as it had during World War I, the anticipated economic downturn in the aftermath did not materialize. Instead of the severe recession that struck after World War I, Canada enjoyed the continuation of wartime prosperity after 1945 for two reasons. First, since many of the important industrial nations lay in ruin with their productive capacities crippled, Canadian products remained in high demand. Second, after 15 years of austerity resulting from depression and war, Canadians were ready to spend their hard-earned money to improve their lifestyles. Having once again helped to preserve the world for democracy, Canadians felt entitled to reap the benefits for themselves. They wanted better wages, more leisure, and the full range of material pleasures that their money could buy. Rising consumerism was manifested in growing sales of automobiles, television sets, and household appliances. Above all, Canadians desired to own their own homes, and the mushrooming suburban communities with their uniform housing subdivisions and shopping plazas afforded them the opportunity. Indeed, not until after World War II were urban Canadians transformed from a society of renters to a society of homeowners. Marriages and families that had been postponed in troubled times could now proceed. And people from war-ravaged nations increasingly viewed Canada as a land of opportunity to revitalize and stabilize their lives.

The postwar boom was sustained and characterized by the remarkable growth of population from 11.5 million in 1941 to 18.2 million in 1961. The national annual growth rate, which had declined to less than 1 percent during the 1930s and early 1940s, approached 3 percent during the so-called baby boom from the late 1940s to the early 1960s, a growth rate comparable to that achieved during the country's wheat boom prior to World War I. The most notable feature of this population growth was an approximately 30 percent rise in the annual birthrate (number of live births per 1,000 population), which resulted in an annual increase in the number of births from fewer than 250,000 in the late 1930s to nearly 500,000 by the end of the 1950s. Equally significant, however, was an almost 25 percent decline in the death rate, highlighted by a more than 50 percent drop in the infant mortality rate, both of which resulted from improved medical sciences and services as well as better nutritional levels, personal hygiene, and housing.

The Canadian population was also bolstered by the arrival of approximately 2 million immigrants in the 15 years after World War II. By contrast to a net loss of nearly 100,000 immigrants during the 1930s when more people left the country than entered it, Canada recorded a net gain of more than 1 million immigrants during the 1950s, the highest level for any decade in Canadian history. The postwar peak was reached in 1957 when 282,000 immigrants arrived in Canada. That only about one-third of the postwar immigrants were of British origin and that most of the remainder came from continental Europe was a concern to the majority of Canadians and to their government. Prime Minister King outlined a new federal immigration policy, which acknowledged "that the people of Canada do not wish, as a result of mass immigration, to make a fundamental alteration in the character of our population." Although the new policy repealed the blatantly discriminatory Chinese Immigration Act of 1923, King rationalized that restrictions must continue:

Large-scale immigration from the Orient would change the fundamental composition of the Canadian population. Any considerable Oriental immigration
would, moreover, be certain to give rise to social and economic problems of a character that might lead to serious difficulties in the field of international relations.

Regarding the less worrisome but still controversial immigration from continental
Europe, King stipulated that government policy would focus "on the admission of the
relatives of persons who are already in Canada, and on assisting in the resettlement of
displaced persons and refugees." Accordingly, about 165,000 displaced persons escaping the tyranny of Nazi Germany, fascist Italy, and the communist regimes of Eastern
Europe were admitted into Canada during the decade after World War II, while another
35,000 refugees of the Hungarian Revolution arrived in 1956.

Most Europeans came to Canada to escape the austerity of their postwar existence
or to find new prospects in a rapidly expanding Canadian economy. Mindful of the economic instability of the prewar era, King assured Canadians in 1947 that immigration
would be related to "our absorptive capacity . . . in response to economic conditions."
As it turned out, a widespread shortage of labor caused by the booming economy
enabled Canada to accommodate far more immigrants than anticipated.

Post-World War II European immigrants were no longer "the stalwart peasants in
their sheepskin coats" seeking a western homestead, as their early-20th century counterparts had tended to be. While some immigrants were directed or lured to the expanding northern and western resource frontiers, the vast majority flocked to the rapidly
growing cities, where factory and construction jobs beckoned. Prominent among the
newcomers were Dutch, Germans, Greeks, Italians, Poles, and Portuguese, who took
advantage of the government preference for immigrants sponsored by relatives already
living in Canada. Indeed, family "chain migration" was so extensive that by 1958 Italy
surpassed Britain as the leading source of immigrants. The tendency for these immigrants to settle in large, closely knit cultural communities within major urban centers—
notably Toronto and Montreal—added a more cosmopolitan quality to Canadian life.
These new Canadians not only brought with them valuable knowledge, skills, and capital but also sustained the vigorous consumer demand for domestic products.

The concentration of population in urban centers and suburban communities was
a major catalyst of the postwar boom. The proportion of Canadians living in urban centers rose from slightly more than 55 percent in 1941 to nearly 70 percent in 1961. Nearly half of the population lived in cities having more than 100,000 inhabitants by 1961,
as compared to about one-quarter in 1941. Montreal and Toronto continued to lead the
way with populations exceeding 2.1 million and 1.8 million, respectively, accounting for
well over one-fifth of the total, while Vancouver was approaching 800,000. Postwar
urbanization in the downtown core of the major cities featured the centralization of service functions, the proliferation of high-rise apartment complexes and office towers, and
the building of public transit systems and expressways to alleviate traffic congestion.

Meanwhile, the fertile countryside was transformed into sprawling suburbs in
response to the construction of asphalt superhighways and improved automobile and
truck technology. With the resulting decentralization of population, retail commerce,
and heavy industry, planned residential subdivision, commercial-industrial parks, and
multiacre shopping centers became standard features of the expanding suburban frontier. The complex challenges of managing these emerging urban agglomerations led to
the adoption of new forms of local or regional authority, highlighted by the creation in

1954 of Metropolitan Toronto as a unique federation of the city and its 12 suburbs (amalgamated into five boroughs in 1967).

Postwar urban and industrial growth was a boon to organized labor. Union membership surpassed the 1-million mark, or about 30 percent of the workforce, in 1950. As industrial demand outpaced the labor supply, unions in the manufacturing sector enjoyed substantial bargaining power and succeeded in negotiating favorable wages. The growing confidence of organized labor and a desire to make up for ground lost during the Great Depression and World War II resulted in a flurry of strike activity in the late 1940s and early 1950s. The most dramatic and bitter industrial conflicts of the era included the Steel Company of Canada (Stelco) strike in 1946, which featured the use of airplanes and boats by management to avoid the picket lines and to transport supplies to the strikebreakers inside the plant in Hamilton; the strike of the Confédération des travailleurs catholiques du Canada (CTCC) in Asbestos, Quebec, in 1949, which lasted five months, resulted in police intervention and government decertification of the union, and contributed to the nationalist fervor that led to the so-called Quiet Revolution of the 1960s; the walkout of 130,000 railway workers, which prompted the federal government to order them back on the job in 1950; and the violent, seven-month confrontation involving copper workers at Murdochville, Quebec, which ended in defeat for the union in 1957.

Labor strength was reflected not only in growing numbers but in greater unity. The merger of the American Federation of Labor (AFL) with the Congress of Industrial Organizations (CIO) in 1955 inspired the union of the Trades and Labour Congress (TLC) with the Canadian Congress of Labour (CCL) to form the powerful Canadian Labour Congress (CLC) in 1956. Many of the CLC unions were affiliated with the AFL-CIO, and Canadian workers employed by American branch plants were not averse to belonging to American-dominated unions.

Contrasting the impressive growth of urban-industrial centers was the persistence of rural depopulation, notably in the western Prairie Provinces where the farm population declined by about 20 percent during the 1940s and 1950s. Foreign demand for western grain remained buoyant until the early 1950s when European agriculture began to recover and the United States decided to dump its accumulated farm surplus onto the world market. As prices fell steadily, the wheat economy could no longer sustain western growth and prosperity. Coincidentally, the discovery of oil and natural gas at Leduc (southwest of Edmonton) in 1947, followed by other major strikes across Alberta and to a lesser extent Saskatchewan and Manitoba, triggered a petroleum boom that strengthened the position of western Canada in the national economy. Western oil and natural gas became the resource base for an expanding Canadian petroleum industry through the construction of a national system of pipelines that transported fuel to markets on the West Coast and in eastern Canada and the United States.

Canada's prospects as a rising industrial power were also enhanced by the continued expansion of the northern resource frontier. The discovery of iron in the Steep Rock Lake district north of Lake Superior in the early 1940s was followed by the unearthing of even richer ore deposits in the Ungava Peninsula around the Quebec-Labrador boundary later in the decade. The opening of the atomic age stimulated an intensive search for new sources of uranium. The discovery of uranium deposits at Beaverlodge in northern Saskatchewan led to the establishment of Uranium City in 1951. In northern Ontario, the Algoma field at Blind River and the Sudbury field at Elliot Lake were also opened up in the early 1950s. The resource frontier extended into the Northwest Territories with the discovery of lead and zinc near Great Slave Lake, tungsten along the Yukon border, uranium and silver near Great Bear Lake, and oil along the lower Mackenzie River. Oil prospecting was even reaching into the distant Queen Elizabeth Islands of the Arctic.

By the early 1950s, Canada was also emerging as the world's second-largest producer of aluminum, with the new smelter at Kitimat, some 500 miles up the mountainous coast from Vancouver, being the world's largest. This development, along with the continued expansion of the pulp and paper industry, which supplied more than half of the world's newsprint, was facilitated by an abundance of cheap hydroelectric power. The new developments of the era included power stations on the Columbia River of British Columbia, the Nelson River of Manitoba, and the Churchill Falls of Labrador.

Because many of the resource developments lay in the heart of the northern wilderness, transportation improvements became important to get machinery, workers, and supplies in and to bring the primary products out. Labrador City and Schefferville, for example, were linked by a 350-mile railway line to Sept-Îles on the St. Lawrence River. These new communities also had to be supplied with housing, schools, churches, electrical power, passable roads, and sanitation and water facilities, among other amenities. Their needs gave new opportunities to the construction and manufacturing industries that could service them.

Resource development in particular and national expansion in general continued to be facilitated by dynamic transportation and communication projects. By 1953 the world's longest oil pipeline ran east from Edmonton to the petrochemical center of Sarnia nearly 1,800 miles away to feed the eastern Canadian market, while another pipeline extended more than 700 miles across the Pacific mountain ranges to Vancouver and eventually on into the United States. Despite generating a storm of political controversy over Canada's dependence on American capital, Trans-Canada Pipeline Limited completed a 2,200-mile pipeline transporting natural gas from Alberta to Quebec in 1958.

Meanwhile, the St. Lawrence Seaway project effectively revived the east-west transport route that had been the backbone of Canadian development from the nation's beginning. Since the early 20th century, Canada and the United States had been negotiating to improve the St. Lawrence system to enable ocean-going ships to travel to the head of the Great Lakes. When negotiations for a joint construction project broke down, the Canadian government proceeded independently in 1951. Recognizing that the St. Lawrence Seaway project would provide vital hydroelectric power to the bordering states and would serve as an efficient avenue for moving iron ore from the Quebec-Labrador region to the American steel mills and western grain to European markets, the United States agreed to participate in 1954, and the project was completed in 1959.

Recalling the building of the CPR and other transcontinental railways of the early 20th century wheat boom, the federal and provincial governments agreed on joint construction of the Trans-Canada Highway in 1949. Although the highway was officially opened in 1962, the billion-dollar project was not completed until 1970. Canadians could now drive, using ferry services on both coasts, from St. John's, Newfoundland, to Victoria, British Columbia. Canadians could also communicate with each other through the new medium of television as the Canadian Broadcasting Corporation (CBC), which began transmission in 1952 and had the capacity to broadcast from coast to coast by 1958. Certainly, the mid-century transportation and communication improvements further diversified and unified the transcontinental economy and linked Canadians more closely together from east to west. But these postwar developments also helped to reinforce Canada's growing economic, diplomatic, and cultural ties with the United States, its powerful southern neighbor.

CONTINENTAL INTEGRATION AND MIDDLE POWER DIPLOMACY

The construction of the St. Lawrence Seaway and a network of pipelines across the country required a volume of private capital that was beyond Canadian means. Indeed, Canada became increasingly dependent upon foreign capital to finance its postwar national expansion. Foreign investment in Canada tripled during the 1950s as American multinational corporations endeavored to avert the high Canadian tariffs on imported manufactured goods by establishing branch plants. Whereas in 1900 some 85 percent of foreign investment in Canada came from Britain and almost all of the remainder came from the United States, by the end of the 1950s, the roles were virtually reversed. Foreign investors controlled nearly three-quarters of the oil industry and one-half of both mining and manufacturing.

Likewise, the American market offered Canada the greatest opportunities for expansion of foreign trade. Nearly 60 percent of Canadian exports went to the United States as compared to about 15 percent to Britain, while more than 70 percent of Canadian imports were from the United States as compared to less than 10 percent from Britain. Canadians debated the relative advantages and disadvantages of this situation. In 1955 the Royal Commission on Canada's Economic Prospects, chaired by Walter Gordon, warned of the dangers to Canadian sovereignty of increasing economic dependence on the United States and urged the pursuit of a broader base of international trade as well as greater controls on foreign investment. On the other hand, C. D. Howe, minister of trade and commerce in the Liberal government, argued strongly for continental integration in 1956:

> Had it not been for the enterprise and capital of the United States, which has been so freely at our disposal in post-war years, our development would have been slower, and some of the spectacular projects about which we are . . . so rightly proud, since they are Canadian projects, would still be far in the future.

Howe favored a policy "to sell as much as possible wherever possible," and thus argued that closer economic ties with the United States created more jobs for Canadians and helped the country's balance of payments by reducing imports. The formation of the European Common Market in 1957, which further limited the prospects of overseas trade, appeared to confirm that continental integration was the best prospect for the Canadian economy.

Continental integration also seemed to be an appropriate response to the new bipolar power structure in the realm of international relations after World War II. Britain was fading as a world power, and thus could not be relied on to protect Canadian interests. The United States had clearly emerged out of its prewar isolationism to assume the role as the leader of the Western democracies competing for global dominance against the Soviet Union and its allied communist regimes. In response to the escalation of the cold war, Canada proved more willing to extend its international relations beyond its traditional limits of defending British imperial interests or asserting North American isolationism.

Canada was alerted to the reality of the cold war in September 1945 when Igor Gouzenko, a cipher clerk in the Soviet Embassy in Ottawa, defected and revealed the operation of a Soviet espionage network in Canada. The rise of Soviet-controlled communist

C. D. Howe (1886–1960), minister of munitions and supply during World War II and minister of trade and commerce in Louis St. Laurent's administration, perhaps the most influential figure of his era, celebrates being named Time *magazine's Man of the Year in 1952.*

regimes in Bulgaria, Hungary, Romania, Poland, East Germany, and Czechoslovakia by 1948, in addition to revelations of Soviet atomic power, aroused Western democracies to take a stand against communist imperialism, which had drawn what British Prime Minister Winston Churchill termed an "Iron Curtain" between East and West. In 1948 Louis St. Laurent, who had been appointed Canada's first full-time minister of external affairs two years earlier, called for "the creation and preservation by nations of the Free World . . . of an overwhelming preponderance of force" that could check Soviet aggression more effectively than the United Nations (UN) had since its inception in 1945. The UN Security Council was stymied in its efforts to maintain international peace and security by the veto power that had been accorded to the so-called great powers, including the Soviet Union, the United States, Britain, France, and China.

Accordingly, the free nations of North America and Western Europe established the North Atlantic Treaty Organization (NATO) in 1949 as a joint defense against Soviet aggression. While the United States preferred a purely military alliance principally committed to the containment of Soviet power, Canada sought to reinforce social and economic links with Western Europe in order to offset American military dominance. Despite Canadian efforts, rising East-West tensions, heightened by the outbreak of the Korean War in 1950, turned NATO into an almost exclusively military alliance. Demonstrating a widening global interest, Canada fulfilled its military obligations to NATO by stationing an army brigade in Germany and an air force division in France, in addition to providing a naval squadron to patrol the North Atlantic.

Canada's cooperation with the United States in NATO was part of a joint program for North American continental defense. As relations between the United States and the Soviet Union deteriorated, Canada became increasingly concerned about the stark reality that the shortest air route between the two superpowers was through its Arctic region. In order to provide warning against air and missile attack on North America from across the North Pole, chains of radar bases were strung across the continent during the 1950s, including the Pine Tree Line in the vicinity of the Canadian-American border, the Mid-Canada Line or McGill Fence along the 55th parallel, and the Distant Early Warning (DEW) Line stretching across the Arctic wilderness. The DEW Line completed in 1959 was built and maintained exclusively by American funds and personnel, and thus aroused controversy regarding possible threats to Canadian sovereignty. The two nations extended their joint military commitments in 1958 by signing the North American Air Defense (NORAD) agreement, which placed continental air forces under an American commander and a Canadian deputy.

Concerned about being viewed as merely an American satellite, Canada was careful to preserve its national identity and to fulfill its diplomatic responsibilities even if it meant occasionally upsetting its continental neighbor and ally. Indeed, the determination to maintain independence from American foreign policy was evident in Canada's active participation in the UN. After winning recognition as a "middle power," Canada went on to perform distinguished service in numerous UN food, health, education, and welfare agencies concerned with the elimination of hunger, disease, ignorance, and poverty throughout the world. Moreover, as a leading supporter of the UN principle of collective security, Canada gained an international reputation for its peacekeeping role. During the Korean War, Canada made the third-largest contribution of troops to support UN efforts to resist North Korean aggression against South Korea. In 1954 Canada served with Poland and India in an International Control Commission to supervise the peace in Indochina.

Recognition of Canada's peacekeeping and peacemaking acumen reached a climax during the Suez Crisis in 1956. Egypt's nationalization of the Suez Canal incited Israel to invade the Sinai Peninsula, while Britain and France launched their armed intervention to regain control of the Canal Zone. With the possibility of American and Soviet military intervention looming, Lester Pearson, who had succeeded St. Laurent as minister of external affairs in 1948 and had been elected president of the UN General Assembly in 1952, introduced a resolution calling for an immediate cease-fire to be supervised by a multinational UN Emergency Force. Pearson's plan was adopted and a Canadian-led UN Emergency Force was stationed in the Canal Zone to act as a buffer between the Egyptians and Israelis until a lasting peace could be negotiated. Through its decisive role in the Suez Crisis, Canada bolstered its status as a middle power unaligned with either Britain or the United States, while Pearson was awarded the Nobel Peace Prize in 1957.

Despite its decision to oppose British military intervention during the Suez Crisis, Canada generally maintained a significant relationship with the Commonwealth as a means of balancing its closer ties with the United States. As partners in the UN and NATO, Canada and Britain were major supporters of the American crusade to check the spread of communism. Moreover, the multilateral General Agreement on Tariffs and Trade (GATT), which Canada signed in 1947, included provisions for lower tariffs with its two principal trading partners, the United States and Britain. Canada also encouraged a reconceptualization of the Commonwealth to accommodate the former British colonies in Asia and Africa that gained their independence after World War II. Canadian initiative helped to replace the concept of common British and Commonwealth citizenship with one based on nationality. The Canadian Citizenship Act of 1947 was the first nationality statute to define the people of Canada as "Canadians" rather than "British subjects." As a result of Canadian efforts, the predominantly white British Commonwealth gave way to the multiracial Commonwealth of Nations. The new Commonwealth included not only the Dominions like Canada, Australia, and New Zealand, which maintained allegiance to the Crown, but also those new republics like India, Pakistan, Ghana, and Nigeria, which merely wished to continue their association with Britain and the Dominions.

In encouraging the acceptance of new Asian and African members into the Commonwealth, Canada rationalized that it was important to persuade these overpopulated nations that their interests were better served by association with the Western democracies rather than with the communist world. Accordingly, Canada joined seven other nations of the Commonwealth in 1950 to formulate the Colombo Plan, a comprehensive program of economic and technical aid to the countries of South and Southeast Asia, a region considered fertile ground for the spread of communism. By the early 1960s, Canada had provided almost $400 million in foreign aid under the Colombo Plan. In essence, the Commonwealth offered Canada the opportunity to retain its traditional "family" ties while it endeavored to influence the broader international order through its middle power diplomacy.

THE POLITICS OF PROSPERITY

Canada's sense of national confidence in the postwar era was bolstered not only by a prolonged economic boom and a growing stature on the world stage but also by the completion of the transcontinental vision of Confederation. After finally rejecting Confederation in 1894, Newfoundland remained a British colony with responsible government until it was granted Dominion status after World War I. Although the Quebec-Labrador boundary dispute was settled in favor of Newfoundland in 1927, Labrador was still only valuable to the island as a mainland coastal strip with whaling and fishing stations. Not for another two decades would the rich iron ore deposits of the interior of Labrador be discovered and developed. During the Great Depression, Newfoundland had to be rescued from bankruptcy by Britain, which suspended responsible government in 1934 and appointed a governor and a commission to rule the island. Prosperity returned during World War II as Newfoundland became a strategic location for American and Canadian military bases. By the end of the war, Newfoundland was in a position to decide whether it would remain under commission rule or return to responsible government under Dominion status. In 1946 the British government arranged for a popularly elected convention to decide the island's future political direction.

Joseph R. Smallwood, a local journalist, introduced a third option for the convention to consider—union with Canada. After initially receiving little support, the Confederation movement began to gain momentum when Britain refused to promise continued financial assistance to restore self-government. In a referendum held in June 1948, 44 percent of Newfoundlanders voted for responsible government, 41 percent for Confederation, and 15 percent for commission rule. A second referendum the following month resulted in a victory for Confederation over responsible government by 53 percent to 47 percent, a margin of fewer than 7,000 votes. The Canadian government then negotiated final terms of the Confederation agreement, and on March 31, 1949, Newfoundland, with a population of about 350,000, became Canada's 10th province. The next day, Smallwood, the leader of the Confederation movement, was fittingly appointed Newfoundland's first premier; as leader of the Liberal Party, he went on to win the inaugural provincial election in the following month.

With Newfoundland's entry into Confederation confirmed, the aging Mackenzie King retired in November 1948 after completing 22 years as prime minister, the longest such service in Canadian and Commonwealth history. King's successor, Louis St. Laurent, proved to be a popular choice as the Liberals captured an unprecedented 190 out of 262 parliamentary seats in the election of 1949. The St. Laurent administration presided over the further clarification of Canadian national sovereignty. The Supreme Court of Canada replaced the Judicial Committee of the Privy Council as the final court of appeal and thus the ultimate judicial interpreter of the Canadian constitution in 1949. The same year, a British statute conferred on the Canadian Parliament the right to amend the British North America Act in matters of purely federal jurisdiction. The right of constitutional amendment, however, did not extend to the alteration of the distribution of powers between the federal and provincial governments and the protection of fundamental rights. For more than three decades, the federal and provincial authorities would continue to search for a mutually agreeable formula for a complete repatriation of the Canadian constitution. Another vestige of British colonialism ended in 1952 when Vincent Massey became the first Canadian appointed governor-general.

The overwhelming reelection of the Liberals under St. Laurent in 1953 reflected not only voter satisfaction in prosperous times but also the sense that the opposition parties offered little alternative. The Conservatives had changed leaders three times since 1935 and had been reduced to little more than an Ontario party, while support for CCF and Social Credit did not extend much beyond Saskatchewan and Alberta, respectively. Only the Liberals could claim to be a national party with support from all parts of Canada. At the provincial level, however, voters were more inclined to express their political opposition. In 1943 George Drew inaugurated 42 years of Conservative ascendancy in Ontario before leaving to lead the national party and being succeeded by Leslie Frost in 1948. The Conservative resurgence continued with triumphs by Hugh Flemming in New Brunswick in 1952, Robert Stanfield in Nova Scotia in 1956, Duff Roblin in Manitoba in 1958, and Walter Shaw in Prince Edward Island in 1959. In British Columbia, W.A.C. Bennett led Social Credit to victory in 1952, while the party continued to dominate Alberta politics under the leadership of Ernest Manning from 1943 to 1968. The CCF continued to rule Saskatchewan under T. C. Douglas from 1944 to 1961 and under Woodrow Lloyd until 1964, while Union Nationale remained entrenched in Quebec from 1944 until the death of Maurice Duplessis in 1959. Only in Newfoundland did the Liberals under Smallwood manage to hold onto power.

The tendency for voters to support one political party nationally and another provincially reflected the strained financial relations between the two levels of government after World War II. Quebec's continuing feud with Ottawa was reflected in the province's Royal Commission of Inquiry on Constitutional Problems (the Tremblay Commission), which in 1954 called for an end to federal "imperialism" and return to "true federalism." In 1957 the federal government introduced a program of equalization payments in an effort to redistribute the national wealth more evenly among the provinces. The federal transfers were designed to ensure that the per capita revenues of all provinces from shared taxes matched those of the wealthiest provinces, at that time Ontario and British Columbia. Negotiations over the extent to which the various provinces were "haves" or "have nots" would become another source of tension in federal-provincial relations.

The constant wrangling with the provinces did not prevent the federal government from extending a variety of health and social services as a safety net against misfortune. A national health programme enacted in 1948 provided federal grants to the provinces to improve hospital care facilities. In 1951 a universal old-age pension scheme was instituted to provide a $40 monthly payment to all citizens over 70 years of age (65 if they were deemed needy). The needs of the unemployed who had exhausted their unemployment insurance benefits or who were not qualified to draw them were addressed in the Unemployment Assistance Act of 1956. The federal government also passed the Hospital Insurance and Diagnostic Services Act in 1957 to provide financial assistance to provinces that established a publicly administered hospital insurance program with universal coverage.

QUEBEC'S VIEW OF FEDERAL-PROVINCIAL RELATIONS AS EXPRESSED THROUGH THE TREMBLAY REPORT, 1954.

ACT TO INSTITUTE A ROYAL COMMISSION OF INQUIRY ON CONSTITUTIONAL PROBLEMS

ASSENTED TO, THE 12TH OF FEBRUARY, 1953

Whereas the Canadian confederation, born of an agreement between the four pioneer provinces, is first and above all a pact of honour between the two great races which founded it and each of which makes a most valuable and indispensable contribution to the progress and greatness of the nation;

Whereas the constitution of 1867 grants to the provinces, and to the Province of Quebec in particular, rights, prerogatives and liberties scrupulous respect for which is intimately bound up with national unity and the survival of confederation, and it imposes on them responsibilities and obligations which imply correlatively the necessary corresponding means of action;

Whereas the Province of Quebec intends to exercise and discharge these rights and obligations, to which end it must safeguard the fiscal resources which belong to it and preserve its financial independence as well as its legislative and administrative autonomy;

Whereas, since 1917, the central power has invaded important fields of taxation reserved to the provinces, thereby seriously limiting the ability of the provinces to exercise their fiscal rights in those fields: . . .

Whereas, in a country as vast and diverse as Canada, only a decentralized administration can meet the needs of every region and ensure the harmonious development of the whole. . . .

Therefore, Her Majesty, with the advice and consent of the Legislative Council and of the Legislative Assembly of Quebec, enacts as follows:

1. The Lieutenant-Governor in Council may constitute a royal commission to inquire into constitutional problems, report its findings to him and submit to him its recommendations as to steps to be taken to safeguard the rights of the Province and those of municipalities and school corporations. . . .

Saskatchewan, whose CCF government had introduced Canada's first universal and compulsory system of hospital insurance in 1947, and British Columbia, which had adopted a similar plan in the following year, immediately qualified for federal assistance. By 1961 all provinces had inaugurated hospital insurance plans and had entered into cost-sharing agreements with the federal government. Aside from these significant advances, postwar prosperity, during which the national unemployment rate ranged from 3 to 6 percent, tended to slow down the popular demand for the expansion of the welfare state.

With a huge majority in Parliament, a popular leader in St. Laurent, and an apparently weak opposition, the Liberals seemed destined to remain the governing party. Heading into the election of 1957, the Liberals had been in power for almost 22 years, the longest unbroken tenure of any national government in Canadian history. But the Liberals had already sown the seeds for their unexpected defeat during the infamous "pipeline debate" of the previous year. Minister of Trade and Commerce C. D. Howe had introduced a bill in Parliament to provide financial assistance to Trans-Canada Pipe Lines to transport gas from Alberta to central Canadian markets. While Howe compared the pipeline to the Canadian Pacific Railway in term of its importance to transcontinental economic development, opposition to the bill focused on the American ownership of Trans-Canada Pipe Lines. Faced with vigorous resistance and a pressing deadline to start construction, Howe resorted to the power of the Liberal majority to cut off debate and to push the bill through Parliament in the absence of the Conservatives and CCF, which had walked out in protest over the allegedly high-handed use of closure. In the subsequent election campaign, the Conservatives adeptly used this incident as evidence that the Liberals had become arrogant and out of touch with the public will after too long a time in power.

Also exploiting regional discontent in the Maritime and Prairie Provinces, the Conservatives, led by Saskatchewan lawyer John Diefenbaker who had succeeded George Drew in the previous year, captured 112 seats to 105 for the Liberals. Although neither party commanded majority support in Parliament, the Liberals decided to relinquish power and to rebuild the party under the leadership of much-celebrated diplomat Lester Pearson. In pursuit of a majority government, Prime Minister Diefenbaker took advantage of Liberal disarray to call another election in 1958. During the campaign, Diefenbaker expounded a vision of "a Canada of the North" and called for "One Canada, wherein Canadians will have preserved to them the control of their own economic and political destiny." Diefenbaker tended to model himself after Sir John A. Macdonald and to view his northern vision as a 20th-century equivalent of the National Policy. Canadian voters responded overwhelmingly to Diefenbaker's strategy as the Conservatives won a record 208 seats, whereas the once omnipotent Liberals were reduced to 49.

In contrast to the more temperate approach of the aging St. Laurent or the eminent but politically inexperienced Pearson, the Diefenbaker vision of Canada on the threshold of national greatness, along with his fiery oratory and his evangelical leadership style, captured the imagination of the millions of Canadians following their first national election on television. In this respect, Diefenbaker ushered in the modern age of mass media politics in Canada. Furthermore, Diefenbaker expressed the optimism that many Canadians felt about their personal lives and their national destiny by the end of the 1950s.

THE ROOTS OF CULTURAL NATIONALISM

Although they were enjoying an improved standard of living and sought to satisfy their basic material needs after World War II, Canadians increasingly hungered for broader cultural horizons, popular entertainment, recreational amenities, and educational opportunities. In 1949 the Canadian government responded by appointing the Royal Commission on National Development in the Arts, Letters, and Sciences, chaired by Vincent Massey, a noted Toronto patron of the arts and culture. The Massey Commission's report in 1951 offered a comprehensive set of recommendations covering all aspects of education, culture, and the mass media. The commission recognized that the amateur, community-oriented, and voluntary character of the nation's prewar cultural life was giving way to a more urban, impersonal, and national orientation. While mourning the passing of traditional Canadian culture, the Massey Commission expressed enthusiasm for the new era of professional "mass culture" that was forthcoming. In the final analysis, the commission not only stimulated government support for future national cultural development but also raised public consciousness of the rich and diverse foundation of artistic and popular cultural accomplishments upon which Canadians could continue to build.

English- and French-Canadian literature came of age in the period from the 1930s to the 1950s. From a "critical realism" perspective, Morley Callaghan's novels—*Such Is My Beloved* (1934), *They Shall Inherit the Earth* (1935), and *More Joy in Heaven* (1937)—portray crime and deprivation in Toronto and Montreal, while Irene Baird's *Waste Heritage* (1939) deals with labor unrest, class conflict, and unemployment in Vancouver during the Great Depression. Hugh MacLennan raised national consciousness through his novels: *Barometer Rising* (1941) focuses on the great Halifax naval explosion of 1917, which killed 1,600 people and injured 9,000 out of a population of 50,000; and *Two Solitudes* (1945), which brilliantly portrays the mutual intolerance of the English and French communities in Quebec, won him the first of three Governor-General's Literary Awards for fiction (inaugurated in 1936). Sinclair Ross's *As for Me and My House* (1941) and W. O. Mitchell's *Who Has Seen the Wind* (1947) capture the struggles of living in the Prairies during the drought-plagued 1930s. Mordecai Richler's *The Apprenticeship of Duddy Kravitz* (1959) depicts the social and moral ambivalence of a young Jewish entrepreneur in contemporary Montreal, while Adele Wiseman's *The Sacrifice* (1956) powerfully captures the Jewish-Ukrainian experience in the Prairies. In a more universal vein, Malcolm Lowry in *Under the Volcano* (1947) and Ethel Wilson in *Swamp Angel* (1954) explore the psychological pressures of alcoholism and women's limited options in society, respectively.

A new generation of English-Canadian poets developed in the shadows of World War II. Dorothy Livesay won the Governor-General's Literary Award for *Day and Night* (1944) and *Poems for Peace* (1947). Earle Birney of Vancouver also won this prestigious award in 1942 and 1945 for his collections of poems and pioneered the teaching of creative writing in Canadian universities. The outspoken and flamboyant Irving Layton produced numerous volumes since the early 1940s, which have given him national and international recognition as a prolific, revolutionary, and controversial poet of the "modern" school. From the 1940s onward, the metaphysical poetry of P. K. Page and Margaret Avison inspired modern generations of Canadian poets. Northrup Frye, a student and colleague of poet E. J. Pratt, went on to become one of the world's leading literary theorists in English following the publication of his book, *Anatomy of Criticism*, in 1957.

French-Canadian literature moved away from traditional rural idealism to express urban realism with the publication in 1938 of *Trente arpents* (Thirty acres) by Philippe Panneton, who wrote under the pseudonym of Ringuet. Unlike Maria Chapdelaine a quarter-century earlier, the novel's hero, Euchariste Moisan, suffers for his stubborn devotion to his small farm, which ultimately can be passed on to only one of his 12 children. His other children must abandon their rural life for an urban existence in Montreal or New England, where Euchariste ends up forlornly living out his last days anguishing over his lost 30 acres. This Governor-General Award-winning novel highlights the reality of the French-Canadian fate and foreshadows the social upheaval in Quebec life that made the Quiet Revolution necessary. Roger Lemelin's *Au pied de la pente douce* (1944, translated as *The Town Below*) and *Les Plouffe* (1950, translated as *The Plouffe Family*) as well as Gabrielle

Roy's *Bonheur d'occasion* (1945, translated as *The Tin Flute*) employ urban working-class settings to convey social realism in mid-20th-century Quebec.

In the visual arts, the influence of the Group of Seven continued to grow with the formation in 1933 of the Canadian Group of Painters whose members included A. J. Casson, Charles Comfort, Edwin Holgate, Yvonne McKague Housser, J.W.G. Macdonald, and Carl Schaefer. Other artists were endeavoring to move away from the rugged landscape nationalism of the Group of Seven. John Lyman of Montreal, who was a key figure emphasizing internationalism, founded the Contemporary Art Society in 1939. In the 1940s and 1950s, a radical group of French-Canadian painters influenced by Parisian surrealism, including Marcel Barbeau, Paul-Emile Borduas, Pierre Gauvreau, Fernand Leduc, Jean-Paul Mousseau, Alfred Pellan, and Jean-Paul Riopelle, were advocating personal freedom and spiritual expression. In English Canada, abstract expressionism was popularized by the 1950s in the work of artists such as Harold Town, Jack Bush, William Ronald, and Alexandra Luke, while Alex Colville was setting a new standard for realist painting. Highlighting the development of sculpture was the unveiling in 1936 of Walter Allward's magnificent Vimy Ridge memorial to Canadian soldiers killed during World War I. Other sculptors who left their mark by mid-century were Alfred Laliberté, Frances Loring, R. Tait Mackenzie, and Florence Wyle.

A major stimulus to Canadian theatrical development was the founding of the Dominion Drama Festival in 1932 under the auspices of Governor-General Lord Bessborough. The Massey Commission recommendations encouraged the opening of the Shakespeare Festival at Stratford in 1953. Opposition from the Catholic Church, which objected to what it deemed to be risqué productions, did not inhibit the success of playwrights such as Gratien Gélinas and Félix Leclerc in Quebec. Playwright, poet, and novelist Robert Choquette became one of the most prolific scriptwriters for radio in the 1930s and 1940s as well as for television in the 1950s. The growing popularity of ballet after World War II led to the establishment of the Royal Winnipeg Ballet in 1949 and the National Ballet of Canada, headquartered in Toronto, under the direction of Celia Franca, in 1951. Symphony orchestras and ballet companies continued to be established as cities reached a population size that could support them and as television exposed more people to its wonders. By the 1930s, Sir Ernest Macmillan had become Canada's first internationally known conductor of symphonic and choral music. Other musicians who achieved international recognition included Edward Johnson, Wilfrid Pelletier, and Healey Willan.

Canada was also producing scholars of international renown in the humanities, social sciences, and the medical sciences. In 1921–22, a University of Toronto medical research team, including Frederick Banting, Charles Best, J. B. Collip, and J.J.R. MacLeod, discovered insulin, which proved to be effective as a life-saving treatment for diabetes. Banting and MacLeod were awarded a Nobel Prize for this scientific breakthrough in 1923. Also at the University of Toronto, Harold Innis became internationally renowned for pioneering communications studies in the 1940s, which in turn inspired Marshall McLuhan's mass media theories in the 1950s and 1960s. While Donald Creighton was revising Canadian historiography with his Laurentian thesis in the 1930s and 1940s, Pierre Berton began to raise Canadian historical consciousness with his popular writing in the 1950s. The founding of the National Library of Canada in 1953 would greatly contribute to preserving and promoting the nation's printed heritage.

Canadians were willing to devote more of their time and money to the enjoyment of popular culture, particularly sports, music, and movies. Even at the height of the Great Depression, hockey retained its popularity to the extent that Conn Smythe built the magnificent Maple Leaf Gardens for his National Hockey League team in Toronto in 1931. The rival Montreal Canadiens had built their own impressive edifice, the Forum, seven years earlier. The national pastime was to follow the exploits of the Toronto Maple Leafs and the Montreal Canadiens as they often battled each other and four American teams for the coveted Stanley Cup. While the Maple Leafs enjoyed their greatest success from 1945 to 1951 when they won five Stanley Cups in seven years, the Canadiens thrived from 1953 to 1960 when, led by the legendary Maurice "Rocket" Richard, they captured six Stanley Cups in eight years, including an unmatched five consecutive wins from 1956 to 1960. Until 1952 Canada could count on its amateur champions (Allen Cup winners) to win the world title, but that changed with the emergence of the Soviet Union as a hockey power.

Although professional football teams competed for the Grey Cup in an annual clash of East against West since the mid-1930s, the Canadian Football League (CFL) formally came into existence in 1958. The popularity of baseball was sufficient to sustain two teams in the Triple A International League, the Toronto Maple Leafs, and the Montreal Royals. In 1946, when major league baseball in the United States was prepared to break the "color barrier" by allowing blacks to play, the Brooklyn Dodgers sent Jackie Robinson to play for the Montreal Royals in order to ease the process of integration. Robinson expressed gratitude for the accolades he received during his outstanding season playing in Montreal, in contrast to the hostility that greeted him in the major leagues the following year. In 1959 Canada won the first official world curling championship and remained a perennial winner until the early 1970s.

Canadians increasingly distinguished themselves in the world of popular entertainment. Don Messer began to play his "down home" Maritime fiddle music on radio in the 1930s and continued to host his "Jubilee" television program in the 1950s. Musicians such as Percy Faith and Guy Lombardo also emerged in Canada during the 1930s, but their worldwide popularity prompted them to depart for the United States. Lombardo and his band the Royal Canadians, with their rendition of "Auld Lang Syne," which had its origins in the Scottish communities of Ontario, became synonymous with American New Year's Eve celebrations. Other Canadian-born entertainers who left to pursue a successful career in the United States include Marie Dressler, Deanna Durbin, Glenn Ford, Lorne Greene, Walter Huston, Ruby Keeler, Art Linkletter, Gisèle Mackenzie, Raymond Massey (brother of Vincent Massey), Leslie Neilsen, Mary Pickford, and Mort Sahl.

The Canadian film industry received a considerable boost in 1939 with the creation of the National Film Board, which went on to produce documentaries that earned an international reputation. The advent of television after 1950 tended to blur the lines between Canadian and American culture to an even greater extent than radio and the movies had already done. Since the vast majority of Canadians lived close to the American border cities, they readily received American television programs. The launching of commercial television broadcasting by the CBC in 1952 was an effort to offset this Americanization of Canadian culture, in addition to providing opportunities for Canadian talent to develop.

To encourage the development of the arts, humanities, and social sciences through systematic public support, the Massey Commission recommended the creation of the Canada Council, which was finally inaugurated by Parliament in 1957. An endowment fund of $100 million was established, half of which would be used to aid university-building programs and the other half to provide scholarships and grants-in-aid of cultural activities. Universities urgently needed federal assistance in the wake of increasing enrollment from 35,000 in 1942 to 58,000 in 1951. Furthermore, it was projected that, as the children of the postwar baby boom hit university age, enrollment would double by 1965 and triple by 1975. Premier Duplessis, of course, was the only provincial leader to reject federal grants because he viewed the funding program as a threat to Quebec's autonomy and to French-Canadian culture.

By 1960, Canadians had much about which to feel optimistic. The memories of the perilous depression and war era were virtually obliterated by the unprecedented national prosperity and international recognition that the nation was enjoying. Canadians were not yet aware that the baby boom was drawing to a close, that the national unity of the previous decade and a half was about to be jeopardized by resurgent regionalism, that they were about to experience profound social changes, and that they would be frustrated in the political wilderness of minority government. Indeed, the new decade would give many Canadians reason to look back nostalgically at the postwar boom years.

CHAPTER 18

THE SEARCH FOR NATIONAL UNITY

Canadians embarked upon their centennial decade confident that a distinct national identity was taking shape and that the economic and political stability of the postwar era would persist. Although they would have much cause to celebrate the achievements of their nation's first century in 1967, Canadians would also feel the disappointment and sense of uncertainty that accompany unfulfilled hopes and ambitions. John Diefenbaker's glowing vision of national expansion through the development of a new northern frontier proved to be more rhetoric than substance. Lester Pearson was hampered by the brokerage politics of minority government and federal-provincial struggles to control the expanding welfare state. National enthusiasm was rekindled with the rise of Trudeaumania and the promise of a "just society" within a bilingual Canada. But Pierre Trudeau, too, was challenged by a federal system strained by conflicting regional interests that potentially threatened national unity. In particular, the resurgence of nationalism highlighted by the so-called Quiet Revolution heralded to the rest of Canada that Quebec was not only a province unlike the others but also that its accommodation within the existing structure of Confederation was in doubt.

THE ELUSIVE POLITICAL CONSENSUS

Following their landslide victory in 1958, the Conservatives under John Diefenbaker struggled to fulfill their lofty election promise: "A new vision! A new hope! A new soul for Canada." The major achievements of the Diefenbaker administration included an ambitious "roads to resources" program that improved access to certain northern areas; a revitalization of western agriculture through increased subsidies and huge grain sales to eastern Europe, the Soviet Union, and communist China; increased old-age pensions and other aid for the needy; the enactment of a Canadian Bill of Rights in 1960; and the granting of the federal franchise to Canada's Native peoples.

Diefenbaker's northern vision also entailed a different approach to world affairs than that of his Liberal predecessors. Like his political hero, Sir John A. Macdonald, Diefenbaker was genuinely devoted to the British connection and was greatly disturbed by the increasing continental integration between Canada and the United States. There-fore, he was actively involved in Commonwealth affairs, particularly as a crusader for racial equality. Diefenbaker actively supported the effort of African and Asian members to block South Africa's application to join the Commonwealth unless the new republic abandoned its racist policy of apartheid. Mounting opposition to this institutionalized segregation of blacks and whites forced South Africa to withdraw from the Common-wealth in 1961. Diefenbaker was less successful in his attempt to reduce Canadian dependence on American capital and commerce by rebuilding trade and diplomatic links with Britain and the Commonwealth. In essence, he hoped to return to a bygone era that could not be revived for two reasons. First, Canada was too deeply committed to the expanding American market whereas Britain's economy, the slowest growing in the industrialized world, had become too small to absorb a significant amount of Cana-dian staple or manufacturing exports. Second, Britain was already moving toward entry into the European Common Market, which would leave little latitude for freer trade agreements with Canada.

Diefenbaker's popularity deteriorated along with the Canadian economy as the pro-longed postwar boom came to an inevitable end. His government came under heaviest criticism for failing to implement policies that could prevent the national unemployment rate from exceeding 11 percent in 1961, the highest level since the Great Depression, or that could prevent the devaluation of the Canadian dollar to 92.5 cents in relation to the American dollar. The fiscal restraints imposed by economic recession effectively limited the Diefenbaker administration from launching policies that would allow the fulfillment of its "northern vision."

Diefenbaker's vision of "One Canada" also came under serious questioning, par-ticularly in Quebec. Although Georges Vanier was appointed governor-general in 1959, French Canadians complained about the relatively few cabinet ministers from Quebec despite the large contingent of Conservative MPs from that province. His impassioned championing of the British connection and of "unhyphenated" Canadianism further alienated French Canadians along with the growing non-Anglo-Saxon immigrant pop-ulation. Under Diefenbaker's leadership, the Conservatives generated strong support in rural and small-town areas, particularly in the Prairie and Maritime Provinces, while alienating the eastern business interests that had been the backbone of the party.

Growing disillusionment with the Conservatives gave the opposition parties a chance to recover from their dismal results in the 1958 election. The Liberals were gaining strength in the urban areas of Ontario and Quebec, particularly among the growing ethnic population, which found Pearson's notion of the Canadian cultural mosaic more appealing. In 1961 the CCF Party formed an alliance with the Canadian Labour Congress. Under the leadership of T. C. Douglas, this merger of traditional socialism and organized labor became known as the New Democratic Party (NDP). Although the platform of the NDP was less socialist than that of the CCF, it continued to advocate government planning and control of economic development, further extension of social security measures, and support for the union movement. After losing all of its federal seats in 1958, Social Credit also reorganized in 1961 by choosing Robert Thompson of Alberta as leader and Réal Caouette of Quebec as deputy leader.

In the federal election of June 1962, Conservative strength was reduced to 116 seats while the Liberals took 100. Social Credit and the NDP, with 30 and 19 seats, respectively, held the balance of power in the new minority government. While the decline of the Conservatives was predictable, the election of 26 Créditistes, as the Quebec wing of Social Credit was known, was the most surprising result. Although Social Credit had never been more than a fringe group in Quebec, Caouette successfully used his weekly television appearances to lure enough rural and small-town voters to support his Créditistes as a protest against the established Conservatives and Liberals. In effect, the emergence of the Créditistes in Quebec stood in the way of a Conservative majority or a Liberal minority government.

While it remained in power with Social Credit support, the Conservative minority government was fearful that decisive measures to deal with the slumping national economy or the emerging continental defense issue in the aftermath of the Cuban missile crisis might lead to its defeat in Parliament. Indeed, Diefenbaker's reluctance to fulfill commitments to NATO and NORAD to install nuclear armaments in antiaircraft missiles on Canadian soil ultimately led to his government's defeat on a general motion of nonconfidence in February 1963. In the consequent election two months later, the fall of the Conservatives was completed as their parliamentary representation dropped to 95 seats, compared to 129 for the Liberals. Now, it was Prime Minister Pearson's turn to draw on support from the 24 Social Credit and 17 NDP members to make a minority government work.

Unlike Diefenbaker, Pearson had the advantage of governing during a period of renewed economic prosperity. Nevertheless, Canadians were divided over many controversial issues that challenged his considerable negotiating skills cultivated during his illustrious career in diplomatic service. The design for a new Canadian flag, consisting of a single red maple leaf in the center with a red border at either end on a white background, triggered a lengthy and emotionally charged debate. Whereas supporters viewed the new design as an assertion of Canadian nationalism, critics, notably monarchists and war veterans, remained fiercely attached to the Union Jack or the Red Ensign. After the Liberals invoked closure to end the great debate, Parliament approved the new flag, which was officially flown for the first time on February 15, 1965. Equally controversial was the integration of the armed forces—army, navy, and air force—initially proposed in 1964 but not officially completed until four years later. Traditionalists argued that the government's preoccupation with efficiency and mobility undermined national military strength and dishonored the glorious achievements and sacrifices of Canadian servicemen and women.

Influenced by the United States's War on Poverty and by the need to maintain the political support of the NDP, the Pearson administration introduced social legislation in 1965–66 that constituted the final building blocks of the welfare state in Canada. The

Canada Pension Plan (1965) together with the Guaranteed Income Supplement (1966) offered a comprehensive program of retirement benefits, disability allowances, and survivors' benefits, the qualification for which was to be reduced to 65 years of age within five years. The effect of these complimentary legislative enactments was to establish a social minimum for the aged at an adequate living standard rather than at a bare subsistence level as was previously the case. The Canada Assistance Plan (1966) consolidated a wide range of federal-provincial programs, including mothers' allowances, blind and disabled persons' benefits, child welfare benefits, and assistance for the working poor into a comprehensive program that would meet financial need regardless of cause. After the CCF government in Saskatchewan again pioneered in the health field by introducing North America's first universal medical insurance plan (often called "medicare") in 1962, the Pearson administration introduced the Medical Care Act (1966). The federal government agreed to pay half of any provincially administered medical-care insurance plan that provided universal coverage for a comprehensive range of general practitioner and specialist services. By 1971 all provinces had agreed to participate in the plan.

The federal government was also called upon to address the rapid expansion of the universities in the wake of the postwar baby boom. As expected, university enrollment doubled from 1951 to 1963 and was projected to more than double again in the following decade, particularly in view of the rising number of women applying to universities and the growing popularity of part-time study. By the early 1960s, women comprised little more than one-quarter of total university enrollment, while part-time students (nearly half of whom were women) made up about one-fifth. Over the next two decades, gender balance would be achieved and part-time enrollment would grow by more than sixfold. Accordingly, provincial governments abandoned their initial strategy to meet these increases by expanding existing institutions, with the result that more funds were needed to build several new universities and community colleges. In response, the federal government replaced its program of direct grants to the universities, initiated in 1951, with a shared-cost contribution to the provinces in 1966. Total government spending on universities increased sevenfold during the 1960s.

The extension of the welfare state further upset the balance between federal and provincial responsibilities, thereby straining the century-old constitutional framework. The economic disparities among the provinces were too great to allow them to decide their own programs and to find the money for them. Only the federal government had the resources and capacity to ensure national minimums in health, education, and welfare. The federal government maintained that it should have wider powers in these fields hitherto reserved for the provinces. The provinces for their part argued that they needed a larger share of the tax revenue to administer their responsibilities, although all except Quebec were willing to allow the federal government to act as the coordinator of social policy in the national interest. Cooperation between Ottawa and the provinces was indispensable if the dichotomy between jurisdiction and resources was to be reconciled.

Accordingly, Prime Minister Pearson emerged as a leading proponent of the concept of cooperative federalism, achieved mainly through federal-provincial conferences. For example, annual federal-provincial conferences in the early 1960s worked out compromises that replaced tax rentals by a tax collection agreement based on proportional sharing of yields, accompanied by equalization payments to the less prosperous provinces in order to bring their income closer to the national average. This arrangement would continue to be a source of federal-provincial tension, resulting in several modifications over the next three decades. Pearson's concept of cooperative federalism also included implementing "shared costs" programs with an "opting out" formula to allow more provincial autonomy to provide social services. Quebec took advantage of this opportunity to establish its own pension plan in 1965. Indeed, securing unanimous consent of 11 different governments on every major issue tended to result in imperfect compromises, which further complicated federal-provincial relations.

The lack of consensus on federalism stalled efforts to "repatriate" the Canadian constitution. No one doubted that continued dependence on the British Parliament to amend the British North America Act was an affront to national sovereignty, but to find an amendment formula agreeable to the federal government and all the provinces proved to be a formidable challenge. In 1964 a federal-provincial conference appeared to have reached agreement on an amending formula. The key provision required unanimous consent for any changes to language rights and provincial legislative authority, while other amendments might be carried with the consent of two-thirds of the provinces representing at least half the population. But after initially agreeing to the formula, Premier Jean Lesage yielded to nationalist opposition in Quebec, which insisted on a veto power over any change that the province disapproved of and yet objected to any veto by other provinces over changes that Quebec demanded.

Prime Minister Pearson decided that his government could not go forward with repatriation of the constitution without unanimous consent of all the provinces. He was particularly cautious to avoid any action that would give further impetus to Quebec nationalism. Responding to the upsurge of nationalism in Quebec, Pearson established the Royal Commission on Bilingualism and Biculturalism in 1963 to address French-Canadian demands for linguistic equality. Through a series of reports over the next eight years, the commission would exert a profound influence on public response to ethnic relations in Canada.

Pearson also presided over and contributed to the lack of national consensus regarding the nature and implications of Canada's relationship with the United States. The newly elected Liberal administration honored previous continental defense commitments to the United States by signing a new agreement with the United States to provide nuclear warheads for Canada's short-range defensive missiles and aircraft. On the other hand, Pearson upset American officials with his open criticism of their Vietnam War policy. Canadian nationalists criticized Pearson for failing to counter American economic domination of Canadian industry, although they applauded his choice of Walter Gordon to serve as minister of finance. His first budget in 1963 included tax measures to limit foreign ownership, but the threat of American retaliation and strong opposition within the Liberal Party forced Gordon to withdraw his proposal.

While Canadians debated the benefits and perils of American investment, the importance of increased trade with the United States was unquestioned. In 1965 the Automotive Products Agreement, known as the Auto Pact, allowed free exchange of vehicles and parts among manufacturers, although not among retailers. Inasmuch as the export of Canadian-made cars to the United States has consistently exceeded American imports to Canada, even the most ardent economic nationalists have conceded that this agreement has been highly beneficial to the Canadian economy, particularly in southern Ontario where most of the automobile industry is located.

The Pearson administration still sought to offset American influence over Canadian foreign policy and economic development through continued involvement in the larger international community. In the United Nations, Canada maintained its peacekeeping role in the Sinai, Cyprus, and the Congo, but international instability generally limited the influence of middle powers after the Suez Crisis of 1956. Commonwealth relations became increasingly incoherent in the wake of military coups in Ghana, civil war in Nigeria, and war between India and Pakistan. Canada found itself at the center of another racial controversy when it demanded that Rhodesia (now Zimbabwe) extend the franchise on a nondiscriminatory basis as a condition for full Commonwealth membership. When Rhodesia rejected these terms upon declaring its national independence in 1965, Canada withdrew recognition, cancelled trade preferences, and embargoed arms shipments. Canada's relations with the Commonwealth during this period were motivated largely by economic prospects. Britain was Canada's second-largest customer, and the hope was that the rest of the Commonwealth could be brought under a system of trade preferences to counterbalance American dominance in foreign trade and investment. Moreover, Canada was concerned about the adverse effects of Britain's decision to join the European Economic Community.

For all his skillful maneuvering on the divisive issues of the day, a majority government eluded Pearson. The election of 1965 gave the Liberals, Conservatives, and NDP two additional seats at the expense of Social Credit and the Créditistes, which had gone their separate ways two years earlier. As Canadians celebrated their centennial in 1967, highlighted by the spectacular "Expo 67" World's Fair which attracted 50 million visitors to Montreal, the face of national politics was in the process of transformation. Robert Thompson left the dying Social Credit to join the ranks of the Progressive Conservatives. In a convention that featured a heated debate over the concepts of "one, united Canada" and "*deux nations*" (two nations), the Conservatives replaced Diefenbaker with former Nova Scotia premier Robert Stanfield. At the end of the year, Prime Minister Pearson announced his intention to retire, and the Liberals chose the charismatic minister of justice from Quebec, Pierre Elliot Trudeau, to assume the role as party leader and prime minister in April 1968.

TRUDEAUMANIA AND THE JUST SOCIETY

The youthful, flamboyant, and decisive image projected by the new prime minister inspired a popular enthusiasm that was dubbed "Trudeaumania." Trudeau's vision of the "just society" held out the promise of a revised Canadian constitution that would guarantee personal and political liberties, protect minority rights, and offer greater opportunities for underrepresented or less privileged regions and social groups. He also envisioned a renewed federalism based not only on a strong central government capable of standing up to the provinces but also on the institutionalization of bilingualism, in order to give French Canada a major role to play in national politics. To Canadians weary of the political chaos of minority government, federal-provincial conflict, and regional polarization, Trudeau rekindled hopes for a new era of national unity and social justice. Consequently, in the election of June 1968, the Liberals won a clear majority with 155 seats, while the Conservatives dropped to 72, and the NDP held firm at 22. Social Credit was completely eliminated from federal politics, although its legacy lived on in Caouette's Créditistes, which took 14 seats in Quebec. For the next 16 years, Trudeau, like Macdonald, Laurier, and King before him, would dominate and define Canadian politics.

The Trudeau administration appeared determined to convert the rhetoric of the "just society" into reality. In 1969 Prime Minister Trudeau asserted that "to build and main-

*Arms raised in victory at the Liberal leadership convention in 1968, Pierre Trudeau (1919–)
went on to serve as prime minister for more than 15 years, longer than any other French Canadian and the third-longest tenure in Canadian history, behind King and Macdonald.*

tain a strong and united country, it is essential that both French- and English-speaking
Canadians should be able to feel at home in all parts of the country, and that their rights
as members of our major language groups should be respected by the federal government." According to the Official Languages Act, based upon a recommendation of the
Royal Commission on Bilingualism and Biculturalism, English and French were to be
coequal languages of the federal civil service, the Crown agencies, and the federal courts.
The act further stipulated that full federal services would be available in both languages
in areas where a minority of either group constituted at least 10 percent of the population. With the exception of a small group of vocal opponents in the West led by Diefenbaker, most Canadians accepted the policy of bilingualism on principle. But over the
years, practical efforts to introduce institutional bilingualism received little support and
aroused much criticism among English-speaking Canadians who, in view of the growing
trend toward unilingualism in Quebec, complained that they had become the victims of
unfair treatment.

   The Royal Commission on Bilingualism and Biculturalism also studied the cultural contributions of non-French and non-British ethnic minorities, who comprised 27
percent of Canada's population of 21.5 million in 1971 (as compared to 21 percent of
14 million in 1951). The changing racial composition of Canadian society was largely
the product of government immigration policy. In 1962 the Diefenbaker administration
made immigration regulations consistent with its Bill of Rights, which two years earlier
had rejected discrimination by reason of race, national origin, color, religion, and gender. The Pearson administration further revised immigration regulations in 1966–67 to
eliminate any discriminatory provisions; to restrict the admission of sponsored depen-
dents and nondependent relatives; and to base selection on a point system employing
such criteria as education and training, occupational demand, age, personal qualities, and

linguistic capacity. Whereas prior to these regulations almost 90 percent of immigrants were of European origin, by the early 1970s about half came from other regions, including the West Indies, Africa, South America, and Asia.

To alleviate concerns that biculturalism relegated all other ethnic groups to second-class status, Prime Minister Trudeau proclaimed in 1971: "A policy of multiculturalism within a bilingual framework commends itself to the government as the most suitable means of assuring the cultural freedom of Canadians." Canada's cultural mosaic would not only be recognized and celebrated but also supported through government grants for some of the activities of ethnic groups. Four provinces with substantial ethnic populations—Ontario, Manitoba, Saskatchewan, and Alberta—subsequently initiated their own multicultural policies. As various ethnic groups competed for government support, critics of multiculturalism soon began to dismiss it as an insidious scheme to buy votes.

The Trudeau government also advocated "the full, free and non-discriminatory participation of the Indian people in Canadian society" in its White Paper on Indian Policy issued in 1969. Minister of Indian Affairs Jean Chrétien called for the end of the Department of Indian Affairs, the repeal of the Indian Act, the elimination of reserves, and the transfer of many federal responsibilities for Indian affairs to the provinces. Legally and administratively, Indians would eventually become like other Canadians. The overwhelmingly critical Native response was summed up in Harold Cardinal's book *The Unjust Society*, which referred to the White Paper as "a thinly-disguised programme of extermination through assimilation." Despite imposing a form of colonialism, the Indian Act at least recognized the special constitutional status of the Native peoples, without which they would be absorbed into mainstream Canadian society. Responding to sustained Native pressure, the government retracted the White Paper proposals in 1971. Inadvertently, the White Paper along with the Trudeau government's refusal to negotiate Native land claims for the approximately one-half of the country that was not already under treaty sparked a dramatic increase in the scope and intensity of political organization and activism among Canada's Native peoples. From 1968 to 1971, four organizations in particular emerged to strengthen the resolve of Native peoples to define their own destiny: the National Indian Brotherhood (reorganized in 1981 as the Assembly of First Nations); the Canadian Métis Society (renamed the Native Council of Canada in 1970); the Indian Brotherhood of the Northwest Territories (renamed Dene Nation in 1978); and the Inuit Tapirisat of Canada.

Women were also emerging as an organized political force and as major economic contributors, as reported by the Royal Commission on the Status of Women in 1970. Chaired by former CBC news commentator Florence Bird, the commission presented 167 recommendations on such matters as employment equity, educational opportunities, and family law, including the decriminalization of abortion. The commission reported that after World War II an increasing number of women pursued a career after marriage or returned to work after raising their children, despite social pressure to surrender their jobs to returning servicemen or to remain occupied in the home. By 1970 married women accounted for more than one-third of the labor force (as compared to one-quarter in 1951), but they were concentrated in white-collar jobs at the lower end of the pay scale. Although some improvements were being made, women were still underrepresented in professional and managerial occupations, political institutions, and higher education, in addition to being subject to a range of discriminatory policies in both the private and public sector. The Trudeau government responded immediately by creating new offices and procedures to deal with women's rights, including a portfolio for the status of women in the federal Cabinet, and by amending federal statutes to remove sections that were discriminatory to women, notably the Canada Labour Code. Nevertheless, dissatisfaction with government progress in implementing the commission's recommendations led to the formation in 1971 of the National Action Committee on the Status of Women, which went on to become the largest umbrella organization of women's groups in Canada.

The "just society" was greatly concerned with the problems of poverty and deprivation. The federal government devised a more systematic and integrated approach to the problem of regional economic disparities with the establishment of the Department of Regional Economic Expansion (DREE) in 1969. The chief purpose of DREE was to help create employment opportunities by providing either grants to individual firms willing to invest in new or expanded manufacturing plants or support for the development of local infrastructure as well as social facilities and services. To provide "individual development coupled with adequate income support," the Trudeau government in 1971 introduced a new unemployment insurance scheme that substantially expanded both eligibility for benefits and levels of support. In effect, unemployment insurance was integrated into the welfare system inasmuch as it became a regular means of income support in the poorer areas of the Atlantic Provinces and Quebec. For all its good intentions, this scheme would be constantly criticized for its steadily rising cost and its negative effects on work incentive.

By the early 1970s, Canadians were becoming more conscious of the adverse effects of dynamic urban and industrial development on their physical environment. Although concerns about the "greenhouse effect," the depletion of the ozone layer, the pollution of air and water, the destruction of the tropical rain forests, the management of rapidly accumulating disposable waste, the hazards of acid rain, and the conservation of natural resources and wilderness areas were largely global in scope, Canadians demanded that their federal, provincial, and local governments be more responsive to environmental protection. Accordingly, the Trudeau administration established the Department of the Environment in 1971, and two years later, the Federal Environmental Assessment Review Office (FEARO) was formed to monitor the biophysical and social impact of major projects on environmental quality in Canada. Within a few years, all of the provinces had established their own departments of the environment and had implemented environmental protection and assessment legislation. Although Canadians would continually debate the adequacy of government responses to environmental issues, the ecological health and well-being of the nation became firmly embedded in the public agenda.

The wave of Trudeaumania and the enthusiasm for the just society that had launched Trudeau into power in 1968 subsided considerably by the time he sought reelection in 1972. The Liberal campaign slogan was "The Land Is Strong," but judging by the results, many Canadians disagreed. The Liberals were reduced to 109 seats, only two more than the Conservatives. Like so many of his predecessors, Trudeau had to account for a faltering economy, this time characterized by a unique concurrence of rising unemployment and inflation, which economists dubbed "stagflation" (stagnation/inflation). That Trudeau did not give this problem the attention that many voters thought it deserved was widely interpreted as further evidence of his growing arrogance and remoteness. Western Canada, where enthusiasm for Trudeaumania ranged from lukewarm to skeptical in 1968, felt thoroughly alienated four years later. Prairie farmers believed that the Liberal government lacked appreciation for wheat-growing, the family farm, and rail transportation. They agreed with others in English Canada that Trudeau had been too preoccupied with bilingualism and rising Quebec nationalism. The Liberals lost almost all of their support in the West and a significant amount in Ontario, mainly to the Conservatives and, to a lesser extent, the NDP. Under the leadership of David Lewis, the NDP cut into urban Liberal support by launching an effective attack on "corporate welfare bums," beneficiaries of the government's policy of granting generous tax concessions to large corporations. The resulting 31 seats not only represented a high-water mark for the NDP or CCF at the federal level but also gave the labor-socialist alliance the balance of power in Parliament. In the final analysis, the land was not as strong as Trudeau believed because he did not fully appreciate the powerful forces of cultural and regional division that were reasserting themselves.

THE QUIET REVOLUTION IN QUEBEC

The dramatic transformation of Quebec politics and society during the 1960s and 1970s provided the most serious challenge to national unity. The floodgates of change broke open shortly after the death of Premier Maurice Duplessis in 1959. For the previous 15 years, Duplessis and his Union Nationale party had governed Quebec as a feudal lord rules over his fiefdom. While the province experienced accelerated urban and industrial growth comparable to neighboring Ontario or the eastern United States, Duplessis implemented social and economic policies that either reinforced traditional values or were unresponsive to the modern realities of Quebec life. His administration became notorious for its political and electoral corruption that helped Union Nationale maintain its grip on power. Duplessis also refused to revise an outdated electoral distribution system that blatantly favored rural over urban areas. Whereas some urban ridings had upwards of 100,000 voters, many rural ridings, which tended to vote Union Nationale, had fewer than 10,000 voters. Furthermore, Duplessis was reluctant to extend education and social services out of a concern that they would undermine the role of the Catholic Church. Instead, he preferred to subsidize church-sponsored schools and social agencies in order to maintain the support of the Catholic hierarchy. The provincial government consistently refused to accept federal assistance to finance education and social programs on the grounds that it was an infringement on provincial rights and autonomy. Economic development strategy focused on inviting foreign capital to exploit the enormous natural resources of the province. Labor unions and legislation to improve working conditions and to protect worker rights were suppressed, often to placate foreign investors. Labor unions, social activists, and other critics of the Duplessis government tended to be branded and persecuted as communists.

By the 1950s growing opposition to the conservatism of Duplessis was led by a new French-Canadian middle class linked to the practical and social sciences as well as to business and administration. Pierre Trudeau was among these "radical" liberal critics of the Duplessis regime who demanded more state intervention to provide better educational opportunities, more housing facilities, improved health care, higher welfare benefits, and equitable labor laws. As the traditional parish organization disintegrated under the impact of urbanization and industrialization, it was no longer practical to expect the church to fulfill fundamental socioeconomic needs. Only the state had the resources and capacity to undertake the complete modernization of Quebec. Without the dynamic leadership of Duplessis, Union Nationale proved powerless to resist the forces of change, and the victory of the Liberals under Jean Lesage in the provincial election of 1960 ushered in an era of political, social, and economic reform that became known as the Quiet Revolution (Révolution tranquille).

The new Lesage administration was determined to enhance the province's capacity to control its own economic development. Most of Quebec's industry was controlled by English-speaking Canadians or Americans, and the province was not well-endowed with private investment capital or entrepreneurial initiative. In an effort to reverse this tendency, Minister of Natural Resources René Lévesque persuaded Lesage to nationalize private electricity companies and to merge them with the Crown corporation Hydro Quebec. This giant corporation standardized hydro rates across the province, coordinated investments in this key energy sector, integrated the electrical system, stimulated industrial development, and inspired greater French-Canadian enterprise. Another success story was the creation in 1965 of the Caisse de dépot et placement du Québec, which successfully administered the Quebec Pension Plan and went on to become one of the largest financial institutions in North America. The Lesage government also established the Société générale de financement to assist small companies experiencing financial difficulty. *Maîtres chez nous* (masters of our own house) was the prevailing philosophy behind government initiatives to promote a more dynamic French participation in the Quebec economy.

In 1961 the average French Canadian annually earned about 40 percent less than his English-speaking counterpart in Quebec. To help bridge this gap and to promote economic progress necessitated reform of the province's archaic education system, which was severely strained by the baby-boom generation reaching adolescence. The Lesage administration, therefore, appointed the Royal Commission of Enquiry on Education in the Province of Quebec, which recommended a sweeping program of reform in 1962 designed to assert state control over a sector in which the Catholic Church had played a powerful role and to equip the youth of Quebec with the knowledge and skills demanded by the modern occupations. The secularization of Quebec education was highlighted by the establishment of the first provincial Department of Education in 1964, almost nine decades after neighboring Ontario had done so. The new department undertook to create and supervise a comprehensive system of primary and secondary education that was accessible to the entire population and to overhaul the school curriculum. The traditional focus on the humanities subjects as preparation for the medical and legal professions or the clergy gave way to greater emphasis on a wide range of scientific, technical, and commercial studies. By the end of the decade, Quebec's universities and colleges were producing their share of economists, managers, engineers, scientists, and other skilled professionals for industry and commerce.

In the social sphere, the government invested heavily in the field of health care, including participation in the federal-provincial hospital insurance program, and inaugurated the Quebec Pension Plan in 1965. To improve labor relations, the government revised the labor code and gave most public-sector workers the right to strike. Political reforms included measures to curb political patronage and electoral corruption, changes to the electoral map to provide better representation for urban areas, and the reorganization of municipal government to promote fiscal stability.

The philosophy of *maîtres chez nous* applied not only to economic development but also to Quebec's relations with the federal government. After creating a Department of Federal-Provincial Affairs with himself as minister, Lesage forced the federal government to accept Quebec's withdrawal from several cost-sharing programs and to compensate the province for them. Unlike Duplessis, who rejected federal-provincial programs as an intrusion on provincial rights, Lesage demanded greater provincial control in the provision of these programs. In his struggles with the federal government, Lesage was seeking not only a further extension of provincial rights but also more money. Indeed, reform proved to be costly as the Quebec budget nearly tripled between 1960 and 1966. Insisting that the federal government was financially starving the provinces, Lesage demanded that more of the tax revenue that it collected should be handed over to Quebec. These federal-provincial quarrels raised the question of the place of Quebec and French Canadians in the Confederation.

Although the Liberal reforms were long overdue, many rural and small-town Québecois in particular found them to be too expensive and too much too soon. In the provincial election of 1966, the Liberals won 50 seats with 47 percent of the popular vote while the Union Nationale under Daniel Johnson captured 56 seats with only 41 percent of the popular vote. To the disappointment of Quebec conservatives, Johnson did not significantly alter the Liberal reforms. In fact, he demanded even greater provincial autonomy based on linguistic equality of Canada's two major ethnic communities or "nations"— "master of our destiny in Quebec and equal partners in running the affairs of the country." Accordingly, Johnson argued for constitutional reform that would involve a redistribution of intergovernmental powers and responsibilities to recognize Quebec as an "associate state." When Prime Minister Trudeau asserted in 1968 that he would pursue linguistic equality without any reduction to federal authority, the battle lines began to be drawn between the forces of Quebec sovereignty and centralized federalism.

The question of sovereignty appeared peripheral to the nationalist aspirations of Quebec through most of the 1960s. Since 1963 the Front de libération du Québec (FLQ), a revolutionary fringe group dedicated to the establishment of an independent and socialist Quebec, had been involved in petty criminal and terrorist activity that did not generate significant popular support. French President Charles de Gaulle seemed to lend support to the cause of independence with his notorious cry of *Vive le Québec libre* during the Expo 67 celebration in Montreal. The sovereignty movement gained more political credibility in 1968 when the widely respected journalist and former Liberal cabinet minister René Lévesque formed the Parti Québecois (PQ), a union of two "separatist" movements that had previously enjoyed limited albeit enthusiastic support. In the provincial election of 1970, the PQ or Péquistes, as they were commonly known, secured almost one-quarter of the popular vote but only seven seats in the legislature.

The noteworthy support for the PQ in its inaugural election, however, was overshadowed by the infamous October Crisis of 1970. Within a span of five days, rival groups of FLQ members kidnapped James Cross, a British trade representative, and Pierre Laporte, a cabinet minister in the recently elected Liberal government. When Laporte was subsequently found murdered, Premier Robert Bourassa requested the assistance of the Canadian Armed Forces to supplement the Quebec police. Prime Minister Trudeau responded by invoking the War Measures Act, which gave the federal government emergency powers to deal with a declared state of "apprehended insurrection." Under this unprecedented peace-time use of the War Measures Act, the FLQ was banned, normal civil liberties were suspended, and about 500 people were detained and arrested on the mere suspicion of being sympathetic to the terrorists (all were later released without being charged). Cross was returned safely, and the crisis passed within three months, but controversy lingered. While the federal response received overwhelming public support outside of Quebec, French-Canadian nationalists and civil libertarians throughout Canada were highly critical of such an extreme measure being adopted for supposedly political purposes in a liberal democracy.

Despite the criticism, neither Trudeau nor Bourassa appeared to suffer politically for their response to the October Crisis. Trudeau retained his strong support in Quebec, which enabled him to survive the federal election of 1972 by the slimmest of margins. Bourassa's Liberals swept the provincial election of 1973, winning 102 seats, while the Union Nationale was reduced to two seats and political oblivion. The PQ managed to increase its popular vote to slightly over 30 percent, yet won only six seats. For the moment, the rest of Canada could breathe a sigh of relief, as the "safe" Liberals appeared well entrenched and the cause of separatism or sovereignty seemed to be languishing.

Nevertheless, the persistence of Quebec nationalism arising from the Quiet Revolution represented a major obstacle to the quest for national unity. In retrospect, the 1960s marked the pinnacle of Canadian optimism and confidence that this goal was fully achievable. The centennial celebration in 1967 was an occasion to reflect upon significant historical accomplishments, which inspired a sense of national pride and hope for even greater prosperity and unity. By electing Pierre Trudeau to lead the nation into its second century, Canadians expected to move beyond the stifling political conflicts of minority government and regionalism to forge a new consensus that would represent the modernity and diversity of their evolving society. When Trudeau's vision of the "just society" failed to meet their expectations, voters accorded him the same fate as they had John Diefenbaker a decade earlier. Trudeau, however, would prove to be more opportunistic in responding to a second chance.

CHAPTER 19

CONFLICT AND CONFRONTATION IN THE AGE OF ANXIETY

From the early 1970s to the mid-1980s, Canadians worried more about the economy than they had at any time since the Great Depression of the 1930s. Stagflation marked by the simultaneous occurrence of high rates of unemployment and inflation slowed down economic and population growth, which in turn intensified conflict among regions, levels of government, and social classes. Although much of Canada's economic difficulties were related to the troubled state of world affairs, Canadians expected, in part because they were promised, decisive action on the part of their federal and provincial governments, which were all too ready to blame each other for the nation's ills. The lightning rod for popular discontent from 1972 to 1984 was Pierre Trudeau, who adeptly took advantage of national anxieties over economic uncertainty, western alienation, and the Quebec sovereignty threat to maintain his dominance over Canadian political life.

THE UNCERTAINTY OF STAGFLATION

Although they continued to enjoy an enviable standard of living during the 1970s and early 1980s, Canadians became increasingly concerned, at times obsessed, about their economic prospects. Much of this economic anxiety was related to the high expectations of a postwar generation, perceiving that the country was not maintaining a growth rate to which it had become accustomed. For example, the rise in Canada's population from 21.6 million in 1971 to 24.3 million in 1981 represented only about a 12 percent increase, as compared to 30 percent between 1951 and 1961 and 18 percent between 1961 and 1971. This slower rate of population growth was largely the result of a steadily declining birthrate. From the peak levels reached at the end of the 1950s, the annual birthrate dropped by almost half and the number of births by about one-third by the early 1970s. Canadians were marrying at a later age and were waiting longer to have children, mainly because women were entering the workforce in greater numbers and had access to better contraceptive measures. Consequently, the postbaby-boom generation (those born after 1965) became known as the "baby bust."

However, Canada continued to be a magnet for immigrants, particularly from less-developed or Third World countries. Approximately 1.4 million immigrants arrived in Canada during the 1970s, about the same number as during the 1960s. Concerned about the country's economic capacity to continue to accommodate high levels of immigration, the federal government produced a Green Paper on Immigration Policy in 1975 as a prelude to the adoption of a new Immigration Act. For the first time, the fundamental objectives of Canadian immigration policy were specified. These objectives included the promotion of Canada's demographic, economic, social, and cultural goals; family reunion; nondiscrimination; the fulfillment of Canada's international obligations in relation to refugees; and cooperation between all levels of government in assisting newcomers to adapt to Canadian society. To achieve better control over the continuing influx of immigrants, the government also introduced annual admission ceilings based on one- to three-year projections of desired immigration levels. By the early 1980s, the annual immigration ceiling was set at 125,000 while, in fact, the number of newcomers reaching Canada was less than 100,000. Among the main determinants of immigration intake was the availability of employment opportunities.

Indeed, the threat or reality of unemployment remained at the forefront of public anxiety about the economy during the 1970s and early 1980s. In the quarter-century after World War II, Canadians had become accustomed to annual average rates of unemployment that fluctuated from 3 percent to 5 percent of the labor force, except during the recession of the late 1950s and early 1960s when the average rate fluctuated from 5 percent to 7 percent. After 1970, however, the national unemployment rate seldom dipped below 7 percent in spite of Canada's success in increasing total employment faster than any other major industrial nation. Of course, cyclical recessions in the early 1970s and 1980s raised the usual but unfounded fear of a return to the conditions of the 1930s. While the national unemployment rate did approach 13 percent in December 1982, the highest recorded level since the Great Depression, the duration of the crisis was short-lived, and its impact was moderated by substantial government assistance to the unemployed. Aside from the cyclical downturns, unemployment levels tended to be higher than expected largely because of the rapid growth of the labor force that had to absorb the postwar baby-boom population and a greater number of women.

Furthermore, the Canadian economy had undergone substantial structural changes since the 1960s. By 1980 half of Canadian workers were employed in the service sector, including government, schools, hospitals, the retail trade, financial institutions, and the communications industry; three out of 10 were employed in manufacturing, construction, and transportation; one out of 20 worked in agriculture; and one in 50 was employed in forestry, mining, fishing, or trapping. This complete reversal of the Canadian economy from the time of Confederation meant that many workers faced painful adjustments that occasionally resulted in unemployment. A worker's prospects could also be adversely affected by the profound regional inequalities in Canadian development, notably in the Maritimes and the northern frontiers. In the final analysis, Canadians in the 1970s and early 1980s felt no greater sense of job insecurity than had their predecessors, but as creatures of the affluent society, they tended to be less tolerant of economic uncertainty.

The threshold of economic insecurity was no doubt heightened by chronic inflation. In the postwar years, the annual rate of inflation in Canada remained relatively stable at an average of about 2 percent until the mid-1960s. In the wake of the Vietnam War as well as rising consumer demand and wage settlements, prices generally rose by 4 percent or 5 percent annually until 1972. The cost of living jumped to 9 percent in 1973 as crop failures in several countries drove food prices up by 17 percent, while the international cartel known as the Organization of Petroleum Exporting Countries (OPEC) quadrupled the world price of oil. In 1979 OPEC again raised the price of oil to more than 10 times the pre–1973 levels. Such a steep rise in the price of one of the key commodities of an industrialized and motorized society had the effect of making double-digit inflation a fact of life. The annual inflation rate reached a postwar high of 12.5 percent in 1981 before gradually beginning to subside.

Although it was a worldwide phenomenon, the inflationary spiral was also aggravated by the responses of business, labor, and government. Some businesses took advantage of the expectation of higher prices to increase their profits, while unions demanded higher wages to meet the escalating cost of living. In both cases, the consumer had to bear the consequent costs, and the diminished purchasing power often resulted in reduced demand for goods and services, which in turn contributed to layoffs and prolonged unemployment. Under popular pressure to take decisive action, the federal government with the cooperation of the provinces attempted with limited success to "wrestle inflation to the ground," in Prime Minister Trudeau's words, through an elaborate scheme of price and wage controls from 1975 to 1978. The Bank of Canada's decision to fight inflation by reducing the rate of growth in the money supply in 1975 resulted in a sharp rise in interest rates, which reached 20 percent in 1981, about four times higher than they had been 15 years earlier. Indeed, confused by the dilemma of which enemy to attack, unemployment or inflation, the federal government adopted a contradictory series of expansionary and restrictive fiscal and monetary policies. Combating unemployment required higher levels of the government expenditure, which had the inflationary effects of driving up budget deficits and interest rates. To fight inflation meant cutting government expenditures, which had the depressing effects of increasing unemployment and public assistance payments while lowering tax revenues. Rather than raise taxes or reduce expenditures, the federal government resorted to borrowing more at historically high rates of interest, thereby prolonging inflation with massive budget deficits. In the end, government seemed powerless to respond effectively to workers who had lost or feared the loss of their jobs, farmers or businesses facing bankruptcy, and homeowners unable to renew their mortgages. The ineffective government responses to economic problems further alienated the postwar generation, which had come to expect that politicians would fulfill their promises and grandiose visions.

Having raised the expectations of Canadians with his meteoric rise onto the national scene, Prime Minister Trudeau became the focus of growing public disillusionment with Canada's political leadership. After the election of 1972, most commentators spoke of a Liberal defeat and a Conservative victory. Some political analysts even speculated that the Liberals were saved from outright defeat by the prevailing mood of national euphoria sparked by Paul Henderson's dramatic last-minute goal that had given Canada the victory in the eight-game ice hockey series against the Soviet Union in the previous month. The Liberal campaign slogan, "The Land Is Strong," would have been even less appealing to the popular imagination had the Canadian professionals gone down to defeat in what is considered to be the national sport. Deciding that a plurality, however small, entitled him to form a government, Trudeau proceeded strategically to cultivate the parliamentary support of the NDP and Créditistes and ultimately to win back voter support.

To appease the NDP, the government greatly expanded public spending on social programs, including higher old-age pension and family allowance benefits in 1973. Appealing to economic nationalists among both the Liberals and the NDP, the Trudeau administration established the Foreign Investment Review Agency (FIRA) in 1974. FIRA was empowered to screen most takeovers and transfers of ownership to foreign interests or among them, to oversee direct foreign investment in new enterprises, and to monitor foreign expansion into any new and unrelated areas of business in order to determine whether they were of "significant benefit" to Canada. Although it immediately satisfied NDP demands, FIRA over the years would inspire more criticism from economic nationalists than from foreign investors. To win support in central Canada, the government promised to keep rapidly increasing oil prices substantially below world levels by developing a national energy policy based on the exploitation of the huge Athabaska tar sands deposits in northern Alberta, the creation of a national oil company, and the construction of a natural gas pipeline up the Mackenzie River valley in the Northwest Territories. The goal of the national energy policy was Canadian self-sufficiency in oil by the end of the 1970s.

The Liberals' uneasy partnership with the NDP ended in 1974 with the defeat of the government budget on a parliamentary motion of nonconfidence. The subsequent election campaign focused on the Conservatives' promise of wage and price controls to fight inflation. A relentless attack on Robert Stanfield's ill-conceived scheme resulted in the Liberals regaining a parliamentary majority with 141 seats, while the Conservatives and NDP were reduced to 95 and 16 seats, respectively. Although they took seats from the Conservatives and NDP in Ontario, Quebec, and British Columbia, the Liberals won only five out of 45 seats in the Prairie Provinces, which did not bode well for the challenges that were forthcoming.

After ridiculing the Conservative scheme of wage and price controls, the Trudeau administration adopted a policy of voluntary wage restraint. Organized labor was in no mood to cooperate, arguing that wage settlements had lagged behind inflation and corporate profits in recent years, and thus substantial raises were in order. In addition to inflationary pressures, labor militancy was spurred on by the doubling of union membership since the mid-1960s. More than 37 percent of nonagricultural workers were members of unions by the mid-1970s, compared to about 30 percent a decade earlier. Most of the newly organized unions were white-collar and service workers, especially those in the public sector, where the newly won right to strike led to highly unpopular work stoppages. For example, postal workers, air traffic controllers, and teachers demanded wage increases that ranged from 20 percent to 80 percent. Such pay demands would invariably lead to higher taxes in the public sector and higher prices in the private sector, thereby fueling the inflation that had precipitated the wage claims in the first place.

Under pressure from business and industry, which maintained that high wage demands undermined the competitiveness of Canadian products in the American market, and from the majority of workers who were unorganized and thus did not receive increases that kept up with the rising cost of living, the Trudeau government felt compelled to reverse its policy in 1975. The Anti-Inflation Board (AIB) was established with the authority not only to roll back excessive prices and wages but also to control the profits and dividends of larger firms. The effectiveness of the AIB controls proved to be inconclusive and the bureaucratic costs associated with this extraordinary state planning of the economy convinced the business community to join labor in urging an end to the unpopular program in 1978.

WESTERN ALIENATION AND THE NEW ENERGY FRONTIER

Meanwhile, the Trudeau administration proceeded with its promised national energy policy designed to shelter Canadians from the impact of world oil-price increases. A Crown corporation known as Petro-Canada (also referred to as Petrocan) began operation in 1975 to engage in energy research and development, to acquire imported oil supplies, and to explore and develop alternative sources of petroleum such as the Athabaska tar sands. The construction of a pipeline to carry gas from the Mackenzie Delta to southern Canada was postponed in 1974 pending Justice Thomas Berger's inquiry into the impact of the project on the northern Yukon and the Mackenzie Valley. His 1977 report, *Northern Frontier, Northern Homeland*, concluded that while a pipeline from the Mackenzie Delta down the Mackenzie Valley to Alberta was feasible, it would cause irreparable damage to the delicate environment of the region and thus would have an adverse impact on the Native population. Accordingly, the Berger Report recommended against the construction of a pipeline across the northern Yukon and urged a 10-year delay in the development of the Mackenzie Valley pipeline. In the early 1980s, a pipeline was built only halfway up the valley to Norman Wells.

The Berger Report called on Canadian governments to settle Native land claims before proceeding with northern resource development. The report specifically advanced the growing Native rights movement by eloquently depicting the North as a distinct homeland for the Native people rather than merely a resource frontier for southern Canada, and by setting the precedent that the Native people should be consulted on major resource development plans. The federal government had already begun to accept the legitimacy of claims to aboriginal rights in the wake of a Supreme Court ruling on the Nishga land claim in northern British Columbia in 1973. Significant agreements on land claims were reached with the Inuit and Cree in northern Quebec in 1975 to open the way for the development of Hydro Quebec's James Bay project and with the Inuit in the Northwest Territories and Labrador.

Progress was also made on claims to aboriginal nationhood, which began in the early 1970s. The Dene people of the western Northwest Territories laid claim to their substantial holdings and declared their right to self-determination in 1975. The following year, the Inuit Tapirisat of Canada proposed the creation of Nunavut (meaning "our land") as a distinct region in the central and eastern Northwest Territories, where the Inuit comprise the majority of the population. The new jurisdiction would administer justice, education, housing, land-use planning, and wildlife management. In his initial response to this proposal, Prime Minister Trudeau insisted that special status was as much out of the question for the aboriginal people as it was for Quebec. Nevertheless, the proposed division was endorsed by the Native majority in the Legislative Assembly of the Northwest Territories in 1979 and by a territory government plebiscite held in 1982. Later that year, the federal government accepted the proposal in principle. The Dene and Métis people of the western district also devised a plan to create their own jurisdiction called Denendeh (an Athapaskan word meaning "land of the people"). Despite this significant progress, Native self-determination would remain an elusive dream.

Besides focusing attention on Native relations, the energy concerns of the 1970s brought the federal government into deeper conflict with western Canada. The Prairie Provinces had become a veritable Liberal wasteland under Trudeau's leadership. Initially, "Trudeauphobia" was the dominant reaction of Prairie farmers frustrated by the mounting wheat surpluses and sagging prices on the world market. Western farmers blamed Trudeau for failing to take appropriate remedial measures, and they never forgave him for responding to them in a moment of mutual exasperation: "Why should I sell your wheat?" The intensity of western alienation, however, reached new heights over the issue of national oil pricing in the wake of the dramatic OPEC increases.

Through the transcontinental pipeline system, Alberta supplied oil to the area west of the Ottawa River, while the eastern provinces depended on foreign sources of supply, which up to 1973 had been cheaper than the domestic product. The initial response to the OPEC price increases was that Canada, as a petroleum-rich country with supposedly a "900-year supply," merely needed to reduce its oil imports and to rely on its natural resources. However, further assessment revealed that the size of the national oil reserves had been greatly exaggerated. Moreover, most of the country's reserves were located in the West far from the largest concentration of population, or in the North where the high cost of exploration and extraction could not provide immediate relief from the world price increases.

As part of its national energy policy, the Trudeau government in 1973 devised a two-price system designed to cushion the Atlantic Provinces, the economically weakest region of Canada, and Quebec, the politically most volatile province, from the shock of OPEC increases. To keep the domestic price of oil lower than the export price, the government levied an export tax on oil, the proceeds of which would help to subsidize the prices paid by the five eastern provinces. The federal government justified its policy by maintaining that oil and natural gas reserves belonged to Canadians as a whole and that Ottawa had an obligation to moderate increases in the domestic price on behalf of the governments of the consuming provinces. Rejecting this argument, the governments of the oil-producing provinces—principally Alberta but also Saskatchewan and British Columbia—countered that the national energy policy interfered with their constitutional right to control their natural resources. Western energy producers felt entitled to seek the world price for their resources, which were in great demand in the United States. Curiously, their free market outlook contrasted with the demand of western wheat farmers for more government support. The western-based oil companies further argued that higher prices were necessary to encourage aggressive exploration, new discoveries, conservation of existing resources, and generally future Canadian self-sufficiency. That Alberta used its rising energy revenues to expand its Heritage Fund for investment in future industrial development infuriated the poorer provinces, which would have to draw on even larger equalization payments from the federal government to afford the higher domestic prices.

After two years of acrimonious dispute and negotiation, the federal government and the energy-producing provinces reached a compromise pricing policy. Although the domestic price of oil would be kept consistently below the world price, it would be adjusted upward periodically to give the producing provinces higher revenues and the oil companies sufficient profits to encourage new exploration and development. Tensions subsided over the next four years as the domestic price rose to within 15 percent of the world price. But another upsurge of OPEC prices in the wake of the Iranian Revolution in 1979 renewed the federal-provincial conflicts over energy pricing in Canada and substantially drove up the cost of federal oil subsidies to the eastern provinces. By then, the Trudeau government was struggling with escalating budgetary deficits and dwindling popular support, which did not bode well for it in the upcoming federal election.

A contributing factor to the mounting federal deficit was the escalating expenditures for unemployment insurance as well as for the three major shared-cost programs with the provinces: hospital insurance, medical care, and postsecondary education. Unable to control provincial expenditures that it had to match dollar for dollar, the federal government attempted to place a ceiling on its contribution to these social programs through the Established Programs Financing (EPF) agreement of 1977. Under the EPF arrangement, the federal government withdrew from the shared-cost aspect of these programs and tied its annual contribution to the growth in per capita gross national product (GNP) rather than to actual provincial spending. After rancorous negotiations in which they typically demanded more money from Ottawa, the provinces agreed to the complicated formula for transfer payments because they saw opportunities to save money through efficient management of established programs without having to share the savings with Ottawa. With the slowing of economic growth in the late 1970s, federal revenue did not keep up with the rise in the per capita GNP, with the result that Ottawa had to make larger-than-anticipated financial transfers to the provinces in order to live up to the terms of EPF. Worse still, the federal government received little political credit for its support of provincial social programs, while it remained an easy target to blame for their shortcomings at election time.

PROVINCIAL POWER AND DISCONTENT

Another source of discontent with the Trudeau government in both English and French Canada was its continued preoccupation with institutionalized bilingualism. Despite the Supreme Court's rejection of a constitutional challenge to the Official Languages Act in 1974, upwards of three-quarters of the anglophone population and one-fifth of the francophone population questioned bilingualism as a government priority. Within this context, the strike of anglophone pilots and air traffic controllers who opposed the sanctioned use of French over Quebec airspace proved to be uniquely popular, despite bringing air travel in Canada to a virtual standstill in 1976. Many French Canadians implied that antipathy toward their language, rather than air safety, was the real motive behind the strike. A commission authorized to investigate the matter reported in 1979 that no risks were attached to the use of both languages in air traffic control. Support for bilingualism was further undermined by a series of provincial enactments promoting French unilingualism in Quebec. In 1979 the Task Force on National Unity criticized the implementation of institutionalized bilingualism in the public service as "costly and relatively ineffective." Indeed, Canadians have continued to debate whether bilingualism has done more to divide or unite the country.

Further evidence of growing antipathy toward the Trudeau administration was the reduction in Liberal provincial governments from five in 1968 to none by 1979. Not surprisingly, the Liberal demise was most pronounced in western Canada. In Saskatchewan, Ross Thatcher's Liberals were defeated by the NDP under Allen Blakeney in 1971, and the party had completely disappeared from the provincial legislature by the end of the decade. The NDP was also triumphant in Manitoba, where Edward Schreyer defeated the Conservatives under Walter Weir in 1969, and in British Columbia, where David Barrett ended the 20-year reign of Social Credit under W.A.C. Bennett in 1972. The defeated parties in both provinces, however, returned to power as William (Bill) Bennett Jr. followed in his father's footsteps by defeating Barrett in 1975, while Sterling Lyons triumphed over Schreyer in 1977. The following year, Schreyer was appointed governor-general, the first in Canada's history who was neither of British nor of French ancestry. His successor as premier of Manitoba, Lyons, fell to the NDP led by Howard Pawley in the election of 1981, when the last remaining Liberal in a western Canadian legislature lost his seat. In Alberta, Peter Lougheed ended Social Credit's 36-year reign and formed the province's first Progressive Conservative government in 1971. The depth of western alienation was further reflected in the emergence of separatist movements in Alberta, Saskatchewan, and British Columbia by 1980.

An indication of how far the Liberals had fallen in eastern Canada was the 1972 defeat of the only living "Father of Confederation," Joseph (Joey) Smallwood, as the Conservatives led by Frank Moores and later Brian Peckford assumed power. In New Brunswick, the Conservatives under Richard Hatfield ended Louis Robichaud's decade-long Liberal administration in 1970, just as Nova Scotia was electing the Liberals led by Gerald Regan. With Regan's loss to the Conservatives under John Buchanan in 1978 and the election of the Conservatives in Prince Edward Island in the following year, the Liberals no longer governed at the provincial level.

Although the Trudeau government was sustained by the votes of central Canada, the provincial Liberals did not fare as well in Ontario and Quebec. The Conservatives maintained their grip on Ontario under the leadership of John Robarts from 1961 to 1971 and William Davis from 1971 to 1985, despite the province's relative economic decline during the 1970s. Beset with a struggling manufacturing sector, particularly the automobile industry, and an economy generally reeling from the impact of rising energy costs, Ontario's status as Canada's wealthiest province was being challenged by oil-rich Alberta and resourceful British Columbia. Yet the Conservatives managed to hold on to power by adeptly deflecting the blame for Ontario's relative decline to the federal Liberals. Meanwhile, Premier Bourassa accomplished what most Canadians thought to be impossible: He squandered the overwhelming Liberal majority in the Quebec legislature and opened the door for a Parti Québecois victory in 1976. Trudeau's powerful defense of Canadian federalism in the face of an avowedly separatist government in Quebec led to a brief resurgence in the prime minister's popularity. But once the shock of René Lévesque's triumph had subsided, Canadians wondered whether Trudeau was too distracted by his crusade against Quebec sovereignty.

Not even the faltering Conservatives could stem the rising tide of Trudeauphobia. When Stanfield stepped down as party leader in 1976, a deeply divided Conservative convention chose little-known Alberta MP Joseph Clark as his successor. In terms of political experience, personal dynamism, and perceived leadership qualities, "Joe Who?" as he was popularly dubbed, suffered by comparison to Trudeau and NDP leader Edward Broadbent. Nevertheless, growing voter antipathy toward Trudeau and the Liberals in the federal election of 1979 enabled the Conservatives to capture 136 seats, while the Liberals dropped to 114, even though their share of the popular vote was actually about 4 percent higher. Liberal support was too heavily concentrated in Quebec, where the party won 67 out of 75 ridings; west of Manitoba it won only one seat and scarcely 20 percent of the popular vote. For their part, the Conservatives captured the West and scored major gains in southern Ontario, but won only two seats in Quebec. To secure a majority of the 282 seats in the House of Commons, the Conservatives only needed the support of all six elected Créditistes or a similar number of the 26 victorious NDP members.

Once in office, the Clark administration realized that some of its major election promises were not fiscally or practically feasible. A series of policy modifications or retreats reduced the popularity of the government and reinforced Clark's image as a weak and indecisive leader. Before it could celebrate its first anniversary, the government fell on a motion of nonconfidence in a budget that included not only a series of oil-price increases to promote new explorations that would lead to energy self-sufficiency by 1990 but also an excise tax on gasoline amounting to 18 cents per gallon. Finance Minister John Crosbie justified the new tax in terms of the need to raise billions of dollars to fight the escalating federal budget deficit. While his reasoning was sound and far-sighted, Canadians were not yet prepared to accept his "short-term pain for long-term gain." Reconsidering an earlier decision to retire from politics, Trudeau led the Liberals to a majority victory with 147 seats compared to 103 for the Conservatives in the election of 1980. The NDP's 32 seats represented an all-time high for the party, while the Créditistes were eliminated from the federal political scene.

The resilient Trudeau immediately launched the National Energy Program (NEP) designed to promote energy self-sufficiency, to redirect a larger share of oil revenues to the federal government, and to encourage greater Canadian ownership of the oil industry. To achieve these objectives, NEP included grants to encourage oil drilling in remote areas, grants to consumers to convert to gas or electric heating, new taxes on the oil industry, an expanded role for Petro-Canada, a requirement of 75 percent Canadian ownership to qualify for new federal exploration grants, and a reduction of foreign participation in oil and gas industry to below 50 percent. Predictably, the NEP was denounced in western Canada for its usurpation of provincial rights and for unnecessary state intervention in the economy, while some American politicians and entrepreneurs threatened retaliatory measures. Ultimately, NEP proved to be ill-timed: the federal government spent billions of dollars purchasing foreign oil companies and assisting oil exploration by Canadian companies only to have world oil prices crash dramatically after 1982. Trudeau's final term as prime minister was also memorable for his continued confrontation with Quebec over sovereignty and the constitution.

QUEBEC SOVEREIGNTY AND THE CONSTITUTION

If Trudeau was overly preoccupied with Quebec, as his critics claimed, political developments in his native province during the 1970s and the early 1980s gave him ample justification. Regardless of which political party governed Quebec, the language question remained at the forefront of public debate. Whereas at the time of Confederation the protection of the Catholic religion had been the chief concern of Quebec, the protection of the French language emerged as the key issue a century later. In response to a decision by the school board of the Montreal suburb of Saint Léonard that all immigrant children should attend French-language schools, the Union Nationale government passed Bill 63 in 1969. The legislation declared French to be the prevailing language of instruction but offered parents the freedom to choose whether their children should be taught in French or English. That immigrants preferred English-language education was disturbing to French Canadians who feared that multiculturalism would lead to the relative decline of their own culture.

The Liberal government of Robert Bourassa took up the language issue in broader terms by passing Bill 22 in 1974. French was decreed to be the official language of the province—the language of business and government—and all immigrant children were required to attend French-language schools. French-Canadian nationalists criticized the measure for failing to make French the sole public language and for permitting English-language education for anglophones. The English-speaking community and ethnic groups denounced the legislation as arbitrary and tyrannical and urged open defiance. The Trudeau government opposed Bill 22 as a challenge to the federal policy of bilingualism. Bourassa thus pleased no one and had to face the consequences of his government's action when he called a premature election in 1976.

Bourassa feared that the PQ was gaining in popularity and that his scandal-ridden administration would not fare well with the voters as the struggling Quebec economy worsened. His strategy of a surprise election with separatism as the issue backfired as the PQ with a little more than two-fifths of the popular vote won 71 seats, compared to 26 for the Liberals and 11 for the resurgent Union Nationale. Apparently, many English-speaking and ethnic Quebeckers voted for Union Nationale to protest Bill 22, thereby splitting the traditional Liberal support. Moreover, Lévesque steered a cautious course by promising that a PQ government would not decide to separate Quebec from Canada without seeking approval in a provincial referendum. Therefore, many antiseparatists voted for PQ because they opposed the Liberals and wanted a change in government. Whatever the case, on November 15, 1976, the Canadian political landscape was undoubtedly complicated and transformed.

At first, the PQ government focused on social and economic legislation that continued the Quiet Revolution and reflected a left-of-center political ideology, more closely resembling the NDP than the Liberals or Conservatives. The PQ intensified the language controversy by passing Bill 101 in 1977. The legislation extended the use of French as the official language to virtually every aspect of Quebec life and further restricted English-language education. By requiring signs to be posted in French only, Bill 101 was anticipating the eventual use of French as the sole public language of Quebec. In effect, Quebec would become as overwhelmingly French as Ontario was English.

Of course, the English-speaking community and ethnic Quebeckers were further outraged, and they responded by launching legal challenges that in some cases the Supreme Court of Canada upheld. Constant political and legal pressure would eventually persuade future governments to moderate some of the provisions of Bill 101. But perhaps the greatest pressure came from the sizable exodus of Anglo-Quebeckers and corporate head offices from the province, citing objections to language restrictions, high taxes, and the threat of separation from Canada. A substantial portion of this migration was to Toronto, which in the census of 1981 surpassed Montreal as Canada's largest city, in addition to becoming the undisputed financial capital of the nation.

As he developed his legislative agenda, Lévesque began referring to the prospect of "sovereignty association" by which a politically sovereign Quebec would enter into an economic association with Canada. To enhance the possibility of winning the provincial referendum scheduled for May 20, 1980, Lévesque composed a shrewdly worded (some would say deceptively worded) question that asked the voters to give his government the right to "negotiate" a sovereignty association agreement with Canada. The outcome of these negotiations would be subject to another provincial referendum. In other words, a *oui* ("yes") vote for the question would not result in a unilateral declaration of independence. Claude Ryan, who succeeded Bourassa as provincial Liberal leader in 1978, led the *non* ("no") forces within Quebec, while Prime Minister Trudeau campaigned on behalf of the rest of Canada. With 82 percent of eligible voters participating, Quebec voted non to the referendum question by a margin of 60 percent to 40 percent. Whereas almost all of the non-French-speaking population voted against the question, the French-speaking community was evenly divided in its response. Nevertheless, Canadians celebrated the defeat of separatism and took comfort in the belief that their nation would remain united.

The rejection of Lévesque's sovereignty association proposal did not prevent the premier from being reelected in the following year. The voters of Quebec overwhelmingly supported Trudeau's Liberals in Ottawa, but they preferred a strong defender of provincial rights in Quebec City. In the early 1980s, Ottawa and Quebec City again clashed over the patriation of the constitution, the achievement of which had eluded Canadian legislators for more than a half-century. Prime Minister Trudeau thought that he had successfully negotiated a proposal for constitutional reform, including an amendment formula and a bill of rights, on which all the provinces appeared to agree in 1971. However, at the last moment, Premier Bourassa rejected the so-called Victoria Charter because it did not grant Quebec sufficient control over social policy. Buoyed by the referendum victory, Trudeau was determined to succeed whether or not the provinces, particularly Quebec, approved of his constitutional proposals. A Supreme Court ruling in 1981 confirmed that the federal government had the legal right to patriate the British North America Act unilaterally but, at the same time, questioned the constitutional propriety of acting without the consent of the provinces. Trudeau pledged to attempt one last time to negotiate a deal with the provinces before he would resort to unilateral action.

A federal-provincial conference finally reached an accord on the terms of the new constitution to replace the British North America Act of 1867. The new Constitution Act (1982) included an amendment formula and a Charter of Rights and Freedoms. The basic amendment formula required the agreement of the federal Parliament and two-thirds of the provinces comprising at least 50 percent of the national population. No longer was it necessary to consult the British Parliament to change the Canadian constitution. Unlike the Bill of Rights of 1960 that it replaced, the Charter of Rights and Freedoms was entrenched into the new constitution in order to ensure that the courts rather than Parliament and the legislatures would have the last word on the protection of liberties and the validity of laws. Again, Quebec refused to sign the constitutional agreement because it was denied veto power as one of the two "national" groups in Canada. Although Quebec was legally bound by the terms of the new constitution, Lévesque spoke of it as a "betrayal" by the rest of Canada and a symbol of the isolation of the province.

After the disappointment of the referendum and the patriation of the constitution, Lévesque abandoned plans for sovereignty association and concentrated on the struggling

THE REVISED CANADIAN CONSTITUTION REPLACING THE BRITISH NORTH AMERICA ACT

CONSTITUTION ACT, 1982

PART I

CANADIAN CHARTER OF RIGHTS AND FREEDOMS

Whereas Canada is founded upon principles that recognize the supremacy of God and the rule of law:

Guarantee of Rights and Freedoms

1. The Canadian Charter of Rights and Freedoms guarantees the rights and freedoms set out in it subject only to such reasonable limits prescribed by law as can be demonstrably justified in a free and democratic society.

Fundamental Freedoms

2. Everyone has the following fundamental freedoms:
   (a) freedom of conscience and religion;
   (b) freedom of thought, belief, opinion and expression, including freedom of the press and other media of communication;
   (c) freedom of peaceful assembly; and
   (d) freedom of association.

Democratic Rights

3. Every citizen of Canada has the right to vote in an election of members of the House of Commons or of a legislative assembly and to be qualified for membership therein. . . .

Mobility Rights

6. (1) Every citizen of Canada has the right to enter, remain in and leave Canada.
   (2) Every citizen of Canada and every person who has the status of a permanent resident of Canada has the right
   (a) to move to and take up residence in any province; and
   (b) to pursue the gaining of a livelihood in any province.

Legal Rights

7. Everyone has the right to life, liberty and security of the person and the right not to be deprived thereof except in accordance with the principles of fundamental justice.

8. Everyone has the right to be secure against unreasonable search or seizure.

9. Everyone has the right not to be arbitrarily detained or imprisoned. . . .

Equality Rights

15. (1) Every individual is equal before and under the law and has the right to the equal protection and equal benefit of the law without discrimination and, in particular, without discrimination based on race, national or ethnic origin, colour, religion, sex, age or mental or physical disability.

Official Languages of Canada

16. (1) English and French are the official languages of Canada and have equality of status and equal rights and privileges as to their use in all institutions of the Parliament and government of Canada. . . .

Minority Language Educational Rights

23. (1) Citizens of Canada

(a) whose first language learned and still understood is that of the English or French linguistic minority population of the province in which they reside, or

(b) who have received their primary school instruction in Canada in English or French and reside in a province where the language in which they received that instruction is the language of the English or French linguistic minority population of the province,have the right to have their children receive primary and secondary school instruction in that language in that province. . . .

(2) Citizens of Canada of whom any child has received or is receiving primary or secondary school instruction in English or French in Canada, have the right to have all their children receive primary and secondary school instruction in the same language.

PART II

RIGHTS OF THE ABORIGINAL PEOPLES OF CANADA

35. (1) The existing aboriginal and treaty rights of the aboriginal peoples of Canada are hereby recognized and affirmed.

(2) In this Act, "aboriginal peoples of Canada" includes the Indian, Inuit and Mtis peoples of Canada.

(3) For greater certainty, in subsection (1) "treaty rights" includes rights that now exist by way of land claims agreements or may be so acquired.*

(4) Notwithstanding any other provision of this Act, the aboriginal and treaty rights referred to in subsection (1) are guaranteed equally to male and female persons.*

PART III

EQUALIZATION AND REGIONAL DISPARITIES

36. (1) Without altering the legislative authority of Parliament or of the provincial legislatures, or the rights of any of them with respect to the exercise of

their legislative authority, Parliament and the legislatures, together with the government of Canada and the provincial governments, are committed to
  (a) promoting equal opportunities for the well-being of Canadians;
  (b) furthering economic development to reduce disparity in opportunities; and
  (c) providing essential public services of reasonable quality to all Canadians.
  (2) Parliament and the government of Canada are committed to the principle of making equalization payments to ensure that provincial governments have sufficient revenues to provide reasonably comparable levels of public services at reasonably comparable levels of taxation.

Quebec economy. This decision upset the more hard-line separatists within the PQ who successfully pressured him into resigning in 1985. The defeat of the PQ at the hands of the Liberals led by a resurrected Bourassa in 1985 appeared to signal again that the separatist movement had run its course. The nationalist lull before the returning storm of sovereignty would prove to be short-lived.

Lévesque's great adversary, Trudeau, also suffered a decline in popularity, which persuaded him to retire from politics in 1984. As he ended his term as prime minister, the third longest in Canadian history behind Mackenzie King and Sir John A. Macdonald, Trudeau ironically achieved some measure of national unity, although not in the sense that he intended. For a brief moment, the nation was united in its antipathy toward Trudeau and all that he and his government represented. As a result, the Liberals went down to an overwhelming defeat in the election later that year to a rejuvenated Conservative Party led by Brian Mulroney. Those who anticipated that the winds of political change would bring more harmonious and prosperous times had their hopes raised for a few years, only to be disappointed again.

CHAPTER 20

🍁

THE ILLUSION
OF CONSENSUS

Just as they had turned to John Diefenbaker in the late 1950s and Pierre Trudeau in the late 1960s, Canadians hailed Brian Mulroney as their political savior in the mid-1980s. In the aftermath of the cultural and intergovernmental confrontations of the Trudeau era, Mulroney's promise of an "era of national reconciliation" was appealing enough to lead the Conservatives to the greatest triumph in Canadian electoral history. A strong economic recovery marked by the steady retreat of inflation offered hope for the development of a new national political consensus. In an ironic reversal of roles and results from nearly a century before, the Conservatives succeeded in convincing voters that free trade with the United States was the key to future national growth, while the Liberals stood in defense of Canadian economic nationalism. But amid the failure to negotiate a constitutional accord with Quebec, a skyrocketing government deficit, and a struggling economy, Canadians became so disillusioned with Mulroney that they decimated his historic political party. With the second Quebec sovereignty referendum ending in a virtual dead heat in 1995, the nation began to consider whether the current arrangement of Confederation was worth sustaining.

THE CONSERVATIVE RESURGENCE

The political landscape of the 1980s and 1990s contrasted sharply with that of the 1960s and 1970s. Canadians grew tired and skeptical of the salient features of Trudeau liberalism. Active state intervention in social and economic life had led to uncontrolled spending and high taxation, while strong centralist rule had incited constant conflict and confrontation with the provinces. Deprived of the opportunity to direct their wrath against Trudeau in the national election of 1984, voters decided to oust his successor, John Turner, after less than three months in office, the shortest term of any prime minister since Charles Tupper in 1896. The Liberals sank to an all-time low of 40 seats, only 10 more than the NDP, prompting predictions of permanent demise for the former governing party. Surpassing the Diefenbaker landslide of 1958, the Conservatives captured 211 seats, including a majority of Quebec ridings, on the strength of Mulroney's vision of a more decentralized federalism emphasizing consensus-building along with a more welcoming and less intrusive environment for free enterprise.

The Mulroney government sought to reduce regional discontent by dismantling the National Energy Program, much to the delight of the West; by granting Nova Scotia and Newfoundland control over their offshore mineral resources; and by promising to negotiate Quebec's acceptance of the constitution of 1982. A recovering economy featuring an annual inflation rate that dropped to 4 percent and a national unemployment rate that was down to an acceptable 6–7 percent range also helped the Mulroney administration in its relations with the provinces, even though prosperity was unevenly distributed. Ontario and British Columbia, particularly the metropolitan centers of Toronto and Vancouver, respectively, were booming in the second half of the decade of the 1980s. Indeed, Vancouver enjoyed international prominence in 1986 when it hosted the World's Fair. On the other hand, Quebec continued to struggle in the wake of the politically induced exodus of business from the province; the Prairie economy was hurt by the decline of energy and agricultural prices; and the Atlantic Provinces remained virtual wards of the federal government, relying more than ever on transfer payments. In response to this disparity of wealth, the Mulroney administration launched a regional development policy that, in contrast to the Liberal program, would be guided by economics rather than politics.

Under the Liberals, the Department of Regional Economic Expansion (DREE) supported a "hodgepodge" of projects that were designed to appease federal-provincial conflict rather than to enhance a national or interprovincial development strategy. With all regions of Canada equally eligible for assistance, Liberal regional development policy tended to move away from its original commitment to the Atlantic Provinces. Under the Conservatives, the Department of Regional Industrial Expansion (DRIE), which had replaced DREE in 1982, was reoriented "to promote the least developed regions." Accordingly, Mulroney established the Atlantic Canada Opportunities Agency (ACOA) in 1987 to ensure that national economic policies were adjusted to correspond to the circumstance of the chronically underdeveloped region and to assist local entrepreneurs in launching new businesses. Later that year, the Western Diversification Office (WDO) was established to assist industrial development and to help move the Prairie economy away from dependence on the volatile resource and agricultural sectors. Major regional development programs were subsequently initiated for Quebec and northern Ontario. Despite their noble intentions, regional development measures became synonymous with government handouts for projects that had dubious economic viability. Like Trudeau before him, Mulroney ultimately succumbed to the temptation to use regional development policy to redivide the national economic pie, with the regions competing against each other for a larger slice.

A generally improving economic climate enabled the Mulroney administration to raise the annual ceiling on immigration from 100,000 to 200,000 in the late 1980s. The Multiculturalism Act of 1988 sought "to recognize all Canadians as full and equal participants in Canadian society" by providing additional funds to promote cultural minorities and to reduce discrimination. So-called visible minorities became a growing segment of the Canadian cultural mosaic: the Caribbean Islands, India, Pakistan, the People's Republic of China, Hong Kong, Taiwan, Vietnam, the Philippines, and Sri Lanka were the major suppliers of immigrants during the 1980s and 1990s. A special welcome was extended to "business-class" immigrants—wealthy entrepreneurs with capital to invest in Canada. For example, Canada encouraged greater capital investment from Hong Kong as the feared communist Chinese takeover loomed closer. The Canadian government also gave special preference to "investor" immigrants from Hong Kong, most of whom chose to settle in British Columbia. Canada continued to be a haven for refugees fleeing war and persecution in their homelands, but public opinion was becoming less sympathetic to their plight. Criticism focused on those who entered Canada illegally and then claimed refugee status in order to short-circuit the immigration review process.

Despite boasting about their multicultural society, Canadians increasingly worried about the impact of immigration on their national identity. The Canadian population rose to 27 million in 1991 thanks to the addition of the 1.2 million immigrants who had accounted for approximately 40 percent of the growth over the previous decade. As a result, the Canadian population was almost evenly divided among the British, French, and "other" ethnicities, and it was only a matter of time before the latter would dominate numerically. Moreover, the fact that the great majority of new immigrants adopted English as their new language contributed to the weakening in the relative position of the country's French-speaking population and to fears of cultural survival in Quebec.

The Mulroney government also endeavored to address the demands of Canada's Native peoples. In 1985 Bill C–31 removed a discriminatory clause within the Indian Act by which a Native woman automatically lost her "Indian" status and became a "Canadian" citizen if she married a "nonstatus" Indian, a Métis, or any other non-Indian. Henceforth, status Indian women could retain their status regardless of their marital decisions, and women who had been so deprived of their Indian status could be reinstated. With Indian status came the entitlement to free medical care, free schooling on the reserve, housing and higher-education subsidies, exemption from federal and provincial taxation for income earned on any reserve, the right to live on the reserve of the Indian band to which one is designated a member, a share of the band's assets, special hunting and fishing rights, and eligibility for federal loans and grants to establish a business on a reserve. A common complaint of Native leaders has been that the already crowded reserves have been hard-pressed to accommodate the influx of reinstated women, their non-Native husbands, and their children. Indeed, this problem intensified the demand for Native self-government inasmuch as Native leaders challenged the power of the Canadian government to determine membership in Native society.

While the Constitution Act of 1982 "recognized and affirmed" the rights of aboriginal peoples, the definition of these rights and of Native self-government remained a source of controversy. The House of Commons Special Committee on Indian Self-Government in 1983 recommended a measure of Native self-government and introduced the concept of "First Nation" into federal negotiations on the issue. By 1987 Prime Minister

Mulroney was prepared to add a clause to the constitution that would acknowledge the fundamental right of Native self-government, but Alberta and British Columbia led the provincial objection to the lack of a clear definition of self-government. The main concern of the provinces was that Native self-government might interfere with their control over natural resources. In 1987 the federal government was more successful in negotiating with the Legislative Assembly of the Northwest Territories the division of that region into two separate jurisdictions—Denendeh and Nunavut. Indeed, Nunavut became Canada's newest territory on April 1, 1999.

The crowning achievement of the Mulroney administration was a new economic direction for Canada. In a spirit reminiscent of C. D. Howe in the decade after World War II, Mulroney declared Canada "open for business." In particular, the Mulroney administration sought to improve relations with the United States, which had varied from strained to lukewarm during the Trudeau era. Liberal attempts to develop a third option, which implied less economic dependence on the United States and greater trade links with other countries, especially countries in Europe, generally failed. Canadian trade with Britain and the Commonwealth declined even further after Britain entered the European Common Market in 1974. As the European trading bloc became stronger and more exclusive, the Mulroney administration realized that, for better or worse, Canada's economic lot was better cast with the United States, the destination for more than 80 percent of exports and the source for more than 70 percent of imports by the mid-1980s.

To signal the changing attitude of Canadian government, the Mulroney administration in 1985 transformed FIRA into Investment Canada, a new agency to encourage foreign investment. At the same time, Canada and the United States began negotiations on a comprehensive free trade agreement, a prospect that was endorsed by the Royal Commission on the Economic Union and Development Prospects for Canada, chaired by former Liberal Cabinet Minister Donald Macdonald. As the usual public debate raged over the merits and demerits of free trade, the two countries concluded an accord in 1987. According to the terms of the Free Trade Agreement that took effect on January 1, 1989, tariffs on various products would be phased out gradually, and both countries would have preferential access to each other's markets. The United States also gained unhindered access for investment in Canadian industries, particularly the energy sector, without any Canadian government surveillance or restrictions. Canada could export energy to the United States without limitations, but the Americans could secure Canadian supplies even in times of shortages. To settle any disputes that might arise, a binational review panel was established to ensure that the trade agencies of each country would abide by the terms of the Free Trade Agreement.

As in 1911, free trade became the major issue of the 1988 federal election campaign, but on this occasion the party roles were reversed. Turner took advantage of the passions raised by the issue to rejuvenate the Liberals as the defenders of Canadian political sovereignty supposedly jeopardized by free trade. The Liberals and the NDP argued that free trade would cost thousands of jobs, particularly if American companies closed down branch plants in Canada since they no longer had tariff walls to climb. Canada might also lose control over pricing of resources, social programs, and cultural industries. In defending the Free Trade Agreement, the Conservatives emphasized the greater economies of scale and lower costs in manufacturing resulting from guaranteed access to the huge American market, more incentives for domestic firms to engage in research and development and to adopt the latest available technology, lower prices for consumers because of the removal of tariffs and higher productivity of Canadian industry, and new job opportunities in the expanding sectors of the economy. Without a viable alternative, the opponents of free trade were no match for the Conservatives, who were reelected with a comfortable albeit substantially reduced majority.

After the free trade election victory, Mulroney's political fortunes and personal popularity began to plummet as his government became tangled in a morass of controversy. Keeping his earlier promise to Quebec, Mulroney presided over a series of federal-provincial conferences that negotiated the Meech Lake Accord in 1987. To secure Quebec's acceptance of the constitution of 1982, the accord included controversial provisions to recognize the province as a "distinct society" and to grant it increased powers over immigration. Having reached an agreement in principle, the federal government and the 10 provinces had three years to ratify the Meech Lake Accord. Expectations were high that Canada's 60-year constitutional odyssey would at last end triumphantly.

However, as the June 1990 deadline for ratification approached, opposition to the accord mounted. Representatives of women, Native peoples, ethnic associations, and northerners complained that their interests and concerns were not adequately addressed by the agreement. Former prime minister Trudeau contended that the Meech Lake Accord would seriously weaken federal authority and promote linguistic ghettos within Canada. Indeed, the fate of Meech Lake was closely linked to the reemergence of the language issue in Quebec. When the Supreme Court of Canada ruled Quebec's law requiring

CONSTITUTION AMENDMENT, 1987

CONSTITUTION ACT, 1982

1. The *Constitution Act, 1867* is amended by adding thereto, immediately after section 1 thereof, the following section:

"2.(1) The Constitution of Canada shall be interpreted in a manner consistent with

(a) the recognition that the existence of French-speaking Canadians, centred in Quebec but also present elsewhere in Canada, and English-speaking Canadians, concentrated outside Quebec but also present in Quebec, constitutes a fundamental characteristic of Canada; and

(b) the recognition that Quebec constitutes within Canada a distinct society.

(2) The role of the Parliament of Canada and the provincial legislatures to preserve the fundamental characteristic of Canada referred to in paragraph (1)(a) is affirmed.

(3) The role of the legislature and Government of Quebec to preserve and promote the distinct identity of Quebec referred to in paragraph (1)(b) is affirmed.

(4) Nothing in this section derogates from the powers, rights or privileges of Parliament or the Government of Canada, or of the legislatures or governments of the provinces, including any powers, rights or privileges relating to language."

French-only public signs to be in violation of the freedom of expression provisions of both the federal and Quebec charters of rights, Premier Bourassa introduced Bill 178 permitting bilingual signs inside an establishment but prohibiting them outside. Anglo-Canadian outrage in response to the passing of the provincial language legislation had the effect of provoking greater opposition to the "distinct society" clause of the Meech Lake Accord. In turn, many within the French community of Quebec questioned whether the accord would give the province sufficient power to protect their language rights and privileges.

Frantic negotiations as the deadline for approving the accord drew near produced an additional commitment by the premiers to work for a reformed Senate that would represent regional interests more effectively. Nevertheless, the accord died as the Manitoba and Newfoundland legislatures could not ratify it before the expiration of the deadline. Canadians outside of Quebec were generally relieved at the demise of the Meech Lake Accord because they felt that it was too favorable to Quebec. Nationalists within Quebec, including many federalists, viewed the failure of the constitutional agreement in terms of English Canada's refusal to accommodate the basic concerns of their province. Lucien Bouchard, a Cabinet minister in the Mulroney government, quit the Conservative Party to form the Bloc Québecois, which was committed to Quebec independence, while sitting in the Canadian Parliament. In response to criticism of his government, Premier Bourassa established a nonpartisan commission that eventually persuaded him to hold a provincial referendum either on independence or on new constitutional offers from Canada.

Prime Minister Mulroney countered by reopening constitutional discussions and subjecting the results to a national referendum. This time the prime minister and the premiers consulted with various interest groups to produce the Charlottetown Accord, which responded to a wide range of proposals for constitutional change, including aboriginal self-government and Senate reform. On the other hand, Quebec, which had vowed to boycott future constitutional talks in the wake of the Meech Lake failure, did not become involved in the negotiations until the late stages. In the national referendum held in 1992, six of 10 provinces, including Quebec, rejected the Charlottetown Accord. Voters in English Canada tended to believe that the accord offered Quebec too much, whereas Quebec voters felt that it offered the province too little. The reality was that too few Canadians actually understood the complexities of their constitution, and after decades of federal-provincial disputes on the issue, too many of them had become cynical about the priorities of their politicians.

THE FALTERING NATIONAL PARTY SYSTEM

By the early 1990s, Canadians were virtually united in their antagonism toward Mulroney and the Conservatives. The government was plagued by a succession of political scandals that reinforced its image as a corrupt regime. Attempts to deal with the mounting budget deficit also proved troublesome. From their Liberal predecessors, the Conservatives inherited a national debt exceeding $200 billion and an annual budget deficit that reached $38 billion in 1985. The Mulroney government's attempt to limit the indexing of pensions to cost-of-living increases was stalled when senior citizens mobilized in protest. Efforts to reconsider the universality of social programs through a "claw-back" of family allowance and old-age pension payments were met with vehement opposition from more affluent Canadians. Rather than further undermine its popularity by cutting expenditures, the government found it easier to raises taxes and to continue to borrow. By 1991 the annual federal deficit still hovered around $40 billion and the national debt approached $500 billion. About 35 percent of federal revenue went to paying interest on its previous borrowings, more than was spent on health and welfare. The Mulroney government provoked its greatest outrage when it endeavored to fight the deficit by replacing the hidden manufacturers' sales tax with a fully visible Goods and Services Tax (GST) of 7 percent starting in 1991.

Compounding the Conservatives' political misery was the onset of a serious economic recession in 1990–91, featuring unemployment again in the 11–12 percent range. Opponents were inclined to blame heavy job losses resulting from plant closures in the manufacturing sector on the Free Trade Agreement, despite evidence that suggested otherwise. Even western Canada abandoned Mulroney, who was regarded as being too fixated on central Canada. The West's dissatisfaction with mainstream parties was again demonstrated by the rise of the Reform Party of Canada, under the leadership of Preston Manning, son of former Alberta Premier Ernest Manning. Formed in 1987, the Reform Party criticized the federal government for its fiscal mismanagement, particularly its costly "welfare-state approach" to social programs, and its commitment to bilingualism and multiculturalism.

Realizing that his party's fortunes in the impending election were dismal under his leadership, Mulroney stepped aside in favor of Kim Campbell, the minister of justice from British Columbia, in 1993. In edging out Jean Charest of Quebec at the Conservative convention, Campbell became the second woman in Canadian history to lead a national party; Audrey McLaughlin had succeeded Ed Broadbent at the head of the NDP in 1989. As leader of the governing party, Campbell enjoyed the distinction of becoming Canada's first female prime minister. But her tenure proved to be short-lived as the Conservatives went down to an unprecedented electoral defeat, returning only two members to Parliament. The historic party of Sir John A. Macdonald lay in ruins.

The Liberals under the leadership of Jean Chrétien, a long-time Cabinet minister in the Trudeau administration, won 177 seats even though he failed to take a majority of seats in his native province of Quebec. There, the Bloc Québecois won 54 seats and, by virtue of having the second-largest number of members in Parliament, became the Official Opposition. Finishing only two seats behind the Bloc Québecois was Manning's Reform Party, which enjoyed its strongest support in Alberta and British Columbia but also managed to win a seat in Ontario. Like the Conservatives, the NDP with only nine seats lost its official-party status in the House of Commons. The unpopularity of NDP provincial governments in Ontario under Robert (Bob) Rae and in British Columbia under Michael Harcourt contributed substantially to the party's poor performance. In effect, Canada had never been so divided, and its political landscape had never experienced such a degree of upheaval. The governing Liberals relied mostly on support from Ontario and the Atlantic Provinces, while two recently formed political parties dominated in Quebec and the West. Indeed, the election of 1993 demonstrated how fragmented and volatile Canadian politics had become.

The volatility of Canadian politics was particularly evident in the provincial government of Ontario. The 42-year reign of the Progressive Conservatives came to an end in 1985 when Premier William Davis retired and his unpopular successor, Frank Miller, was narrowly defeated by the Liberals under David Peterson. The Liberal minority government depended on the support of the NDP until winning an overwhelming majority of seats in the election of 1987. The NDP led by Bob Rae formed the Official Opposition, while the Conservatives appeared headed for political oblivion. Fearing that an impending downturn in the economy might seriously erode his popularity, Premier Peterson called a surprise election in 1990. This tactic backfired and resulted in a stunning upset victory for the NDP, which had deliberately toned down its socialist-labor rhetoric to increase its voter appeal. Rae's decision to fight the recession with massive spending, particularly on social welfare payments, proved to be his undoing. In the election of 1995, Ontario politics came full circle as the Conservatives under Michael (Mike) Harris returned to power, promising a "neoconservative" agenda of social spending cuts and lower taxes as to reduce the mounting provincial deficit and debt load as well as to restore business confidence. Clearly, the era of party loyalty had given way to unbound voter restlessness.

The West remained a Liberal wasteland, particularly in Alberta, where the Conservatives remained entrenched. Donald Getty, a former Edmonton Eskimos player in the Canadian Football League, replaced Peter Lougheed in 1986 and was succeeded by former Calgary Mayor Ralph Klein six years later. In Manitoba, the Conservatives under Gary Filman returned to power in 1988, while in Saskatchewan Grant Devine's Conservatives lasted from 1982 until defeated by the NDP under Roy Romanow in 1991. Social Credit maintained its hold on British Columbia as Bill Bennett gave way to William Vander Zalm in 1986 who, as a result of serious conflict of interest allegations, was forced to resign in 1991 in favor of Rita Johnson, the first female provincial premier in Canadian history. The NDP soon returned to power under Mike Harcourt, who was succeeded by Glen Clark in 1996.

By contrast, Maritime politics featured a veritable Liberal revival in the late 1980s. In 1986 Joe Ghiz became premier of Prince Edward Island, and the Liberals remained in power for a decade until unseated by the Conservatives under Patrick Binns. The Liberals led by Frank McKenna swept every seat in the New Brunswick election of 1987, marking only the second time a provincial party had performed such a feat (the first occurrence was the Liberal sweep in Prince Edward Island in 1935). Clyde Wells brought Newfoundland back into the Liberal fold in 1989 and was succeeded by Brian Tobin in 1996. John Savage led the Liberals out of the political wilderness in Nova Scotia in 1993, but his successor, Stewart MacLennan, had to form a coalition with the Conservatives in 1998 to stave off the challenge of the rising NDP under John Hamm. The success of the Nova Scotia NDP in the federal election of the previous year was a signal that Maritime politics might be ready to break away from the traditional two-party system.

The winds of political change were also blowing in Quebec as ill health forced Premier Bourassa to step aside for Daniel Johnson, son of the Union Nationale leader of the 1960s. The Liberals then fell to the Parti Quebecois led by Jacques Parrizeau in the provincial election of 1994, even though the two parties finished virtually tied in the popular vote count. Nonetheless, Parrizeau interpreted his solid majority of seats in the National Assembly as a mandate to hold another referendum on sovereignty scheduled for October 30, 1995. Again, Quebec voters were asked to respond to a vaguely worded question empowering the government to negotiate terms of independence with Canada. Passions ran high as an early federalist lead in public opinion polls dwindled into a cliffhanger that left both sovereigntists and federalists claiming victory. The actual vote was 50.3 percent to 49.7 percent in favor of the "non" forces, which supported federalism, but the improved support for the "oui" forces compared to the 1980 referendum was cause for celebration among the sovereigntists.

But their moment of triumph was tempered by the racist inferences of an exuberant but inebriated Parrizeau, who blamed "money and ethnics" for denying sovereigntists an outright victory. Parrizeau was expressing what many Canadians suspected all along—that the sovereignty movement was sustained by an underlying French intolerance for the English-speaking and ethnic minorities within Quebec. Official Opposition leader Bouchard, who was the driving force behind the pro-sovereignty movement during the referendum campaign, left federal politics to replace a disgraced Parrizeau at the head of the PQ and as premier of Quebec. The PQ again scored a majority victory in terms of seats in the provincial election of 1998, even though the Liberals led by former federal Conservative leader Jean Charest held a 1 percent lead in popular votes.

Although the prospect of yet another sovereignty referendum looms at the beginning of the new millennium, the Quebec independence movement faces an uncertain future for demographic and economic reasons. Quebec society is far from homogeneous, and it will become more deeply divided in the 21st century. Demographers predict that Quebec's population will continue to fall, and the provincial government will necessarily resort to immigration to sustain growth, thereby perpetuating a clash between multiculturalism and unilingualism. Already the notion of partitioning the province is popular among those living in the Montreal and Ottawa River regions as well as among the Native peoples of the vast northland. Support for sovereignty is strongest in the less-developed part of the province east of Montreal and focused on Quebec City. Furthermore, Quebec's declining importance in terms of its share of the national population and the national wealth does not bode well for its political influence. Indeed, the rest of Canada is becoming increasingly indifferent to an insular and disaffected cultural (and at times racist) fragment that appears to be oblivious to the realities of continentalism and globalization.

Prime Minister Chrétien received much of the blame for the near defeat of the federalist forces in the Quebec referendum campaign. Some critics felt that he had become too involved in the political affairs of his native province, while others thought that he was not sufficiently active in advancing the federalist cause. His government also came under fire for reversing election promises. After severely criticizing free trade during the election campaign, the Chrétien government adopted the North American Free Trade Agreement (NAFTA) with the United States and Mexico in 1994. Although they denounced the Conservatives' "obsession" with fighting inflation and the budget deficit, the Liberals reduced the size of the federal civil service and substantially cut unemployment benefits as well as grants to the provinces for health and higher education. Chrétien also reversed his electoral promise to abolish the despised GST, which had become a vital revenue-producer for the federal treasury. A conservative fiscal strategy combined with the general economic recovery enabled the Chrétien administration to achieve a budgetary surplus by the late 1990s, thereby bringing an end to a quarter-century of deficit financing and refocusing the public debate on whether to use the surplus to reduce the national debt or to revitalize social programs.

While Chrétien endured heavy criticism from within his party for deviating from the Liberal agenda that had built the welfare state, his personal popularity remained strong enough to secure reelection with a reduced but comfortable majority in 1997. With 60 seats, the Reform Party moved ahead of the Bloc Québécois with 44 seats as the Official Opposition. The election was also noteworthy for the improved performance of the

NDP (21 seats) under Alexis McDonagh and the Conservatives (20 seats) led by Charest. When Charest left federal politics to lead the Quebec Liberals in the following year, Joe Clark returned to lead the party he had guided into power nearly two decades earlier. The federal election of 1997 confirmed the regionalization of national politics at the end of the 20th century. The Liberals were the party of Ontario, capturing all but two of the province's 103 seats; the Bloc Québécois still dominated Quebec; and the Reform Party won by a landslide in the West. Only the Liberals had representation in all regions of the country, although its support in the West was rather meager. Temporarily at least, the national system built by the Conservatives and Liberals had broken down, and Canadian politics had entered a process of realignment, the result of which will not be evident for decades to come.

THE CANADIAN CULTURAL REVOLUTION

The post-1960 era featured a veritable explosion of Canadian cultural achievement as the talents of numerous writers, artists, and musicians became internationally recognized. Certainly Canada Council grants and other government support programs have been instrumental in allowing artistic energy to find expression and the public's appetite for Canadian culture to be satisfied. From an inaugural budget of $1.5 million in 1957, the Canada Council grants across the whole range of cultural activities escalated to $114 million in 1997–98. Furthermore, various government measures set specific guidelines and quotas to give priority to the promotion of Canadian culture. For example, Canadian musicians received a substantial boost in 1970 when the Canadian Radio-Television and Telecommunications Commission (CRTC) established Canadian content rules for broadcasters. Canadian cultural development also benefited from the growing diversity of Canadian society. By the 1980s, the Anglo-dominated cultural establishment was making room for a more socially diverse elite that better reflected the Canadian mosaic. The rise of French-Canadian nationalism in the wake of the Quiet Revolution and the sovereignty movement provided the inspiration for artistic expression in Quebec.

A plethora of writers have had an impact on the literary world since the 1960s with work that moved away from realist fiction focusing on the preoccupations, attitudes, and aspirations of Canadians toward more experimental prose exhibiting the qualities of late modernism. Many of the most popular novelists have been women offering insights into the social alienation and personal struggles of their gender. Margaret Laurence's *The Stone Angel* (1961) and *The Diviners* (1974); Margaret Atwood's *The Edible Woman* (1969), *The Handmaid's Tale* (1985), and *Alias Grace* (1996); Alice Munro's *Who Do You Think You Are?* (1978) and *The Love of a Good Woman* (1998); Mavis Gallant's *From the Fifteen District* (1979); Joy Kogawa's *Obasan* (1981); Marie-Claire Blais's *Une Saison dans la vie d'Emmanuel* (1965); and Anne Hébert's *Kamouraska* (1970) are read throughout the world. Carol Shields's novel *The Stone Diaries* (1993) won not only the Governor-General's Award but also the Pulitzer Prize. Other famous Canadian novels of the period include Robertson Davies's *Fifth Business* (1970) and *The Rebel Angels* (1981), Timothy Findlay's *The Wars* (1977) and *Famous Last Words* (1981), Rudy Weibe's *The Temptations of Big Bear* (1973), Roch Carrier's *La Guerre, Yes Sir!* (1968), Yves Beauchemin's *Le Matou* (1981), Hubert Aquin's *Prochaine Épisode* (1968), and Rohinton Mistry's *Such a Long Journey* (1991) and *A Fine Balance* (1995). The international recognition of many Canadian novels has been enhanced by their adaptation into feature films, such as Michael Ondaatje's *The English Patient* (1992), which won the Academy Award for best motion picture in 1997.

Canadian poetry continued to be enriched and diversified by the lyric and prose verse of Margaret Atwood, Nicole Brossard, Anne Carson, Leonard Cohen, Robert Kroetsch, Anne Michaels, Michael Ondaatje, Fernand Ouellette, and Al Purdy, among other notables. Quebec playwright Michel Tremblay's works are performed around the world, while Marcel Dubé has made major contributions to French-language theater. With the founding of the Stratford Festival and the Shaw Festival at Niagara-on-the-Lake, along with alternative theater companies such as Theater Passe Muraie and the Tarragon Theater in Toronto, the Prairie Grain Exchange in Winnipeg, the Neptune Theater in Halifax, and Centaur Theater in Montreal, English-speaking drama came into its own with the emergence of playwrights such as David French, John Gray, Sharon Pollock, George Walker, Judith Thompson, and Tomson Highway.

The blossoming of Canadian visual arts in the post-1960 period is evident not only in the number of internationally prominent artists but also in the proliferation of galleries and exhibitions as well as the development of art magazines. The Canada Council and the provincial art councils played a crucial role in this development, as did the growth of museums and art departments in Canadian colleges and universities. The diversification of styles and themes over the past half-century has produced not so much a "Canadian art" as a dynamic Canadian art scene. The major contemporary Canadian artists include Eli Boorstein, Patterson Ewen, Dorothy Knowles, William Kurelek, Charles Pachter, Christopher Pratt, Otto Rogers, Jack Shadbolt, Michael Snow, Takao Tanabe, Joanne Todd, Claude Tousignant, Joyce Wieland, and Bill Reid, the internationally acclaimed Haida sculptor. The danger of such a list is that it invariably excludes numerous other artists whose work deserves recognition.

The same dilemma occurs in highlighting the spectacular growth of Canadian musical achievement over the past four decades. The emergence of world-rank performers, ensembles, and composers performing in splendid new concert halls and arts centers across the country is also attributable to Canada Council support and the development of music education programs and scholarly research in colleges and universities. Such groups as the Orford String Quartet, the Festival Singers of Canada, the Canadian Brass Quintet, Tafelmusik, and the Elmer Iseler Singers are internationally acclaimed. Individual performers of world repute include opera singers Maureen Forrester, Ben Heppner, Richard Margison, Lois Marshall, Teresa Stratas, and John Vickers; pianists Angela Hewitt, Anton Kuerti, André Laplante, Louis Lortie, John Kimura Parker, and the legendary Glenn Gould; cellist Ophra Harnoy; violinist James Ehnes; guitarist Liona Boyd; jazz musicians Maynard Ferguson, Diane Krall, and Oscar Peterson; composers Murray Adaskin, Jean Coulthard, Alexina Louie, R. Murray Schafer, and Harry Somers; and conductors Mario Bernardi and Boris Brott.

Likewise, Canadians have been prolific in the realm of popular music. A host of English-Canadian singer-songwriters emerged in the 1960s, including Paul Anka, Leonard Cohen, Tommy Hunter, Gordon Lightfoot, Joni Mitchell, and Neil Young. In Quebec, Robert Charlebois, Pauline Julien, Ginette Reno, and Gilles Vigneault expressed the powerful nationalist current of the Quiet Revolution through their songs. Anne Murray was the first star of the Canadian Radio-television and Telecomunications Commission era, but her popularity proved to be enduring inside and outside of Canada. Other performers of the 1970s, 1980s, and 1990s who have left their mark on contemporary music include Bryan Adams, The Band, Bruce Cockburn, Céline Dion, composer David

Foster, The Guess Who (including Burton Cummings), Sarah McLachlan, Rita McNeil, Alanis Morissette, The Rankin Family, Rush, The Tragically Hip, Shania Twain, and Roch Voisine. The Canadian recording industry has become a multibillion-dollar business, producing music that is popular well beyond the relatively small national market and that is no longer dependent on Canadian content regulations.

A growing number of Canadians have become household names around the world as movie and television performers. The major dramatic actors include Geneviève Bujold, Martha Henry, William Hutt, Margot Kidder, Dora Mavor Moore, Kate Nelligan, Gordon Pinsent, Christopher Plummer, Kate Reid, William Shatner, Donald Sutherland and his son Keifer, R. H. Thompson, and Al Waxman. Canada has had a penchant for producing comedians and comedic actors, including Dan Ackroyd, John Candy, Jim Carrey, Michael J. Fox, André-Philippe Gagnon, Rich Little, Andrea Martin, Mike Myers, Catherine O'Hara, Martin Short, and the team of (John) Wayne and (Frank) Shuster. Major film directors and producers include James Cameron (who won an Academy Award for *Titanic* in 1998), David Cronenberg, Atom Egoyan, and Norman Jewison. Unlike their predecessors, most of these performers have maintained their Canadian ties and identity even though their work may require them to live in the United States.

Another form of popular culture that has become a multibillion-dollar industry is sports. Hockey continues to be considered the national sport with additional NHL teams located in Vancouver (1971), Calgary and Edmonton (1979), and Ottawa (1993). Quebec City and Winnipeg also entered the NHL in 1979, but escalating player salaries along with higher taxation levels in Canada forced the franchises to move to U.S. locations in the 1990s. How long the other six Canadian teams can remain economically competitive with the 24 American-based franchises is a pressing question as the century draws to a close. Over the past two decades, hockey fans have been thrilled by the scoring exploits of Wayne Gretzky of Brantford, Ontario, who has rewritten the record book in virtually every offensive category. After leading the Edmonton Oilers to four Stanley Cups in five years from 1984 to 1988, Gretzky was traded to the Los Angeles Kings for financial reasons—yet another Canadian who found it necessary to continue his career south of the border. In the wake of Canada's dramatic last-minute victory in the 1972 series with the Soviet Union, the Canada Cup was inaugurated in 1976 as a tournament to be held every four years to determine international hockey supremacy. Canada has won four of the six competitions.

In recent times, hockey has had to share the limelight with baseball and basketball. Major league baseball came to Montreal in 1969 and Toronto in 1977. The Toronto Blue Jays, operating since 1989 out of a magnificent and expensive retractable-roofed stadium known as Skydome, became the first foreign team to win the World Series in 1992 and 1993. On the other hand, the Montreal Expos have fallen on financial hard times as a "small market" franchise and may be forced to move to an American city as early as 2000. Financial problems also plagued the Canadian Football League as Montreal and Ottawa were temporarily forced to curtail operations in the late 1980s and the mid-1990s, respectively. As in hockey and baseball, the Canadian teams have had to overcome competition from the American-based National Football League (NFL). In 1996 the Toronto Raptors and the Vancouver Grizzlies joined the ranks of the National Basketball Association (NBA). In the late 20th century, Canadians have been inclined to support only major league professional sports, even though the Canadian market may not be large enough to sustain a team.

The international sporting spotlight shone on Canada when Montreal hosted the Summer Olympic Games in 1976 and Calgary hosted the Winter Olympic Games in 1988. The organizational success of the Calgary games could not make up for the financial disaster of the Montreal games in the minds of many Canadians, who have questioned the wisdom of Toronto's unsuccessful effort to host the 1996 Summer Olympic Games and the pending attempt to secure the 2008 Olympic Games. After World War II, Canada became an important figure skating nation. Canadian world champions in individual competition have included: Barbara Ann Scott (1947–48), Donald Jackson (1962), Donald McPherson (1963), Petra Burka (1965), Karen Magnusson (1973), Kurt Browning (1989–91, 1993), and Elvis Stojko (1994–95). Canadian world champions in pairs competition have included: Frances Dafoe and Norris Bowden (1954–55), Barbara Wagner and Robert Paul (1957–60), Maria and Otto Jelinek (1962), Barbara Underhill and Paul Martini (1984), Isabelle Brasseur and Lloyd Eisler (1993). During the 1980s, Toronto, Montreal, and Vancouver became regular stops on the major international auto racing circuits. In the 1990s, Jacques Villeneuve achieved the world championship recognition in auto racing that eluded his legendary father Gilles Villeneuve, who was killed in a racing accident two decades earlier. Indeed, Canadians at the end of the millennium have such high expectations of their athletes because so many of them have achieved world championship distinction in their sports.

A FINAL REFLECTION

Each year from 1992 to 1999, the United Nations Development Program has ranked Canada first among nations in a survey on quality of life. Other major international surveys have rated Canada highly as a safe, healthy, and stable place to live and work. Despite the fact that the rest of the world views the opportunity to live in Canada with envy, political cynicism, regional discontent, and anxieties about economic security and social diversity continue to pervade national life. Rightly or wrongly, Canadians have come to have high expectations of their country, and they are not reluctant to express their disappointment when their hopes are not fulfilled. In this respect, Canadians have not changed a great deal even though their nation has evolved into a much more complex society than the one that existed in colonial times.

The early explorers expected to find gold and other precious metals or a route to India or China but were disappointed when they found neither. Full appreciation of the land's existing agricultural, mineral, forest, and hydroelectric power potential, and the possibilities opened up by the St. Lawrence–Great Lakes water route, was a long time in coming. In fact, Canada was not initially the favored destination of immigrants. The majority of overseas immigrants either went directly to the United States or moved there after being disappointed with what Canada had to offer them. Only in the 20th century did Canada begin to compete favorably with its southern neighbor as a land of opportunity. Still, Canadians have felt a sense of economic insecurity, primarily because of their tendency to measure the prospects and achievements of their country against those of their neighbor to the south.

While admiring the dynamism of the United States, Canadians have tended to feel threatened by its power and influence. Whether it was the Huron facing the mighty Iroquois attack from the south, the St. Lawrence River traders competing against the Hudson River traders, the armed forces of the thirteen colonies invading New France, the American army invading British North America, the prospect of reciprocity leading to annexation, or the perceived threat of American capital and culture to national independence, Canadians have continuously believed that they need special protection from southern encroachments. In effect, Canadians have carried on an ambivalent relationship with their American neighbors.

Yet Canadians have been no less ambivalent toward relationships within their own society. Canada has always been a multicultural society in search of cultural homogeneity. In prehistoric and colonial times, the diverse Native cultures that inhabited the land were not immune to intertribal warfare. Then came the French, British, and other European cultures to complicate the mix and to enhance the possibilities of conflict. On the other hand, the various cultures have always found reason to cooperate and collaborate, whether it was the French-Native or the French-English partnerships in the fur trade, the diverse British peoples endeavoring to open up the settlement frontier in the 19th century and the multitude of other ethnic groups seeking a new start in the 20th century, or the French and the English resisting an American invasion or forming a political coalition to seek or maintain power. Indeed, the formidable challenges of Canadian development have often forced people to set aside their differences and to work together to achieve their aspirations.

Canadians have always been divided into regional communities often separated by geographic barriers or vast distances to travel. In addition to their sense of nationality, Native peoples had a regional consciousness that defined the parameters of their nomadic existence. In the days of New France, the St. Lawrence colony had little contact with Acadia to the east or the itinerant fur traders seeking their fortunes in the western interior wilderness. Likewise, in British North America, Newfoundland was isolated from the Maritime colonies, which in turn were divided by culture from Lower Canada and by distance from Upper Canada. The settled communities were in turn far removed from the fur trade domains of the North West Company and the Hudson's Bay Company stretching from the upper Great Lakes to the Pacific and Arctic shores. So, when the Dominion of Canada was formed out of these isolated and alienated colonial societies, it was not surprising that regionalism persisted, that federal-provincial relations would be constantly strained, and that national unity would be elusive.

Nevertheless regionalism has had some unexpected benefits. It has encouraged negotiation and compromise rather than aggression and dominance. The evidence of the early fur trade suggests that the Native peoples, despite their suspicions of the European interlopers and the bitter warfare that occasionally had to be waged, were prepared to bargain in good faith. The British imperial authorities preferred to negotiate the transfer of land from the Native peoples rather than to beat them into submission as the Americans did in their western frontier. Ultimately, the British governors adopted a conciliatory relationship with the French colonists despite the specter of military conquest. The achievement of self-government and nationhood in the 19th century was also a product of compromise, as opposed to the confrontation that had led to the American Revolution. Even the federal government after Confederation, armed with a constitution designed to reduce the provinces to purely local authorities, could only advance its national agenda through legislative compromise. In essence, regionalism has been prevalent in Canada not only because of the formidable barriers of geography but also because no single force has been powerful enough to impose its continuous will.

Perhaps the most powerful force in Canadian life has been government. Whether it was the authoritarianism of royal government in New France, the British imperial administration reluctant to encourage democracy, or the federal government attempting to maintain its power over the provinces after Confederation, Canadians have always been ambivalent toward government authority. Governments and the politicians who represent them have engaged in wars that endanger the lives of their citizens, have imposed high taxes, and have restricted individual freedom. The habitants of New France often suffered in the wake of the imperial authority's military crusade against Britain, while the Loyalist settlers were victims of the American-British conflict during the Revolutionary War and, to a lesser extent, the War of 1812. In the 20th century, French Canadians have been highly critical of the national government's willingness to become entangled in overseas warfare. Canadians of every generation have complained about excessive taxation whether levied on land, imports, purchases, income, or profits. The public outrage directed toward the GST is the most recent manifestation of this tendency. Canadians have also resisted various government attempts to limit political liberties, religious freedom, language rights, free enterprise, and the right to strike, among others. On the other hand, the public outcry could be just as loud if government failed to restrict such liberties.

Indeed, Canadians have tended to expect and to demand a greater measure of government intervention into their social and economic lives than have Americans. Initially, the role of government was to offset geographical disadvantages, to support colonization, and to defend against foreign invasion. The paternalistic absolutism of royal government extended to virtually every aspect of life in New France. The fur trade and subsequent resource developments depended on the state's grants of monopoly rights or generous subsidies. The settlement of the Upper Canadian frontier and the western prairies was also stimulated by government grants of free land, while the development of the transcontinental transportation and communication network was wholly or heavily dependent on public subsidization. In the 20th century, the state added to its role the promotion of social justice and economic security. Demanding so much from the public sector, Canadians have been deeply disappointed when it has failed to fulfill expectations.

The ambivalent responses of Canadians and the tensions that have sustained them are not about to change. Canada is destined to remain a multicultural and regional society in which private and state enterprise collaborate to maximize the potential of the nation's abundant natural and human resources. Furthermore, the course of Canadian development will continue to be influenced by external forces beyond national control. The 18th century was the century of imperialism, and within this context, Canada developed as a colony. The 19th century was the century of nationalism, during which Canada became a nation. The 20th century was the century of globalism, during which Canada participated fully in world affairs and earned international recognition as a defender of democracy, as a peacekeeper and haven for oppressed people, and as one of the leading places to live and work. Whatever the 21st century may bring is bound to add to the richness of Canadian history.

SUGGESTIONS FOR FURTHER READING

GENERAL WORKS

Barman, Jean. *The West beyond the West: A History of British Columbia.* Toronto: University of Toronto Press, 1991.

Bercuson, David J. *Colonies: Canada to 1867.* Toronto: McGraw-Hill Ryerson Ltd., 1992.

Bliss, Michael. *Northern Enterprises: Five Centuries of Canadian Business.* Toronto: McClelland & Stewart Ltd., 1987.

Brown, Craig. *The Illustrated History of Canada.* Toronto: Lester & Orpen Dennys, 1998.

Buckner, Phillip A. and John G. Reid, eds. *The Atlantic Region to Confederation: A History.* Toronto: University of Toronto Press, 1994.

The Canadian Encyclopedia. CD ROM. Toronto: McClelland & Stewart Limited, 1998.

Conrad, Margaret and Alvin Finkle. *History of the Canadian Peoples: Beginnings to 1867.* Vol. 1. Toronto: Addison-Wesley, 1998.

Dickason, Olive P. *Canada's First Nations: A History of the Founding Peoples from Earliest Times.* Toronto: McClelland & Stewart Ltd., 1992.

Dictionary of Canadian Biography. 14 Volumes. Toronto: University of Toronto Press, 1966–98.

Finlay, J. L. and D. N. Sprague. *The Structure of Canadian History.* Scarborough: Prentice Hall, 1989.

Francis, R. Douglas and Donald B. Smith. *Readings in Canadian History: Pre-Confederation.* Toronto: Harcourt Brace & Company, Canada, 1994.

———. *Readings in Canadian History: Post-Confederation.* Toronto: Harcourt Brace & Company, Canada, 1994.

Francis, R. Douglas, Richard Jones, and Donald B. Smith. *Destinies: Canadian History since Confederation.* Toronto: Harcourt Brace & Company, Canada, 1996.

———. *Origins: Canadian History to Confederation.* Toronto: Harcourt Brace & Company, Canada, 1996.

Friesen, Gerald. *The Canadian Prairies: A History.* Toronto: University of Toronto Press, 1984.

Gentilcore, R. Louis, ed. *Historical Atlas of Canada, Volume 2: The Land Transformed, 1800–1891.* Toronto: University of Toronto Press, 1993.

Granatstein, J. L. *Nation: Canada since Confederation*. Toronto: McGraw-Hill Ryerson Ltd., 1990.

Granatstein, J. L. and Norman Hillmer. *For Better or Worse: Canada and the United States to the 1990s*. Toronto: Copp Clark Pitman, 1991.

Harris, R. Cole, ed. *Historical Atlas of Canada, Volume 1: From the Beginning to 1800*. Toronto: University of Toronto Press, 1987.

Harris, R. Cole and John Warkentin. *Canada before Confederation: A Study in Historical Geography*. Ottawa: Carleton University Press, 1991.

Heron, Craig. *The Canadian Labour Movement: A Short History*. Toronto: James Lorimer, 1989.

Kerr, Donald and Deryk Holdsworth, ed. *Historical Atlas of Canada, Volume 3: Addressing the Twentieth Century, 1891–1961*. Toronto: University of Toronto Press, 1990.

Knowles, Valerie. *Strangers at Our Gates: Canadian Immigration and Immigration Policy, 1549–1990*. Toronto: Dundurn Press, 1992.

Neary, Peter and Patrick O'Flaherty. *Port of the Main: An Illustrated History of Newfoundland and Labrador*. St. John's: Breakwater Books, 1983.

Norrie, Kenneth and Douglas Owram. *A History of the Canadian Economy*. Toronto: Harcourt Brace, 1996.

Owram, Doug. *Canadian History: A Reader's Guide*. Vol. 2, *Confederation to the Present*. Toronto: University of Toronto Press, 1994.

Prentice, Alison et al. *Canadian Women: A History*. Toronto: Harcourt Brace, 1996.

Rowe, Frederick W. *A History of Newfoundland and Labrador*. Toronto: McGraw-Hill Ryerson Ltd., 1980.

Taylor, Graham and Peter A. Baskerille. *A Concise History of Business in Canada*. Toronto: Oxford University Press, 1994.

Taylor, M. Brook. *Canadian History: A Reader's Guide*. Vol. 1, *Beginnings to Confederation*. Toronto: University of Toronto Press, 1994.

Trofimenkoff, Susan Mann. *The Dream of Nation: A Social and Intellectual History of Quebec*. Toronto: Gage, 1983.

Winks, Robin. *The Blacks in Canada: A History*. Montreal/Kingston: Queen's-McGill University Press, 1985.

EXPLORING THE NORTHERN AMERICAN FRONTIER

Dickason, Olive P. *The Myth of the Savage and the Beginnings of French Canadian Colonialism in the Americas*. Edmonton: University of Alberta Press, 1984.

Kehoe, Alice B. *North American Indians: A Comprehensive Account*. Englewood Cliffs, N.J.: Prentice-Hall, 1992.

McGhee, Robert. *Ancient Canada*. Ottawa: Canadian Museum of Civilization/Libre Expression, 1989.

———. *Canada Rediscovered*. Ottawa: Canadian Museum of Civilization/Libre Expression, 1989.

Morrison, R. Bruce and Roderick Wilson, eds. *Native Peoples: The Canadian Experience*. Toronto: McClelland & Stewart Ltd., 1995.

Morison, Samuel Eliot. *The European Discovery of North America: The Northern Voyages, AD 500–1600*. New York: Oxford University Press, 1971.

Quinn, David B. *North America from Earliest Discovery to First Settlement: The Norse Voyages to 1612.* New York: Harper & Row, 1977.

Rogers, Edward S. and Donald B. Smith, eds. *Aboriginal Ontario: Historical Perspectives on the First Nations.* Toronto: Dundurn Press, 1994.

THE FRENCH EMPIRE IN NORTHERN AMERICA, 1608–1760

Eccles, W. J. *Canada under Louis XIV, 1663–1701.* Toronto: McClelland & Stewart, 1964.

———. *The Canadian Frontier, 1534–1760.* Toronto: Holt, Rinehart & Winston, 1969.

———. *Essays on New France.* Toronto: Oxford University Press, 1987.

———. *France in America.* Markham, Ontario: Fitzhenry & Whiteside, 1990.

Griffith, Naomi. *The Acadians: The Creation of a People.* Toronto: McGraw-Hill Ryerson Ltd., 1973.

———. *The Contexts of Acadian History, 1686–1784.* Montreal/Kingston: Queen's-McGill University Press, 1985.

Grant, John Webster. *Moon in Wintertime: Missionaries and the Indians of Canada in Encounter since 1534.* Toronto: University of Toronto Press, 1984.

Jaenen, Cornelius. *The French Relationship with the Native Peoples of New France and Acadia.* Ottawa: Department of Indian and Northern Affairs, 1984.

———. *The Role of the Church in New France.* Ottawa: Canadian Historical Association, 1985.

Miquelon, Dale. *New France: 1701–1744.* Toronto: McClelland & Stewart Ltd., 1989.

———. *The First Canada: To 1791.* Toronto: McGraw-Hill Ryerson Ltd., 1994.

Ray, Arthur. *Indians in the Fur Trade.* Toronto: University of Toronto Press, 1974.

Stanley, G. F. *New France: The Last Phase, 1744–1760.* Toronto: McClelland & Stewart Ltd., 1968.

Steele, I. K. *Warpaths: Invasions of North America.* New York: Oxford University Press, 1994.

Trigger, Bruce G. *Natives and Newcomers: Canada's "Heroic Age" Reconsidered.* Montreal/Kingston: Queen's-McGill University Press, 1985.

———. *The Indians in the Heroic Age of New France.* Ottawa: Canadian Historical Association, 1989.

Trudel, Marcel. *The Beginnings of New France, 1524–1663.* Toronto: McClelland & Stewart Ltd., 1973.

THE BRITISH NORTH AMERICAN COLONIES, 1760–1867

Brown, Wallace and Hereward Senior. *Victorious in Defeat: The Loyalists in Canada.* Toronto: Methuen, 1984.

Buckner, Philip A. *The Transition to Responsible Government: British Policy in British North America, 1815–1850.* Westport, Conn.: Greenwood Press, 1985.

Careless, J. M. S. *Union of the Canadas: The Growth of Canadian Institutions, 1841–1857.* Toronto: McClelland & Stewart Ltd., 1967.

Cowan, Helen. *British Immigration before Confederation*. Ottawa: Canadian Historical Association, 1968.

Craig, Gerald M. *Lord Durham's Report*. Toronto: McClelland & Stewart Ltd., 1963.

———. *Upper Canada: The Formative Years, 1784–1841*. Toronto: McClelland & Stewart Ltd., 1963.

Creighton, Donald. *The Road to Confederation: The Emergence of Canada*. Toronto: Macmillan, 1964.

Francis, Daniel. *A History of the Native Peoples of Quebec, 1760–1867*. Ottawa: Department of Northern and Indian Affairs, 1984.

Lawson, Philip. *The Imperial Challenge: Quebec and Britain in the Age of the American Revolution*. Montreal/Kingston: Queen's-McGill University Press, 1989.

MacNutt, W. S. *The Atlantic Provinces, 1712–1857*. Toronto: McClelland & Stewart Ltd., 1965.

Martin, Ged, ed. *The Causes of Canadian Confederation*. Fredericton: Acadiensis, 1990.

McCalla, Douglas. *Planting the Province: The Economic History of Upper Canada, 1784–1870*. Toronto: University of Toronto Press, 1996.

Miquelon, Dale, ed. *Society and Conquest: The Debate about the Bourgeoisie and Social Change in French Canada, 1700–1850*. Toronto: Copp Clark, 1977.

Moore, Christopher. *The Loyalists: Revolution, Exile, Settlement*. Toronto: Macmillan, 1984.

Morton, W. L. *The Critical Years: The Union of British North America, 1857–1873*. Toronto: McClelland & Stewart Ltd., 1964.

Neatby, Hilda. *Quebec: The Revolutionary Age, 1760–1791*. Toronto: McClelland & Stewart Ltd., 1968.

Ouellet, Fernand. *Lower Canada, 1791–1840: Social Change and Nationalism*. Toronto: McClelland & Stewart Ltd., 1979.

———. *Economic and Social History of Quebec, 1760–1850*. Toronto: Macmillan, 1980.

Pannekoek, Frits. *The Fur Trade and Western Canadian Society, 1670–1870*. Ottawa: Canadian Historical Association, 1988.

Paquet, Gilles and Jean-Pierre Wallot. *Lower Canada at the Turn of the Nineteenth Century. Restructuring and Modernization*. Ottawa: Canadian Historical Association, 1988.

Read, Colin. *The Rebellion of 1837 in Upper Canada*. Ottawa: Canadian Historical Association, 1988.

Rich, E. E. *The Fur Trade and the Northwest to 1857*. Toronto: McClelland & Stewart Ltd., 1967.

Sagar, Eric W. and Lewis R. Fischer. *Shipping and Shipbuilding in Atlantic Canada, 1820–1914*. Ottawa: Canadian Historical Association, 1986.

Waite, P. B. *The Confederation Debates in the Province of Canada, 1865*. Toronto: McClelland & Stewart Ltd., 1963.

Wilson, Bruce. *As She Began: An Illustrated Introduction to Loyalist Ontario*. Toronto: Dundurn Press, 1981.

THE FOUNDATIONS OF CANADIAN NATIONHOOD, 1867–1931

Allen, Richard. *The Social Passion: Religion and Social Reform in Canada, 1914–28*. Toronto: University of Toronto Press, 1971.

Armstrong, Christopher and H. V. Nelles. *Monopolies Moment: The Organization and Regulation of Canadian Utilities, 1830–1930*. Philadelphia: Temple University Press, 1986.

Beal, Bob and Rob Macleod. *Prairie Fire: The 1885 North-West Rebellion*. Edmonton: Hurtig Publishers, 1984.

Berger, Carl. *The Sense of Power: Studies in the Ideas of Canadian Imperialism, 1867–1914*. Toronto: University of Toronto Press, 1970.

Bothwell, Robert, Ian Drummond, and John English. *Canada, 1900–1945*. Toronto: University of Toronto Press, 1987.

Brown, R. C. and R. Cook. *Canada, 1896–1921: A Nation Transformed*. Toronto: McClelland & Stewart Ltd., 1974.

Careless, J. M. S. *The Rise of Cities in Canada before 1914*. Ottawa: Canadian Historical Association, 1978.

———. *Frontier and Metropolis: Regions, Cities and Identities in Canada before 1914*. Toronto: University of Toronto Press, 1989.

Cook, R. *Provincial Autonomy, Minority Rights and the Compact Theory, 1867–1921*. Ottawa: Queen's Printer, 1969.

Eagle, John A. *The Canadian Pacific Railway and the Development of Western Canada*. Montreal/Kingston: Queen's-McGill University Press, 1989.

Forbes, E. R. *Aspects of Maritime Regionalism, 1867–1927*. Ottawa: Canadian Historical Association, 1983.

Granatstein, J. L. and J. M. Hitsman. *Broken Promises: A History of Conscription in Canada*. Toronto Copp Clark Pitman, 1985.

Harney, R. F. and H. Troper. *Immigrants: A Portrait of the Urban Experience, 1890–1930*. Toronto: Van Nostrand Reinhold, 1975.

Linteau, Paul André, René Durocher, and Jean-Claude Robert. *Quebec: A History, 1867–1929*. Toronto: James Lorimer, 1983.

Rutherford, Paul. *Saving the Canadian City, 1880–1920*. Toronto: University of Toronto Press, 1974.

Silver, Arthur. *The French-Canadian Idea of Confederation, 1864–1900*. Toronto: University of Toronto Press, 1982.

Stacey, C. P. *Canada and the Age of Conflict: A History of External Relations*, Vol. 1, *1867–1921*. Toronto: Macmillan, 1977.

Stelter, G. and A. Artibise, eds. *The Canadian City: Essays in Urban History*. Toronto: McClelland & Stewart Ltd., 1977.

Struthers, James. *No Fault of Their Own: Unemployment and the Canadian Welfare State*. Toronto: University of Toronto Press, 1983.

Waite, P. B. *Canada, 1874–1896: Arduous Destiny*. Toronto: McClelland & Stewart Ltd., 1971.

Zaslow, Morris. *The Opening of the Canadian North*. Toronto: McClelland & Stewart Ltd., 1971.

AFFLUENCE AND ANXIETY IN THE MODERN ERA

Bothwell, Robert, Ian Drummond, and John English. *Canada since 1945: Power, Politics and Provincialism*. Toronto: University of Toronto Press, 1989.

Creighton, Donald. *Canada, 1939–1957: The Forked Road.* Toronto: McClelland & Stewart Ltd., 1976.

Granatstein, J. L. *Canada, 1957–1967: The Years of Uncertainty and Innovation.* Toronto: McClelland & Stewart Ltd., 1986.

Guest, Dennis. *The Emergence of Social Security in Canada.* Vancouver: University of British Columbia Press, 1981.

Horn, Michiel. *The Great Depression of the 1930s in Canada.* Ottawa: Canadian Historical Association, 1984.

Jones, Richard. *Duplessis and the Union Nationale Administration.* Ottawa: Canadian Historical Association, 1984.

Linteau, Paul André. *Quebec since 1930.* Toronto: James Lorimer, 1991.

McRoberts, Kenneth. *Quebec: Social Change and Political Crisis.* Toronto: McClelland & Stewart Ltd., 1988.

Neatby, H. Blair. *The Politics of Chaos.* Toronto: Macmillan, 1972.

Stacey, C. P. *Canada and the Age of Conflict.* Vol. 2, *1921–1948: The Mackenzie King Era.* Toronto: University of Toronto Press, 1981.

Thompson, John with Allen Seager. *Canada, 1922–1939: Decades of Discord.* Toronto: McClelland & Stewart Ltd., 1985.

Wilbur, Richard. *The Bennett Administration.* Ottawa: Canadian Historical Association, 1969.

Zaslow, Morris. *The Northward Expansion of Canada, 1914–1967.* Toronto: McClelland & Stewart Ltd., 1988.

PHOTO CREDITS

PAGES 34, 46, 61, 86, 90, 104, 122 left, 122 right, 135 upper left, 135 upper right, 186, 216, 225, 232, 242, 258. Courtesy of the National Archives of Canada, Ottawa.
PAGE 78. Courtesy of the National Gallery of Canada.
PAGE 135, bottom left. Courtesy of the Archives of Ontario, Toronto.
PAGES 159, 171, 223. Courtesy of the Glenbow Archives, Calgary.

INDEX